DATE DUE

Mating Intelligence Unleashed

Mating Intelligence Unleashed

The Role of the Mind in Sex, Dating, and Love

GLENN GEHER

and

SCOTT BARRY KAUFMAN

OXFORD
UNIVERSITY PRESS

OXFORD
UNIVERSITY PRESS

Oxford University Press is a department of the University of Oxford.
It furthers the University's objective of excellence in research, scholarship,
and education by publishing worldwide.

Oxford   New York
Auckland   Cape Town   Dar es Salaam   Hong Kong   Karachi
Kuala Lumpur   Madrid   Melbourne   Mexico City   Nairobi
New Delhi   Shanghai   Taipei   Toronto

With offices in
Argentina   Austria   Brazil   Chile   Czech Republic   France   Greece
Guatemala   Hungary   Italy   Japan   Poland   Portugal   Singapore
South Korea   Switzerland   Thailand   Turkey   Ukraine   Vietnam

Oxford is a registered trademark of Oxford University Press in the UK and certain other
countries.

Published in the United States of America by
Oxford University Press
198 Madison Avenue, New York, NY 10016

© Oxford University Press 2013

Library of Congress Cataloging-in-Publication Data
Geher, Glenn.
Mating intelligence unleashed: the role of the mind in sex, dating, and love / Glenn Geher,
Scott Barry Kaufman.
p. cm.
Includes bibliographical references and index.
ISBN 978-0-19-539685-0 (hardback : alk. paper)
1. Mate selection.   2. Mate selection—Psychological aspects.   3. Man-woman relationships.
4. Sex.   5. Dating (Social customs)   6. Love.   I. Kaufman, Scott Barry, 1979–   II. Title.
HQ801.G388 2013
306.82—dc23
2012026352

3 5 7 9 8 6 4
Printed in the United States of America
on acid-free paper

CONTENTS

THE NEW "MODERN SYNTHESIS"

Foreword by Helen Fisher, Biological Anthropologist, Department of Anthropology, Rutgers University

With breakthroughs in genetics in the 1930s and 40s, Mendel's theory of genetic inheritance and Darwin's theory of evolution by natural selection became integrated. With this "modern synthesis," as it is hailed, our intellectual forebears finally began to understand how speciation and evolution actually work. But I have come to believe we are now in the midst of a far greater synthesis of scientific ideas.

Researchers have begun to understand some of the brain pathways associated with feelings of romantic love, attachment, social conformity, and religiosity. Others have uncovered some of the neurochemistry of trust, altruism, and wanderlust. Some of the genes linked with curiosity and creativity have been established. The mental machinery that guides our mating strategies is becoming understood. And with inroads into epigenetics, scientists have begun to show how environmental forces turn genes on and off, affecting how we—and our offspring—are likely to behave. The nature/nurture argument is dead. We are witnessing the true fusion of biology and culture, of psychology and brain architecture, of personality, neurochemistry, genetics and evolution, of brain and mind.

This synthesis is not complete. Some therapists cling to the concept that we emerged from the womb as "blank slates," that our childhood makes us who we are. Some psychologists still overlook the importance of functional magnetic resonance imaging (fMRI) and other forms of brain research, regarding the brain as just a standard toolbox that can tell us nothing about what makes us tick. Many neuroscientists study brain activity without considering why these activation patterns evolved. And many deride evolutionary psychology as a ream of just-so stories.

I find this narrow focus strange, for both practical and intellectual reasons. I work regularly with the press. And in my 30 years of fielding their queries, I have never once found a journalist who resisted the evolutionary, neurochemical, or genetic approaches to explaining why we do the things we do; journalists and many others outside the scientific community want holistic explanations. Moreover, uncovering the biological foundations of human behavior does not threaten the social sciences. On the contrary, I suspect that the more we come to understand the biological and evolutionary forces that drive human cognition and conduct, the more we will discover the powerful role that culture plays in sculpting human action.

Regardless of these naysayers, the growing fusion of the social and biological sciences is ushering in a vastly wider and deeper view of humanity. And this book by Geher and Kaufman is a wonderful contribution to this new synthesis.

Evolutionary psychologist Geoffrey Miller has written that "the mind evolved by moonlight." He was referring to Darwin's brilliant idea of sexual selection, the concept that many of our thoughts, feelings, motivations, and aptitudes evolved to win the mating game. Take poetry. One doesn't need the poetic skills of Shakespeare, Frost, Baudelaire, or Akhmatova to survive another day. Like the peacock's elaborate tail feathers, our outsized poetic talents (and many other seemingly unnecessary human capacities) most likely evolved to enchant a potential mating partner. Those forebears who were more talented with words, song, or some other exaggerated human trait won more sex, bore more young, and passed along their extravagant abilities to us.

Geher and Kaufman go further down this road. Using data from many disciplines, including evolutionary biology, behavior genetics, neuroscience, sociology, anthropology, developmental psychology, social psychology, and personality psychology, they discuss the myriad unconscious neural mechanisms and evolutionary forces that prime us to do the things we do. I agree with them when they write in their preface that "human mating is arguably the single most important behavioral domain of human functioning." To this end, they neatly unclothe many of our human sexual motivations, stripping them of the standard psychological explanations, then dressing them in their true evolutionary garb.

We are living in a thrilling time of scientific discovery. "Ah-ha" is on the lips of many who investigate the mental machinery of human thought and action. And I suspect that when our descendants look back, they will regard the modern synthesis of the 1930s and 40s as just the first step in the emergence of a far broader scientific synthesis—in which those of many disparate disciplines shed light on that ultimate palimpsest, the human mind. Darwin would tip a glass to Geher and Kaufman for their contribution to this growing enlightenment.

PREFACE

"Not another Intelligence!" If this is how you reacted when you saw the title of this book, we don't blame you. These days, there seems to be an intelligence for everything—general intelligence (e.g., IQ), emotional intelligence, social intelligence, spiritual intelligence, executive intelligence—ad infinitum.

Some of these intelligences, such as general intelligence, are supported by a wealth of solid peer-reviewed journal articles, whereas others are linguistic inventions that capture the popular eye, but aren't necessarily grounded in empirical reality. We, the authors of this book, believe that *mating intelligence* falls into the former category. Enough research findings from evolutionary psychologists have culminated on the topic of human sexuality and intimate relationships to reach an important threshold. This threshold marks the need for the field of intelligence to pay a bit more attention to the work of evolutionary psychologists, for evolutionary psychologists to pay a bit more attention to the work of intelligence researchers, and for everyone else (including you, the reader!) to pay attention to both.

Consider a recent analysis of articles of the journal *Intelligence* conducted by members of our research team. Since its inception in 1977, nearly 33 full volumes of this journal have been published. To examine the extent to which this journal (essentially the premier international journal on the topic of intelligence) includes content that pertains to human mating, members of our research team coded all articles published in the journal as having some mating-relevant component or not. The coding was specifically conducted on the titles, keywords, and abstracts of these articles. Guidelines for inclusion were relatively lax; any article that seemed to have something to do with mating and/or sexual relationships at all was to be included. Despite these relatively lax criteria, only eight articles (of 970; 0.8%) dealt with any issues regarding mating. In fact, "mating" is less likely to be associated with "intelligence" (121 papers) than with "cockroach" (168 papers), "Norway" (178), or "steel" (182). Thus, "mating" and "intelligence" do not seem very closely connected in the minds of scientists (we will refrain from speculating as to why this unfortunate state of affairs exists!). Until the advent of the mating intelligence framework, theories of intelligence across the entire history of psychology have had little to say about human mating.

Now, why should intelligence researchers care about human mating? To the general reader who isn't locked up in the ivory tower, the answer to this question is pretty obvious. Nonetheless, we'll take the question seriously and provide two answers. First, from an evolutionary point of view, the domain of human mating is arguably the single most important behavioral domain of human functioning. Every single one of you reading this book comes from a long line of mating-successful individuals. Well done. The second reason is that for most human beings, mating success is important. Research on happiness shows that the quality of intimate relationships (especially sexual relationships) is a major predictor of overall life satisfaction—often more important than education, income, or occupational status! Therefore, although intelligence researchers have gleaned important insights into human intelligence by looking at people's performance at solving abstract puzzles in paper-and-pencil format, we suggest that they may have neglected the investigation of how intelligence operates in a domain that has a lot of importance to most people.

In this book, we will describe various cognitive processes that relate to the mating domain. Many of these processes are involved directly in understanding the mating world, but some processes are *attractors*—traits that tend to show a lot of variability among humans and are considered sexy. We hope that talk of a sexy brain is a refreshing topic in a society that is constantly bombarded with images and products relating to the more superficial aspects of sexual attraction, such as body type or facial structure. Yes, humans have deeper qualities as well, and they *are* immensely attractive.

Before we let you get on with this book, we— your "guides" to the scientific understanding of mating intelligence—thought we should add a personal note. We are both young scientists who are truth seekers. We are also male. As much as we've tried to write this book from a gender-neutral perspective, at the end of the day, we remain males. We are very interested in discussing the ideas and findings we present in this book with our female and male readers, and hope this book stimulates discussions that lead to positive change in society.

We, like you, have been fascinated with human mating behavior our entire lives and are excited to apply the scientific method to obtain answers that can't be obtained by any other method. At the same time, we humbly admit that the mating intelligence framework proposed in this book is a work in progress. We also must acknowledge that most of the studies on human mating from an evolutionary perspective have been conducted on college undergraduates (typically sophomores) in the United States. To make more confident generalizations to all of human nature and to more fully investigate the breadth and depth of individual differences will require much more research.

Nonetheless, we felt it was time to put all the research together under a single framework. This does not mean that we have solved all the riddles of the mating world, or that future research won't show that some of the past research was misguided. Throughout the book, we posed new questions and hinted at potential avenues for future research. If the mating intelligence framework stimulates thought, research, and new directions within our field and allied fields, then we will be ecstatic. At the very least though, we hope to share our enthusiasm of the power of science to answer some of life's deepest and most important questions. Enjoy.

ACKNOWLEDGMENTS

First and foremost, we thank the great Lori Handelman, our initial publisher on this book at Oxford, whose intuitive and experienced style helped shape this project from top to bottom—and she always helped with a smile. And we thank our new publisher, Abby Gross, whose ability to pick things up and move forward from where things left off has proved outstanding. Oxford runs a tight ship—and this book has benefited accordingly throughout this project.

We also thank the folks at *Psychology Today*—including, primarily, Kaja Perina, whose support of the idea of mating intelligence has been enormous for the growth of research on this topic as well as for our ability to produce this book. Kaja's consistently bright, competent, and supportive style puts her as a shining star in the industry—and this book is better off as a result of her support.

Geoffrey Miller's groundbreaking ideas on the interface of intelligence and human mating played a pivotal role in shaping the ideas of this book—and we're deeply grateful for his scholarly contributions, which largely serve as a foundation to much of the content in this book. We'd also like to thank one of our collaborators on prior projects related to mating intelligence: the great Maureen O'Sullivan. Maureen's work on deception as a slice of mating intelligence has led to some of the most interesting research on this topic. Having the support and collaboration of someone as respected as Maureen has really been inspirational for us as we've moved forward on this project. The antithesis of the stuffy, arrogant academic, Maureen was simply the most down-to-earth, friendly, and supportive collaborator going. She was a beacon among humanity—and we like to think that including her ideas in this book helps her spirit live on. When the world lost Maureen in May of 2010, a silent mourning was felt across the globe. We miss her deeply—and hope that this book comes close to matching her exacting standards!

We are very appreciative to the following people for kindly providing feedback on earlier sections of the manuscript as well giving us relevant references: W. Keith Campbell, Colin DeYoung, Marco Del Giudice, Ryan Johnson, Lee

Kirkpatrick, Pranjal Mehta, Lars Penke, and David Schmitt for kindly providing feedback on earlier parts of the manuscript and providing us with relevant references. Several colleagues and students have collaborated with us on our various projects related to mating intelligence, and we'd be remiss if we didn't acknowledge them here. From Scott, acknowledgements go to Melanie Beaussart, Colin DeYoung, Jane Erickson, Ben Irvine, James C. Kaufman, Aaron Kozbelt, Michael Magee, Elliot Samuel Paul, and Sheela Ramesh. From Glenn, appreciation goes out to Alice Andrews, Mike Camargo, Rachael Carmen, Rosemarie Chang, Ben Crosier, Jason Diffenderfer, Haley Dillon, Mary Finn, Maryanne Fisher, Andy Gallup, Justin Garcia, Dan Glass, Mandy Guitar, Abbey Kurtz, Laura Johnsen, Ashley Peterson, Sarah Strout, and Stephen Williams. Special thanks to the great Briana Tauber for her outstanding editorial help! And Glenn gives a special thanks to Jane Lehman, the real boss of the psychology department—who makes sure that everything gets done so that I have time to work on fun projects like this one! Jane, you are one of a kind!

COPYRIGHT NOTES

1. Parts of this book are adapted from Scott Barry Kaufman's blog for *Psychology Today*, "Beautiful Minds." Scott owns the copyright to all this content, and the content is being reproduced with the expressed written consent of *Psychology Today*.

2. Sections of Chapter 6 are adapted from Glenn Geher's article titled "Oversexualization in Cross-Sex Mind-Reading: An Adaptationist Approach" from the 2009 volume of *Evolutionary Psychology*. Glenn is the owner of the copyright to this material, and the content is being reproduced with the expressed written consent of the editors-in-chief of *Evolutionary Psychology*.

3. The Mating Intelligence Scale, presented in the Epilogue, is adapted from the January 2007 issue of *Psychology Today*. This scale was written for the magazine by the authors (Glenn Geher and Scott Barry Kaufman), and they were given expressed written consent to reproduce and adapt that information for the purposes of this book—this consent was given by the editor-in-chief of *Psychology Today*.

Mating Intelligence Unleashed

1

Introduction

Cupid's Cognitive Arrow

LARRY KING: What, Professor, puzzles you the most? What do
you think about the most?
STEPHEN HAWKING: Women.
LARRY KING: Welcome aboard.
—Larry King Live Weekend *(December 25, 1999)*

Sex is constantly on the mind. When we're not thinking about sex, we are thinking about how to get it. Let's face it: the mating world doesn't play by simple rules. Contradictions, paradoxes, and ambiguities are apparent at every stage. The consequence is that we are consumed by thoughts related to mating. Early in relationship formation, we are focused on physical attractiveness and the overall value of potential mates as well as our own mate value. In this mate-selection phase of mating, we often ask questions such as, *Is she into me? Is she attractive?...Is she attractive enough? What would my friends and family think of her? How can I get her into bed tonight? Is she long-term material?*

As we move further into courtship, other universal questions consume us: *Am I ready to have sex with him? Is that thing he does when he eats cute? quirky? benign?...or downright gross!? Does he always wear shirts like that? Is his apparent kindness genuine? Is he really going to quit smoking? Is he going to be a success?*

When in the throes of a long-term relationship, a host of other thoughts consume the normal adult mating mind: *Does he really love me? Do I really love him? What has happened to our sex life? Is he interested in what's-her-name sexually— and, if not, why does it feel like he is? Why am I not turned on anymore? Why do I no longer find him funny? Does he still find me sexy?...Am I sexy? I wish he would pay more attention to me and the kids. Does he really "have to" go out on three business dinners this week? Why does he always have "business meetings" with her?*

Human mating is complex. Mating psychology involves an intricate combination of emotions, physical responses, deep (and often uncontrollable) urges, and many cognitive mechanisms. Many times in your life you have undoubtedly shaken your head in confusion while watching or participating in the mating domain.

Believe it or not, there is hope for understanding many of these mating puzzles. Modern scientists who study human mating from the perspective of our evolutionary origins have developed a framework for understanding mating processes that has led to an extraordinary accumulation of discoveries regarding the nature of our mating mind. Recently, mating researchers have documented qualities of human faces that are universally appealing, qualities of human behavior that are attractive, factors that lead to conflict in relationships, variables that lead to aggression and hostility in relationships, the effects of hormone levels on mating behaviors, and many other puzzling aspects of human mating.[1] In short, evolutionary psychology is unlocking mysteries of human mating that precede the existence of *Homo sapiens* on the African savanna.

As you'll see, evolution has provided us with some mental machinery that, when properly developed in the right context, can help us navigate the fascinatingly complex domain of mating. Even though humans share many instincts with lower animals, we are unique in our capacity for complex problem solving and reflection. Unlike many other species, we don't just look at each other, see a body we like, and have sex with that body—certainly not typically, in any case. Rather, the behaviors that constitute mating in our species generally require a great deal of high-level conscious and unconscious cognitive work. Therefore, intelligence is at play somewhere in the mating domain.

In thinking about how conscious forms of intelligence make their way into human mating, consider the different phases of mating—from initial attraction, to courtship, to a long-term relationship. High-level cognitive processes—often involving consciousness and verbal expression—are present at each step. Consider the case of initial attraction. In initial attraction, we think about our own mate value—often quite consciously. In fact, we often even discuss this issue with others (*Am I good enough for her? Tell me what you really think—be honest—I'm serious—really—no, I mean it ...*). We think about the mate values of potential partners (*Is he rich? He was pretty loud at that party—is he confident because he's a great guy...or just a jerk? What kind of dad would he be?*). We also use quite a bit of our mind to *display* our mate value—from the creative use of pick-up lines to displays of charisma, intelligence, humor, personality, and compassion.

Despite what it may seem by opening up the latest issue of *Maxim, Playboy, Vogue,* or *GQ,* or by turning on *MTV or VH1,* physical attractiveness isn't the whole story. We have all faced situations in which our physical attraction to a person has seriously diminished the second the person opened his or her mouth and situations in which someone with less than matinee-style looks suddenly started looking very nice through their personality. All these examples are cognitions—thoughts—building blocks of human intelligence—designed to optimize one's own lot in the mating game.

A domain as complex as mating requires a framework that is equally complex. Therefore, in this book we draw from many different disciplines—evolutionary biology, behavioral genetics, behavioral ecology, sociology, anthropology—and from subdisciplines of psychology—evolutionary psychology, developmental psychology, creativity, intelligence, social psychology, personality psychology—and more. Many of these threads may appear to conflict, such as the study of individual differences and the study of universal instincts. But science thrives on contradictions; in fact, only by putting various pieces of the puzzle together can we come to a deeper understanding of behaviors as complex as mating behaviors. Still, every new framework owes its debt, so before we get ahead of ourselves, the basic principles of evolutionary psychology and the field of human intelligence deserve particular attention because each is a major foundation of that framework.

Darwin and Peacocks

Evolutionary psychology is a perspective that underlies all of psychology—it's not a traditional area of study within psychology, such as, for instance, developmental psychology, which focuses on the development of psychological processes across the life span, or social psychology, which focuses on how people influence the thoughts and behaviors of an individual. Evolutionary psychology is a set of ideas, rooted in evolutionary theory, that can be applied to any psychological issue or question—it is, in essence, a way of understanding all aspects of mind and behavior.

Evolutionary psychology is traced back to Charles Darwin, whose theory of evolution was nearly as much about psychology as it was about biology. Darwin's theory of evolution by natural selection, which he based on extensive naturalistic studies of plants and animals in varied parts of the world, provides an extremely logical and powerful explanation for why (and how) species of plants and animals take the forms that they do. In his best-known work, he studied the beaks of finches on the Galapagos Islands. The important riddle that he initially asked regarding these birds concerned his observation that their beaks seemed specialized to particular circumstances of their localized environments. The species of finches at the rocky coast, for instance, had relatively long beaks that seemed *designed* for pulling food out of holes between rocks. Finches in the rain forests had beaks that seemed *designed* for getting food out from the bark of trees. How did these birds come to have such remarkably optimized features?

Darwin's answer came in the form of his theory of natural selection, which suggests that qualities of organisms (which are partly inherited from parents) vary and, further, that certain qualities will ultimately be more likely to lead to survival and reproduction (i.e., *reproductive success*) than others. Importantly, factors that lead to reproductive success are specific to particular environments—a chick with a relatively long beak at the coast is likely to prosper, whereas a chick with a relatively long beak in the rain forest is not.

A quality that is thought to increase the likelihood of reproductive success is called an *adaptation* (and is referred to as *adaptive*). Adaptations are, thus, qualities of organisms (often referred to as *phenotypes*) that increase reproductive success. Additionally, such qualities reflect a good *fit* between an organism and an environment. As such, scientists often refer to such adaptations as phenotypes that *increase fitness* (or, often, *qualities that increase genetic fitness*).

An additional important point regarding natural selection concerns the idea of change or *mutation*. With the advent of the field of genetics in the early part of the 20th century, evolutionary theory and research on genetics were ultimately synthesized (an event now referred to as the *great evolutionary synthesis*, largely attributed to the work of the biologist Ernst Mayr[2]). During the sexual reproduction process (or any reproduction process), copying errors are possible. When a copying error takes place in the genes during the reproductive process, the outcome is considered a mutation. Although the lion's share of mutations are deleterious (a fact that corresponds to the modern-day connotation of the word), an occasional mutation leads to a phenotypic quality that is relatively adaptive. For instance, the first finches near the coast of the Galapagos Islands that had, by chance, mutations coding for relatively long beaks were more likely to eat, survive, and, ultimately, reproduce compared with their "normal" *conspecifics* (i.e., members of their same species). Thus, the long beak (because of its effective fit with localized environmental conditions) would be naturally selected (and would be likely to stay in the gene pool). Ultimately, through many generations of this process, the adaptive phenotypic quality (i.e., the long beak) will come to typify the entire species (i.e., only long-beaked finches will exist on the rocky coast).

One of Darwin's most important psychological theories pertains not to natural selection but rather to *sexual selection* (sexual selection is really just a particular type of natural selection). The puzzle that led to Darwin's theory of sexual selection was the peacock's tail—colorful and beautiful on the one hand and conspicuous, wasteful, and seemingly maladaptive on the other. How could evolution by natural selection favor such a wasteful feature? Peacocks with a large, colorful tail are surely more likely to be picked out by predators than are their dull-tailed counterparts. Further, imagine how much the body of a peacock would have in terms of physiological resources if it didn't have this gaudy appendage to maintain! Darwin once said, "The sight of a feather in a peacock's tail, whenever I gaze at it, makes me sick!"

Darwin's reaction to the existence of the bright plumage of the peacock led him to one of his most important insights. Given how sexual reproduction works, he concluded that reproduction is, ultimately, more important than survival! If one animal (let's call it a *survivor*) has a feature that improves survival a great deal (but that inhibits reproduction) and a competing animal (let's call it a *reproducer*) has a feature that tends to inhibit survival but facilitates reproduction, the reproducer will leave more offspring than the survivor. Accordingly, any feature that is, for whatever reason, desirable to potential mates will be selected—regardless of its survival value. Thus, the preferences of the opposite sex (preferences that, clearly, fall under the umbrella of psychological phenomena) select the qualities that will be reproduced in offspring. Why do peacocks have such a bright tail? Because peahens think a bright tail is a *hot* commodity.

Once Darwin came up with the notion of sexual selection, he concluded that it exists in *two* important domains: courtship between members of opposite sexes (*intersexual selection*) and competition for mates between members of the same sex (*intrasexual selection*). A typical example of intrasexual selection concerns the large horns of grazing mammals such as caribou. Male caribou have antlers that often exceed 4 feet in length and 20 pounds in weight. These antlers often grow at the rate of an inch a day during the summer season and require so much calcium that the animal's body often taps calcium from the skull to use in the creation of the antler![3] How then, could such an obviously costly and handicap-inducing characteristic be selected by the great optimizing forces of evolution? Answer: intrasexual competition. Bulls use the antlers to fight for access to females. Bulls who win these competitions reproduce. Bulls with relatively large antlers are more likely to be such victors. The genes coding for their ornamental headgear get reproduced along the way.

Intrasexual selection is also observable in humans every time a socially dominant male derogates a competitor's strength, social status, intelligence, personality, or physical qualities (e.g., penis size). Similarly, intrasexual selection is at work when a woman paints a competitor as overly promiscuous, overly prudish, catty, or unattractive. One of the great—and simple—insights of modern evolutionary psychology is this: It is often the case that features of human behavior parallel those found in other sexually reproducing species. We can learn an awful lot about ourselves by looking to the nature of other animals that were shaped by the same kinds of evolutionary forces that created us.

In terms of both his theory of sexual selection (which suggests that the psychological preferences of one sex can come to shape the phenotype of the other sex over evolutionary time) and his theory of emotional expression across species as having been shaped by evolutionary forces (described in his 1872 book,

The Expression of the Emotions in Man and Animals), Darwin was keenly aware of implications for his theory of evolution on the psychology of animals—including humans. Thus, from the get-go, evolutionary theory was designed to be a theory of psychology.

Modern evolutionary psychology, which represents a revolution within psychology, has many different forms. At its core, however, evolutionary psychology is the application of evolutionary principles to an understanding of psychological processes and behavior. Evolutionary psychologists examine psychological questions by addressing what the great evolutionary ethologist, Nikolaas Tinbergen, called *proximate* and *ultimate* questions. Proximate questions address the immediate causes of behavior, often including stimuli in the immediate environment of the organism or physiological mechanisms inside the organism. Ultimate questions about behavior lead into the ancestral past of an organism's species, addressing how some behavior or psychological process would have been adaptive (in terms of survival-based natural selection or reproduction-based sexual selection) for the organism's ancestors.

Consider, for instance, the ability to present oneself as attractive to potential mates—surely important to mating success. We all try to present ourselves as attractive, with varying success. Consider the woman who wears way too much make-up, the guy who uses too much cologne, or the woman who wears the all-too-visible thong at the family reunion. When it comes to this aspect of mating intelligence, some of us just miss the boat (although the thong display may be adaptive in certain short-term mating contexts).

The ability to effectively present oneself as attractive in the mating domain likely has its roots in environmental upbringing. Some of us were raised in households that focused on the perspectives of others and on the impressions that we give of ourselves. Others (like us) were raised in households that focused much less on the importance of such impressions. For instance, Glenn Geher (hereafter referred to as GG) didn't realize that it was a good idea to own more than one pair of shoes until he was about 26—and those "shoes" were, in fact, sneakers! This could partly explain his challenged mating life before that point in time. Likewise, Scott Barry Kaufman's (hereafter referred to as SBK) mom always labeled his clothes drawers while he lived at home. When he first arrived at college, she labeled all his clothes drawers in his dorm room as well. SBK never thought twice about this until one day when he found his date laughing hysterically at the "underwear drawer" label his mom had applied to his clothes bureau. When he never heard from that date again, he became aware of his need to modify aspects of his mating behavior.

From an ultimate perspective, this ability to know how to present oneself to appear attractive clearly makes sense as having been shaped from evolutionary forces. Ancestral humans who not only *tried* to present themselves as attractive but also were *intelligent* and, as such, *successful* in these efforts were more likely to attract mates and, thus, more likely to reproduce and leave genes in future generations.

Understanding the *proximate* origins of this ability allows us to think about ourselves and the factors in our own lives that shape our mating psychology. On the other hand, understanding the *ultimate* origins of this ability encourages us to consider why this ability matters in a big-picture sense. A superficial analysis of this ability may lead a misguided individual (or *individuals*, such as GG and SBK a few years back...) to say something like, *"Any woman who judges me by the number of shoes I have or by the relationship I have with my mother isn't worth my time!"*

The ultimate explanation helps us see all this in a wider perspective—it allows us, for instance, to realize that women's psychology has been shaped by evolution to pay careful attention to behavioral and physical features of men in making choices of mates. This tendency is not capricious—and it's not really *superficial*, at least from an ultimate evolutionary perspective. Ancestral females who didn't engage in such discriminating mental work were less likely to mate with a high-quality male and were less likely to become our ancestors. Accordingly, working on skills associated with being perceived as attractive by potential mates is worthwhile for anyone. Such an ultimate-origin insight provides practical lessons regarding why presentation matters—and why it should matter. By understanding behaviors at each of these levels (proximate and ultimate), evolutionary psychologists can paint a relatively deep and multifaceted portrait of the causes of some psychological processes that typify our species.

Thus, evolutionary psychology seeks to understand both proximate and ultimate causes of species-typical psychological processes in light of the basic ideas of evolutionary theory. Using this approach, evolutionary psychologists have shed light on many questions about human nature that were rather puzzling before the application of evolutionary principles to an understanding of human behavior.

For instance, consider Michael Cunningham's work on qualities that we find attractive in female faces.[4] By examining photographs of women from the Miss Universe contest, Cunningham was able to address features of women who are considered beautiful in a truly cross-cultural, universal sense. The results were clear: the most beautiful women were those with full lips, large eyes, thick hair, and smooth skin. In his evolutionary analysis of the data, Cunningham applies an evolutionary lens: a major feature of reproduction in our species has to do with menarche and menopause—the reproductive years of women are limited. Men under ancestral conditions who happened to, by chance, have psychological preferences for women who were fertile were more likely to mate with such women and were more likely to successfully reproduce—sending such preferences into subsequent generations (to the extent that such preferences have a heritable basis). Focusing on such qualities as full lips and thick hair makes sense from an evolutionary perspective because these are precisely the physical features that degrade with aging (relatively older women tend to have relatively thin lips and hair). Thus, using these particular physical qualities as an attractiveness cue would have been adaptive in our ancestral environment.[5]

Importantly, the evolutionary forces that created the human nervous system ultimately underlie all aspects of our psychology—from the nature of a baby's cry, to the fear that young children have of strange men, to the foods that we find particularly yummy, to our most common fears, such as those of spiders, snakes, and heights. However, mating behaviors are those behaviors in particular that bear directly on the ultimate evolutionary outcome: *reproduction*. Accordingly, many evolutionary psychologists focus on the nature of human mating.

One piece of mating intelligence comes from evolutionary psychology. The other major area of psychology that inspired the mating intelligence framework is the field of human intelligence. Where does mating intelligence fit in with all the other "intelligences" that one hears about? There are very active research programs on a number of other intelligences, which have relevance for mating intelligence. As such, we would expect some overlap with other existing theories of intelligence, but not complete overlap. Let's take a brief tour of the highly active, constantly evolving, and fascinating field of human intelligence.

The Scientific Study of Human Intelligence

General Intelligence

At the turn of the 20th century, the British psychologist Charles Spearman[6] made a startling discovery. He noticed that performances across a number of different school subjects were positively related to one another. In other words, students who tended to get good grades in one class tended to get good grades in other classes, and vice versa. This pattern has been found over and over again, across school subjects as well as diverse tests of cognitive ability.[7]

What is particularly interesting about this phenomenon (sometimes referred to as the *positive manifold*) is that the tests that appear to correlate with each other are seemingly different from each other in terms of surface content. Some tests measure the ability to form analogies, whereas others measure the ability to manipulate images in one's mind. The fact that all sufficiently large and diverse arrays of cognitive tests tend to positively correlate with each other suggests that they are all measuring a similar process or set of processes. Spearman hypothesized that all of the tests measure a core reasoning process, which transcends particular content. He labeled this the *general factor of intelligence*, or the *g factor* (not to be confused with the *G-spot*) for short. He labeled the abilities specific to each tests as *s* (for *specific*).

Although there is accumulating evidence that the *g* factor does not comprise a single, unitary process or cognitive mechanism,[8] there is wide acceptance that *g* in an aggregate statistical sense is a very real phenomenon and does a good job predicting academic achievement,[9] occupational success in professional fields such as physics, medicine, and law,[10] and even health and longevity.[11] As we noted in the preface, most *g* factor theorists haven't conducted too much research on how *g* operates in the mating domain. But what *is* the relationship between IQ (often used as a proxy for *g*) and mating intelligence?

Are Those with a High IQ Clueless About Mating?

The relevance of IQ to mating depends on the mating intelligence component in question. As we discuss in more detail later, the mating intelligence framework distinguishes between the *display* of traits and the use of those traits to navigate the mating domain. These two sets of skills don't necessarily correlate, a state of affairs that presents an intriguing irony: those with the sexiest mental and personality traits may also be the most clueless when it comes to navigating the turbulent waters of the mating domain! Alternatively, very intelligent people may use their intelligence to learn about the mating domain in order to conquer it (there are cottage industries devoted to this,[12] and we have no doubt many of our readers fit this category).

Humans are highly sensitive to behavioral cues of potential mates that reveal *good genes,* in the evolutionary sense that they reveal a relatively low mutation load (a relatively low number of genetic mutations) and good health, survival, and successful reproductive abilities.[13] There is accumulating evidence that the *g* factor is at least partly an indicator of deleterious mutation load, a situation that affects many interacting genes and has an effect on the entire biological system.

The *g* factor has shown correlations with biological traits such as height, health, longevity, bodily symmetry, and even sperm quality.[14] Many of these correlations are very small and in some instances have not replicated,[15] but the results suggest that *g* may at least partially reveal a person's deleterious mutation load and level of instability during development.

We do want to point out that we are not suggesting that intelligence is *entirely* genetically determined—not by a long shot. We agree with Steven Pinker, who has argued in his 2003 book, *The Blank Slate: The Modern Denial of Human Nature,* that both extreme genetic determinism and extreme environmental determinism are misguided and pernicious. Our understanding of the latest research in epigenetics suggests that nature and nurture are always interacting and can never be separated.[16] This means that even though intelligence has substantial heritability,[17] and genes do play a role in building brains capable of intelligent functioning,[18] there are most certainly *many* interacting genes that play a role,[19] and the expression of genes is affected by many environmental variables and life experiences.[20] We will continually be highlighting the flexible and contextual nature of human intelligence throughout this book, thereby revealing the subtle and intricate ways in which biology (e.g., genes, the brain, and hormones) and context interact to contribute to mating outcomes.

Still, all selection pressures require at least a reasonable amount of genetic variation to do their job. If these relations between *g* and various measures of developmental stability replicate, much of human mate choice may be best conceptualized as an evolutionary adaptive and unconscious fear of heritable mutations, something we can refer to as *mutation phobia*. The basic idea of mutation phobia is that people are put off sexually by mental and physical traits that indicate an extremely high mutation load. Examples frequently given in the biological literature are body asymmetry or dullness of plumage.[21]

This may sound discriminatory, but every time you choose one mate over another, you *are* discriminating against the person you didn't choose. We also admit that this isn't a very romantic way to talk about mate selection. Certainly other systems, such as the attachment system, can come online, and powerful bonding emotions relating to love are certainly possible.[22] But keep in mind that natural and sexual selection mechanisms aren't as romantic as you and I have the potential to be! Increasing reproductive outcomes is their bottom line, regardless of how that is achieved. So, we have a lot of emotions and cognitive adaptations mixed together in one body. Humans are complicated.

We understand now that IQ may be related to the *display* component of mating intelligence. But is someone with an IQ of 160 much sexier than the person with an IQ of 120? In general, probably not. It is likely that our mate preferences were shaped more to *avoid* mating with people with an extremely high mutational load, than to finely discriminate among individuals with roughly similar levels of mutation load.[23]

With that said, there are certainly individual differences. IQ may play an important role in finding a good match—those with similar IQ levels tend to marry each other.[24] This could be due to a number of factors, including that people with similar levels of IQ may feel more comfortable being with one another, sharing similar values and enjoying similar intellectual pursuits and conversations (see Chapter 3, where we discuss individual differences in mate preferences). We must also take into consideration the existence of other personality traits and cognitive abilities. Someone who has a high IQ but isn't particularly interesting, creative, or entertaining may not be attractive to a lot of people (although that person may certainly be interesting to others with a similar personality). Likewise, someone with a low IQ can compensate by highlighting other traits.

Indeed, research shows that IQ is only moderately correlated with creativity, with the relationship differing significantly depending on the domain.[25] Also, IQ shows little relation to personality traits, with the notable exception of the openness to experience domain, which is related to higher IQ.[26] In the next Chapters 2 and 3, we consider the roles of creativity and personality in mating intelligence.

The fact that IQ may matter for different people suggests the importance of researchers studying mating intelligence in populations from all strata of society. College sophomores, who are typically studied in mating research, tend to have higher IQs than the general population, so firm conclusions shouldn't be made based solely on these studies. Also, more research needs to be conducted cross-culturally. Many of the studies (but certainly not all) summarized in this book are from North American college sophomores. We hope this book sparks researchers around the world to investigate this important topic.

Finally, what about the relation between IQ and the mating mechanisms component of mating intelligence? Those with higher IQs tend to discount immediate rewards in favor of longer-term goals.[27] Perhaps those with higher levels of general intelligence are better able to prioritize their immediate goals in the service of obtaining their longer-term goals. In recent years, neuropsychologists have located a set of brain areas in the frontal lobe (around the forehead) of humans that support self-control. These "executive functions" were the last bit of our brain to evolve and include the ability to plan, inhibit, and delay responding.[28] Whenever someone must focus hard on a task and ignore distractions, this area is particularly active. The extent to which these areas light up in a person predicts a lot of important outcomes, including whether people are likely to follow the norms of society, resist a wide variety of temptations, and engage in risky behaviors. Executive control even predicts the willpower to resist the urge to eat M&M's when on a diet![29]

Individual differences in these very same self-control cognitive mechanisms have been used to explain mating-specific behavior, such as why some people cheat on their partners and others stay faithful. A recent study found that performance on tests measuring various aspects of executive functioning were positively related to the reported tendency to stay faithful, actual flirting behavior, and desire to go on a date with someone other than one's partner.[30] In this book, we provide some hints to how intelligence plays itself out in terms of mating strategies, but more research needs to be conducted to see how intelligence affects species-typical mating mechanisms.

Now, let's briefly consider the relationships of mating intelligence to other "intelligences" that have been proposed by researchers.

Multiple Intelligences

During the past 30 years, various researchers have emphasized additional "intelligences" that are tied to a specific context or domain of intellectual functioning. This approach is in line with the idea from evolutionary psychology that humans possess a variety of modules, information-processing devices, or biological propensities, which are designed to react to particular environmental stimuli.[31,32]

One of the first to go beyond *g* was Howard Gardner[33] when he introduced his theory of multiple intelligences. According to the latest version of his theory, there are eight independent cognitive abilities: linguistic, logical-mathematical, spatial, musical, bodily-kinesthetic, interpersonal, intrapersonal, and naturalist.

Gardner's theory has profoundly influenced educational psychology, although the theory's impact on psychological testing is not nearly as strong, garnering criticism from *g* factor theorists that when they try to measure his intelligences, most of his so-called independent intelligences are highly correlated with one another.[34] Gardner's intelligences can be conceptualized as talents or "domains of mind" that evolved to solve recurrent problems in the environment,[35] with general intelligence playing a role in all domains to different degrees, depending on how much explicit, on-the-spot novel reasoning is involved.

At any rate, Gardner's theory paved the way for others to propose additional intelligences. In the early part of the 20th century, Edward Thorndike defined social intelligence simply as the ability to understand and interact with others. In recent years, John Kihlstrom has generated scholarly work on social intelligence, and the study of how the brain is related to social interactions ("social neuroscience") is a burgeoning field. In his book, *Social Intelligence: The New Science of Human Relationships,* Daniel Goleman argues for the need for the latest social neuroscience research findings to affect the construct of social intelligence and our understanding of relationships. We also see its relevance to our understanding of mating.

A major issue addressed by researchers on the topic of social intelligence is whether social intelligence is related to general intelligence. Are those of us who score higher on traditional measures of intelligence better able to navigate the wavy waters of the social world? In addressing this issue, some researchers have emphasized that intelligence is specific to each context in which it is applied.[36] Goleman has argued that social intelligence cannot be measured properly by paper-and-pencil tests but rather must gauge the individual's ability to be socially appropriate in actual social interactions.[37] Gardner has echoed this sentiment in response to critiques that his intelligences correlate with each other when administered in test format.[38] Cognitive psychologist Robert J. Sternberg proposed a distinction between *analytical intelligence* (the type of intelligence mostly measured by IQ tests) and *practical intelligence* (the type of intelligence one uses in the real world to solve problems relevant to one's own life).[39,40] We agree that to fully capture human intelligence in its many guises one must go beyond laboratory testing. Perhaps nowhere is this more relevant than in regard to the mating domain (for obvious reasons)!

Social intelligence may therefore be specifically geared toward solving problems presented in social life. As noted earlier, Gardner includes social intelligence in his theory of multiple intelligences. He splits social intelligence into *intrapersonal* and *interpersonal* intelligence, defining intrapersonal intelligence as the ability to know your own internal mental and emotional state and interpersonal intelligence as the ability to understand and distinguish those whom surround you in the social world. In support of the idea of a distinct kind of intelligence designed for social purposes (i.e., social intelligence), Gardner points to people with brain damage that impairs their ability to recognize the internal states of others but does not necessarily impair their performance on nonsocial cognitive tasks (e.g., math).

What role would social intelligence play in mating? A socially intelligent individual would successfully communicate with other individuals and accurately represent the internal world of his or her acquaintances. Mating clearly includes socially relevant tasks such as acquiring and keeping a mate, and it inevitably involves a degree of social interaction and navigation. Not only must an individual possess the ability to read another's thoughts and feelings, but this individual must also possess a proficiency in interpreting complex social stimuli. We take up these issues more in Chapter 7 when we discuss mind-reading. The mating-intelligent individual must be able to gauge the social standing of potential mates as well as evaluate his or her own status in society and thereby identify realistically who he or she can potentially acquire as a mate (although, as we note in later chapters, a modicum of self-delusion can be adaptive!). In sum, mating intelligence may be construed as a special case of social intelligence.

Emotional intelligence is another newcomer on the scene.[41] Emotional intelligence— generally comprising cognitive abilities tied to emotional processes— is closely related to social intelligence, yet it has received more attention by scientific researchers. Peter Salovey and John Mayer, who developed the idea of emotional intelligence (popularized by Daniel Goleman in 1997), see this kind of intelligence as consisting of four main components: the ability to identify emotions, the assimilation of emotions into thought, the understanding of emotions, and the management of emotions. Like for many of Gardner's and Sternberg's intelligences, tests of emotional intelligence correlate with tests of general intelligence, but these also are partially separate.[42] Emotional intelligence relates to additional variables that clearly play a role in the mating domain (and that we touch on throughout the book), such as openness to experience, agreeableness, social competence, quality of relationships, interpersonal sensitivity, work relationships, drug use, deviancy, aggressiveness, and psychiatric symptoms.[43] Many of these relationships still exist even after controlling for the effects of general intelligence and personality.

It is not difficult to imagine the impact of emotional intelligence on the mating domain. On average, a person who cannot control his emotions will not likely be as successful in obtaining a desirable mate compared with his emotionally savvy counterpart. In fact, several recent scientific papers that examine the relationship between emotional intelligence and success in intimate relationships—conducted by Marc Brackett and his colleagues at Yale—suggest that emotional intelligence does correspond to success and happiness in relationships. There is no doubt: emotional intelligence is an important facet of mating intelligence (see Chapter 7 for more on the link between emotional intelligence and mating intelligence).

In light of the importance that emotions play in the mating game, it is easy to see how emotional abilities may underlie mating intelligence. For instance, think about how much emotional processing takes place when people engage in the crucial task of assessing interest of potential mates. *Does he like me? Does he like me that way?* Suppose you're a college student at the bar with some friends for a night of dancing and laughs. You see Christopher from your statistics class. *Nice guy. What a big, warm smile he gives you! Wasn't expecting that...hmm. And it's not just his smile—his posture when he comes over to talk with me is very warm and approachable—his emotional expressions are telling me something.* Clearly, emotional intelligence, including the kinds of emotional-cognitive tasks given in this example, represents an important slice of mating intelligence.

Theories of emotional and social intelligence get us closer to explaining intelligence applied to the mating world. However, researchers studying these kinds of intelligence have not traditionally focused on mating-relevant issues and therefore have not been as effective in helping us understand intimate relationships as they could be. Current theories of intelligence provide us with great potential for understanding the psychology of human mating. We think it's time for this potential to be tapped. By drawing on past work on human intelligence and a deep understanding of our evolutionary past, the mating intelligence framework takes us a step further in our ability to understand the psychological aspects of human mating. It was from this fusing of evolutionary psychology and intelligence that *mating intelligence* was born.

Mating Intelligence Unleashed

Mating intelligence consists of the entire set of psychological abilities designed for sexual reproduction. For instance, the thought-work that one engages in when trying to figure out whether a romantic partner might engage in an act of sexual infidelity is the particular kind of thought-work that falls under the umbrella of mating intelligence. Mating intelligence is not a single adaptation, nor is it located in a single brain region or a single gene. It is a collection of dozens or hundreds of distinct psychological processes and learned skills that affect the mating domain based heavily on context.

Such cognitive processes include memories (*I do remember her talking with that guy Andrew extensively at the Taylors' party* ...), perceptions of others' behaviors and emotions (*She kept smiling and doing that hair thing when they were talking—she just seemed so happy and into him, now that I think about it* ...), perceptions of one's own emotional states (*Gosh, now that I think about, something really didn't feel right to me about that interaction at all—I was totally pissed off about it even though I tried not to be* ...), attention (*I so noticed that she took the phone upstairs—why?!!—Maybe I'll check the caller ID*), and, often, excessive planning that taps cognitive resources (*OK—we'll cancel our other plans so we can go to the Hills' party on Friday—Andrew and his wife are ALWAYS at the Hills' parties—that'll give me a chance to reassess this situation* ...).

Crucially, there are *gender differences* as well as *individual differences* in all of these cognitive processes, and these differences relate to mating outcomes. People aren't always going to behave the same way or make the same decisions. Consider the idea of cognitive resources. There are a lot of ways for our cognitive resources to be depleted,[44] and the mating domain is no exception. For some people, just *talking* to someone of the opposite sex can be a cognitively demanding task. A recent study by Karremans and colleagues in the Netherlands found that mixed-sex interactions temporarily cause a decline in cognitive functioning.[45] Men, but not women, were the ones who showed the decline in cognitive performance after interacting with a woman. Men also reported higher levels of impression management in mixed-sex interactions relative to same-sex interactions.

Unfortunately, the researchers did not explore individual differences, but we surmise that the guys who did not get anxious or lose their head (literally!) while talking to women would fare better in the mating domain. They would undoubtedly come across as more attractive to women—more confident as well as more sexually experienced. These are important mating intelligence skills.

When our cognitive resources are depleted, we are also more at risk of cheating. Simone Ritter and her colleagues[46] found that under normal conditions, romantically involved heterosexual individuals reported less interest in attractive opposite-sex individuals than those who were single. All bets were off though, when they were cognitively taxed by the experimenter; for example, if they were under heavy time pressure while completing a task. In these situations, with their executive-control guards down, there was no longer a difference between single and romantically involved individuals. Other research shows that people in monogamous relationships whose minds are fatigued spend more time looking at attractive potential mates,[47] are more likely to accept a coffee date from an attractive person who is part of the experiment,[48] and report a greater likelihood of cheating.[49] It appears, then, that it's much easier for romantically involved people to reject attractive potential partners when they have enough cognitive resources and time to consciously make that decision to control their impulses.

We are also not at our best cognitively when we have too many options. Researchers Alison P. Lenton and Marco Francesconi[50] looked at 84 speed-dating events and found that when people faced abundant choice (larger speed-dating events), they were not able to use as may cues to make a decision—so they paid attention to the most quickly and easily assessed characteristics such as height and weight. These findings were the same for both males and females. Yes, both males *and* females can get cognitively overloaded.

The idea that cognitive processes play a role in mating is actually a rather new development.[51] In 1998 Geoffrey Miller and Peter Todd published their seminal paper "Mate Choice Turns Cognitive," in which they reviewed the accumulating research on the role of perception, judgment, and search strategies in the mating domain. Note, however, that cognitive processes that constitute mating intelligence can be deliberate and conscious, or they can be unconscious. Importantly, the unconscious elements of mating intelligence need not be considered unintelligent. Indeed, many of the mechanisms, such as cue integration (see Chapter 4) and mind-reading (see Chapter 7), operate at a level that isn't typically accessible to conscious awareness.

There is strong consensus in psychology that humans possess two quite distinct modes of thought—one controlled and the other more automatic.[52] Many automatic processes may lie outside our conscious awareness, but they still can be very adaptive.[53] Dual-process theories of cognition have greatly increased our understanding of a wide range of cognitive, personality, social, developmental, and cross-cultural phenomenon. In fact, one of the newest theories of human intelligence to come onto the scene makes just this point. According to SBK's Dual-Process Theory of Human Intelligence, the key to predicting differences in any slice of human intelligent behavior is to understand differences in the mix of goal-directed and spontaneous cognitive processes that make up that behavior.[54] According to this theory, neither mode of cognition is more important than the other; it all depends on the context. As we will demonstrate in this book, many spontaneous processes that draw on our unconscious mind are heavily tied to mating issues and have an underlying evolutionary logic that is quite smart.

The Mating Intelligence Framework

The flavor of human courtship is markedly different from that of other species. We will do just about anything to attract mates, from singing and dancing to writing poems and painting marvelously complex and aesthetic pictures. We also are unique in the number of dates we go on before we make a commitment to a mate. Orangutans and turtles don't tend to go to many classy restaurants where they engage in witty banter and have long conversations about preferences and values. The interesting question, though, is, *Why do we bother*?

Surely most humans are looking for a mate whom they can connect with on a "deep, personal level" and who shares similar hopes, desires, values, goals, and fears. But even so, mate preferences aren't *arbitrary*. In humans, fitness can be demonstrated in a lot of ways, and we certainly adopt many different strategies to attract potential mates. This book focuses on two major types of courtship displays: *cognitive* courtship displays and *personality* courtship displays. Now, let's briefly look at the other component of mating intelligence: *mating mechanisms*.

Mating mechanisms allow us to navigate the complex, emotionally laden, and often-treacherous sea of human mating. These mating mechanisms are comparable to the adaptations for mating that many evolutionary psychologists write about. For instance, David Buss and his colleagues provide evidence suggesting that men are particularly astute at detecting signs of a female partner engaging in sexual infidelity compared with females (who are more astute than men at many other social-cognitive tasks). For instance, these researchers found that men remember more details regarding sexual infidelity than women do. Buss argues that men's astuteness regarding this issue is an evolutionarily shaped adaptation.[55]

The evolutionary reasoning that Buss and colleagues apply suggests that males in our evolutionary past were faced with the problem of paternity certainty—unlike females, who were always sure that their offspring were indeed their genetic kin. Males have never been 100% sure that their offspring are their own. As such, evolution would favor men with cognitive capacities that helped them reduce the likelihood of a mate's sexual infidelity. One mechanism that helps with this task is awareness of information that may reliably predict whether a female will have sex with another man. This mechanism is one of the many psychological processes that together represent mating intelligence.

Other mating mechanisms addressed in detail in this book include the ability to effectively judge a partner's mate value, the ability to detect deception in the sphere of mating, and the ability to modify one's mating strategies in light of existing conditions of the local mating market, in addition to a plethora of others. In combination, these cognitive processes that bear on mating outcomes make up the mating mechanism component of mating intelligence.

Mating mechanisms differ markedly from courtship abilities. Whereas mating mechanisms are explicitly about the mating game, courtship displays are explicitly about something altogether different (such as music, art, poetry, extraversion, and kindness). Thus, our twofold theory of mating intelligence suggests that half of mating intelligence—mating mechanisms—is dedicated to helping us deal with stimuli tied to mating, whereas the other half—courtship displays—is only indirectly related to mating and is, essentially, designed to help us acquire high-quality mates by advertising ourselves as good mating prospects. See Table 1.1 for a breakdown of these domains of mating intelligence.

Table 1.1 **Defining Features of the Two Main Domains of Mating Intelligence**

	Courtship Displays	*Mating Mechanisms*
Definition	Displays of intellect, personality, emotions, and creativity that are attractive to potential mates	Cognitive processes that deal with mating-relevant issues
Example	Ray Charles' vocal and piano virtuosity	Paying attention to cues regarding whether one's mate has cheated sexually
Relationship to mating	Indirect	Direct
Focus	Focus is on some area that is not tied directly to mating (e.g., social extraversion, linguistics, art, poetry)	Focus is on specific aspects of mating (e.g., assessing mate value, analyzing cues of infidelity)
Purpose	To help attract high-quality mates	To help people navigate the waters of human mating

Of course, there can be overlap among the two components. For instance, conscientiousness can be used both as a courtship display and as a mechanism for maintaining a healthy, harmonious relationship. Or consider one of the most important areas of mating: mate selection. In the mate-selection process, we engage in courtship displays and use our mating mechanisms to assess the courtship displays of others. In the process, there are several universal issues that we face. When trying to attract a mate, what courtship displays should you use? How should you go about displaying your physical qualities, such as strength, virility, fertility, and athleticism? What psychological traits are important to convince your desired partner that you have the capacity for kindness, intelligence, creativity, resourcefulness, and social status? How accurate are we at evaluating the courtship displays of potential mates? Likewise, how well can we deceive in our own efforts to present ourselves as an amazing mate? Perhaps most importantly, how should we differ in how we present ourselves depending on what kind of mating outcome we are seeking (short term vs. long-term)?

It is important to note that mating intelligence doesn't predict that all cognitive processes relating to mating should relate to each other. Some skills or strategies that increase an individual's chances of obtaining a short-term fling may backfire when trying to acquire a high-quality mate and maintain that relationship. The mating intelligence framework should help us make predictions based on mating strategy (short-term vs. long-term) and other important variables, such as the age, gender, personality, attachment style, and life history of the person. We hope that further research will bear out the full structure of the mating intelligence framework. We are just laying the groundwork.

This Book

Mating intelligence combines two approaches—the study of individual differences that intelligence researchers are focused on, and the study of universal adaptations that concern evolutionary psychologists.[56] By bringing together both perspectives, we can come to a more complete understanding of human mating.

We first discuss courtship displays in the cognitive domain (Chapter 2) and in the personality domain (Chapter 3), before turning to cognitive mechanisms that are used in different phases of human mating. Chapter 4 looks at the various traits that are generally considered attractive and how these traits integrate and play out in the real world. Chapter 5 discusses the numerous mating strategies that exist among humans, all of which are highly dependent on context. In Chapter 6, we discuss adaptive biases such as overconfidence. Sometimes, self-delusion can be quite adaptive in the mating domain! In Chapter 7, we discuss the important role of emotional intelligence in mating intelligence as well as the conditions under which we deceive in our relationships. We also focus on the psychology of catching a lying mate. In Chapter 8, we use the mating intelligence framework to figure out whether nice people finish last.

A major goal of this book is to help people take knowledge gleaned from psychology so that they can succeed in their own mating-relevant goals. In our final chapter, Chapter 9, we explore implications of mating intelligence for real-life situations. Because different readers will be in different life stages, this book focuses on two important mating contexts: short-term mating (the singles scene) and long-term mating (the mysterious world of long-term relationships). Chapter 9 also discusses implications of mating intelligence for reducing socially undesirable mating behaviors such as violence and for increasing cross-communication between the sexes.

In the Epilogue, we present the "world-famous" Mating Intelligence Scale that will allow you to test your own mating intelligence. The chapter also brings together a lot of ideas presented throughout this book. We hope that by the end of your journey through this book, you will have some answers to the many puzzles of human mating.

2

"I'm Too Sexy for This Canvas"

Why Creativity Is Sexy

On any reasonably sunny summer day, you can visit Washington Square Park to witness a phenomenon. All sorts of performance acts, from juggling to jazz to jiu-jitsu, are presented to the social world in full peacock display. The combination of sounds is not too pleasant, but some of the individual acts are quite good (whereas others are definitely not as good). But as you walk around, you'll notice a look of determination in each of the performer's eyes, whether it's the grunge-rocker wannabe playing guitar and singing his heart out or the sword swallower trying to hide his grimace as he tries to push the sword down his throat. Without question, women also engage in all kinds of courtship display activities[1]—but when it comes to overt mating displays, we see men competing with each other much more for the spotlight.

This phenomenon, of course, doesn't start and stop at Washington Square Park—it's happening everywhere. Been to a gym lately? It's like a tidal wave whenever a cute woman walks down the line of bench press machines. Each guy she passes pumps faster and more ferociously. On the mats, guys lying down next to flexible women look like Mexican jumping beans as they consciously or unconsciously display their fitness. The second the women leave the mat, the men flop down defeated. It's funny to watch.

Humans possess a variety of ways to display mate value and employ many strategies to attract a potential mate. We aren't arguing that everything people do is for the purposes of mating (for instance, children are very creative even though they have no interest in mating), but consciously or unconsciously, once the mating motive is activated, people are driven more to showcase their biological fitness. Fitness need not be purely physical though. This chapter is all about *mental* courtship displays. The mating motive can be quite a potent force for creativity. Hester Thrale inspired Samuel Johnson. Yoko Ono inspired John Lennon. Woody Allen has had a number of muses. Lou Andreas-Salomé inspired Friedrich Nietzsche, Rainer Maria Rilke, and Sigmund Freud.

To capture the mating motive in the laboratory, Vladas Griskevicius, Robert Cialdini, and Douglas Kenrick[2] conducted a clever study on college students. First, they tested the baseline creativity levels of their participants by asking them to write a short story about ambiguous cartoon and abstract images. Then they asked students to choose the most desirable romantic partner from a series of photos taken from Match.com. With their selected picture visible in front of them on the screen, participants were told to imagine going on a first date with the person in the photo and write a story about their idea of the perfect date with that person. The stories were rated by a panel of expert judges on creativity. In the control condition, participants looked at photos of a street with several buildings and imagined being on that street (a scenario that doesn't activate the mating motive in most normal humans!) and were told to write stories about what they thought about the most pleasant weather conditions to walk around and look at the buildings (sexy!).

Men's stories tended to be more creative in the mating motive condition than in the control condition. In fact, across multiple studies these researchers conducted, the mating motive had strong effects on men, even when a more objective measure of creativity involving the ability to access remote associations was used. Also, the mating motive had an effect on actual creative ability that couldn't be attributed to increased effort on the creativity tasks or changes in mood or arousal. The mating motive was even more powerful an incentive for being creative than a condition that involved just monetary incentive! This study shows how potent the mating motive can be and how it exerts its effects on creative performance even when the person knows that he is in a psychology experiment and isn't actually going to date the person who appears on the computer screen. All it took was for the mating motive to become activated. But what about the women? Did the mating motive boost their creativity as well?

The researchers didn't just ask participants to imagine a short-term or a long-term mating scenario. They also varied the level of commitment of the potential romantic partners in the imagined romantic scenarios. While men increased their creativity in every single condition (it doesn't take much to activate the mating motive in men!), women only increased their creative output in *one specific condition*—after imagining wanting to attract a clearly trustworthy and committed long-term mate, whom friends agreed was awesome (see Chapter 5 for more on mate-copying effects). This suggests that women do indeed respond to the mating motive (women are human, too!), but that they require a bit more assurance that their partner might be good relationship material.

These results make sense within the context of differential parental investment[3]: when pursuing a short-term mating strategy, women tend to be more guarded than men because they have a lot more at stake, reproductively speaking (that is, women risk getting pregnant, whereas men don't). But when pursuing a long-term mating strategy, men and women are much more similar in their mating goals and preferences—both expect to invest significantly in the offspring and want a partner who shows signs of dependability.

This finding may also explain why there are more female muses than male muses: it just might be easier and faster to turn on a male's mating motive. This is not to say that male muses don't exist though. Victorian poet Elizabeth Barrett Browning wrote her greatest work, *Sonnets from the Portugese*, in the throes of a relationship with a committed male fan, the poet Robert Browning. And there is no doubt that in many long-term committed relationships, both individuals continue to inspire each other creatively, spiritually, and emotionally.

Still, the initial passion that increases the mating motive naturally decreases during the course of a relationship and may require constant work to keep both the creative and mating sparks alive. As a demonstration of this, Kelly Campbell, James C. Kaufman, and Jacinta Gau[4] found that individuals in short-term relationships demonstrated higher levels of creativity compared with those in long-term relationships. Relationship length, however, was negatively associated with creativity, with the amount of passion in the relationship being an important moderating variable of this effect. The researchers concluded that long-term relationships, which tend to get more companionate than passionate as they proceed, require work to stay passionate.

Other research confirms the effects of the mating motive. In their paper "Bikinis Instigate Generalized Impatience in Intertemporal Choice," Bram Van den Bergh, Siegfried Dewitte, and Luk Warlop[5] found that the presence of sexy cues (e.g., a sexy television commercial) led to an urgency to consume rewarding stimuli (e.g., money, food) and an increase in divergent thinking ability in men compared with a nonsexual control condition. The same effect was not found for women. Interestingly, individuals with a sensitive reward system were more susceptible to the sexual cues, and those who had eaten recently were less susceptible to the cues. These findings highlight the importance of taking into account individual differences and contextual factors when looking at the effects of the mating motive. Similarly, Margo Wilson and Martin Daly[6] found that men who viewed attractive women chose a smaller sum of money the next day rather than a larger sum at a later date. Men were told that they could have between $15 and $35 immediately (depending on experimental condition) or between $50 and $75 in a week or more (depending on experimental condition). There was a significant effect for choosing the immediate reward in the attractive-face condition. The same effect was not found among women, or for men viewing cars instead of women.

The mating motive has been shown to have an effect even in domains as diverse as skateboarding and chess. In one study, increased levels of testosterone were found in male skateboarders who were being observed by an attractive female—causing the young men to increase their risk-taking (as well as crash landings!).[7] In another recent study, Anna Dreber, Christer Gerdes, and

Patrik Gransmark[8] found that male chess players chose riskier strategies when playing against an attractive female opponent, even though it didn't help them improve their performance. Women's strategies were unaffected by the attractiveness of their opponent. Overall, even though prior research has shown that sexual arousal has an effect on sexual judgment and decision making,[9] the mating motive can also be quite a potent force for creativity and innovation. But why—in the first place—is creativity sexy?

Creativity as a Mental Courtship Display

The wonderfully complex and abstract qualities of the human mind that separate us from other beasts likely did not evolve solely because of their assistance in survival. How do the abilities to tell a clever anecdote, play a classical score on the piano without missing a note, sculpt an emotionally provocative piece of art, or write an articulate and interesting poem help in survival? In particular, how did these kinds of behaviors help our hominid ancestors survive under ancestrally natural conditions on the African savanna? They didn't. At least not *directly*.

According to Geoffrey Miller's notion of mental courtship displays, these high-level manifestations of creative intelligence have come to typify our species, and not only because they aided in survival.[10] An emotionally provocative poem would not help much in the event of a lion attack. Musical prowess is the last thing you need when the storm comes through the village. A particularly clever wit is more likely to get you punched in the face by a competing male compared with a wit that's altogether dull. However, remember that Darwin's theory of evolution suggests that there are *two* major forces that come to shape the nature of organisms—*natural selection* (which selects for qualities that aid in survival) and *sexual selection* (which selects for qualities that increase reproductive output). Perhaps, as Miller's theory of courtship display suggests, the creative intelligence that uniquely characterizes humans was heavily influenced by sexual selection.

Under this account, a feature such as our ability to write poetry or fiction arose not because these skills helped in survival but rather because they helped in the domain of life that's even more important than survival (from a Darwinian perspective): *mating*. Perhaps creative writing is sexy. Perhaps highly creative writers were more likely to acquire mates than those without imagination across the part of the history of our species that included poetry and fiction.[11] Not everyone is good at creative writing, but humans differ from each other in many different ways, and high levels of skill in any of a number of domains can be sexy from a sexual selection perspective. Indeed, in *The Mating Mind*, Miller[12] argues that sexual selection may have played a greater role than natural selection in shaping our species' talents for storytelling, art, music, sports, dance, humor, and leadership. The idea that music may have been shaped by sexual selection can be traced back to Darwin:

> It appears probable that the progenitors of man, either the males or females or both sexes, before acquiring the power of expressing mutual love in articulate language, endeavored to charm each other with musical notes and rhythm. (Darwin, 1871, p. 880)

On the face of it, this all certainly seems valid. There is plenty of sexual hysteria relating to rock stars, writers, and artists. Throughout history, many creative people (some with less than amazing looks) have had high reproductive success: Aphrodite, Woody Allen, Germaine Greer, Tori Amos, Jimi Hendrix, Charlie Chaplin, Pablo Picasso, Ray Charles, Albert Einstein, and Russell Brand just to name a few.

So if there is indeed a link between creativity and mating success, then it does not matter if poetry is a totally wasteful handicap when it comes to survival. Genes for the qualities that underlie poetic abilities will be selected by the fact that they increase reproductive opportunities—and, ultimately, reproductive success.

Miller's theory is certainly tantalizing. However, it begs the question: *Why would poetry and other uniquely human cognitive abilities be considered attractive in potential mates? From an ultimate, evolutionary perspective, what's sexy about ornamental displays of creativity?* The answer lies in part with the complex interaction of genes, the brain, and behavior. For many of the traits in our species, the genes are fixed and lead to little variation among people. In fact, most of the genes that are fixed in our species are identical to the genes found in other primate species. Genes coding for the number of appendages and the number of bones in the body, for example, show no variability across people. However, there are some traits for which there is great variability between people—at the level of genes coding for such traits and their corresponding phenotypes (or outward manifestations). For instance, there is a lot of variability in height (with adult North American males ranging from approximately 5 feet, 3 inches to 6 feet, 6 inches). Females who show a preference for relatively tall males (a common preference among females) are actually demonstrating a preference for certain genes—the genes coding for tallness over shortness. Thus, sexual choice for an observable feature of a potential mate actually selects (through sexual selection) certain genes to be more likely than others to propagate in the future.

According to this theory of sexual selection, it makes sense that we would be particularly focused on qualities of potential mates that effectively discriminated those with good genes versus others. Thus, people would be selected to focus on qualities of potential mates that show a good bit of variability between people. Using a feature that shows virtually no variability across people, such as number of fingers, would not lead to much discrimination in mate choice. But that's not what we focus on. Rather, we focus on qualities that show large variability between people—and such qualities tend to correspond to traits with ample genetic variability underlying them.

Enter the brain. About 84% of the roughly 20,000 genes in the human genome is expressed in the brain. The brain is, therefore, an organ that is telling of genetic quality like no other. How can we assess the quality of a potential mate's brain (in attempts to secure a high-quality mate with good genes that would combine well with our genes in the form of high-quality progeny)? Any Psychology 101 student at any university *should* be able to tell you: brain phenomena manifest in behavior. Thus, the cognitive courtship display theory suggests that a major component of human courtship focuses on assessing behavioral patterns of potential mates.

Which behavioral patterns should matter in our efforts to find mates with the best genes? The logic of Miller's theory is clear on this point. Some aspects of human behavior are universal. Our ability to discriminate happiness from anger, for instance, varies little. Thus, it makes little sense that we would focus on such features of others in courtship. However, think about how wildly people vary on so many dimensions tied to creative intelligence and personality. Think about musical ability, for instance. We vary quite a bit on that! From virtuosos with perfect pitch who can master any instrument to adults who can't clap to the beat of "Old McDonald"—and everyone in between. Miller's list of sexually selected mental indicators, including such qualities as musical ability, drawing ability, humor, and verbal ability, all share this same fact: they vary tremendously from person to person.

According to Miller's theory of courtship displays, such dimensions of human behavior are exactly the kinds of qualities that are telling of that person's combination of traits. Singers who profess their love on stage through a ballad are openly displaying a variety of abilities that all show substantial heritability and therefore are partly transmitted through genes—an extraverted personality, a relatively high intelligence, an ability to express emotions, an ability to obtain social status and resources, and so forth. Thus, they are exactly the kinds of features that we pay careful attention to in the area of courtship. In fact, we may have been selected by years of hominid evolution to do so.

There is evidence that intelligence and creativity are sexually attractive traits. Renowned evolutionary psychologist David Buss[13] investigated mate preferences across 37 cultures and found that intelligence was the second-most-desired trait in a sexual partner, right after kindness. Other studies show that creativity is also universally ranked very high on people's list of mate preferences.[14]

Creative people do have more sex partners. Daniel Nettle and Helen Clegg[15] looked at differences in sexual success for creative professionals compared with those not involved in a creative occupation. They found that professional artists and poets had about twice as many sexual partners as other people (a proxy for reproductive success). In a follow-up study, Clegg, Nettle, and Dorothy Miell[16] found that more successful artists had more sexual partners compared with less successful artists. The effect was only found among male artists, however, and remained even after taking into account income. This suggests that the higher number of sexual partners among male artists wasn't driven solely by high social status. The researchers speculate that perhaps professional female artists are more interested in seeking quality over quantity.

They also found that the more successful male artists were more interested in longer-term relationships. To explain the apparent contradiction, the researchers propose that more successful artists may have a greater choice of sexual partners, and successful male artists in particular may sample a larger number before settling down. They also raise the very real possibility that successful male artists may just cheat more on their partners.

The preference doesn't relate only to creative quality but also to engagement in creative activity. In one study, Melanie Beaussart, SBK, and James C. Kaufman administered a number of items measuring engagement in different types of creative activities in the performing arts, science, writing, and visual arts. They found that people who tended to engage in a wide variety of creative activities had a higher number of sexual partners. Consistent with the other studies just mentioned, this effect held only for men.

The reasons for these correlations are numerous. Perhaps creative men have more mating success than less creative men because they have assertive, outgoing personalities that make them more likely to seek out multiple mates (see next chapter), or perhaps women are attracted to creative men because of their exciting personalities and cognitive skills and actively seek them out for short-term encounters. It's most likely that a combination of both factors is operating.

Nevertheless, the link between creativity and mating success remains. Obviously, there are many ways a person can display his or her creativity. Some forms of creativity, like creative writing, take many years to master and many more to be great.[17] Other forms of creativity, such as humor, can be displayed right away. In fact, humor just might be one of the most effective and useful tools in the mating intelligence arsenal.

Humor as a Courtship Device

Many of us use wit and humor to woo, and for good reason: people report desiring humor and intelligence in a potential mate.[18] Humor serves many different functions, many of which affect the mating domain. Before we look at humor's many functions, let's first look at sex differences in humor display.

Sex Differences in Humor Display

Sex differences exist in both the production and appreciation of humor. Recent research suggests that while both men and women say they like a "good sense of humor" in a potential mate, they differ in what they mean by this phrase. Women tend to prefer men who make them laugh, whereas men tend to prefer women who laugh at their jokes.[19]

Consistent with this, Robert Provine[20] analyzed more than 3,000 singles ads and found that women were more likely to describe their good humor appreciation ability whereas men were more likely to offer good humor production ability. In another study, Eric Bressler and Sigal Balshine[21] found that although women rated funny men as better potential partners and as more friendly, fun, and popular, they didn't have the same preference for humorous women as potential friends. Additionally, a man's views of another man or woman's personality attributes were uninfluenced by how funny he or she was.

In general, females tend to demonstrate significantly more apprecia-tion of humor than men[22]; these differences begin in early childhood[23] and appear to reflect differences in sexual choosiness. For instance, Grammer and Eibl-Eibesfeldt[24] found that the amount of synchronized laughter during spon-taneous male/female conversations predicted mutual initial attraction, but the amount of laughter the woman produced was most predictive of mutual interest in actually dating. Clearly, woman's laughter is a good index of humor appreciation and has an impact in a mating context.

Other evidence for sex differences in humor appreciation comes from brain research. In one study, researchers looked into the brain as men and women responded to various cartoons.[25] In this study, participants looked at a num-ber of cartoons and were instructed to press a button if they found the car-toon funny. They also rated the humor value of each cartoon. Both men and women found about 80% of the cartoons funny and showed no reliable dif-ference in their ratings or response times. Women did, however, show deeper verbal analysis of the cartoons and derived more pleasure from the humor than men, as evidenced by higher activations in the left prefrontal cortex and the nucleus accumbens. Women were also faster to rate low-humor cartoons as unfunny.

In other research, Jennifer Hay[26] observed, based on historical sources, that males produce humor in courtship much more so than females. Helga Kotthoff[27] likewise reported evidence that males were more likely than females to pro-duce verbal humor in informal social situations. Of course, funny women can be immensely sexy, and many men do value humor ability in women (this quality tops each of our lists!). But taken together, the results suggest that females, on average, are more discriminating than men when it comes to humor and that men, on average, are more motivated to be funny.

Humor as a Mental Indicator, or the "Woody Allen Effect"

Earlier in this chapter, we presented Geoffrey Miller's hypothesis that various forms of creativity are partial indicators of mental "fitness." Based on this hypothesis, if humor and intelligence are significantly correlated, perhaps humor is an honest signal of intelligence. And if humor indeed is an honest mental indicator, humor ability may have evolved as a result of sexual selection through mate choice.[28]

Indeed, studies have shown a correlation between humor ability and general intelligence[29] and there is some evidence that humor is related to mating outcomes. Gil Greengross and Geoffrey Miller[30] found in a sample of 400 university students that general intelligence and verbal intelligence both predicted humor production ability (writing captions for cartoons), which in turn predicted lifetime number of sexual partners (a proxy of reproductive success). They found, however, that males showed higher average levels of humor production ability, which is consistent with the sexual selection perspective. From these results, Greengross argues that a sense of humor evolved at least partly through sexual selection as an intelligence indicator.

SBK, Jane Erickson, Sheela Ramesh, Aaron Kozbelt, Michael Magee, and James C. Kaufman[31] found similar results looking at the IQ, personality, sexual, and relationship correlates of humor production ability using a large, ethnically diverse sample. In the study, participants completed captions to four cartoons that were then rated by a judge for how funny they were. Although men, on average, were rated as funnier than females (consistent with Greengross's study), there was no difference between males and females in IQ, and humor was significantly related to IQ for both males and females. This suggests that men are not funnier than women but instead are more *motivated* to showcase their humor ability, even in a boring psychology experiment where the mating motive wasn't intentionally activated!

The researchers also found that at the group level, IQ, openness to experience, and creative potential were each separately related to humor ability. Humor ability was also related to a desire for short-term mating and to relationship length of up to 1 year. These relations held even after controlling for self-perceived physical attractiveness (which was used as a proxy for actual physical attractiveness). The researchers refer to this finding as the "Woody Allen effect" because humor can facilitate relationships regardless of physical attractiveness. Indeed, Woody Allen seems to have done quite well for himself in the mating domain, despite his looks! The researchers also found that for males only, humor ability was related to a measure of self-reported mating intelligence, which measures various aspects of the mating intelligence framework (see Epilogue).

Of course, humor doesn't just signal intelligence. In addition to general intelligence, humor may also signal a person's *playfulness*, *insight*,[32] *creativity*,[33] *openness to experience*,[34] *extraversion*,[35] and *sociability*.[36] The fact that humor can signal so many attractive traits makes it a candidate for the mating intelligence hall of fame!

Humor as an Interest Indicator

Humor does not always have to be used in the service of sexual goals. More generally, humor can be used to form and regulate relationships and can play an important social bonding role in a variety of social domains, including relationship maintenance, family relations, friendships, status hierarchies, and self-protection.[37]

One way humor can play a role in relationship formation and maintenance is by signaling interest. Norman Li and colleagues[38] argued that "humor also functions to indicate interest in social relationships—in initiating new relationships and in monitoring existing ones." In their first study, they found that both males and females reported initiating humor and laughing at someone's jokes when they were *already attracted* to the individual but not when they were *not* already attracted to the person. In their second study, they found that judgments of humor were affected by a person's initial attraction and interest in a potential relationship. In their third study, participants rated speed-dating interactions. In general, encounters in which humor was initiated and responses to humor were positive were rated as more likely to be successful. The researchers also found that initial attraction to a person led to greater perceptions of interpersonal warmth coming from that person's humor, which were then associated with more positive reactions to the humor. Taken together, their results suggest that humor initiation can function as an indicator of relationship interest by signaling cooperative potential.

At first, these findings may seem to counter the sexual selection theory of humor courtship displays we discussed earlier. But as Li and colleagues noted, the two models are not incompatible. Perhaps humor is sexy because it signals, in part, mental ability, but it is only effective if the potential mate is already attracted to the person attempting the humor. In some first encounters, people may already have their minds set that they are not going to like a person, so they are not receptive to humor, even if it is the most brilliant comedy ever.

Their second study, which found that humorous audio introductions led to increased attraction toward targets who were rated physically *unattractive* and least preferred for romantic relationships, provides further support for the Woody Allen effect. The researchers suggest that humor can exert its powerful effect by increasing perceptions of interpersonal warmth. Therefore, humor may be a powerful tool in the mating intelligence arsenal for those who are not much to look at or who, for other reasons (e.g., job, income), are lower in social status. On the flipside, the research suggests that if you happen to be high in social status, *self-deprecating* forms of humor may be your most valuable tool in the mating marketplace.[39]

It is interesting that Li and colleagues found similar effects of humor as an interest indicator for both men and women. Perhaps men are motivated to produce more humor only in sexual courtship. When it comes to marriage, though, both men and women may be equally motivated to be funny. The use of humor on the part of both partners certainly affects the quality of relationships.[40] For instance, Lorne Campbell, Rod Martin, and Jennie Ward[41] recorded couples having live conversations and found that affiliative humor was associated with relationship satisfaction, whereas aggressive humor was related to relationship dissatisfaction.

Humor serves many functions in the mating domain and can signal many attractive traits as well as indicate interest. Humor, however, is only a slice of verbal creativity. Perhaps one of the most widespread uses of verbal creativity is to initiate banter in the first place. And as many women can tell you, some guys don't have a clue how to properly approach a woman.

Humor as a Form of Intrasexual Competition

As we mentioned in Chapter 1, sexual selection tells us that people can maximize their reproductive success in two primary ways: (1) by having traits that are attractive to the opposite sex (*intersexual selection*) or (2) by derogating same-sex rivals (*intrasexual selection*). In many species, animals display their dominance by physically hurting or even killing their sexual rivals. Humans, thankfully, have many different ways they can display dominance that don't involve physical aggression, and a person can become the "top dog" solely through the use of humor and wit.[42]

In a real-world study conducted by Nicolas Gueguen, three attractive 20-year-old male confederates (i.e., they were part of the study) went to a bar in France and waited until a female was in earshot. All female participants were between the ages of 20 and 26 years. The men then began their experimental script, first by discussing their summer jobs. After 3 minutes, one of the confederates said to the others, *"That's enough talking about work; I've got some good jokes to tell,"* to which another confederate responded, *"Alright, go ahead! You always have some good jokes for us.*" Then, the first male confederate told three jokes. One joke clearly involved derogation:

> Two friends are talking:
> *"Say, buddy, could you loan me 100 Euros?*
> *Well, you know I only have 60 on me.*
> *OK, give me what you've got and you'll only owe me 40."*

After each joke, the two other confederates laughed loudly and said things like "*That's amazing*" or "*You always have good jokes!*" After all the jokes were told, the two other confederates noted that they had to leave, and then left. The first male confederate stayed, waited a minute, and then approached the female participant, saying "*Hello. My name's Antoine. I noticed you when I arrived here. I just want to say that I think you're really pretty. I have an appointment now, but I was wondering if you might give me your phone number. I could phone you later, and we could have a drink together someplace to get to know each other.*" After this request, the confederate waited 10 second while gazing and smiling at the participant. If the confederate got the phone number, he said "*See you soon.*" If the participant refused to give him her phone number, he said "*Too bad. It's not my day. Have a nice evening!*" In the "no humor" condition, the person who did the approaching was not the joke teller but one of the other confederates who laughed at the jokes. Shortly after the female participant left, a young female who was also part of the experiment approached the participant and asked her to rate her impression of the man on a number of dimensions.

Men in the "humor" condition received phone numbers from 42.9% of the female participants and were refused 57.1% of the time. In comparison, men in the "no humor" condition were refused 84.6% of the time and were only accepted 15.4% of the time. In other words, men who were observed as the humor producers of the group were nearly *three times as likely* to receive a phone number than those who were observed as laughing at a friend's joke instead. Additionally, those who were observed telling the funny jokes also had a higher probability of being perceived as attractive (as a person, as for a long-term relationship), funny, intelligent, and sociable. When analyzing all the variables at once, it was found that levels of compliance were most directly related to perceptions of funniness and sociability. Therefore, funny people may be signaling not only high intelligence and wit but also a particularly social form of intelligence.

What's going on here? Our interpretation is that the man in the "humor" condition was signaling that he was the most socially adept person in his group. He was also receiving what psychologists refer to as "social proofing" every time his friends laughed and commented on how awesome his jokes were (although you may not find the jokes very funny at all). Both these factors will raise his social status in the eyes of observers, and we know that research shows that people are attracted to social status in a potential mate. In our view, the moral of the Gueguen study has just as much to do with *intra*sexual selection as it does with *inter*sexual selection. Those who are physically bullied on a regular basis, take heart and know that you can rise above it all someday by learning a socially valued skill such as humor (also see Chapter 8).

We do want to emphasize, however, that it's *not necessary* to derogate your rivals to gain social status and the reproductive benefits that can come with it. Displays of skill and social dominance were probably attractive to many female participants in Gueguen's study, but research shows that empathy and prosociality are also key components of the *prestigious* path to social status (see Chapter 8). In the study, the comparison groups involved either a socially dominant humor producer or a receiver who laughed at the jokes. There was no third condition in which the confederate was the humor producer and was also kind to his friends. We predict, based on the research on the sexual attractiveness of prestigious men (see Chapter 8 for a review) that men in this condition would have been the *most* successful at obtaining phone numbers from the female participants.

Chat-Up Lines as a Courtship Display and a Screening Device

Deciding to approach a potential mate is the most important step in the mating process. Just as in basketball, where you miss 100% of the shots you don't take, in mating, you miss 100% of the mating opportunities you don't attempt. But coming up with a good pick-up line (or as they call them in Europe, a "chat-up" line) on the spot, that is witty and contextually appropriate, is not always easy.

In the 1980s, Chris Kleinke, Frederick Meeker, and Richard Staneski analyzed the effectiveness of 100 pick-up lines across a number of different settings, including bars, restaurants, supermarkets, laundromats, and beaches. They found three main categories of openers: *direct gambits*, which are honest and get right to the point (e.g., *"I'm sort of shy, but I'd like to get to know you"*), *innocuous gambits*, which hide a person's true intentions (e.g., *"What do you think of this band?"*), and *cute/flippant gambits*, which involve cheesy, unwitty, canned humor (e.g., *"Do you have any raisins? No? Well then, how about a date?"*).

Both men and women agreed that cute/flippant pick-up lines were the least attractive. Women, however, preferred innocuous lines and had a greater aversion to cute/flippant lines than men, whereas men had a greater preference for direct opening gambits than women. This basic pattern has been found repeatedly in a variety of settings, including bars.[43]

A person's state of mind also matters. After all, we're not machines, with a steady supply of cognitive resources on command. Receptivity to chat-up lines involves cognitive processing, and cognitive resources can be depleted (see Chapter 1).[44] This is important because a certain amount of mental energy is required to follow the conversation and decipher a person's intentions. For example, in a recent study, Gary Lewandowski and colleagues[45] gave 99 undergraduates a 5-minute writing task in which they were asked to describe a recent trip. In the ego-depletion condition, students were told they couldn't use the letters A or N anywhere in the story, whereas in the nondepletion condition, they weren't given this cognitively taxing instruction. After the writing task, participants looked at a picture of an attractive person of the opposite sex and rated how they would respond if the person approached them using one of three categories of openers: direct, innocuous, and cute/flippant. What did they find?

Those who were cognitively fatigued were less receptive to cute/flippant openers than those in the nondepletion condition. In the context of cute/flippant lines, those in the depleted group were more likely to "ask the initiator to leave them alone" and "ignore the initiator." For innocuous gambits, the depleted students were less likely to ignore the person and ask the person to leave them alone. Receptivity to direct gambits was unaffected by being cognitively depleted. There were also gender effects consistent with prior research. Men were more receptive to direct openers, and females were more receptive to innocuous openers. Women were least receptive to cute/flippant openers.

What explains these cognitive depletion effects? The researchers argue that when it comes to cute/flippant openers, less mental effort is required to figure out the person's intentions. Mix that in with the fact that a depleted, frazzled individual may have less tolerance for obvious pick-up attempts, and you have an enhanced aversion to cheesy lines. When it comes to innocuous chat-up lines, however, the person's intentions are much more ambiguous. This requires more cognitive resources. As the researchers noted, it's less socially awkward for the ego-depleted individual to continue the conversation until the person's intentions become more obvious.

Although cognitive fatigue makes the effectiveness of different kinds of pick-up lines more salient, the basic pattern of findings remains—which raises the question, *Why do some kinds of opening lines tend to universally work, whereas others universally tend to fall flat?* A key to this mystery involves the notion of trait perception, the characteristics that people infer from behavior (see Chapter 4).[46] One study found that people perceive those who use innocuous lines as smarter and sexier than those who use cute/flippant lines.[47] Another study found that although women perceived men who use cute/flippant lines as more sociable, confident, and funny, they also perceived them as less trustworthy and intelligent. All these traits certainly influence mate choice, but research shows that low trustworthiness and low intelligence are deal breakers for a long-term relationship, overriding other "luxuries," such as humor and confidence (see Chapter 5).[48]

Women are rightfully skeptical of cute/flippant pick-up lines; research shows that those with a long-term mating strategy do tend to use supportive and honest pick-up strategies, whereas those with a short-term mating strategy tend to use manipulation and dishonesty (also see Chapter 8).[49] When women are looking for a short-term fling, however, it may be a different story. One study conducted on college students found that women favored men for a short-term fling if they found the men attractive regardless of the content of their pick-up lines![50]

Under the mating intelligence framework, opening gambits can be conceptualized as a form of courtship display that signal various traits. In this view, trait perception isn't capricious: there's a deep, evolutionary logic underlying such perception. Viewing "chat-up lines" as a form of courtship display, Christopher Bale, Rory Morrison, and Peter Caryl[51] set out to determine the effectiveness of a broad range of opening gambits, using principles of evolutionary psychology. In their study, 205 undergraduates at the University of Edinburgh in Scotland read 40 vignettes in which a man approached a woman and then judged on a scale of to 1 to 5 the extent to which they thought the women would continue the conversation. Each vignette differed in the type of courtship display. Here is an example of a male's attempt to display his *wealth*:

> *A woman has just ordered a drink at the bar of a busy and trendy night-club. A smartly dressed man, who is standing beside her, tells the barman that the drink is on the house. He turns to the woman, offering his hand:*
> MALE: *Hi, my name's William, I'm one of the owners here, would you like to dance?*

Here's a *sexually charged* chat-up line:

> *A club in Ibiza. It's hot, sweaty, and people pretty much only go there for one thing. A man saunters up to a woman sitting on a stool at the bar:*
> MALE: *Well hey there, I may not be Fred Flintstone, but I bet I can make your Bed Rock!*

Here's an example of a male displaying his *musical talent* as well as his *knowledge* of high culture:

> There is an elegant society dinner in a large country house. A man and woman, who have just met for the first time, are standing having drinks before the meal. The man turns to the woman and points out the large grand piano occupying a corner of the room.

> MAN: *It's a fine instrument, wouldn't you say? A Steinway concert grand if I'm not mistaken.*

WOMAN: *Oh really...do you play then?*

MAN: *Just a little, for myself. I'm not really good enough to perform...unless, that is, you would like me to ...*

WOMAN: *Well, I wouldn't want to force you into it...But I've always loved Beethoven's Moonlight Sonata ...*

MAN: *Ah...yes, the Moonlight Sonata, or to give it it's true name, Sonata Quasi Una Fantasia. A fittingly beautiful piece for a beautiful lady. I will try, but I can only hope that my attempt will do justice to you.*

Chat-up attempts differed in their rated success in leading to further conversation. The attempts that received the highest ratings included items in which a man displayed his helpfulness; ability to take control of a situation; wealth, education, or culture; and spontaneous wit. Direct requests for sex received low ratings, but attempts involving sexually based humor or scripted opening gambits taken from websites received even lower ratings.

In terms of sex differences, opening gambits that revealed a man's wealth, talents, generosity, ability to take charge, and physical fitness appealed to women. Wit was attractive to women, but instances in which a man used wit to make fun of a woman, or instances in which a man told pre-planned jokes and one-liners, or told jokes that were sexually charged, were generally not effective.

Note that the researchers made the important distinction between *wit* (which they defined as "spontaneous jokes that fit the context exactly, are genuinely funny, and require intelligence") and *humor* (which they defined as "the pre-planned jokes and one-liners which were ineffective and do not demonstrate intelligence.") The former is a genuine mental indicator, as well as an indicator of the ability to be sensitive to interpersonal context, whereas the latter merely indicates the ability to memorize canned jokes.

The researchers suggest that some unattractive opening gambits may serve a useful function, however, in that men can use them to screen out women with a long-term mating orientation from woman with a short-term mating orientation. For example, if a woman laughs at a man's sexually charged humor attempt, she may be open to negotiating a short-term liaison that evening. Indeed, in one observational study at a bar where male humorous sexual remarks ran rampant, it was noted that the women who laughed at such jokes did indeed seem sexually interested in the men,[52] whereas (obviously) the women who didn't laugh were not sexually interested. These humorous sexually loaded attempts could be conceptualized as a test to gauge interest and receptivity to a sexual encounter.

Chat-up lines can also be used to screen the potential mate on other dimensions, such as personality. For example, chat-up lines can serve the function of finding similarly extraverted or introverted others,[53] those who share the same mating orientation (short-term fling vs. long-term committed relationship),[54] as well as finding others who share a similar sense of humor.[55] A person's attachment style may even play a role (see Chapter 5).[56] One study found that people with a dismissive-avoidant attachment style tend to distrust others and see potential mates as more untrustworthy than securely attached individuals who are more forthcoming during initial interactions.[57] Individual differences are just as important to the mating intelligence framework as biological sex differences.

Using a larger and more diverse age-related sample than their other study, Matthew Cooper, David O'Donnell, Peter Caryl, Rory Morrison, and Christopher Bale conducted a study in 2007 in which they further investigated the effect of personality and gender on judgments of various opening gambits. Just as in the 2006 study by Bale and colleagues, they found that stereotypical chat-up lines were less effective than opening gambits that reflected the context of the interaction and revealed something about the man's character, personality, interests, or wealth. Females rated the humorous items as more effective than men did (consistent with the idea that women are more discriminating when it comes to humor) and rated the sexually charged items as less effective than men did. Among females, extraversion was positively related to the rated effectiveness of humor, and psychoticism (a personality trait characterized by aggressiveness, impulsiveness, risk taking, and social hostility) was negatively related to chat-up lines that revealed that the person would be a good mate. Among males, extraversion was negatively related to the rated effectiveness of humor and was positively related to chat-up lines that were sexually charged.

Additionally, it was found that men *underestimated* the extent to which woman liked opening gambits that revealed a man's willingness to hand over control of the interaction to the woman, revealed his wealth, or revealed his willingness to help someone in a way that showed his character. Males also *overestimated* the extent to which women would like sexually charged items as well as the extent to which women would like an over-the-top display of their talent. Building on Bale and colleagues' ideas, the researchers suggested that unattractive opening gambits can serve an important screening function. As they note,

> *A male will incur opportunity costs when he invests time and effort on one woman in an attempt to form a relationship: therefore, men should be selective in their choice of target. While the woman's attractiveness will be known in a face to face encounter, the man may need to make a rapid assessment of her personality, and he could potentially achieve this through his opening remark.* (Cooper et al., 2007, p. 1083)

Of course, women can also be successful in their opening gambits. Although Cooper and associates' study[58] suggests that sexually charged openers are particularly effective for women, it may be the case that any form of direct opener can be effective for women. In support of this idea, T. Joel Wade, Lauren Butrie, and Kelly Hoffman[59] administered a questionnaire to 40 women, aged 18 to 23 years, and asked them to record five statements that they have said or would say to a man to indicate to him that they are interested in dating or spending time with him. Their study also explored the likelihood of a woman approaching a man to initiate a romantic interaction.

Both men and women agreed that a woman directly asking a man on a date, hinting at a date, giving a man her phone number and requesting a call, or trying to find out what things they may share in common are the opening lines that are most effective for attracting a man. In addition, both sexes perceived lines that directly ask for a date, ask whether the man is single, or convey a phone number as the most direct lines.

Why do direct openers work best for women? The researchers suggest that direct openers may work because it may be hard for a man to gauge interest from a woman within the first few minutes of an interaction. In support of this idea, Karl Grammer, Kirsten Kruck, Astrid Juette, and Bernhard Fink[60] found that women who stated an interest in a man did not send significantly more signals of interest in the first few minutes of an interaction than women who stated low interest in a man. The message here is clear: women, be direct! Wade and colleagues conclude that their results "show that women can use opening lines to attract men and that they are likely to do so. Additionally, these findings further indicate that it is no longer unacceptable for a woman to be seen as the direct or overt initiator of a dating relationship."

Of course, people don't just have different tastes in humor and in chat-up style, they also have different tastes in creativity. It is to these differences that we turn next.

I Heart Nerds

Some people dig nerds, some dig artists, some dig nerdy artists. Gregory Feist[61] makes the important distinction between *ornamental-aesthetic* forms of creativity and *applied-technological* forms of creativity. Feist argues that throughout the course of human evolution, natural selection sculpted applied or technological aspects of creativity that had clear survival benefits, such as advances in science and engineering, whereas sexual selection acted more on ornamental or aesthetic aspects of creativity, including art, music, dance, and humor.

On the face of it, this certainly seems to be the case. Artists, musicians, and poets, whose products don't have a clear survival value, certainly seem to attract more sexual partners than computer programmers, mechanical engineers, and doctors. You can also see this at work in celebrity obsession. Why do we put celebrities on such a high pedestal, care about them so much, and gossip about them so much more than we do about the cardiologist who lives next door? Why do the final three contestants on *American Idol* get a parade in their hometown, receive the keys to their city, and even get days named after them, whereas the person who gets a Ph.D. in, say, psychology, gets a parade upon graduation involving mainly his grandmother and other family members?

Building on the ideas of both Feist and Miller, SBK, Aaron Kozbelt, Melanie Beaussart, and Geoffrey Miller[62] argued that ornamental-aesthetic forms of creativity may be sexually attractive because they are indicators of mental fitness, but that's not the whole story. Creators in the ornamental-aesthetic realm also tend to have other desirable traits, such as the displays of emotion and openness to experience that are more "in-your-face" than applied-technological forms of creativity. This ability to combine multiple displays in ornamental-aesthetic forms of creativity may be a key to its higher sexiness. Highly skilled engineers may simply not be connecting with as many people as the musician who can speak directly to a wide swath of society.[63]

Think about the sex appeal of the Backstreet Boys. Their song "I Want It That Way" (SBK's favorite karaoke song!) is arguably creative, but it is clearly emotive and vulnerable. The singers are broadcasting not only their general intelligence but also their openness to experience and capacity for empathy. Such displays may have been sexually selected. This doesn't just apply to the Backstreet Boys, of course (which is no doubt a relief to many!).

The idea that musicality may have been sexually selected is supported by recent research conducted by Katharine Eskine.[64] Eskine had 92 undergraduate participants read a neutral, short-term mating, or long-term mating vignette before completing a musical aptitude task. She found that being primed for long-term mating increased the display of musicality for both men and women, but only men showed increases in the short-term mating condition. Most interestingly, music performance wasn't associated with IQ, general mental flexibility, nor the ability to generate a lot of ideas. In short: music ability was not associated with cognitive traits and showed domain specificity. This leaves open the possibility that music production was primarily sexually selected to serve as an indicator for other displays, such as empathy and emotional expressiveness.

As a further test of these notions, SBK, Jane Erickson, Julie Huang, Sheela Ramesh, S. Thompson, Aaron Kozbelt, Elliot Samuel Paul, and James C. Kaufman[65] administered a checklist of a variety of different creative acts, from "playing sports" to "writing music" to "writing an original computer program." Participants rated how sexy they found each creative activity in a potential mate. Various behaviors clustered together to form three factors: ornamental-aesthetic creativity, applied-technology creativity, and personal creativity. There were a variety of creative preferences. Although most of the differences in preferences were accounted for by the ornamental-aesthetic creativity factor, a proportion of participants were attracted to those achieving in applied-technology forms of creativity and an even smaller proportion were attracted to people who engage in personal forms of creativity. At a group level of analysis, though, ornamental-aesthetic creativity was the sexiest factor. Also, females, more than males, found ornamental-aesthetic forms of creativity (but not applied-technological forms of creativity) in a potential mate sexy. Therefore, we agree with Feist's idea that it's important to distinguish between various forms of creativity when talking about the sexual attractiveness of creativity.

Even so, there were also important individual differences found *within* each sex. For males, a preference for ornamental-aesthetic forms of creativity in a mate was positively related to a preference for intuition, openness to experience, and self-reported creative achievement in the domestic arts and negatively related to a preference for intellectual achievement. In contrast, in females, a preference for ornamental-aesthetic forms of creativity in a mate was positively related to self-reported creative achievement in the arts, IQ, neuroticism, and openness to experience and negatively related to self-reported creative achievement in the domestic arts.

In terms of a preference for applied-technological forms of creativity, for males, such a preference was related to self-reported creative achievement in the sciences as well as intellectual and rational thinking styles. For females, a preference for applied-technological forms of creativity was related to self-reported creative achievement in the arts and sciences and a rational thinking style but was additionally related to conscientiousness. Note that openness to experience was not an important predictor of a preference for applied-technological forms of creativity in a mate for either males or females. This is consistent with the idea that there is something related to an openness to aesthetics and emotions that is sexy about the arts.

Finally, a preference for personal forms of creativity in females was associated with a preference for rational thinking, agreeableness, perceiving oneself as creative, and self-reported creative achievement in the domestic arts. For males, none of the variables predicted a preference for personal forms of creativity in a mate. Taken together, these results suggest that in addition to looking at a preference for creativity in general, it's also important to look at *individual differences* in a preference for creativity.[66]

"I Want His Artistic Genes *Now*!"

Do women prefer creative talent or the wealth that comes with it? In a clever study, Martie Haselton and Geoffrey Miller[67] assessed these preferences across the ovulatory cycle. Their reasoning was as follows: When selecting a long-term mate, women tend to value "good dad" indicators such as the ability and willingness to invest in protection, provisioning, and care to potential offspring. Some women with a very high mate value may be able to have their cake and eat it too—good genes *and* good dad potential—but most women will end up with a committed partner who is not their ideal at all levels. Because the benefits of "good genes" can only be obtained during the high-fertility phase just before ovulation, women in the high-fertility phase who are seeking short-term mates can be expected to value good-genes indicators (creativity, intelligence) *relative to* good-dad indicators.[68] Therefore, Haselton and Miller expected to see ovulatory cycle shifts in female preference for fitness indicators such as creativity versus indicators of resources, particularly in a short-term mating context.

Participants (41 heterosexual female college students) read vignettes about potential male mates in both art and business, and each participant's fertility was estimated based on menstrual cycle information collected. One vignette depicted a man who had high creative talent but who was poor, owing to bad luck and circumstances. The other vignette depicted a man average in creative intelligence but wealthy owing to good luck and circumstances. In each vignette, it was clear that each man's level of creativity reflected raw, natural talent but that his level of wealth was largely accidental, not associated with merit.

For instance, in one vignette, the male artist enjoys the accolades of his art professors, who agree that he is their most talented student. However, his paintings do not earn him much money. In another vignette, the art student enters the art world by chance after just "fooling around" with paint and canvas. He accidentally spills paint on the canvas, and the result wins him a $100,000 commission. Both these artists are considered highly desirable by other women on campus, and friends say they are dependable, kind, and generous. Which fictional man do you think women in their most fertile phase chose for a short-term liaison: the poor, struggling artist or the rich abstract painter without much skill?

When women were most fertile, they tended to pick the guy with natural talent for short-term mating over the rich guy with very little skill. Fertility did not have an impact on preference for long-term mating. This supports the idea that displays of creativity, at least in the short term, act as good-genes indicators.

This study, along with other studies on the relationship between fertility and mate preferences, shows that human female sexuality adapts to trade-offs between cads and good dads. When women are at the low-fertility stage of their cycle, they tend to shift their preferences toward males who offer resources, an evolutionarily adaptive preference because those resources would be beneficial under circumstances in which good genes cannot be readily obtained.[69] Note that a preference for female resource-acquisition ability also evolved in part through male mate choice for a long-term partner because women who forage more effectively and reliably offer better returns on male investments of mating and parental effort.

The preferences shown by the women in Haselton and Miller's study are not simply the result of increased sex drive or increased choosiness around ovulation. If this were the case, you would expect that increased libido and choosiness would have made men displaying creativity and wealth in both art and business more attractive for short-term and long-term mating. Instead, very specific effects were found in specific mating contexts for specific types of men. It's worth noting that there's very little chance that these decisions were conscious. Women rated the vignettes before they saw the menstrual cycle questions, and the study wasn't explicitly about the effects of ovulation on mate preferences.

The women's preferences also cannot be explained solely by cultural conditioning. As the researchers note, it is unlikely that popular culture, parenting, or peer pressure would cause women to unconsciously favor creativity on high-fertility days but not on low-fertility days of their menstrual cycles, and only for short-term mating. If anything, social conditioning by men would probably favor long-term mating to wealthy men all of the time and disfavor short-term mating with creative but poor men.

These fertility effects may not be limited to artistic or business displays of creativity; many different displays of creativity can serve as good-genes indicators. An unpublished pilot study suggests that humor may also be affected by fertility effects.[70] Two hundred and six female participants read vignettes about potential male mates that varied in their levels of humor-production ability. Men who were described as being funnier were rated by the women participants as significantly more socially sensitive, adaptable, extroverted, exciting, happy, and able to play well with kids as well as more intelligent, kind, tall, healthy, masculine, and muscular. As we noted earlier in this chapter, being funny clearly signals quite a lot of sexy things!

The researchers also found that among women who were not taking birth control pills (i.e., were naturally cycling), female fertility significantly increased the short-term attractiveness of the men who were considered the funniest but had no effect on the long-term attractiveness of these men nor on the attractiveness of the men who were considered only medium or low in humor-production ability. There were no cycle effects for women using hormonal contraception: they weren't more attracted to humor at peak fertility. Women on hormonal contraception, however, did show the same personality trait inferences given different sense of humor levels as the naturally cycling women.

Also, consistent with the study by SBK, Erickson, and colleagues[71] mentioned earlier, among women in a steady sexual relationship, the funniness of their current male partner significantly predicted their general relationship satisfaction, expected relationship length, and expected future likelihood of having children together. This suggests that the ability to be funny serves as both a good-genes indicator and as a way of keeping the flame alive. It should be noted that although suggestive, the effects in this study weren't strong, and there weren't a large number of participants. All the findings need to be replicated before they should be taken too seriously. Also, note that none of this research suggests that creative and funny women cannot be sexy or that humor ability in women is unimportant in the maintenance of a relationship. The results just suggest that women's mate preferences, owing to their fluctuating fertility, may be more likely to fluctuate from one day to the next than are men's preferences.

If we have learned anything by this point, it is that human mating intelligence is extremely complex. As Haselton and Miller noted in their article in *Human Nature,*

> Far from reducing human sexuality to a list of simple mating instincts, evolutionary research is revealing the profoundly flexible nature of person perception in the mating domain—flexibility that is responsible not only to the external costs and benefits of short-term vs. long-term relationships, but also to the internal physiological milieu of women's bodies, and their fertility cycles that regulate their reproductive lives. (Haselton & Miller, 2006)

In this chapter, we demonstrated the ways in which human mating intelligence involves the mind just as much as the body, the many ways creative traits can be displayed, the contexts in which these traits tend to be displayed, and individual and sex differences in a preference for those traits. Cognitive courtship displays, however, rarely act in isolation. As we alluded to throughout this chapter, displays of creativity and intelligence are combined with other personality dispositions. In the next chapter, we look at the equally important domain of personality in understanding human mating intelligence.

3

Wanted! Neurotic Mess

The Role of Personality in Mating

It's not unusual to encounter a couple and note how different the two are from each other. On the extreme end, we have the HBO show *Curb Your Enthusiasm*. The neurotic and disagreeable Larry David—whose catchphrase whenever he does something inappropriate is "what—*no good?*"—couldn't be more different than his emotionally stable wife Cheryl. Yet, somehow, they made it work (for the most part—and yes, we are aware it's just a TV show). In humans, you'll find all sorts of interesting combinations of personality traits. Personality variation is a major component of mating intelligence. Together with intelligence and creativity, personality plays a critical role during courtship by signaling traits that men and women consider important in a mating partner. Many even rate dispositional variables (e.g., intelligence, creativity, humor, personality) as *more important* than situational variables (e.g., wealth, social status) or physical attractiveness in selecting a mate.[1]

An evolutionary perspective allows us to look at different combinations of personality traits. We can see how they cluster in evolutionarily predictable ways, how they may have been differentially related to reproductive success among our distant ancestors, and how they play out in today's mating marketplace. For instance, although we normally think of emotionally stable, agreeable, and conscientious people as "well adjusted," the evolutionary perspective allows us to stand back and ask, well adjusted for *what*?

Why Differences in Personality?

In the last chapter, we argued that the display of cognitive abilities such as artistic creativity and humor is sexy, at least in part, because they reveal an individual's total load of rare, mildly harmful deleterious mutations. Evolution is constantly trying to keep up with new genetic variants introduced through mutation. When selection cannot keep up and remove all of the variants, it is not able to optimize a trait. Because complex traits like intelligence and creativity are the result of many interacting genes (i.e., polygenic), it is particularly difficult for selection to keep up with all the new variants in personality, so differences remain in the general population.

As we hinted at in the prior chapter, many forms of creativity are sexy not just because of the cognitive abilities they signal but also because of the personality traits they are broadcasting. For instance, when the cellist Jacqueline Du Pré played the Elgar Concerto with the Philadelphia Orchestra, she was displaying her intelligence and creativity *as well as* her dispositions for expressiveness, kindness, tenderness, and compassion. According to mating intelligence, both cognitive displays and personality dispositions play a role in courtship display. However, from an evolutionary genetics perspective, we think about cognitive abilities a bit differently from personality.

When it comes to the development of cognitive abilities, a low mutation load will *always* be beneficial, regardless of the environment. In contrast, the reproductive consequences of having various personality traits are more dependent on environmental conditions. For instance, high levels of extraversion may be more conducive to reproductive fitness in unstable environments where exploration is crucial, whereas the other end of the spectrum—introversion—may be more conducive to reproductive success in stable environmental conditions.

The fact that environments have varied so much throughout the course of human evolution means evolution was not able to find one single optimal trait conducive to reproductive fitness across all contexts. Increasingly, evolutionary psychologists agree that individual differences in personality traits are best conceptualized from this mating trade-offs perspective.[2]

The fact remains that people only have limited time and energy, so there will be trade-offs for any mating strategy. Here are some common trade-offs involved in human mating faced across our species and, for some of them, even across other species[3]:

- Should you spend time attracting new mates or invest all your time and energy in the one you're with?
- How much time and energy should you invest in detecting mating-relevant threats, such as cues that your mate is cheating or has lost interest, status, resources, or health?
- How patient should you be regarding future mating opportunities? Because life is finite and uncertain, how much should you weigh your current reproductive opportunities against future opportunities or costs?
- How much empathy should you have for significant others? What's the best balance to strike between caring about the well-being of significant others versus being opportunistic and caring about your own immediate advantage?
- How much time and energy should you invest in developing courtship displays? It takes a lot of time and effort to develop social-valued skills

and then become creative and productive in those skills enough to attract a wide range of potential mates.

From an evolutionary perspective, there is no *absolute* answer to each trade-off. Because physical and cultural ecological conditions varied quite a bit during the course of human evolution, it makes sense that human mating strategies would also be variable. Every culture, and every person within that culture, must strike its own right balance for each of these mating trade-offs. And each culture does.

Owing to such trade-offs, the most likely candidate mechanism for maintaining personality differences in the human population is *balancing selection*. Balancing selection only works on traits that are balanced in the sense that both extremes of the same trait are conducive to reproductive success to the same degree depending on the environment. To take our earlier example, extraversion would be a good candidate for balancing selection if high levels of extraversion were conducive to fitness in certain environments and low levels of extraversion were equally as conducive to fitness in other environments.

This delicate balancing act can happen in a number of different ways, but the best candidate for how this works with personality traits is through a process called *negative frequency-dependent selection*.[4] This balancing act typically occurs in social environments (as opposed to just focusing on the physical environment) and only selects genes that are rare in frequency.[5] This type of selection is particularly relevant to human personality, which is particularly social in nature and involves many genes that are differentially conducive to reproductive fitness depending on the social environment and situations in which the genetic variants are rare in any one particular context. *Bottom line*: you cannot understand the existence of differences in personality without taking into account the social context.

In this chapter, we adopt this mating trade-offs approach and link personality to the mating intelligence framework. Before we take a look at the direct relationship between personality and mating outcomes, let's start by looking at how personality traits are intimately intertwined with other behaviors to form a person's mating strategy. Although personality is an important courtship display for mating intelligence, it is part of a larger system that evolved for specific survival and reproductive purposes.

Do You Live Life in the Fast or Slower Lane?

According to the *life history perspective*,[6] a wide range of traits and behaviors—from self-control and personality to attachment style, reproductive strategies, growth, longevity, and fertility—cluster together in evolutionarily predictable ways and represent different mating strategies that were adaptive for reproductive success among our very distant ancestors. Even today, these ancestral genes play a role in certain contexts.

Areas that are more safe and stable (such as many reasonably high socioeconomic suburban areas) are more conducive to holding resources and long-term planning. In these areas, you find that people tend to be physically larger (because they have the time and energy to invest in health); focus on offspring *quality* instead of quantity; have delayed sexual development, lower fertility, higher interbirth intervals, higher parental investment, lower infant mortality, and greater longevity; and have more intense competition for scarce resources. They also tend to take fewer risks, are less impulsive, and are more likely to follow group norms and have high group cohesion. Entire species, such as elephants, exhibit this pattern of development because in the ecologies in which they evolved, these long-term strategies paid off. These species are referred to as *K-selected* species.

Areas that are more harsh and unpredictable, however, tend to be more conducive to a short-term, impulsive strategy. In these areas, you find that the people tend to be physically smaller; focus on offspring *quantity* rather than quality; have early and fast sexual development, higher fertility, and lower longevity; and have little competition for scarce resources. They also tend to take more risks, are more impulsive, are less likely to follow externally imposed rules of conduct, and have lower group cohesion. Entire classes of animals, such as rabbits, exhibit this pattern of development because in the ecologies in which they evolved, these short-term strategies paid off. These species are referred to as *r-selected* species.

Human ecologies differ quite a bit from each other. Consider the Canela people of Brazil. The women of Canela pursue a short-term mating strategy (in the parlance of evolutionary psychology, they are "sexually unrestricted"). They have public ceremonies at which women are *encouraged* to have sex with multiple partners. Men in this society support this behavior and must hide their jealousy. They certainly don't give women derogatory labels for their promiscuous behavior. Why are things the way they are in Canela society?

Life history theory lends a cue here. Canela society is a matrilineal society (resources are passed along the female lineage), the environment is unpredictable, resources are scarce, and males experience high rates of mortality. When a women finds out she is pregnant, she engages in extramarital affairs with high-status men to confuse paternal certainty. As a result, none of the men can ever be assured he is the father of the child. This guarantees that the surviving men will invest in the child and not kill, abuse, or neglect the child because it *could be* theirs. This is a much smarter strategy on the female's part than relying on assistance from one mate who is likely to die early. This situation results in several men investing in or protecting their children.[7] If Canela women do get married, the couple is expected to remain married until all their children are adults. Additionally, the husband is expected to tolerate his wife's affairs, and the general attitude among members of Canela society is that the welfare and survival of children is more important than a man's control over a women's sexuality.[8] The characteristics of Canela society, including high levels of sexual promiscuity, uncertainty about future resources, and high rates of mortality, suggest that the people of Canela have shifted their life history strategy closer to the r-selected side because of their ecological conditions.

This example of a matrilineal, harsh, unpredictable, and resource-poor society was used to illustrate the extreme end of the fast-slow life spectrum. It turns out that humans cross the entire spectrum, from fast to slow and everywhere in between (compare North American New England suburbia to the Canela society, for instance!). This is because all of the crucial environmental dimensions (*matrilineal vs. patrilineal, resource rich vs. resource poor, unpredictable vs. stable, harsh vs. safe*) can vary independently of the others.

For instance, resource scarcity, by itself, has the *opposite* effect of a harsh and unpredictable environment and is more conducive to living the slower life. When resources are scarce, it is important to use long-term planning skills to save what you've got and conserve valuable energy and calories. In fact, resource-poor but safe ecologies are relatively stable, monogamous, and equitable in terms of contributions from both parents. In these societies, it makes more sense for a pair to settle down and work together to invest in the long-term survival of their children. It is to neither partner's benefit to mate with many different partners under these circumstances. In these societies, people actually have a fair chance of being rewarded for their long-term investment in resources.[9]

During the course of human evolution, natural and sexual selection sculpted and coordinated various traits to make sure they did not strategically interfere with one another. For example, risky, impulsive attempts at mating effort (i.e., seduction) may interfere with the careful, long-term planning that is beneficial for survival and long-term pair bonding. As a result, evolution selected various psychological traits to cluster together in adaptively coordinated ways. These clusters were selected and sculpted by evolution to maximize reproductive fitness within particular environments.

Because those living life in the fast lane tend to focus on short-term gains at the expense of long-term costs, their core adaptive psychological traits should involve rebelliousness, risky behaviors, impulsivity, and a focus on mate quantity and reduced parental investment. On the contrary, because those living a slower life focus on the long-term, their core adaptive psychological traits should involve careful risk considerations, a preference for monogamy, high parental investment, and conformity of social rules. Note that when we say "should" here (and throughout this book), we mean "can be expected to, from an evolutionary perspective." We are not in the business here of telling anyone how they should act in life.

The evidence suggests that personality traits do cluster in just these ways among humans. A. J. Figueredo and colleagues[10] administered a wide range of indicators of life history strategy to 222 psychology undergraduates. All of these indicators were reasonably correlated with each other, forming an over-arching "K-factor."

Those scoring higher on this K-factor (i.e., those living a *slower* life) tended to report *feeling higher levels of emotional closeness as a child toward a father figure* (e.g., "I want to be like my biological father"), *higher levels of security in adult romantic attachment* (e.g., "I do not often worry about being abandoned"), *lower levels of mating effort* (e.g., "I would rather date one boy at a time than several boys at once"), *lower levels of Machiavellianism* (e.g., "I tend to trust people"), and *lower levels of risk-taking attitudes and behaviors* (e.g., "I wouldn't approach someone very attractive if I thought it were a long shot"). Those scoring higher on the K-factor also tended to report lower levels of neuroticism and psychoticism, and there was nearly a positive association with extraversion.

Further research revealed that this K-factor does have a heritable basis. Analyzing a nationally representative sample of 309 identical twins and 333 fraternal twin pairs aged 25 to 74 years, Figueredo and colleagues[11] looked at 30 scales of *life history traits* (e.g., quality of family relationships, altruistic behaviors), *medical symptoms* (e.g., thyroid disease, ulcer), *personality traits* (e.g., neuroticism, extraversion, conscientiousness, openness to experience), and *social background* (e.g., financial status). They found that all the items were moderately related to each other and that people scoring higher on this over-arching K-factor tended to live a slower life, whereas those scoring lower on the K-factor tend to live a faster life. This higher-order K-factor explained most of the genetic correlations among the scales, was 68% heritable, and accounted for 82% of the genetic differences among the lower-order factors. According to the researchers, these results suggest that life history strategy may be influenced by a large number of genes that coordinate the activation of a wide array of traits. Regulatory genes don't just activate themselves, though—they require environmental triggers, or else they won't be expressed. What are the important environmental triggers?

Environmental Triggers

External Environments

Barbara Brumbach, Jose Figueredo, and Bruce Ellis[12] found that two environmental factors in particular explained a considerable amount of the differences found in life history strategy among thousands of adolescents followed up from youth to young adulthood (see Chapter 5 for other environmental conditions that can influence a person's mating strategy). Both *environmental harshness* ("self-reported exposure to violence from conspecifics") and *unpredictability* ("frequent changes or ongoing inconsistency in several dimensions of child-hood environments") independently explained a large part of the differences in a K-factor consisting of an intertwined number of life history traits such as mental and physical health, relationship stability, sexual restrictiveness, social deviance, and economic success. Life history traits in adolescence were fairly stable across time and were significantly related to life history strategy in young adults. According to the researchers,

> ... *by the time people reach their mid-twenties, they have formed a coherent life history strategy that is characterized by their overall health, approach to romantic and sexual partners, and the amount of effort they have put into education and employment.*

This research suggests that the interaction of nature and nurture exerts its most potent effects during youth. The unpredictability of the environment can take many forms, but a particularly important contributor to the development of a person's life history strategy is his or her early family environment. Let's take a look at those familial influences.

Family

Although it is certainly true that human parental investment is extremely high compared with other species,[13] there are many circumstances in which children are raised in unpredictable family environments with little parental care. Various studies, including those that have controlled for the effects of genetic transmission, show that stressful parent-child relationships and nega-tive parenting have a significant effect on pubertal timing. This effect seems to be strongest for females, although family stress can accelerate adrenarche (a stress hormone) in males as well.[14] There is also research on the effects of total parental absence on the development of life history strategy. In general, when fathers don't invest in parental care, there is a tendency for boys to live the fast life—increased delinquency, aggression, and other indicators of high mating effort.[15]

In a large review of the literature, Bruce Ellis[16] presented evidence that girls who grow up in a home where the father is absent or negligent in their par-enting are more likely to go through their first menstrual cycle (i.e., "menar-che") by the age of 12 years and, compared with their peers, to show increased fertility, greater levels of manipulative and exploitative attitudes, greater risk-taking behavior, higher incidence of affective disorders, social aggression, sexual promiscuity, preference for sexual variety, lower adult attachment to romantic partners, and less parental care devoted to one's offspring. In fact, the age in which "father-absent girls" tend to go through menarche is related to the number of years of father absence, the amount of time fathers spent taking care of daughters during the first five years of life, and the amount of affection observed in parent-child relationships.

Framing the effects of parental absence on life history strategy in an evolutionary context, Belsky and associates[17] and Chisholm[18] argue that children in the first few years of life use their level of family stress, unharmonious parent-child relationships, father absence, and marital conflict as cues of risk and uncertainty, which then influences the development of their reproductive strategy.

A safe and predictable environment (neighborhood, social, and parental) will tend to trigger a *slower* reproductive strategy, with a focus on later reproduction, high parenting effort, longer-term couple relationships, and more secure, trusting, mutually beneficial close relationships. A dangerous and uncertain environment, on the other hand, will tend to trigger the *fast* life, involving earlier reproduction and physical maturation, higher mating effort, less parental investment, a higher incidence of short-term and uncommitted relationships with partners, and increased opportunism and risk-taking.

Insecurely attached adults do report shorter estimates of their own life expectancy,[19] so there does appear to be a link between adult attachment security and perceptions of the harshness of the environment.

Building on the work of Belsky and associates[20] and Chisholm,[21] Marco Del Giudice[22] has shed light on the developmental time course leading from infant attachment styles to mature, sexually differentiated strategies. Del Giudice proposes that life history strategies develop in a flexible, multistage fashion.

According to this view, life history strategies remain open to continual modification depending on life stage and context (although some people may be more flexibly adaptive than others). Del Giudice also proposes that throughout human development, there are developmental switch points when an individual's genes are calibrated with information from the environment, and this integration then shapes an individual's choice of life history strategy.[23]

The complex, dynamic interplay between nature and nurture is mutually reinforcing. People's genes, which are partially shared with their parents, may influence to a certain extent what aspects of the environment they engage in, and those environments can in turn trigger and reinforce the expression of those genes. This can be unfortunate in situations in which, for example, the genes that predispose someone to living the fast life cause that person to take dangerous risks that make his or her environment even more dangerous, causing a dangerous cycle. Therefore, when looking at the development of life history strategy, neither the environment nor genetic make-up can be viewed in total isolation.[24]

Cutting-edge research in evolutionary biology is addressing issues central to child development, such as plasticity and genotype-by-environment interactions (GxE).[25] The study of organismic development is even becoming a major foundation of the new theoretical synthesis in evolution.[26] The field of developmental evolutionary psychology has much promise for shedding light on data that may not have made sense before, such as why attachment patterns correlate with such a wide range of developmental outcomes as aggression, sexuality, cooperation, and psychopathology.[27]

For example, recent epigenetic research looking at genotype-by-environment (GxE) interactions suggests that not all people may be *equally influenced* by environmental conditions; some girls and boys may be more reactive to stressful early environments than others because their highly reactive and negatively emotional temperament may be more affected by parenting than that of other children.[28] Indeed, revisions of Belsky and associates'[29] and Chisholm's[30] models put these genetic effects back into the picture. This doesn't mean, however, that all people can't use a wide range of cues to adjust their life history strategy. Most people can, and do.

This mutually reinforcing pattern of nature and nurture assures that neither the genes nor the environment alone is destiny. Just because your life history strategy at a certain age is rather stable does not mean you can't change your strategy (if you so desire); life history strategies are plastic and highly sensitive to environmental triggers (although this doesn't mean change is necessarily going to be easy): change the triggers, and you increase the chances that you will change the pattern of gene activations. Evolution "designed" humans to be highly sensitive to environmental cues and built in a great deal of plasticity into the human genome. Such plasticity would be more adaptive than rigidly "hard-wiring" at birth a person's life history strategy or allowing the environment to exert complete control. As Figueredo and colleagues[31] point out, evolution would favor developmental plasticity to allow for a wide range of possible environments.

The bottom line is that humans are extremely flexible strategically when it comes to mating because the adaptive value of different mating tactics depends on the ecology of the individual. What is an adaptive mating tactic in one society may be considered counterproductive in another. Every society has to solve reproductive trade-offs, such as whether to spend time investing in mating effort or to spend time and energy investing in parenting, *in their own way.* Different ecologies call for different ways of solving the unique reproductive trade-offs people face.

This strategic flexibility means that evolution was never able to settle on a stable solution and optimize any particular mating function in humans, allowing for individual differences to remain. So far, we discussed the broader picture of clusters of personality traits and how they tie in with a variety of other life history variables. Now it's time to focus solely on the major personality dimensions, starting at the broadest level of personality description.

Do You Grab Life by the Horns or Sit on the Sidelines?

Personality psychologists have agreed on five main personality dimensions that people differ on (dubbed the "Big Five"): extraversion, neuroticism, agreeableness, conscientiousness, and openness to experience.[32] Before we dive into the reproductive consequences of each of these factors individually, we will stand above the Big Five for a moment and look at two "meta-traits" that account for much of the shared variance among the lower-order dimensions.[33] We will be looking at these meta-traits with an eye toward implications for reproductive success.

The first meta-trait can be referred to as *stability* and is a blend of emotional stability (low neuroticism), conscientiousness, and agreeableness. This factor is all about self-control. Those who score high in stability have a need to maintain a sense of order in their lives. To help them accomplish this goal, they restrain themselves from engaging in a wide variety of behaviors. Individual differences in stability have been linked to the serotonergic neuromodulator. Serotonin has regulatory or inhibiting effects on mood, behavior, and cognition. Serotonin helps increase a person's vigilance while also reducing the negative affect that might get in the way of a person's effort to control the environment. One research study found that the association between serotonin and impulse control was the most consistent association found between serotonin and personality.[34]

The second meta-trait can be referred to as *plasticity* and is a blend of extraversion and openness to experience. High scorers on plasticity have a drive to engage in the world, and they soak up novelty from the environment like a sponge. Differences in plasticity have been linked to functioning of the dopaminergic neurotransmitter system. Dopamine can have activating effects on behavior and cognition and is linked to approach behavior, sensitivity to rewards, and breadth of thinking. Dopamine has shown linkages to positive affect, broad thinking, and mental flexibility.

It is possible for any one person to have any combination of these two meta-traits; stability and plasticity are *not* opposites. The opposite of plasticity is rigidity, and the opposite of stability is instability. What are the implications of each meta-trait for reproductive success? To provide clues, let's take a deeper look at how people scoring on each dimension tend to act in the real world.

Jacob Hirsh, Colin DeYoung, and Jordan Peterson[35] measured the two meta-traits in a community sample of 307 participants. Personalities were rated both by participants and three of their friends. Participants were given 400 behaviors and were asked to check off which ones they frequently engage in.

Those scoring higher on the stability meta-trait tended to engage less in a wide variety of behaviors. Of all the significant relations with stability

(82), 90% were negative. Here's a sampling of the top 10 behaviors people high in stability tended to *avoid*:

1. Tried to stop using alcohol or other drugs
2. Drank alcohol or used other drugs to make myself feel better
3. Swore around other people
4. Hung up the phone on a friend or relative during an argument
5. Lost my temper
6. Spent an hour at a time daydreaming
7. Yelled at a stranger
8. Rode a motorcycle
9. Awakened in the middle of the night and was unable to get back to sleep
10. Became intoxicated

These behaviors cluster together to enable self-control and long-term gains and would therefore be potentially conducive to a long-term reproductive strategy. Indeed, one of the most consistent findings in the literature is that both men and women report wanting high levels of agreeableness, conscientiousness, and emotional stability in a long-term mate.[36] Of course, this makes sense— these are all traits that are conducive to bonding and mutual satisfaction.

Not only do people desire these traits in a mate, but they also tend to seek mates who are somewhat *higher* than themselves in terms of their own perceived mate value in levels of extraversion, agreeableness, conscientiousness, and emotional stability.[37] People apparently want to feel as though they "acquired" a partner of higher quality than themselves. This situation leads people during courtship to hide their own levels of neuroticism and exaggerate their levels of emotional stability, conscientiousness, and agreeableness.[38] In turn, women, perhaps because of their higher biological cost of mating, report being skeptical about such displays.[39]

In a recent study, Portia Dyrenforth, Deborah Kashy, Brent Donnellan, and Richard Lucas[40] looked at the personality predictors of relationship and life satisfaction in three very large, nationally representative samples of married couples in Australia, the United Kingdom, and Germany. They looked at three different effects: *actor* effects, which refer to the association between a person's personality and their own satisfaction; *partner effects*, which refer to the association between a person's personality and his or her partner's satisfaction; and *similarity effects*, which refer to the association between the similarity of both partners and each partner's satisfaction.

They found that actor effects on relationship and life satisfaction were large, and partner effects were small, but still substantial. Taking actor and partner effects into account, similarity effects were minimal. The three best personality predictors (what they refer to as the "Big Three") for both actor and partner effects were agreeableness, conscientiousness, and emotional stability. These findings provide further support for the notion that the meta-trait of stability is well suited to meaningful, long-lasting relationships and life satisfaction. The higher your level of stability, the higher the likelihood that you will be satisfied in your relationship and in life, and the higher the likelihood that your partner will be satisfied. The research also suggests that your own level of stability does a better job of predicting relationship and life satisfaction regardless of your partner's similarity.

What about plasticity? Whereas those scoring high in stability tended to *avoid* engaging in a lot of behaviors, those scoring high on the meta-trait plasticity tended to *engage* in a wide variety of behaviors. Here's a sampling of behaviors people high in plasticity tend to engage in:

1. Was consulted for help or advice by someone with a personal problem
2. Planned a party
3. Attended a public lecture
4. Told a joke
5. Gave a prepared talk or public recital (vocal, instrumental, etc.)
6. Spent an hour at a time daydreaming
7. Wrote a thank you note
8. Wrote a love letter
9. Attended a city council meeting
10. Entertained six or more people

Actually, one of the behaviors on the list not included here might just be our favorite—perhaps the one *most conducive* to reproductive success: *Lounged around my house without any clothes on!* Anyway, you get the idea. All of these behaviors involve an active exploration and engagement in the world. As can be seen by the previous list, the plasticity dimension can manifest in a number of ways and may facilitate a fast life history strategy. People who engage in the world may increase their opportunities for short-term mating in a number of ways. By being more proactive, they may increase their overall chances by just approaching more people. Also, by being more inclined to display their creativity and abilities, their personality traits might acts as "amplifiers" that increase their chances of being noticed, and as we saw in Chapter 2, creative displays are highly valued in a potential mate. Also, people may be attracted to those high in plasticity (especially for a short-term encounter) because of their outgoing, "exciting personalities."[41]

Therefore, at the broadest level of description it seems as though differences in human personality reflect *restraint* and *engagement*. Stability is associated with avoiding engaging in potentially disruptive impulses, whereas plasticity is associated with engaging with the world, creatively and socially. The former may be more conducive to a long-term mating strategy, whereas the latter may be more conducive to a short-term mating strategy.

In short, there are advantages and disadvantages of each profile for reproductive success; it depends on your mating goals. Also, just because you tend to display one profile over another does not mean you can't change your behavioral patterns. Change your patterns of behavior and context, and your neurotransmitters will change as a result. Because a wide range of behaviors tend to cluster together to form a particular evolutionary adaptive strategy, to make a change requires formulating higher-order rules. These can take the form: "*I want to like to like engaging,*" or "*I want to want to be more stable,*" or even "*I want to like to be more stable and engage more in the world.*" Or whatever is consistent with your goals.

The meta-trait framework explains a lot of personality differences, but it does not explain everything. Even in Hirsh's study,[42] the researchers found that each of the Big Five traits offered unique prediction of behaviors. Also, recent research in the emerging field of personality neuroscience[43] suggests that each trait of the Big Five (except for the openness/intellect domain) is associated with the volume of different brain regions.[44]

In one study, the researchers found among 116 healthy adults, extraversion was associated with volume in the *medial orbitofrontal cortex* (a region involved in reward); neuroticism was associated with reduced volume in a number of brain regions typically associated with threat, punishment, and negative affect; agreeableness was related to reduced volume in various regions involved in theory of mind; and conscientiousness was related positively to volume in the *middle frontal gyrus* in the *lateral prefrontal cortex*, a region involved in self-regulation, planning, and self-control. Note that these gray-matter correlations are not fixed—volume in different areas of the brain changes constantly throughout the life span as a person accumulates experiences.

Each of the Big Five dimensions has important implications for reproductive success. Building on the work of MacDonald, Nettle has argued that variations in each of the Big Five dimensions can be conceptualized as variations in mating strategies that had different reproductive consequences under different environmental conditions in our ancestral past.[45] Let's now put each of the Big Five traits in the spotlight (they've been waiting very patiently!) and see how each one relates to reproductive outcomes.

The Stability Suite

Emotional stability, agreeableness, and conscientiousness together make up the stability suite. Let's look at each dimension separately.

Emotional Stability

Emotional stability (the opposite of neuroticism) is associated with reduced levels of negative emotions, such as fear, sadness, concern, wariness, anxiety, and guilt. Hirsh and colleagues[46] found that emotionally stable people tend to report *avoiding* the following real-world behaviors: taking medication for depression, taking tranquilizing pills, visiting a psychiatrist or psychologist, taking three or more different medications in the same day, sharing a problem with a close friend or relative, misplacing something important, participating in a self-help group, giving money to a panhandler, taking a sleeping pill, and trying to stop using alcohol or other drugs. It's clear: emotionally stable people are definitely stable!

Emotionally stable people also tend to display fewer occurrences of negative outcomes such as depression, stress, social isolation, and impaired physical health.[47] In fact, emotional stability is a very strong positive predictor of a spouse's martial satisfaction and relationship quality.[48] In the sexual domain, Nettle and Clegg[49] note, "neurotic individuals undermine their own sexual relationships through relentless worry, suspicion, jealousy, and neediness." And when it comes to courtship, neurotic individuals may overthink issues so much that they do not act, having too much "approach anxiety" to even get a chance in the mating marketplace. What, then, could be the benefits of low levels of emotional stability for reproductive success?

A person's level of neuroticism represents his or her threshold for detecting biologically related threats. Anxiety, a major component of neuroticism, increases detection and attention of potentially threatening predators by speeding up reaction to such threats and interpreting ambiguous stimuli as negative.[50] Within the mating intelligence domain, neurotic individuals tend to be hypervigilant to potential cues of mating-related threats. In the words of Nettle and Clegg,[51] neurotic people have "hair-trigger threat-detectors" that evolved to be safer more than sorry.

The evolutionary logic of the neurotic person is actually quite sound. Take jealousy, something neurotic people are particularly prone to. Although imaginary cases of cheating may cause some relationship difficulties, a few genuine cases may slip through the cracks. Because the costs of cheating are so great for reproductive success, it may well be worth it to worry, at least at a moderate level.

Neuroticism is also related to competiveness and academic success.[52] Therefore, the negative effects of neuroticism on reproductive success can also be positive when directed toward the goal of increasing one's position in the mating domain. For those who can deal with their levels of neuroticism (without it becoming too much of a burden), high neuroticism can be beneficial to reproductive success.

Taken together, in terms of reproductive success, emotional stability can have its benefits and disadvantages. High levels of neuroticism can have disadvantages but can also be adaptive in detecting mating-relevant threats and can be a source of motivation in competition for mates. Let's look at the next two traits that make up the stability suite.

Conscientiousness and Agreeableness

Scoring high in conscientiousness and agreeableness may seem socially desirable. However, like all the other traits mentioned in this chapter, social desirability is a different animal than the positive effects on fitness (see also Chapter 8).[53] Whether we like it or not, natural and sexual selection favors traits that increase reproductive success, including many cases in which this success comes at the expense of others. Fitness can be enhanced, under certain circumstances, by breaking rules and cheating.

It is with these trade-offs in mind that we discuss the highly correlated traits of conscientiousness and agreeableness. Nettle and Clegg[54] reported that in a sample of 545 people, men (but not women) with low levels of agreeableness and conscientiousness tended to have a higher number of sexual partners. It has also been found cross-culturally, across 10 world regions, that low levels of agreeableness and conscientiousness are related to higher levels of sexual promiscuity and relationship infidelity,[55] so there may be reproductive benefits to those on the low end of these traits (also see Chapter 8). To further explore these correlations, let's look at conscientiousness and agreeableness separately.

Conscientiousness involves orderliness and self-control in the pursuit of goals.[56] Those high in conscientiousness are good at delaying immediate short-term rewards in favor of greater long-term payoffs. Hirsh and colleagues[57] found that those scoring higher in conscientiousness tended to report engaging *less* in variety of behaviors, such as discussing sexual matters with a friend, lounging around the house without any clothes on (if you recall, our favorite!), picking up a hitchhiker, reading a tabloid paper, driving or riding in a car without a seatbelt, swearing around other people, spending an hour at a time daydreaming, shopping at a second-hand thrift store, telling a dirty joke, and listening to music. *Bottom line*: people high in conscientiousness take better care of themselves and avoid risks. Indeed, conscientiousness is associated with life expectancy.[58]

People scoring *extremely* high in conscientiousness tend to have high levels of moral principle, perfectionism, and self-control. This is reflected in the discovery that conscientiousness is found among patients with eating disorders and obsessive-compulsive personality disorder.[59] Conscientiousness may be very beneficial to a highly competitive modern world in which high achievers get ahead. Directly in terms of reproduction, those higher in conscientiousness ought to be better parents and more dutiful when it comes to taking care of their children.

According to Robert Sternberg's triarchic theory of love,[60] different components of love can combine to produce different types of love. Intimacy alone is "liking," passion alone is "infatuation," and commitment alone is "empty" love. Intimacy and passion combine to form romantic love, intimacy and commitment combine to form compassionate love, passion and commitment combine to form fatuous love, and if you can combine all three components, you get consummate love. Research shows that conscientiousness is positively correlated with both the intimacy and commitment components of Sternberg's theory of love,[61] which would make conscientiousness very well suited to a compassionate form of love. In the words of Engel, Olson, and Patrick,[62] "conscientious persons tend to be motivated workers in their love relationships."

Reasonably high levels of conscientiousness can certainly be conducive to long-term reproductive success. But in some contexts in the modern world, and especially in *most* of the unpredictable and harsh environments in which our ancestors evolved, high levels of conscientiousness and the extreme self-control associated with it may be *harmful* to fitness. In unpredictable environments, it may make more sense, evolutionarily speaking (again, we are not prescribing anything here), to be more open to spontaneous opportunities to enhance reproductive success.

Low levels of conscientiousness may therefore be more conducive to short-term mating success. But why? As Nettle and Clegg[63] note,

> Less conscientious individuals favor immediate opportunities, with little regard for their future consequences. They are impulsive about pleasures and procrastinate about work. In mating, they are more promiscuous, more likely to be unfaithful, and more likely to have impulsive, unsafe sex under the influence of alcohol or drugs.

Maybe those with low conscientiousness are just more impulsive and opportunistic, and that is why they have a higher number of sexual partners. Research shows that highly conscientious people report fewer short-term mating partners as well as avoiding opportunities to take an immediate reward that could be to their short-term advantage.[64] Low conscientiousness is related to delinquency, antisocial behavior, impulsiveness, unfaithfulness, and sexual intercourse under the influence of drugs or alcohol.[65] There's no doubt: conscientious people exert greater self-control.

Like all the other traits mentioned in this chapter, there are clearly trade-offs to reproductive success. Clusters of traits that orient the person toward working for long-term payoffs will tend to reduce opportunistic immediate rewards but may also decrease risk for getting a sexually transmitted disease, jealous partners, and a bad sexual reputation.[66] Depending on the context, the relative weighing of the costs and benefits for reproductive success will differ.

Whereas conscientiousness has to do more with responsibility and a sense of duty, agreeableness is more tied to empathy and the desire to please others. Indeed, agreeableness, empathy, and theory of mind are intimately connected (see Chapter 7).[67] Those who register others' emotions, can feel others' pain, and are aware of others' mental states tend to also be highly agreeable. Hirsh and colleagues[68] found that those scoring higher in agreeableness tended to report giving more money to panhandlers, participating in more self-help groups, taking more tranquilizing pills, drinking less in a bar, producing less works of art, riding fewer horses, misplacing things that are important, riding less in taxis, using thermometers more to take temperature, and drinking less beer. In general, women tend to score much higher than men on measures of agreeableness,[69] and agreeableness is related to higher-quality friendships, successful parenting, better academic and career performance, health, and life satisfaction.[70]

We humans (with apologies to the orangutans reading this book) appear to be unique among mammals in how well we cooperate with people not genetically related to us. Because humans are such a social species, we may have been under strong evolutionary selection pressures to pay attention to the mental states of others.[71] Agreeableness is associated with *all three* of Sternberg's love dimensions—passion, intimacy, and commitment[72]—which would make agreeableness the Big Five trait most directly associated with a consummate form of love. This is not surprising because agreeableness and its associated mental states and emotions are highly advantageous to facilitating harmonious relationships and avoiding violence, aggression, and hostility.[73]

Although highly agreeable individuals display less infidelity and show increased loyalty to mates, they also have fewer lifetime sexual partners.[74] Agreeableness may even sometimes be *detrimental* to short-term mating success (see Chapter 8 for more on the allure of the bad boy).[75]

Therefore, highly agreeable people are very much valued as friends and long-term partners but may also miss out on sexual opportunities and have impaired status competition, both outcomes potentially relating to reproductive outcomes. A study of male business executives found that agreeableness negatively predicted career success, with nice guys finishing last in the competition for status and money.[76] Of course, agreeable individuals may just not be as driven to have a high number of sexual partners, which could explain their lower total number of sexual partners (see Chapter 8).

It seems unlikely that always caring for the needs of others is conducive to fitness under every circumstance. Although having empathy is surely helpful for most of social life, it also bears costs in terms of leaving one open to exploitation and inattention to personal fitness gains.[77] The balance of advantages and disadvantages between different levels of agreeableness will therefore depend on the context. In small, isolated groups with a limited number of people and where contributions are public,[78] high levels of conscientiousness and agreeableness may be more evolutionarily adaptive than in a big city where there are looser social connections or in situations where competition is required (as opposed to cooperation). We take up these issues again in Chapter 8.

The Plasticity Package

Extraversion and openness to experience form the core of plasticity.

Extraversion

Extraversion is intimately tied with *exploration*, particularly in social situations.[79] Extraversion is also associated with positive emotions. As part of the plasticity factor, extraversion is tied to the dopaminergic neurotransmitter system.

Extraversion is associated with short-term reproductive outcomes in men.[80] Men who are more extraverted tend to be more popular in a speed-dating context,[81] have a higher number of sexual partners,[82] and also tend to cheat on their current mate or end their current relationship for another.[83] Extraverted women, compared with introverted women, get more sexual invitations from men.[84] Extraverted women also tend to show reduced levels of choosiness in a speed-dating context.[85]

Although extraversion preferences tend to be equally strong in both sexes in student samples,[86] when one looks at members of dating agencies, people dating, and newlyweds, one finds a tendency for men (more than women) to prefer introversion in their mates.[87] What is clearer is that both men and women prefer extraversion for a short-term encounter relative to a long-term encounter.[88]

The high energy and positive mood of extraverts may allow them to obtain mates of higher quality than someone who may be more introverted and not as prone to seek out other mating opportunities. Extraversion is also related to sensation seeking, the passion component of Sternberg's triarchic theory of love, and people high in extraversion are more likely to have more social support and gain reward from social engagement.[89]

In the study by Hirsh and colleagues,[90] those higher in extraversion were more likely to tell a dirty joke, plan a party, entertain six or more people, volunteer for a club or organization, get a tan, attend a city council meeting, color their hair, go to a night club, and drink in a bar. Clearly, extraverts engage more in the social world and exhibit behaviors (e.g., coloring their hair) that have social and mating implications.

The very same advantages of extraversion for a short-term mating strategy, in certain contexts, may be disadvantages. For instance, having too much sexual diversity and social exploration can be risky in terms of health as well as forming and maintaining a long-term relationship. Those who are higher in extraversion tend to be hospitalized because of an accident or illness more frequently than those lower in extraversion.[91] Those high in extraversion also tend to be arrested more and become involved in criminal or antisocial behaviors.[92] Also, the extraverted tendency to jump from relationship to relationship means that the children of extraverts may have a higher probability of being exposed to stepfathers, a known risk factor for child well-being.[93]

Clearly there are reproductive trade-offs for extraversion. Reproductive goals and environmental circumstances call for different levels of the extraversion continuum. This constant fluctuation of the "optimal value" during the course of human evolution meant that natural and sexual selection could not settle on an optimal value, allowing individual differences in extraversion to remain.

Openness to Experience

Of all the Big Five domains, the openness to experience domain of personality (sometimes referred to as openness/intellect) is the most cognitive. Therefore, this particular dimension of personality may undergo the highest mix of selection pressures, including both *mutation selection* and *balancing selection*.

Intellect and openness are substantially correlated with each other and reflect an interest in truth and beauty, respectively.[94] Consistent with this, Hirsh and colleagues[95] found that those scoring higher in the openness/intellect domain tended to report higher levels of the following: producing works of art, reading poetry, painting a picture, writing poetry, buying a book, reading a book, attending an art exhibition, making a gift for someone, attending an opera or orchestra concert, and attending a ballet performance. Considering the mix of intellectual and creative aspects of the larger openness/intellect domain, Gerard Saucier's[96] suggestion that "imagination" is a better label for this domain seems quite reasonable.

Although openness is often combined with intellect, the two constructs can also be separated from one another. In fact, this separation is *crucial* to mating intelligence. In a recent analysis, researchers conducted a large-scale analysis of 15 scales measuring facets of openness/intellect.[97] Even though the two facets were related to each other, they also were at least partially separate in terms of their correlations with more than 2,000 personality items taken from the *International Personality Item Pool*.[98]

The kinds of items that related to *Intellect* reflected engagement in intellectual matters and perceived intelligence (e.g., "*Like philosophical discussions,*" "*Am quick to understand things*"). On the other hand, openness was related to personality traits reflecting engagement in sensation and perception (e.g., *"Believe in the important of art," "See beauty in things that others might not notice"*).

Recent brain and behavioral research provides further support for the partial separation of intellect from openness. In one sample of 104 healthy adults, intellect, *but not openness,* was related to the ability to update working memory representations and the brain areas associated with that activity in the left lateral anterior prefrontal cortex and posterior medial frontal cortex.[99] Intellect was also associated with IQ scores. The association of intellect with brain activity could not be entirely explained, however, by cognitive ability. This is most likely because intellect reflects both the ability and the desire to engage in the intellectual realm.

If openness, by itself, is not related to conscious, rational, deliberate thinking, what *is* it related to? From a personality perspective, we already noted that openness is related to extraversion, and both may be tied to the functioning of the neurotransmitter dopamine. However, personality dispositions affect cognition (and vice versa). Dopamine can affect both behavior and thought. Cognitively speaking, openness is associated with apophenia (seeing patterns where they do not exist),[100] an enhanced ability to implicitly learn the probabilistic rule structure of the environment,[101] and an inability to ignore stimuli that were previously tagged as irrelevant (the technical term for this is *latent inhibition.*[102])

But here's where things get really interesting. On the one hand, people with high levels of openness tend to be more creative, particularly in the arts.[103] Indeed, many creative pursuits require a heightened engagement and sensitivity to the sensory world, and individuals with higher levels of openness, and its associated state of cognitive disinhibition, may be more likely to see connections that others may not notice.[104] On the other hand, openness and its associated cognitive states also show linkages to a proneness to psychosis.[105] Openness is associated with altered states of consciousness and unusual perceptual experiences such as vivid imagery and magical thinking.[106] These traits are sometimes referred to as the *positive aspects* of schizotypal personality disorder, a milder form of schizophrenia.

What does all of this have to do with mating? Well, schizotypy is also related to short-term mating success. One study on practicing poets, artists, and control subjects found that perceptual-cognitive distortions predicted creative output, which in turn predicted lifetime number of sexual partners.[107] Another recent study found that among males, a general tendency to engage in creative activities across the performing arts, science, writing, and visual arts, was related to total number of sexual partners within the past year. Schizotypy was indirectly related to number of sexual partners through its relationship with creative activity.[108] Other research has confirmed this link between positive schizotypal traits and a short-term mating strategy, as indicated by reduced levels of long-term investment (see also Chapter 7).[109]

Therefore, the unusual thinking style characteristic of openness can lead to highly creative and imaginative ideas about the world, or to full-blown psychosis. Although there is still some debate about the precise nature of the relation between openness to experience and schizotypy,[110] and this is still very much an open area of exploration, the bulk of the evidence suggests that the effect of openness on mating depends on other traits of the individual.

Individuals high in openness but in poorer condition without protective functions such as intelligence and working memory[111] can appear disorganized, incoherent, delusional, low in emotional expression, and impaired in perspective taking and can appear to have a bizarre, unfunny sense of humor. This combination (high openness and low condition) may repel potential mates and represent what Shaner, Miller, and Mintz[112] refer to as a "catastrophic failure of mating intelligence." Indeed, there is evidence that people with schizophrenia do have lower levels of reproductive success.[113]

On the other hand, those with high levels of openness, who exhibit schizotypal-like traits and who can deal with the influx of emotions and cognitions they experience, can be extraordinarily attractive to potential mates, exhibiting a terrific sense of humor, an accurate theory-of-mind, emotional expressiveness, and the ability to tell engaging stories. Indeed, many creative people of great recognition and accomplishment display the positive symptoms of schizotypy (the milder form of schizophrenia), and these individuals have plenty of mating success, particularly in short-term contexts (also see Chapter 7).[114]

Because the fitness payoffs to openness to experience seem so highly dependent on environmental conditions and other mental and personality characteristics of the individual, it would make sense for balancing selection to maintain a significant source of variation of openness in the general population.

Summary

Understanding the evolutionary origins of variations in personality is highly relevant to understanding human mating intelligence. Traits cluster in evolutionarily predictable ways that served fitness-enhancing functions among our ancestors in a number of different contexts. Each particular trait also can be related to trade-offs in reproductive strategy. Throughout the course of an individual's life span, different contexts can differentially activate different genes. The dynamic interplay between nature and nurture within an individual's life span is highly complex and mutually enforcing. How personality affects mating depends both on the context and condition of the individual.

Biology, Personality, and Attraction

Mate choice often happens fast, with men and women (often unconsciously) deciding whether a person is an appropriate long-term partner within the first few minutes of meeting him or her.[115] Although a number of social, economic, ecological, and psychological forces certainly play a role in this initial attraction,[116] *biological* forces are at play as well (see Chapter 4), including bodily and facial symmetry, ovulatory cycle effects, and the scent of those with dissimilar histocompatibility complex (MHC) genes involved in the immune response.[117]

A particularly understudied biological process is the contribution of biological systems that are likely to underlie universal human *personality traits*. People are typically (but certainly not always) correct in their initial perceptions of personality, even after meeting someone for only a few seconds (also see Chapter 8).[118] Since personality perception happens fast, and plays a role in mate selection, an interesting question is: *what kinds of personalities tend to be attracted to one another, and what are the biological systems that make up the relevant personality factors?*

To explore this question, Helen Fisher and colleagues[119] examined the role of temperament in the initial attraction phase of mate choice. They identified four interrelated yet different neural systems that are associated with a unique suite of biobehavioral traits and developed a self-report measure to tap into individual differences in each of these systems. The four systems are (1) the *dopamine and norepinephrine* systems, which are related to each other and are linked to the meta-trait plasticity, (2) the *serotonin* system, which is linked to the meta-trait stability, (3) the *testosterone* system, which is linked to heightened attention to detail, intensified focus, restricted interests, spatial acuity, aggressiveness, and social dominance, and (4) the *estrogen and oxytocin* systems, which are associated with each other and are linked to verbal fluency, empathy, nurturance, bonding, social connection, and other prosocial skills.[120] Of course, these four hormone systems interact, and it is possible for individuals to score high on more than one dimension. Still, people differ in terms of which hormones are most dominant.

In a sample of 28,128 participants taken from the dating website *Chemistry. com*,[121] the researchers found that men and women who reported higher levels of traits associated with the dopamine/norepinephrine system were more likely to seek out others with similar traits.[122] The same pattern was found for those reporting higher levels of traits associated with the serotonin system. On the other hand, those expressing traits associated with the testosterone system were more likely to choose to meet those expressing traits associated with the estrogen/oxytocin system. In sum, they found that like tended to attract like in terms of those expressive of dopamine/norepinephrine and serotonin, but opposites attracted among those expressive of the testosterone and estrogen/oxytocin systems. The researchers concluded that aspects of biology play significant roles in the initial phase of mate choice (of course, environmental and cultural factors play a huge role here as well).

Therefore, it would seem that the predictors of attraction are very specific to the individual, and are not necessarily the same predictors of relationship and life satisfaction. Fisher's research suggests that those who like to explore the world tend to be attracted to like-minded explorers. Those who are dutiful and emotionally stable tend to be attracted to others who are stable. Those expressive of testosterone may be drawn to those high in estrogen because these partners have the verbal and social skills and the compassion that the higher-testosterone individual needs. At the same time, those predominantly expressive of estrogen may be drawn to those expressive of testosterone because they need the high-testosterone person's decisiveness, directness, and analytical and spatial skills. We hope that in the future researchers will investigate the impact of hormones on attraction and how initial attraction affects short-term and long-term mating success.

Of course, hormones are constantly changing in every individual and are influenced by contextual factors, such as age, stage of a relationship, and even particular interactions. For instance, research shows that men exhibit a spike in testosterone after trying to impress an attractive woman.[123] Hormones also naturally fluctuate through the course of a relationship and as people age.[124] These fluctuations can affect the mating domain. For instance, one study reported that as people age, they tend to report lower levels of passion and higher levels of intimacy and commitment,[125] a personality profile that is no doubt influenced by hormonal changes. Therefore, it may not be such a surprise that initial attraction is not always be the best predictor of long-term relationship satisfaction and that the person we are initially attracted to does not always make the best long-term mate.

For instance, although extraversion is associated with passion, passion is *negatively* associated with relationship length.[126] Therefore, two people high in extraversion may be attracted to each other, but their relationship can fizzle out once the passion fades. To keep the relationship going may require high levels of other personality traits, such as agreeableness and conscientiousness. Indeed, both agreeableness and conscientiousness are related to the intimacy and commitment components of love, and intimacy and commitment are positively correlated with relationship length. There seem to be only minor differences between males and females in these personality-relationship correlations, so both sexes can benefit in relationships by working on their personality (which can alter their hormones).

We told you mating intelligence was complex! But hopefully we have demonstrated the usefulness of mating intelligence in making sense of the complex

role personality plays in human mating, especially in terms of individual differences. In the previous chapter, we took up the role of cognitive abilities in
human mating, and in this chapter we took up personality. That concludes the
courtship display aspects of mating intelligence. For the remainder of the book,
we turn to the many mechanisms humans have in place for selecting a mate
and navigating the windy road of mating. Next up, we'll discuss other traits
that can increase attraction, how all of these various cues become integrated in
perception, and how this all plays out in the real world.

4

What's Your Cue?

Attractiveness and Mate Choice in the Real World

Attractiveness is possibly the single-most-studied area of human mating from an evolutionary perspective. A topic that fascinates people of all persuasions, attractiveness has held center stage in much of evolutionary psychology in the past two decades. Researchers on this topic represent some of the top behavioral scientists the world over—including such academic pugilists as David Buss, Helen Fisher, Gordon Gallup, Steven Gangestad, Karl Grammer, Martie Haselton, and Devendra Singh. Consequently, many questions on this topic have been illuminated by research and have become common knowledge.

It makes good sense that attractiveness has been so well studied. Attractiveness has been shown to be related to all kinds of important outcomes, including income,[1] rising to leadership positions,[2] general perceptions of one's character,[3] and hiring,[4] to name just a few.

In one classic study, Snyder, Tanke, and Berscheid[5] manipulated the situation so that a group of males, based on a coin flip, thought they were talking to either a very attractive or a less attractive female by phone (attractiveness was manipulated by providing the males with different photographs of their ostensible conversation partners). Independent judges listened to tapes of either the male or the female half of the conversation and then rated the participants on a variety of dimensions related to sociability. The males who thought they were speaking to a physically attractive female were rated more positively by these independent judges. Not so surprising. But the females in the *attractive photograph* condition were also rated as having more positive and sociable personalities compared with their counterparts in the *not-so-attractive-photograph* condition. The actual women in these different conditions did not differ from one another and were, like the men, randomly assigned to experimental conditions. Looks matter. And apparently, looks create self-fulfilling prophecies.[6]

Imagine going through life and having everyone you meet treat you as *very likely to have a positive personality and great social skills*.[7] This might affect who you are. Looks matter, attractiveness matters, and we can demonstrate the differences in how people of various levels of attractiveness are treated by society.

The evolutionary perspective on attractiveness has, thus far, focused largely on determinants of physical attractiveness. This work often has a specific focus on either (1) features that are attractive in females or (2) features that are attractive in males. This work is also often divided into (a) features attractive in short-term mates and (b) features attractive in long-term mates—sometimes these coincide within the sexes; sometimes they do not.

In the first part of this chapter, we'll review some of the traditional research from evolutionary psychology on cultural universals of physical attractiveness. We fully acknowledge that preferences vary quite a bit from one culture to another, from one person to another, and even from one moment to another.[8] Even so, such variability isn't infinite and is usually explained from an evolutionary perspective.

What Makes a Woman Physically Attractive?

From a societal standpoint, this is not a frivolous question. Several major industries depend crucially on understanding attractiveness. The entire cosmetics industry, which grosses over $15 billion per year in North America alone,[9] hinges on this question. Pornography and prostitution bear on this question. Madison Avenue—in its efforts to advertise everything from beer to computers to cellular phones to pillows—eyes this question.

In brief, attractive features of female faces and bodies tend to be features that are typical of women who are of reproductive age. Features shared by females between their late teens and their late 40s tend to be features that are attractive. The evolutionary reasoning here is clear and statistically oriented. Evolution is a gambler, or, more accurately, evolution creates gamblers who make good bets. Because there is no socially acceptable, nonmedical means of gauging when a woman is fertile (a slightly separate issue from when she is *currently ovulating*), natural selection has shaped males to gamble. On average, under ancestral conditions, women between the ages corresponding to post-pubertal to pre-menopausal were more likely to be able to bear offspring compared with other women. Beyond about the age of 30, the probability of conception decreases, and the probability of birth complications increases.[10] Attraction to a woman whose features signal that she is likely in the fertile time of life has clear adaptive value.

All things considered, imagine two stone-age male hominids—Buffy and Sly. Buffy is, for some reason, attracted to the relatively young women in the clan (except for those who are close genetic relatives—we have adaptations that reduce such attraction).[11] Buffy likes long blonde hair. He likes smooth skin. He likes large, round, symmetrical breasts of the nondrooping variety.

Sly, for reasons unbeknownst to himself (and Darwin), is really into the older women in the clan (and there are only a few left!). To him, gray hair is a real turn-on. He likes the skin wrinkly. Thin lips are just plain hot. And he is sexually excited by an older woman's waist-to-hip ratio, which is hard (even for Sly himself) to objectively distinguish from the waist-to-hip ratio of the older men in his clan.

Buffy and Sly are sharks with the ladies. Both are real lookers with smooth moves who often end up with the women they seek.

Question: Who's more likely to leave genes into future generations? Buffy, obviously. Given his preferences, Buffy is more likely to mate with women who are fertile and more likely to pass on his genes to offspring. And, further, he is more likely to pass on genes predisposing his offspring to find youthful features in females as attractive. Sly may well get a lot of action, but given his preferred type, he's not too likely to pass on his genes—and the genes coding for an attraction to relatively elderly features are likely to go the way of the dodo bird.

This reasoning bears strongly on features of female faces and bodies that are generally perceived as attractive (although there are certainly individual and cultural differences), including the following:

- Relatively large eyes[12]
- Smooth skin[13]
- Lustrous, nongray hair[14]
- Full lips[15]
- A curvy figure (approaching a 0.7 waist-to-hip ratio)[16]
- A symmetrical face and body[17]

Although these features vary across cultures considerably, attraction is still universally predictable from an evolutionary perspective.[18] Research on women at Miss Universe contests (along with other convergent research) has demonstrated that many of the qualities rated as attractive (such as a waist-to-hip ratio of 0.7) are considered attractive across all corners of the globe.[19]

Indeed, evolutionary psychology theories of beauty have overturned much conventional wisdom among social scientists and have suggested that, although there are definitely cultural influences, physical attractiveness is not *arbitrarily socially constructed*.[20] Even so, this doesn't mean that such evolved preferences can't be dangerous to women. Feminists and evolutionary psychologists agree that they can be.[21] In this modern environment, it appears as though men's evolved preferences for female beauty have facilitated a destructive run-away female-female competition that causes women to unhealthily attempt to attain a standard of beauty that men don't even find attractive.[22]

Importantly, another thing that seems to make women look, sound, smell, and behave in an attractive manner is simply being at or near the time of peak ovulation.[23] As described in detail in the next chapter on mating strategies, a great deal of variability in mating processes is tied to a woman's ovulatory cycle—a point that seems to result from the fact that women can only be impregnated within a small window of time each month. Evolutionary forces have shaped women to display subtle cues of their ovulatory status.

Female Short-Term Versus Long-Term Attractiveness

One of the great insights of modern mating research is that people seem to have different psychologies when it comes to thinking about short-term versus long-term mates.[24] What makes a woman attractive as a short-term mate is often quite different from the characteristics that make her attractive as a long-term mate.

For a male seeking a short-term mate, any woman who signals accessibility tends to be relatively attractive. Along with this accessibility component, females who are successful in short-term mating often show the hallmarks of physical attractiveness—but in a crowded bar on a Saturday night, the evidence does suggest that standards go down, particularly toward closing time.[25]

That said, a body of current research suggests that what may *appear* to be a short-term mating strategy may not always be the case. Females who engage in short-term hook-up behaviors quite frequently report that they were hoping for the hook-up to turn into something a bit more long-term.[26] As such, although female attempts to appear attractive in short-term contexts can be documented, such attempts may sometimes be part of a larger female strategy designed for long-term mating. This finding points to the fact that the split between a short-term and long-term mating strategy isn't always so clear-cut. After all, we are dealing with humans with complex emotions!

Some of the same features that are attractive in females during short-term mating contexts are repulsive in long-term contexts. Being conspicuously sexually accessible often leads to derogative comments such as being called a *slut*—a signal within a social community that a particular female is more appropriate as a short-term partner than a long-term mate. In coming across as attractive in a long-term mating context, many of the qualities that matter are *characterological*. Kind, easygoing, altruistic, intelligent, humorous, conscientious—these are all features that are attractive in females in long-term mating contexts.

What Makes a Man Physically Attractive?

Although males are generally more likely than females to focus on looks in the process of searching for a mate,[27] the physical attractiveness of a male does matter. Women tend to focus on whether a male is a capable of providing resources for offspring, is sending honest signals of interest and commitment, is a genuinely kind person, and is someone who's near the top of the social totem pole in his local world.[28]

Beyond this, though, a male's physical attractiveness is certainly noted and plays a factor in mating. In particular, there is mounting evidence that women focus more on a male's physical attractiveness if she is (1) near ovulation,[29] (2) engaging in an extra-pair copulation (i.e., is cheating),[30] (3) engaging in a decidedly short-term mating strategy,[31] or (4) looking for a sperm donor.[32] These four contexts share a common feature—they all may be associated with a high probability of conception. If a woman is seeking a male primarily for his genes (as opposed to his parental ways or his ability to acquire resources), all the research suggests that the physical attractiveness of the potential mate matters more. Some researchers talk about this in terms of being attracted to a *cad* compared with a *dad*.[33] If you're likely to get pregnant, go for the "good genes"—this seems to be the evolutionarily shaped rule. Of course, displays of humor, intelligence, and creativity are also displays of good genes (see Chapter 2), but good genes appear to be most readily observable in physical features.[34]

Specific qualities of men that are generally considered physically attractive (again, individual and cultural differences exist) include the following:

- Symmetrical face[35]
- Masculine face with square jaw line (reflecting high testosterone levels)[36]
- Tall height (which correlates with strength, likeliness to hold a leadership position, and intelligence)[37]
- Muscular build[38]
- High shoulders-to-hips ratio, approaching a V-shaped upper body[39]
- Relatively deep voice[40]

Male Short-Term Versus Long-Term Attractiveness

As with women, there seem to be somewhat different features of males that are attractive in short-term versus long-term contexts. As mentioned earlier in this section, male features that are attractive in short-term contexts tend to correspond strongly to physical qualities. Men who are successful in short-term mating are often tall, masculine, muscular, facially attractive, and socially dominant.[41] According to Gangestad and Simpson's[42] theory of *strategic plural-ism in human mating*, males who do not have this constellation of features are not likely to be successful in short-term mating and would probably be best off using alternative tactics in trying to secure a partner (we would suggest developing other good genes indicators such as humor, intelligence, and creativity).

There seem to be a host of qualities that make a man attractive as a long-term mate. Several of these pertain to signals of kindness, warmth, and loving.[43] Further, a reputation as a genuine altruist is attractive[44]—and being someone who is seen as likely to attend to children and who has *dad* features (as opposed to *cad* features) makes a man attractive as a long-term mate.

There is also plenty of evidence suggesting that for a male to be attractive as a long-term mate, he should show signs of the ability to secure resources. Qualities such as ambitiousness, intelligence, and resourcefulness are all rated as important in male attractiveness as a long-term partner.[45] Similarly, being considered at or near the top of a social hierarchy is considered attractive (in fact, evidence suggests such power is, as Kissinger famously said, such an aphrodisiac that it's attractive in both short-term and long-term contexts[46]).

Finally, the bulk of the evidence suggests that men who look like dads (as opposed to cads) are preferred at certain times during the menstrual cycle, particularly when risk for conception is high.[47] In one study, Japanese participants were asked to select the face they considered most "physically attractive" out of a series of faces that included five Caucasian and five Japanese men.[48] Each face had a different degree of femininity. Participants preferred faces that were less feminized in the high-conception-risk phase than in the low-conception-risk phase of their menstrual cycle. No effect of ethnicity (Caucasian or Japanese) was found, although there was an overall preference for faces that were more masculine.

In another study,[49] British participants were asked to choose the most attractive face for a "long-term relationship" or a "short-term relationship." When it came to a short-term relationship, the preferred face shape was less feminine during the high-conception-risk phase, whereas preferences remained constant when women judged attractiveness for a long-term relationship. All of these findings make sense from an evolutionary perspective because there are reproductive costs and benefits associated with mating with different kinds of people. As the researchers noted, such ovulatory effects may allow women to have their cake and eat it too: causing them to seek a primary partner whose low masculine facial features indicate cooperation and parental care while occasionally mating with a more masculine-looking male when conception is most likely.

We should note that the good genes hypothesis is not the only possible explanation for these findings.[50] Other researchers have suggested that these ovulation shifts occur because of women's increased levels of self-perceived mate value when they are actually more reproductively valuable, which is at ovulation.[51] Yet other researchers have found that hormonal changes in women's estradiol concentrations across the menstrual cycle explain these effects.[52] James Roney, Zachary Simmons, and Peter Gray argue that their findings suggest that women's estradiol is particularly important in promoting attraction to androgen-dependent cues in men (a finding also seen among females in nonhuman species). Future research is needed to further elucidate the precise mechanisms by which these effects are found.

Attractive Behaviors

To this point, this chapter has focused mainly on mating psychology traditionally presented. One of the ways in which mating intelligence offers a fresh perspective pertains to the idea of behavioral patterns that are attractive and that play important functions in mating. Addressed in detail in our chapter on courtship displays (see Chapter 2), the notions of mental, dispositional, and behavioral courtship displays[53] serve as a core concept that sets mating intelligence apart and that forges new ground in our understanding of human mating psychology from an evolutionary perspective.

Behavioral courtship displays can be so powerful that they can override cues of physical attractiveness, a point that is highlighted in a very intriguing study conducted by the evolutionary psychologists Kevin Kniffin and David Sloan Wilson.[54] These researchers argue that from an evolutionary perspective, even though beauty is an assessment of fitness value, the fitness value of a potential social partner can be influenced by both physical and *nonphysical* traits. Each of us has met someone whose "objective" rating of physical attractiveness changed quite drastically after interacting with that person.

To empirically test this phenomenon, Kniffin and Wilson ran a set of studies to test the influence of personality and behavioral displays on perceptions of physical attractiveness. In their first study, they had participants rate the photographs of classmates in their high school yearbooks for physical attractiveness, familiarity, liking, and respect. The researchers then had strangers who had never met the people in the yearbook photos of the same sex and approximately the same age rate the same photographs for physical attractiveness. How much difference was there between the ratings of the strangers and the ratings of those who actually knew the people?

Even though nonphysical factors made the biggest difference for women rating men, nonphysical factors (particularly liking) significantly influenced men's perceptions of the physical attractiveness of the women. There were also women in the sample who were heavily influenced by physical attractiveness.

To illustrate their effect, the researchers looked at the photograph of the male whom a particular female participant rated as *least* physically attractive. To both the researchers and the strangers who rated this man, he was about average in physical attractiveness, and certainly not ugly. When the researchers showed the photograph to the participant and asked her why she rated him so ugly, her faced turned to one of disgust as she explained how horrible a person he was. She was apparently physically disgusted by the image of this guy, even though his personality had nothing to do with his physical features. What is even more striking is that this woman's perception of this man's physical attractiveness remained this intense, even after 30 years since she had last interacted with him!

The researchers found the same effect in another study in which they asked members of a university rowing team who spent a year with each other to rate all the other team members in terms of talent, effort, respect, liking, and physical attractiveness. Strangers also rated the same people by looking at a team photograph. Just like their first study, perceptions of physical attractiveness were heavily influenced by nonphysical traits in both males and females, and ratings by the strangers and the team members were markedly different from each other. In one case, a male team member who was considered a slacker by the rest of the team was unanimously rated as physically ugly, whereas in another case a member of the team who was considered a hard worker was rated by everyone as physically attractive. Perhaps most telling was the fact that according to the strangers who knew nothing about these two individuals, there was no difference between both of them in terms of their levels of physical attractiveness.

A third and final study was conducted at the beginning and end of an intensive 6-week summer archaeology course where the students worked with each other intimately on a dig site. The researchers asked these students to rate each other in terms of familiarity, intelligence, effort, liking, and physical attractiveness. By this point, you should be able to figure out what the researchers found. Nonphysical traits (particularly liking) predicted the ratings of physical attractiveness at the end of the course above and beyond the effects of the initial impressions of physical attractiveness. In one case, a woman who received a below-average rating of 3.25 by the other members of the class on the first day ended up with a mean rating of 7.0 by the last day of class. From the first day to the last day, she became more popular, was well liked, and was regarded as hardworking. The traits significantly boosted others' perceptions of her physical attractiveness, even though she probably didn't do one thing to alter her physical appearance throughout the course. Taken together, these results suggest that our initially "hardwired" gut reactions to appearance can be overwritten by mental and dispositional fitness indicators of the sort we've been describing thus far in this book. The researchers concluded with a beauty tip: "If you want to enhance your physical attractiveness, become a valuable social partner." In other words, if you want to increase other's perceptions of your mate value, a bit of mating intelligence couldn't hurt!

In short, behaviors that display complexity, exceptional abilities, and valued personality traits (e.g., kindness) are attractive to both males and females—and there is even evidence that they are attractive in both long and short-term contexts.[55] Art, poetry, musical ability, dance, storytelling, humor, kindness, and so on—these are all qualities of our species that exist universally across cultures (albeit in culturally specific incarnations)[56] and that sometimes serve no direct survival function. As discussed in other sections of this book and elsewhere,[57] these qualities likely evolved partly as courtship display signals in a species with complex brains that are controlled by a large share of the genome. It's important, however, to distinguish cognitive displays from dispositional displays. Just as mental and dispositional courtship displays can override cues of physical attractiveness in perceptions of mate value, so can cognitive courtship displays override cues of disposition.

Consider the Woody Allen effect that we raised in Chapter 2. Woody Allen is hardly the best-looking guy out there. He's neither particularly tall nor muscular. He's not really a very positive person. He's probably not screaming "kindness" to the ladies. And some might call him creepy, to boot. A quick look at his mating history tells a story of having at least some level of success. Guess what: it's not the creepiness, neuroticism, and mediocre looks! Clearly, his abilities in the domain of writing, cinema, and humor are elite—and these mental abilities are attractive—even attractive enough to compensate for some pretty dramatic dispositional deficits!

Want to attract a mate? Want to rekindle a spark in a long-term pair-bond? Don't worry so much about diets, or make-up, or steroids. Work on developing either creative behaviors—many classes of creative behaviors will do—or personality traits that are valued by your "type" (see Chapter 3). There is almost always room for improvement.

Intrasexual Competition—A Fact of Mating

Attracting a mate or maintaining a relationship is always done in a broader social context. Looking good is not enough if all the others look great. Having a reputation as someone who's pretty helpful falls short when most people in your community have reputations as saints who'd rip the shirts right off their backs for a stranger.

To succeed in the mating domain, you not only need to appear attractive to appropriate targets but also need to appear *more* attractive relative to the competition (see Chapter 2 for an example of the use of humor). And any steps that you can take to bring the competition down a notch would be beneficial.

Now this all sounds a bit Machiavellian—and, often, it is. One theory of human intelligence, in fact, suggests that the most interesting thing about human intelligence is its Machiavellian nature. This construct, named after

Niccolo Machiavelli of Italy in the 16th century, focuses on the tendency to manipulate others in a social environment for one's own gain, just as Machiavelli's *Prince* did famously—so famously, in fact, that he now has a personality construct in modern psychology named after him.[58]

As we mention later in this book, Machiavellianism does seem to play an important role in human mating, especially in the courtship phase (see Chapters 7 and 8).[59] The entire idea of getting a mate to select you partly by derogating the competition may be Machiavellian, but all the research suggests that it's also quite human.

And as is true of many facets of human mating, rival derogation seems to be a bit sex differentiated. The nature of rival derogation within each sex makes sense when examined from an evolutionary perspective.

In the world of male-male derogation, males hit one another where it counts. Physical stature matters in terms of physical attraction of women to men—so men will derogate other males physically, calling one another such endearing terms as *wimp*, *geek*, or *fat ass* (yes, we males use these terms!). Males will refer to other males as *losers*, painting a rival as someone who's not near the top of the status totem pole, who'll never get a good job, and who's just, well, *not a winner*. Females are highly attracted to males who are altruistic and who show signals of kindness. To address this issue, males will refer to rivals as *assholes*, *jerks*, or even *dickheads*. Each of these words, in a single utterance, paints an individual as selfish and non-other oriented—not exactly what you might want in a husband.

In a series of studies on female-female intrasexual competition, Maryanne Fisher and her colleagues have shown that females are hardly the kinder sex when it comes to rival derogation. A host of research shows that female-female derogation may be subtler than male-male derogation, but it's there. When shown photographs of other women and given a mating scenario to think about, women can be very explicit and critical of one another's looks. In fact, while features of female attractiveness seem to have evolved as a result of males' evolved desires, females appear to be exquisitely attuned to the constellation of characteristics that correspond to female attractiveness—and they use this information in partner derogation.[60]

In addition to putting down other women in terms of physical shortcomings, women are much more likely than men to comment on the sexual reputation of intrasexual rivals. Referring to rivals as *sluts* paints these rivals as no good for long-term mating—and in a species that is primarily about long-term mating, such a reputation can be extremely detrimental to social prospects.

But does this mean that derogating one's rival is the *only* path to mating success? Not at all. In Chapter 8, we discuss more prestigious paths.

Attraction as a Big Piece of the Mating Intelligence Puzzle

So how does attraction from an evolutionary perspective relate to mating intelligence? According to the research, this happens in at least two important ways.[61]

Remember that there are two important classes of ideas that constitute mating intelligence. First are courtship displays.[62] To a large extent, behavioral displays of intelligence, creativity, and personality are products of our evolution—shaped as ornamental fitness displays for courtship. Second, mechanisms that underlie attraction in the domain of mating may be conceptualized under the *mating mechanisms* part of mating intelligence.

In attracting a potential mate or in retaining a mate and staying attractive within a mateship, creative and intelligent behavioral displays are crucial. Being a physical beauty with all fluff between the ears (come on, you know at least one!) may well allow someone to attract a certain number of mates, but it doesn't bode well for attracting a long-term mate, nor for maintaining an exciting and interesting relationship as things progress. As Geoffrey Miller[63] cleverly pointed out in *The Mating Mind*, TVs, radios, books, and (certainly) the Internet did not exist during 99% of human evolutionary history. If you wanted to be entertained in this scenario, you'd better find someone interesting. And because there are only 150 of us in this clan (in terms of *Dunbar's number*, which is considered a reliable estimate of clan sizes in ancestral *Homo sapiens*), we might have a tough time finding Jerry Seinfeld!

Creative displays, including various art forms such as singing, storytelling, and dance, have ancestral roots.[64] With the intense complexity of the human mind, entertainment became almost necessary at some point in evolution. And with the fitness-indictor capacity of these kinds of behavioral displays, these sorts of activities ultimately evolved to serve important functions in courtship. Long, shiny blonde hair may be attractive, but so is the ability to make a whole group laugh aloud with a story about something that would be otherwise mundane ("You wouldn't believe what this lady did in front of me in line at the grocery store!"). From Jimi Hendrix to Einstein to Sarah Silverman to Helen Fisher (shh, don't tell her!), people who engage in exceptionally high-quality displays of intelligence or artistic abilities are attractive as mates.

The mechanisms of romantic attraction in the mating world are important mechanisms of mating intelligence. Being attracted to potential mates who would be beneficial for long-term reproductive fitness is a component of mating intelligence. Some people are just consistently attracted to the wrong *type*. Being able to spot this kind of thing is a hallmark of mating intelligence. Someone high in mating intelligence should also be better than average at detecting deceptive courtship displays. Natural blonde hair and dyed blonde hair look pretty similar—someone high in mating intelligence should be able to pick out the fake blonde (along with the guy with the toupee and the woman with the breast enhancements). Being able to tease apart a false courtship display from a genuine courtship display is a central component of mating intelligence.

Further, processes involved in intrasexual competition are integral to mating intelligence. Realizing that one is being derogated by same-sex rivals is likely an important part of mating intelligence, and future research would definitely be helpful in documenting the nature of this process. Are some people better at detecting such derogation than others? What are some of the skills needed to make this realization without stepping into the world of paranoia? Similarly, tactics designed to diffuse attempts at reputation damage represent an important element of mating intelligence. And the ability to effectively derogate rivals without coming across as a gossipy jerk seems like it would require a good bit of intelligence as well!

Attraction and mate selection happen in broad social contexts that include (1) being attractive to potential mates, and (2) coming across as attractive relative to rivals in the same mating pool. A good bit of mating intelligence is needed to navigate the waters in the ocean of mate attraction.

Integrating Multiple Cues

So far, we've treated all of these various cues to attractiveness in isolation. Obviously, in the real world, all of these cues have to be integrated somehow to form an overall impression of the person in terms of how attractive he or she is.[65] A lot of mate selection involves making inferences. A guy picks up your groceries, and you *infer* that he's a nice guy. A woman tells a funny joke, and you *infer* that she's generally funny. You don't know for sure, but you are constantly on the lookout for cues that reveal underlying traits about that person.

This cue-based strategy has its roots in Egon Brunswik's[66] original lens model, in which perception first involves the weighting of each cue (e.g., the telling of a joke), depending on how strongly it is related with it's distal variable (intelligence), and then all the cues are combined. Brunswick was interested in investigating visual perception, but we can apply Brunswik's lens model to the mating domain and think of various categories of cues that influence mate choice. Geoffrey Miller and Peter Todd[67] distinguish among the following cues: health/fertility, neurophysiological functioning, provisioning ability/resources, and capacity for cooperative relationship. All of these cues are aspects of mate quality and have to be integrated to form an assessment of overall attractiveness. How is this done?

The jury is still out on this one, but various ways of integrating cues can be modeled on computers, and these simulations have been helpful in comparing various theories. One possibility is that people integrate cues in a linear way, going from one cue to the next in forming their judgments. This doesn't seem to be the way humans integrate cues, however, because many cues interact in a nonlinear fashion. For instance, those with lower levels of physical attractiveness may devote more of their energy to increasing their sense of humor. Another problem with linear models is that they assume that all the cues are available all at once when forming a judgment. This is not realistic. Some cues are more readily assessed (e.g., physical attractiveness), whereas others take more time (e.g., kindness).

Another possibility that overcomes some of these limitations is a sequential-aspiration model, in which cues are used to make inferences as soon as they become available. In this model, we start with the most easily assessable traits and keep modifying our perceptions as new cues become available. The late, great Herbert Simon won a Nobel Prize for his work on "satisficing" that highlighted the fact that people don't tend to make "optimal" decisions, but instead make decisions that are "good enough."[68] This idea also seems to apply to the mating domain. Each piece of new information we learn about a potential mate helps guide our decision to continue chatting with (or dating) that person, and people differ from one another in terms of what level of each cue is good enough for them. A major variable that affects aspirational levels for each cue is the type of relationship sought. The more serious people are about a relationship, the higher they tend to raise the bar in terms of intelligence, kindness, earning capacity, and physical attractiveness.[69]

Dating in the Speed Lane

To more fully understand human mating intelligence, it is necessary to look both at stated preferences cross-culturally (which provide insight into universally evolved mating mechanisms) and real-life interactions (which put constraints on the possibilities attained in the mating marketplace) across a wide age range. Thankfully, there are a number of fascinating studies looking at mate selection in real-world contexts.

Recent research using large speed-dating samples has investigated the predictors of both mating (short-term encounters) and relating (long-term relationships). Jens Asendorpf, Lars Penke, and Mitja Back[70] set up a speed-dating event in Germany in which they invited a total of 190 men and 192 women who were between the ages of 18 and 54 years. All of their participants were real singles whose sole motivation for participation in the study was to find a real-life romantic or sexual mate. Participants went on a series of 3-minute dates and indicated whom they would like to see again. They were followed up by the researchers 6 weeks and 1 year after the speed-dating session.

Consistent with parental investment theory, women, on average, tended to state interest in long-term mating more so than men. This was only relative, however: both men and women reported a desire for long-term mating, and most men in this dating context did choose a long-term mating orientation. This suggests that a speed-dating context is one that generally attracts people pursuing long-term mating tactics (or at least report that they do!).

Who was the most popular? Popularity was heavily influenced by easily perceivable physical attributes such as facial and vocal attractiveness, height, and weight. Sex differences were also evident, with men mainly basing their decisions on physical attractiveness and women using more criteria, including high levels of sociosexuality (willingness and desire to engage in short-term sexual encounters), low levels of shyness, and cues of current or future resource-providing potential, such as education, income, and openness to experience.

Interestingly, sociosexuality (the extent to which someone has a short-term mating orientation) was *the most important predictor* of popularity once physical attributes were already taken into account. Because most women expressed interest in long-term mating, it is surprising that they would be attracted to men with a short-term mating orientation. The researchers raised the possibility that a male's sociosexuality may indicate his history of successful mating experiences or mating skills (i.e., high mating intelligence) and that this is attractive to women. It should also be noted that the relationship between shyness and popularity was *negative*: the more shy the man appeared, the less popular the man. The researchers suggested that this may be due to traditional male sex roles, which require men to be assertive and proactive in the mating domain, skills that may not come as easily to shy guys.

The researchers also found that the popularity of the speed-dater was positively related to the choosiness of that speed-dater—but this correlation only held for men. As the researchers noted, this finding is consistent with the idea that highly popular people are thought to be more careful in their choices, whereas unpopular people are thought to be less discriminating.[71] Interestingly, they found an age effect: the older the woman, the less choosy she was; and the older the man, the *more* choosy he was. We'll explore this in more detail in the next chapter. Surprisingly, the researchers found a rather weak effect of similarity—like didn't tend to attract like, although this finding is probably due to the brief interactions these individuals engaged in. Most certainly, it takes longer than 3 minutes to form a deep connection.

When the researchers followed up, they found that the chance of having sex with a speed-dating partner was 6%, whereas the chance of ending up in a long-term relationship with a speed-dating partner was 4%. These numbers were influenced by the mating orientation of the *other* sex, however. The chances of a woman mating (i.e., having sex) increased if her partner had a short-term mating orientation, and the chances of a man mating increased if his partner had a long-term mating orientation. This finding was confirmed both 6 weeks and 1 year after the speed-dating event.

Are there practical implications of these findings? The researchers put their data in perspective. They figure that the chances of finding a sexual romantic partner will be lower than speed-dating if one visits a café for 2 hours actively in search of a partner and higher than speed-dating if one visits bars (or, we would add, nightclubs) with a certain reputation. The researchers converted their percentages into the time and money spent on multiple speed-dating events, assuming that all the events were independent in terms of outcome and that each event cost 30 Euros (roughly $40) and lasted 3 hours. With these assumptions in place, to have the same chances of finding a relationship partner *without* speed dating would require investing 75 hours and 750 Euros (roughly $1,000) on average. For busy people, speed dating may indeed be worth it.

As you can see, not all of the theories and findings we've presented are purely theoretical. Mating intelligence can be studied in the real world, and evolutionary theories can be tested. How people form judgments of others, who are the most attractive individuals, and the predictors of mating and relating are all important questions and can be treated scientifically and explored.

As we've repeatedly stressed, humans are an extremely flexible species, with many different mating strategies up our sleeves. In the next chapter, we will look at some of those strategies and the conditions that make those strategies more likely to be employed.

5

Game Plans

The Highly Contextual Nature of Human Mating Strategies

When it comes to human mating, evolutionary psychologists have cracked much of the code. The evolutionary perspective has elucidated many elements of human mating, including the nature of physical attraction,[1] the nature of love,[2] the interface of parenting and courtship,[3] infidelity,[4] relationship conflict,[5] and pretty much any other aspect of human mating that you can think of. All elements of human mating follow from basic principles derived from Darwin's big idea.

But one of the most exciting themes to emerge from all of this research is that human mating patterns are strategic, predictable (i.e., not random), and largely designed by evolutionary forces to increase reproductive payout across future generations.[6] This is not to say that the evolutionary perspective predicts that all humans (or all members of any species, for that matter) are designed to create as many offspring as possible during a lifetime. In fact, from a behavioral ecological perspective, optimal patterns of offspring production within a species are capped by ecological factors.[7] For women, increasing the number of sex partners decidedly does not increase the number of viable offspring who make it to reproductive age[8]—and for men, who live in a social world with ground rules set by females' high levels of obligatory parental investment and high levels of discrimination in mate selection, efforts to have sex with as many women as possible usually fall quite flat. Also, individual differences play a role here. Sex drive levels certainly vary *within* both males and females as a function of personality, attachment style, genetics, hormones, daily stressors, time of month, culture, and many other factors. What is clear is that humans have a lot of mating strategies at their disposal, and context (both internal physiology and external factors) strongly influences which strategies are prominent at particular points in the human life span.

Indeed, human mating strategies were shaped by selection pressures to take these complex factors into account. In the original formulation of Sexual Strategies Theory, Buss and Schmitt[9] advanced nine hypotheses and made 22 empirical predictions. Since then, the theory has been tested in many different ways, it has influenced related theories, and it has been extended to incorporate individual differences, sex-specific adaptive issues surrounding love and commitment, and a wider array of social, cultural, personal, and ecological variables.[10]

In this chapter, we discuss the complex suite of factors that underlie human mating and discuss how mating strategies may be conceptualized as residing at the core of human mating intelligence.

What Are Mating Strategies?

In terms of the psychology of human mating, *mating strategies* are optimized patterns of behavior that are relatively likely to lead to long-term reproductive success based on typical environments faced by our ancestors across human evolutionary history. Such strategies include, for instance, males being attracted to females who show signs of youth[11] (e.g., lustrous hair, smooth skin; see Chapter 4) because such signs were correlated with fertility across ancestral contexts. Mating with women who were most likely able to produce children (as opposed to mating with women who probably could not) would clearly be an adaptive mating strategy. A female tendency to seek high levels of commitment from a partner before consenting to sexual relations would be an adaptive strategy because women benefit greatly from mating with partners who are faithful and who have the ability to provide resources for a growing family. Thus, females would be expected to screen carefully through signals of commitment—and research on the nature of female mating intelligence has found that this is exactly what they do.[12]

To understand the evolutionary perspective on human mating strategies, we have to understand the appropriate use of the word *strategy* in this context. Importantly, *strategy* does *not*, here, correspond to a conscious game plan implemented to achieve some stated goal. It would be inaccurate and inappropriate, for instance, to talk about the male tendency to desire multiple partners (relative to females' desires)[13] as reflecting *a conscious effort* on the part of all males to deceive women and to turn up multiple sex partners—and to destroy families across the globe along the way. Such an inappropriate interpretation would easily lead to the implication that *all* men are pigs. Indeed, the evolutionary perspective explains the urge to do so, but there are certainly good men who use their conscious capacities to override their instincts and minimize hurting others and getting hurt themselves.

Therefore, when evolutionary psychologists refer to a *strategy*, they are typically talking about a behavioral pattern that is *largely unconscious* in nature. Thus, evolutionary psychologists might talk about tendencies that are common in males across cultures regarding desiring multiple partners—but that is very different, of course, from saying that men across all cultures consciously *choose* to be pigs. Many of the unconscious forces that pull us toward certain stimuli and repel us from other stimuli are at times quite potent and are predictable from an evolutionary perspective. This chapter is all about those unconscious strategies that evolutionary psychologists are at the forefront of understanding. Once you start reverse-engineering the human mind, you discover just how intricate and intelligent these forces really are.

The Evolutionary Roots of Human Mating Strategies

Although the evolutionary origins of human mating are addressed in our introductory chapter, we believe it's important to revisit these basic issues here because they are particularly pertinent to our understanding of human mating as strategic. The evolutionary roots of human mating strategies are perhaps best understood in terms of Robert Trivers'[14] theory of parental investment. Trivers, trained at Harvard as a biologist in the 1960s, has become one of the world's leading voices on the topic of evolution. He has been particularly lauded for the powerful nature of his theories and their ability to generalize to explanations of humans. His theory of parental investment may well be evolutionary theory sine qua none in the field of evolutionary psychology.

Interestingly, parental investment theory was not designed as a theory about humans at all. In fact, this theory was initially conceptualized as an explanation of parenting across species. In some species, such as robins, offspring are particularly *altricial*—the young are helpless at birth and need a lot of assistance. So much so, in fact, that multiple adult helpers are nearly required for the young to get enough in the way of worms to reach adolescence. In such a species, it would make sense that adults would form pair-bonds and would both contribute to raising offspring—such a species-typical arrangement would benefit not only female robins (who secure nice, helpful, dad-like partners) but also male robins, who benefit from siring offspring that don't die horrible deaths in their first few days and who, rather, grow up to reach adulthood and become successful in the mating domain themselves. When these ecological conditions are met, and parental costs are relatively high, long-term mating strategies should come to typify the species. Thus, the pair-bonds that robins form each spring—along with their beautiful songs brought us all summer long—provide the prototype of long-term mating.

Not all species have young that require intensive help from multiple adults. White-tailed deer, which, like robins, are prevalent in so many regions of North America, give birth to young who typically can walk during their first day of life (they are, thus, *precocial*). Like all mammals, the young seek proximity to their mothers for the first several months of life, being fed exclusively by her

for quite a while. So here we have a case of a species for which obligatory parental investment is relatively low. A fawn needs help from fewer adult conspecifics than does a robin hatchling. Guess what? Bucks don't get married or settle
down. In deer, mating is typified by short-term strategies—efforts to choose
high-quality mates coupled with zip in the way of expectations of long-term
pair-bonding.

Trivers' great insight, thus, is this: In species in which parental investment
is high, long-term mating systems are expected to evolve. In species in which
parental investment is low, short-term mating systems are expected to evolve.

Where are humans on this continuum? Good question. Well, without a
doubt, human offspring are altricial. A newborn human needs at least as much
adult help as does a robin hatchling. If you're a parent, you do not need us to
tell you that.

So with humans, we have a relatively altricial species and relatively high levels of parental investment required for individuals to ultimately rear offspring
that are capable of ultimately reproducing (successfully) themselves. Based on
this reasoning, it is little wonder that human cultures are permeated with variants of monogamy. As a species, humans are long-term strategists.

Female Versus Male Mating Strategies

One of the most prominent areas of research in evolutionary psychology—
and one of the most controversial[15]—pertains to work on sex-differentiated
behavioral patterns between men and women in the mating domain. Study
after study that examines differences between the sexes in mating-relevant
behavior has found important differences that are generally consistent with
predictions based on the evolutionary perspective.

Although long-term mating strategies definitely characterize human mating
in a general sense, research does suggest that it is appropriate to differentiate
between a specific male mating psychology and a specific female mating psychology.[16] Importantly, just as differences among mating systems of different
species can be well understood in terms of Trivers' theory of parental investment, differences between the sexes (within a species) can also be understood
in terms of parental investment.

In most sexually reproducing species, females invest more in parenting than
do males. This point partly is made necessary by the fact that the biological
definition of the female of any species is the sex that has the larger gamete
(referred to as the *egg*). Contributing the larger gamete to offspring (in other
words, being female) sets the stage for relatively high parental investment. Eggs
provide developing zygotes with all the nutrition needed in the earliest stages
of life. Sperm cells generally simply activate the egg and start the process of

fertilization. They do not contribute to the nutritional resources of the developing zygote. As a result of this biology, females in most sexually reproducing species[17] tend to have higher obligatory parental investment than do males.

Female Mating Strategies

In humans, the idea of females having relatively high obligatory parental investment compared with males is apparent in many facts. At the gamete level, the egg is considerably bigger than is the sperm—and sperm are considerably more common. Females release approximately 350 eggs in a lifetime; males release approximately half a billion sperm cells in a single ejaculate. For males, the physiological costs of pregnancy are nonexistent. For females, these include dramatic effects that bear on all bodily systems and that have potentially dangerous consequences. In all societies (especially pre-westernized societies),[18] childbirth is a significant cause of death of women (but, obviously, not of men). In pre-westernized societies, women tend to nurse children through about 3 years. Men do not. Even beyond the very early years, when women, across cultures, spend a disproportionate amount of time in childraising relative to men, women still expend more energy on parenting compared with men. And this sex difference holds true for grandmothers versus grandfathers, as well.[19]

In our species, women invest more in parenting than do men. Further, given how altricial human newborns are, child care provided by multiple adults offers an important advantage on the road to survival and reproductive success. According to Trivers' theory of parental investment, then, women, on average, should be more likely to utilize long-term strategies compared with men. In an unconscious effort to reproduce most effectively, optimal female mating strategies would include efforts to secure high-quality mates that are (1) faithful and monogamous, (2) able to provide material resources for offspring, and (3) likely good and kind in the domain of parenting and relationships.

Research on this topic bears these predictions out. In a study with thousands of young adults across more than 30 cultures, David Buss and colleagues[20] found that, regardless of geographic region, women consistently rate *education, ambition, intelligence,* and *kindness* as crucial in potential mates. These qualities clearly are features that would be highly desirable in a long-term mate. In follow-up research in this same area, Li[21] found that women who are told to imagine that they have a *limited mating budget* tend to emphasize these same kinds of qualities. In this research, participants are given a certain amount of mating budget dollars—either an extravagant or a highly restricted budget. They then allocate mating dollars to different qualities based on how important these qualities are (e.g., 5 mating dollars on looks, 3 on wealth). With a large budget, males and females come out as very similar—wanting all good features regardless of whether they're looking for long-term or short-term mates. However, we see something very interesting in the restricted budget conditions—in such conditions, men allocate a disproportionate amount of dollars to attributes related to physicality, and women allocate a disproportionate amount to markers of wealth, status, trustworthiness, and resource-acquisition ability. Li's[22] big insight is that core sex differences in mating strategies emerge under restricted budgetary conditions. Under such conditions, females trade off looks for status and security.

Another important element of female mating psychology has to do with choosiness and relative discrimination when it comes to mate selection. In recent years, several studies have used a speed-dating paradigm to create an ecologically valid microcosm of human mating in action. In a particularly intensive study done in this way, Penke, Todd, Lenton, and Fasolo[23] found that women are much more discriminating than men—being about half as likely to agree to a second date to any particular individual compared with men. In fact, a great deal of prior research bears this prediction out—in humans[24] as well as a host of other species in which females are relatively high in parental investment compared with males.[25]

In fact, female mating strategies across the gamut of the mating domain seem to speak to a general long-term strategy that typifies female mating psychology. As mentioned earlier, female mate preferences seem to be honed to draw women to faithful, honest, intelligent men who can provide for their young.[26] Deeper into a relationship, there's further evidence that women are relatively sensitive to a partner's investment of time and emotional resources.[27] In addition, when it comes to infidelity, there is evidence that females are more concerned about partners cheating in an emotional fashion (e.g., falling in love with another) compared with males.[28] This makes sense from an evolutionary perspective because a male partner who falls in love with another may be showing signs of withholding resources from a mate and her children. Although both men and women have both long-term strategies and short-term strategies at their disposal (and do use both strategies), compared with men, women (on average) tend to primarily employ long-term mating strategies.

Male Mating Strategies

Two major forces bear on male mating strategies. First, given the fact that women are highly discriminating in the mate-selection process,[29] women are the gatekeepers of human mating, and males must deal with the fact that females set the ground rules. A second point to consider is the fact of relatively low obligatory parental investment associated with being male. So, although all human males are part of a species with high parental investment costs and altricial offspring, compared with females, males are the lower-investing sex (in terms of obligatory parental investment).

Given these factors in combination, males should be biased toward relatively short-term mating strategies (compared with females), but they should, in important ways, be biased toward long-term mating as well (because women, who are generally armed with long-term mating strategies, set the ground rules).

Being prone to short-term mating strategies seems to be manifest in several features of male mating psychology. In a classic study on this topic, male and female college students were approached by an attractive member of the opposite sex (really a psychology research confederate)—who, at random, asked one of three questions: (1) Will you go on a date with me? (2) Will you come back to my apartment? or (3) Will you have sex with me? For the question about the date, males and females both showed a 50% hit rate—half the men asked and half the women asked, consented. The other questions may be taken as a proxy for proclivity toward short-term sex—and the data were clear. For the apartment question, 6% of women consented, compared with 69% of men. And for the sex question, none of the women consented, compared with 75% of the men.[30] These results were replicated soon after the first study.[31] Of course, college women may have *desired* an encounter just as much as men, but because of societal expectations at that time, women may have been under more pressure to say no. Thankfully, there have been many more studies conducted since then to assess the extent to which males, on average, are tilted toward a short-term mating orientation.

A much more recent study aimed to replicate the original study conducted by Russell Clark and Elaine Hatfield, but also to go beyond it by looking at additional factors, such as the influence of age, relationship status, confederate attractiveness, and type of sexual invitation.[32] In this study, 389 participants (173 men and 216 women) from Denmark were approached outdoors either at a university campus, a pedestrian area, or a park area between the hours of 11:00 a.m. and 5:00 p.m. during a 2-day period. Twenty-one, moderately attractive first-year psychology students (11 women and 10 men; the "confederates") approached a stranger of the opposite gender and said: "*Hi, my name is _____.*
I am sorry to disturb you like this, but I have been noticing you around and find you very attractive." The confederate then asked one of three questions: (1) "*Would you go on a date with me tonight or during the week/weekend?*" (2) "*Would you come over to my place tonight or during the week/weekend?*" or (3) "*Would you go to bed with me tonight or during the week/weekend?*"

The confederates were told to only approach strangers who were walking by themselves and whom they could imagine would follow through on their request. Each confederate approached up to 30 subjects during a 2-day period. After participants received the request from the confederate, they were approached by one of the other members of the research team, were told about the purpose of the study, and were asked to anonymously disclose their age, current relationship status, and awareness of the point of the study and to rate their own attractiveness as well as the attractiveness of the confederate on a nine-point scale.

Their results were very similar to those of the Clark and Hatfield study.[33] Men, on average, responded more favorably to the two most sexually explicit invitations than women did. There was also an effect of confederate attractiveness, but only for females. Men did not seem to be much swayed by physical attractiveness differences; as long as the female was of moderate level of attractiveness, the males tended to accept the invitation for an immediate sexual encounter. The researchers argue that the finding that females were more likely to accept a sexual invitation of an attractive stranger is consistent with the Good Genes Hypothesis, which states that women are more likely to engage in causal sex with men who exhibit traits (such as physical attractiveness, creativity, etc.) that signal they have a genotype that contributes to offspring viability or reproductive success.[34]

The researchers additionally found an effect of relationship status. Males who were not in a relationship were 20 times more likely to consent to one of the sexual invitations compared with males who were involved in a relationship. Here, there were relative gender differences: females who were not in a relationship were more than 8 times more likely to consent to one of the sexual invitations compared with females who were in a relationship. When they stratified the entire sample by relationship status, they found that the overall percentile rates for both men and women who were not in a relationship were not significantly different from the aggregated findings of Clark and Hatfield[35] and Clark.[36] In sum, different time periods (1990 vs. 2010) and different locations (U.S. college-aged participants vs. Denmark college-aged students) found the same basic findings.

Since the Clark and Hatfield study, psychologists have accumulated an exceptionally large body of evidence across multiple continents, across a wide range of age groups, and using extremely large samples, to suggest that males, on average, have a higher desire for sexual variety than females. Here are some of the most notable findings[37]:

1. Men across the globe in 48 nations report an interest in having more lifetime sex partners compared with women.[38]
2. Men in 53 nations show higher levels of sociosexuality (a proxy for promiscuity) than women, and women were more variable than men in their sex drive.[39] Although gender equality predicted sex differences in sociosexuality, the extent to which the culture was equitable did not affect sex differences in sex *drive*.

3. Men select more partners in a speed-dating context.[40]
4. When asked how early in a relationship it would be okay to have sex, men's answers came in much earlier compared with women's answers.[41]
5. Men report more reasons for having sex, and their reasons centered more on physical appearance and physical desirability (*"The person had a desirable body"*), experience seeking (e.g., *"I wanted to increase the number of partners I had experienced"*), mere opportunity (e.g., *"The person was 'available'"*), pure physical pleasure (e.g., *"I was horny"*), utilitarian reasons (*"to improve my sexual skills"*), and social status (*"I thought it would boost my social status"*) than females.[42]
6. Men are more likely than women to engage in extradyadic sex (i.e., sex outside of a relationship).[43]
7. Men are more likely than women to be sexually unfaithful multiple times with different sexual partners.[44]
8. Men are more likely than women to seek short-term sex partners who are already married.[45]
9. Men are more likely than women to have sexual fantasies involving short-term sex and multiple opposite-sex partners.[46]
10. Men are more likely than women to pay for short-term sex with (male or female) prostitutes.[47]
11. Men are more likely than women to enjoy sexual magazines and videos containing themes of short-term sex and sex with multiple partners.[48]
12. Men are more likely than women to desire, have, and reproductively benefit from multiple mates and spouses.[49]
13. Men desire larger numbers of sex partners than women do over brief periods of time.[50]
14. Men are more likely than women to seek one-night stands.[51]
15. Men are quicker than women to consent to having sex after a brief period of time.[52]
16. Men are more likely than women to consent to sex with a stranger.[53]
17. Men are more likely than women to want, initiate, and enjoy a variety of sex practices.[54]
18. Men have more positive attitudes than women toward casual sex and short-term mating.[55]
19. Men are less likely than women to regret short-term sex or "hook-ups."[56]
20. Men have more unrestricted sociosexual attitudes and behaviors than women.[57]
21. Men generally relax mate preferences (whereas women increase selectivity for physical attractiveness) in short-term mating contexts.[58]
22. Men perceive more sexual interest from strangers than women do.[59]

To be sure, there have been studies here and there that seem to contradict this overall pattern of results, and each of the studies reviewed in this section has some methodological limitations (there is no perfect study). Even so, all of the research taken together points to an inescapable conclusion: compared with females, males, *on average*, are more likely to demonstrate short-term mating strategies. With that said, these are average group differences and mask a lot of variability in behavioral outcomes. In addition to documenting these overall sex differences, the most recent cutting edge research also suggests that both male and female mating strategies are *highly contextual*, vary quite a bit *within each sex* (although males may be more variable in terms of number of sexual partners),[60] and in many cases, are *more similar than dissimilar*. In the rest of this chapter, we discuss the evidence for these important points.

Men Are from Springfield, Women Are from Springfield—Sex Similarities in Mating Strategies

From an evolutionary perspective, men and women are only expected to differ in areas where they faced recurrently *different* adaptive problems over evolutionary history (e.g., the biological consequences of short-term mating). This means that they are expected to be *similar* in all areas where they faced similar adaptive problems. According to Buss and Schmitt, "Although the final scientific word is not yet in, we suspect that the similarities outnumber the differences."[61]

Mating researchers have developed a reputation for documenting sex differences in behavior. Sex differences are interesting, important, and have significant effects on many aspects of human life. And sex differences in human mating behavior have been documented by a dauntingly large set of studies across the past several decades.[62] But this all needs to be tempered by a fact of human cognition: the human mind seems to be prepared to see differences more easily than similarities.[63] Perhaps psychological researchers are more likely to, accordingly, focus on differences than on similarities.

In fact, much of the same research that documents differences between the sexes documents similarities as well. It's often forgotten, but in the classic Clark and Hatfield[64] study on short-term mating we just mentioned, males and females were *equally as likely* to consent to an offer of a date from an attractive member of the opposite sex. Also, even though Cindy Meston and David Buss[65] found that men gave more reasons for having sex than women, there still was quite a lot of similarity among the sexes: 20 of the top 25 reasons given for having sex were identical for both men and women! Also, no sex differences were found in their two subfactors relating to emotional reasons for having sex: Love and Commitment, and Expression (even though at the item level, women did endorse more emotional motivations for sex). As the researchers note, this finding counters the stereotype that men always want sex detached from emotion and "supports a growing body of clinical evidence suggesting that both men and women at times desire intimacy and emotional connectedness from sexual activity."[66]

In another study looking at the link between sexual motivations and sexual satisfaction, Kyle Stephenson, Tierney Ahrold, and Cindy Meston[67] found that love and commitment motives were positively correlated with satisfaction for both men and women and that having sex to boost self-esteem and gain resources were negatively associated with satisfaction for both men and women. Therefore, men and women show a lot of similarities in terms of what makes them sexually satisfied.

Among college samples in the United States, similarities between the sexes may be particularly pronounced. A recent study found that modern-day college-aged men and women invest the same amount of mating effort toward short-term mating and that both lower their standards for sex partners the same amount.[68] These results suggest that today's college-aged men and women may be a lot more similar than different when it comes to mating orientation, at least in the United States (see Chapter 9 for more discussion on the possible causes for the increase in hook-up behaviors found among college students in the United States).

Another recent study focusing on college students also found many similarities between men and women in willingness to engage in a short-term sexual encounter.[69] Psychologist Terri Conley argues that a major confound inherent in the original Clark and Hatfield study is that female participants were judging whether they wanted to have sex with men, whereas male participants were judging whether they would want to have sex with women. According to Conley, "by considering the gender of the participants independently of the gender of the proposer, one may overlook crucial information about the reasons behind the gender differences in casual sex."[70] To overcome this potential confound, Conley conducted a series of studies in which her focus was on the perceived characteristics of the *proposer.*

Looking just at the likelihood of accepting casual sex proposals from the participant's own life experiences, men accepted the casual sex offer 73% of the time, whereas women did so only 40% of the time. These overall gender differences are consistent with the original Clark and Hatfield studies, although they do suggest that in thinking about hypothetical naturalistic sexual scenarios, women are much more likely to accept offers of casual sex. Also, lesbian women were equally as likely to accept a casual sex offer as men were, and bisexual women were more likely to accept an offer from a woman than from a man.

Above and beyond these overall gender effects, Conley found a number of interesting *contextual* findings that extend the original Clark and Hatfield study. First, she found that males who approached women for a sexual encounter were uniformly perceived as less desirable compared with females who approached men. Such "approaching" men were perceived by women as more physically dangerous and as less likely to provide them sexual satisfaction. They were also perceived as having relatively low status and as being cold individuals. This finding suggests that the gender differences found in the Clark and Hatfield studies may have been strongly influenced by the gender of the proposer in addition to the gender of the receiver, with perception of risk being an important factor.[71] Of course, gender differences in risk perception may still be an evolved difference, with the risk perception difference being the proximate means by which the ultimate function is achieved.[72]

Conley also found a number of situations in which male and female college students were equally likely to engage in a short-term affair. Conley investigated how much *familiarity* could reduce these effects. Using stories of famous people, the participant's best opposite-sex friend, and strangers, she found that women (but not men) perceived less risk from the familiar individual making the sexual proposal than from a stranger. When women considered the familiar (and thus less risky) proposer, they were just as likely to agree to casual sex as men were.

While testing the importance of familiarity as a variable in mating, Conley found that men were as *unlikely* to accept an offer from Roseanne Barr as women were to accept a sexual offer from Carrot Top or Donald Trump. Regardless of how rich and successful these individuals are, they just weren't considered sexually attractive! This finding is consistent with Sexual Strategies Theory because women wouldn't be expected to be as interested in resources for short-term mating and would be more interested in indicators of good genes. The familiar man who the women did (hypothetically) agree to have a short-term encounter with is Johnny Depp—someone clearly with many good genes! The good genes of Johnny Depp probably *would* have given women pleasure. That women weren't as interested in Carrot Top is interesting in light of our argument in Chapter 2 that good humor ability is an indicator of good genes. Perhaps the women in the sample didn't find Carrot Top particularly funny! Likewise, Roseanne's humor ability wasn't good enough to overshadow her less than stellar physical attractiveness. Men preferred to sleep with Christie Brinkley and Angelina Jolie instead—not a huge surprise.

We must stress that this sample consisted of college-aged students who, as a group, were probably not as interested in finding a long-term mate with earning potential than they were in sexually experimenting and having pleasure. Older female samples may find Carrot Top and Donald Trump more enticing propositions (although see the section below on age effects)! Taking all the results together, Conley suggests that "for women, feeling 'safe' contributes to their likelihood of accepting a sexual offer, which is why familiar proposers are more likely to receive favorable responses to their sexual proposals than unfamiliar proposals."[73]

Across studies involving actual and hypothetical sexual scenarios, Conley also found that men and women were equally likely to accept an offer of casual sex if the approacher was perceived as *sexually capable* (i.e., "good in bed"). Therefore, anticipated pleasure may be a stronger predictor of short-term sexual engagement than the sex of the participant. This is consistent with pleasure theory,[74] as well as evolutionary psychology, because gender differences in pleasure (like risk) may be the proximate means by which the ultimate function is achieved.[75] Therefore, in the real world, women on average may accept fewer offers of casual sex than men because they think they will be less likely to experience pleasure from such an encounter. Indeed, as Conley notes, this assumption may not be unwarranted because research does demonstrate that women have orgasms only 35% as often as men do in a first-time casual sexual encounter situation.[76]

Conley's clever studies suggest that college-aged men and women are equally as likely to accept a short-term sexual invitation if the person doing the approaching is a gorgeous celebrity, the perceived risk of the person doing the approaching is low, and there is high anticipation that pleasure will ensue from such an interaction. Importantly, Conley also found that women were much more likely to agree to have sex with Johnny Depp than a complete stranger, whereas men were only slightly more likely to agree to have sex with Angelina Jolie than a complete stranger. These results are similar to those from a study conducted by Schützwohl and colleagues[77] who found among a sample of men and women from three countries (Germany, Italy, and the United States) that physical attractiveness had a much greater effect on women's than on men's willingness to accept an explicit offer for casual sex. These findings are quite consistent with a Sexual Strategies Approach but also show specific proximal conditions that may cause men and women to be more likely to agree to a short-term sexual encounter.

Along similar lines, Pamela Regan[78] found that when it comes to a casual sex partner, both men and women undergraduates were most willing to compromise intelligence and social status but were unwilling to compromise physical attractiveness; and when considering a romantic partner, both men and women were least willing to compromise on interpersonal skill and responsiveness and were most willing to compromise on social status. When it comes to short-term flings, the data are in: *both men and women are highly likely to consent if the person is physically attractive* (shocking, we know!). So, amidst reporting of sex differences, it is sometimes too easy to ignore the great amount of overlap that exists among the sexes.

When it comes to the long-term, the data are even clearer: men and women want the same things. Research on mate-selection factors and personality in the mating arena suggests that males and females, on average, converge considerably in factors that they prioritize in seeking mates. Kindness, mutual love, sense of humor, and intelligence are considered among the most important features of a potential long-term mate for both men and women—and this fact has been documented clearly across 37 disparate cultures.[79]

A recent study including nearly 300 young adults also showed marked similarities in the sexes regarding many facets of human mating. In this study,[80] men and women showed no significant differences in the following:

- How much overall distress they experienced thinking about their partners cheating sexually
- How much distress they experienced thinking about their partners cheating via vaginal versus oral sex
- How much distress they experienced thinking about their partners cheating with a friend versus a stranger
- How much distress they experienced thinking about their partners using a condom or not in an instance of infidelity

The bottom line of this study is that people tended to be more distressed by thoughts of their partners cheating with someone from their intimate social circle compared with a stranger—and this effect replicated across the sexes. The researchers interpreted these findings as showing that one of the main evolutionary costs of infidelity pertains to adverse consequences to one's social bonds, beyond the obvious adverse effects to one's pair-bond. Relevant to the point at hand, the sexes responded very similarly to one another.

It's rarely been stated, and may seem relatively uninteresting to some, but we think this point is extremely important for understanding human mating intelligence: *males and females show considerable similarities in nearly all areas of the mating domain.*

Some Women Are from Springfield, Some Are from the Bronx—Within-Sex Differences in Mating Strategies

Sex differences may also mask important differences *within* each sex. As we mention repeatedly throughout this book, *individual* differences are essential to the mating intelligence framework. Humans vary among one another in their sexual preferences and behavior. Consider the fact that people differ quite a bit in their motivations to have sex.[81] In the Meston and Buss study we mentioned earlier,[82] the researchers found 237 reasons why male and female college students have sex! They condensed the reasons down to 4 broad factors and 13 subfactors.

The first broad factor was *Physical Resources*, which consisted of Stress Reduction (e.g., *"I was frustrated and need relief"*), Pleasure (e.g., *"It feels good"*), Physical Desirability (e.g., *"The person had an attractive face"*), and Experience Seeking (e.g., *"I was curious about sex"*). The second broad factor was *Goal Attainment*, which consisted of Resources (e.g., *"I wanted to get a raise"*), Social

Status (e.g., "*I wanted to be popular*"), Revenge ("*I wanted to get back at my partner for having cheated on me*"), and Utilitarian reasons (e.g., "*I wanted to get out of doing something*"). The third broad factor was *Emotional*, which consisted of Love and Commitment (e.g., "*I wanted to feel connected to the person*") and Expression ("*I wanted to welcome someone home*"). The fourth and final broad factor was *Insecurity*, which consisted of Self-Esteem Boost ("e.g., "*I wanted to feel powerful*"), Duty/Pressure (e.g., "*I didn't know how to say 'no'*"), and Mate Guarding (e.g., "*I wanted to keep my partner from straying*").

Some of the top reasons for having sex for both men and women included "*I was attracted to the person,*" "*It feels good,*" "*I wanted to show my affection to the person,*" and "*I was horny.*" As the researchers noted, the less frequently endorsed reasons for having sex are equally as important. Some of the most infrequent responses for both men and women included "*I wanted to give someone else a sexually transmitted disease (e.g., herpes, AIDS),* "*Someone offered me money to do it,* "*I wanted to get a raise,*" "*It was an initiation rite to a club or organization,*" "*It would get me gifts,*" "*I wanted to punish myself,*" "*I wanted to feel closer to God,*" "*I wanted to be used or degraded,*" "*I wanted to break up a rival's relationship by having sex with his/her partner,*" and "*I felt sorry for the person.*" We don't yet know what traits or life experiences predict these kinds of responses.

The researchers analyzed the personality variables that predicted the various factors. The more extraverted the woman, the higher she tended to score on the Pleasure subfactor. The more disagreeable, less conscientious, and neurotic the woman, the higher she tended to score on all four broad factors. Interestingly, there was no relation between openness and any of the factors or subfactors among women. Unsurprisingly, the more unrestricted the women's sociosexuality (the more she reported a short-term mating strategy), the higher she tended to score on every single factor and subfactor except for one exception: the Love and Commitment subfactor. The strongest correlates of sociosexuality (an orientation for short-term mating) for women related to Physical Resources: stress reduction, physical desirability, experience seeking, and pure physical pleasure (which is consistent with the Conley study mentioned previously).

For men, there were less meaningful individual differences than for women, but some still existed. Although extraversion and neuroticism did not correlate with any of the factors or subfactors among males, agreeableness was associated with the Emotional factor and the Love and Commitment subfactor. Lower levels of conscientiousness were associated with the Duty/Pressure subfactor, and openness was associated with reduced levels of Social Status and higher levels of Love and Commitment. Sociosexuality was associated with the Physical, Goal Attainment, and Insecurity broad factors, but not the Emotional factor. As the researchers note, the relations between personality and reasons for having sex may be more apparent among women than men because of the gender appropriateness of sexual promiscuity in our culture.

Meston and Buss's work may be interesting in light of Robert Sternberg's theory of love as a story.[83] According to Sternberg, each of us creates a love story unconsciously at a young age. As we age, our relationships, and the type of people we are attracted to, tend to be influenced by these stories. Sternberg identified 26 love stories, from the fantasy fairy tale story to the war story. Perhaps many of Sternberg's love stories are associated with the different reasons for having sex that Meston and Buss document. For instance, maybe those who are attracted to a war love story are also the ones who tend to have sex purely for goal-attainment purposes. This is pure speculation, but we think this would be an interesting future line of research.

Another important individual-differences variable that affects mating strategy is *intelligence*. As we mentioned earlier, the parental investment theory predicts (among other things) that men, on average, will have more of a short-term mating orientation than women and that women, on average, will care more about financial resources in a long-term mate than men. But are these effects just as strong for women who have greater access to resources and therefore not as high of a biological cost if they become pregnant?

Christine Stanik and Phoebe Ellsworth[84] found that verbal SAT scores were negatively related to college-aged women's reported desire for a man with resource-earning potential. In another study, they replicated this finding but also found that as women's verbal intelligence increased, the more college-aged women tended to favor uncommitted sexual encounters and the less they reported adhering to and supporting traditional gender roles in marriage that view the man as provider and the women as caretaker.

Although these results must not be generalized too far because of their restricted sample (college females), they still point to the potentially moderating effect of intelligence on a women's mating psychology. Further research should try to pinpoint exactly why intelligence has an effect. Does it have to do with the enhanced ability for prioritization that high intelligence affords? Does it have to do with increased access to career opportunities? What about men? How does higher intelligence affect a man's mating strategy and views of traditional gender roles in marriage? Do these results replicate across a wide range of ages, and not just in college students? These are the sorts of questions that can be pursued from a mating intelligence perspective.

Another important individual-differences variable is how much shame a person feels reporting sexual fantasies. Cultural and familial expectations can strongly influence reporting on a psychological experiment. To investigate this issue, a recent study had college students click a golf tally every time they thought about food, sleep, or sex over the course of a full week.[85] Men, on average, thought about sex more than women (about once an hour, or less than 19 times a day, compared with once every 2 hours for women). Although there was variability among both males and females (ranging from single-digit weekly totals to reports in the thousands), males did show greater variability in how much they thought about sex. Also, even though men did think more about sex, they also thought more about food and sleep.

Interestingly, social desirability and erotophilia (the extent to which a person responds to sexual cues and is comfortable sexually) were significant predictors of frequency of sexual cognitions for women, but not for men, and overall, erotophilia was a better predictor of frequency of sexual cognitions than the sex of the participant. The researchers argue that these findings suggest that culture exerts a strong influence on the reporting of sexual fantasies, with culture exerting more of an influence on women than men. Further research should control for these two variables when looking at sexual fantasy differences among males and females.

Yet another important individual-differences variable is *attachment style*. John Bowlby's attachment theory revolutionized developmental psychology and our understanding of parent-child relationships.[86] As brilliant as his theory was, he was missing one crucial component. Focusing entirely on the role of attachment for survival, he completely ignored the roles the attachment system plays in *reproduction*. This is understandable because Bowlby focused on infant attachment, and obviously infants are not interested in reproducing. The game changes, however, when we start looking at stages of development that involve the struggle for reproduction.

Modern evolutionary psychologists, building on Bowlby's important work but incorporating Darwinian principles of sexual selection, conceptualize the attachment system as evolving for two related but distinct adaptive reasons: survival and reproduction. Certainly, adult attachment styles serve a different function than childhood attachment styles. In children, attachment styles help elicit care from parents in order to survive, whereas in adults, attachment styles serve to maintain long-term pair-bonds that can increase reproductive success.[87]

Although other drives surely come into play in adult relations (e.g., sexual attraction), the evidence suggests that the motivational system that underlies parent-infant bonds may have been at least partially co-opted during the course of human evolution to promote long-term bonding in an adult context. The attachment system is closely linked to the stress response system and helps regulate a child's feelings of distress, pain, fear, and loneliness, with secure attachment buffering external sources of stress to some degree, and with secure and insecure infants showing different types of stress responses to separation. Some research has investigated the link between stress responsiveness and romantic attachment in adults, and the results so far seem to be consistent with those found in children.[88]

Securely attached individuals have fewer problems with intimacy and worry less about being alone or being rejected by others. In contrast, there are two types of insecure attachment. Those with an *anxious-preoccupied* insecure attachment style are inclined to increase their signaling of need and distress, show a constant preoccupation with the presence and availability of attachment figures, and tend to be clingy. An anxious-preoccupied attachment style predicts a mix of impulsive sexual attitudes, early age of intercourse (mostly for women), and intense desire for intimate, committed relationships. Anxious-preoccupied adults show higher dependency and are powerfully motivated to search for exclusive, intimate relationships.

Those with a *dismissive-avoidant* attachment style tend to show higher levels of self-reliance, a reduced signaling of need for others, and a distancing, detached attitude toward parents or partners. In children, avoidance is related to aggression, antisocial behaviors, and inflated self-esteem. In adults, avoidance is related to low commitment in romantic relationships, avoidance of intimacy, higher levels of sexual coercion, and a more promiscuous, sexually unrestrained orientation.[89] Dismissive-avoidant attachment bears the hallmark of a low-parenting strategy, favoring short-term relationships over intimate, long-term bonding.

Now consider the well-replicated finding that men, on average, are more likely than women to find sexual infidelity more distressing than emotional infidelity.[90] A recent study on an undergraduate sample of 99 men and 317 women replicated this finding, but also found interesting relations between attachment style and reaction to jealousy that went beyond the biological sex of the individual.[91]

These investigators found that men, on average, were between 3 and 4 times more likely than women to report greater sexual jealousy compared with emotional jealousy, thus replicating the already well-documented finding of sex differences in reaction to jealousy. But here is where things get interesting. They also found that both men and women with a secure attachment style tended to find emotional infidelity more distressing than sexual infidelity, whereas both men and women with a dismissive-avoidant attachment style tended to find sexual infidelity more distressing than emotional infidelity. Therefore, attachment style predicts reaction to jealousy.

Does this make the sex differences they did find irrelevant? No! They found that biological sex and attachment style each made *independent* predictions on reported reaction to jealousy. Also, although they found small sex differences in the secure and anxious-preoccupied attachment style groups, they found sizeable sex differences in the dismissing-avoidant and fearful-avoidant attachment style groups, with fearful-avoidant men being roughly *5 times more likely* than fearful-avoidant women to experience greater sexual jealousy compared with emotional jealousy and dismissing-avoidant men being *26 times more likely* than dismissing women to report experiencing greater sexual than emotional jealousy. Just comparing a dismissing-avoidant attachment style with a secure attachment style within each sex, the researchers found that dismissing-avoidant women were roughly 4 times more likely than securely attached women to report greater sexual than emotional jealousy, whereas dismissing-avoidant men were nearly 50 times more likely than secure men to report experiencing greater sexual than emotional jealousy!

These findings are quite consistent with other recent studies. For instance, Marco Del Giudice[92] analyzed the combined results of 113 samples (66,132 participants) on romantic attachment from various countries and found that overall, males showed higher levels of a dismissive-avoidant attachment style and lower levels of an anxious-preoccupied attachment style than females. Sex differences in an anxious-preoccupied style peaked in young adulthood, whereas sex differences in a dismissive-avoidant attachment style increased throughout the life course, with men being even more likely to be avoidant in relationships compared with women as people age.

Ample other research suggests that attachment style predicts sexual behaviors above and beyond the effects of gender. Birnbaum[93] found that an anxious-preoccupied attachment style predicted frequency of submissive sexual fantasies. Anxiously attached women were also particularly likely to report fantasies of sexual relations with partners other than their current partner, whereas anxiously attached men were particularly likely to report romantic fantasies. Those with a dismissive-avoidant attachment style reported less romantic fantasies.

Another study found that attachment style predicted actual extradyadic involvement (i.e., infidelity), but that the effect depended on gender.[94] Overall, undergraduate females reported more intimacy motivations than males, and males reported more casual motivations than females. Additionally, there was an interaction with attachment style. Dismissive-avoidant males had the most extradyadic partners over the prior 2 years relative to all other groups, whereas preoccupied-anxious females reported more partners than secure females.

What is going on here? Why do men and women tend to become insecurely attached in different ways? Del Giudice[95] presents an intriguing hypothesis. Because males have less at stake, reproductively speaking, from sexual intercourse, it is predicted that males living under conditions of high environmental stress will show higher levels of avoidance than females, which is part of a low-investment, low-commitment strategy. Anxiety, on the other hand, may be a way for females living under the same environmental conditions to secure and extract investment from both family members and sexual partners. These differences, however, should *only* emerge at key points in development that are related to sexual development. In support of this prediction, research does show that insecure attachment in juvenility predicts the early appearance of flirting and sexual contacts, even in prepubertal children.[96]

To succeed in mating, an organism needs to out-compete same-sex rivals and attract members of the opposite sex. For males, this involves status-seeking displays of dominance and aggression or investment in traits and displays that are attractive in short-term mates, such as humor, intelligence, and creativity (see Chapter 2). For females, this may involve relatively more investment in forming alliances, increasing displays of physical attractiveness, and becoming popular.

Therefore, different styles of insecure attachment may be conducive to social status, depending on one's sex. Because avoidant attachment is related to traits such as aggression and inflated self-esteem, it may be part of a status-seeking strategy for young insecure males living the fast life. Such a strategy would center on mating effort, early reproduction, and selfish risk taking. For females, dependent and closeness-oriented behaviors may be advantageous in female group relationships. Some researchers have suggested that anxious attachment in females may relate to relational and indirect aggression, which makes evolutionary sense in the context of female peer competition. This hypothesis hasn't been directly tested yet, however.

According to this theory, the mechanisms regulating strategic variation are sex differentiated, and the same cues may exert quite different effects, depending on the person's sex. A key environmental variable that affects this sex difference is the level of stress and risk in the environment. At moderate levels of risk, it is predicted that insecure males (but not females) will adopt short-term strategies; but under high levels of risk, it is more evolutionarily adaptive for both males and females to adopt a short-term mating, low-parenting strategy.

The implications here are huge, not just for our understanding of the development of attachment styles but also for our understanding of sex differences in sexuality, dominance seeking, aggression, trust, cooperation, and risk taking. For more on Del Giudice's hypothesis and to get a sense of the multiple viewpoints in this debate, check out Del Giudice.[97]

So, where does this leave us? As Levy and Kelly point out, it is possible that individuals' biological sex causes them to react differently to harsh and unpredictable environments, and these reactions can in turn influence the development of their attachment style and consequently their reaction to jealousy. As we discussed in Chapter 3, attachment styles are related to life history strategy. Those growing up in harsh and unpredictable environments tend to become insecurely attached, whereas those growing up in stable environments tend to become securely attached. Perhaps males and females react to harsh environments in different ways, influencing *how* their attachment style is expressed. Only further research will be able to test these ideas.

This all sounds complex, but that's just our point. Biological sex differences can be explained in a number of ways and can sometimes mask even more fascinating and specific sex differences that are in line with evolutionary theorizing. In our mating intelligence approach, we advocate multiple levels of analysis to get at what is really going on. We wholeheartedly agree with Meston and Buss that "human sexuality is motivated by a complex and multifaceted psychology. Efforts to reduce sexual motivation to small number of variables are doomed to fail."[98]

A little-talked-about feature of research on human mating psychology is that sex differences, although real and significant, are only part of the story.

If X, then Y—The Conditional Nature of Human Mating Strategies

As we discussed in the prior section, we believe that seeing females as long-term strategists—and males as short-term strategists—misses the boat. In fact, given how wonderfully complex and adapted the human mind is, and how central mating is to every aspect of life, it only makes sense that any *individual*, regardless of sex, will use a variety of mating tactics across his or her lifetime.

Evolutionists often refer to organisms as behavioral strategists, employing different behaviors under different ecological conditions. Without question, humans are not above this basic rule—there is wealth of data suggesting that, regardless of sex, people modify their mating strategy as a function of ecological conditions. And, as we discuss at the end of this chapter, it makes sense to see mating intelligence as the ability to modify mating strategies optimally as a function of the environment.

We've already mentioned some important contextual factors that affect mating strategies, such as perception of risk and expectation of pleasure. Many other fascinating context-relevant factors have also been demonstrated as affecting mating strategies. This section offers a sample of some of these.

Life History Strategy

As we've discussed in this chapter and in Chapter 3, a person's life history strategy has an enormous bearing on his or her mating strategy. Individuals from relatively unstable backgrounds are considered as having a *fast* life history strategy.[99] Individuals from backgrounds that are highly stable and resource rich are more likely to develop *slower* life history strategies.[100] Such individuals are more likely to pursue long-term mating strategies[101] and to avoid risk-taking behaviors.[102]

An important implication of the life history strategy work is that the background of a person's upbringing and his or her personality (which is steeped in both that background and individual genetic make-up) may well have more of a bearing on the use of long-term versus short-term mating strategies than his or her biological sex. Being a male or a female may actually matter less in determining a person's mating strategy than that person's life history strategy—which is largely the result of a person's past environmental experiences and individual genetic heritage.

Sex Ratio Matters

Another major ecological variable that affects mating strategies is the prevailing sex ratio. Although we often think of sex ratio as being 50/50, it's often not. Consider many colleges these days with imbalanced sex ratios. The current first-year class at SUNY New Paltz is 70% female. The current first-year class at Clarkson University, known for its formidable programs in engineering, is 27% female. And if you are a student at one of these schools, it's a good bet that the prevailing sex ratio at your school matters plenty in terms of optimal mating strategies for you and the thousands of other students there.

Data back this point up. In one of the largest-scale cross-cultural studies ever conducted, David Schmitt[103] studied the impact of a nation's prevailing sex ratio on the average sociosexuality (promiscuity) scores of the country's inhabitants. Sex ratio matters. In countries with an overabundance of men, male sociosexuality scores go down. Men in such a context cannot afford to be short-term strategists. Women are setting the ground rules—with a home-field advantage. They can pick and choose. In such a context, males have fewer options—and the tendency for males to be short-term strategists diminishes dramatically. Interestingly, under such conditions, women's scores turn toward promiscuity—under such conditions, they can actually afford to implement short-term strategies without incurring the high costs of male abandonment—remember, males in such a situation are not in a position of power.

When the tables turn and there happens to be an overabundance of women, male sociosexuality scores skyrocket—whereas female scores do not. In such a context, males can have their druthers, and that tends to play out in short-term mating strategies.

Although this research, like any research done by Schmitt, is of extremely high quality, it may only scratch the surface. If nation-level sex ratios are this sensitive to variability in mating strategies, it seems that more localized sex ratios (such as on specific college campuses, which vary quite a bit on this variable) likely have even more dramatic effects on mating strategies. Research on this question should yield fruitful information about the true impact of sex ratios on behavior.

Are You Hot or Not? The Impact of (Self-Perceived) Mate Value on Mating Strategies

We can't all get what we want. Sure, we may all *want* the man or woman who scores high on every single desired attribute, but (a) not everyone can have this person, and (b) honestly, do you really think that perfect mate actually exists? Think again! Because of the realities of the mating market, many of us "satisfice" or end up with a partner that strikes the most reasonable balance of traits we value (see Chapter 4).[104] Indeed, research does show that our stated preferences often diverge from what we actually choose.[105] Sometimes compromises have to be made.

But how many dates should we go on before we know we've found "the one" (to satisfice with)? There is no easy answer. According to the "37% rule," determined by the "secretary search problem," first estimate the number of potential mates you are likely to meet in your life, go on a date with the first 37%, assess the best one from that batch, and then marry the next one who comes along who exceeds the "best" one's value![106] Very romantic, huh? Although this method may be feasible for those who live in a small, rural area, what about city dwellers? A person is likely to meet many more people in New York City than they can keep track of and use to make a statistical calculation!

Does this mean we all settle? Probably not. The truth of the matter is that someone better will *always* be there, just around the corner (again, unless you live in a really small village). At the end of the day, if you want to be in a committed relationship with someone you love and care for, and you don't want to always be looking over your shoulder, you will have to convince yourself that this person is the best "fit" for you. Everyone has to believe this—even movie stars (look at the high rate of divorce among them)!

Still, the question of how people decide to stop their search and commit is an important question. Some researchers have suggested that people use their self-perceived mate value as a cue to where they should set their aspiration levels.[107]

In a sense, mate search is parallel to optimal foraging in wild animals.[108] In the process, one scans the environment, calibrates his or her selection criteria, uses past feedback and information to help optimize the current situation, invests time in some areas but doesn't waste time in others, and so forth. Including self-assessed mate value in such calculations likely helps optimize mate search in humans.

More generally, using one's own self-assessed mate value in making mating decisions is an important element of mating intelligence. Calibrating decisions based on one's self-assessed mate value likely affects several kinds of mating decisions, including the following:

- Which mates to pursue for short-term relationships
- Which mates to pursue for long-term relationships
- When to stop searching for a mate and settle on a particular individual
- How much effort to expend in courtship
- How much effort and investment to put into shared investments such as children and materials

A person's self-assessed mate value is influenced by a number of factors, including physical attractiveness, financial and professional success, and the accumulation of a lifetime of responses from others. A person's self-perceived mate value can even be influenced by whom else is around.

For instance, Sara Gutierres, Douglas Kenrick, and Jenifer Partch[109] found that after men in their sample were exposed to highly socially dominant men, they lowered their rating of their own desirability as a marriage partner, but their self-evaluations had no effect after being exposed to physically attractive men. The reverse occurred for women: women lowered their self-evaluations as a marriage partner after exposure to physically attractive women, but their self-ratings were not affected after being exposed to socially dominant women. The researchers suggest the effects may have been caused by changes in the perceived distribution of physically available or highly dominant people available to members of the opposite sex in one's local community.

Keep in mind that one's current self-perceived mate value can be completely off. As Gutierres and colleagues note, the media plays a huge role here:

> ... we may see in 1 hour dozens of individuals who are more attractive and more successful than any of our ancestors would have seen in a year, or even a lifetime. The results of this program of research suggest that our mental mechanisms may trick us into using such extraordinary individuals as comparison standards for ourselves and our potential mates. (Gutierres et al., 1999, p. 1133)

There are other ways a person's self-perceived mate value can be highly inaccurate. Consider the girl who grows up with a lot of pimples and is mocked by others and then grows up to become a beauty queen. In her mind, she still may be that 10-year-old awkward girl. Or consider narcissists (whom we discuss at great length in Chapter 8), who have an overly inflated view of their mate value. What matters sometimes is not your actual mate value, but what you *truly believe* your mate value to be (see Chapter 6) because this influences who you seek out, how quickly you rebound after a rejection, and how you interpret ambiguous information (and quite a lot of the mating game is ambiguous).

Regan[110] found the higher that women perceived themselves on various dimensions (e.g., intellect, family orientation), the less willing they were to compromise those traits for a romantic partner as well as a casual sex partner. This effect was not found in men, perhaps because men are more willing to make compromises to increase the likelihood of finding a willing casual sex partner.

Other studies in a real-world context have found similar effects. In their study of speed dating behavior in German adults, Penke and colleagues[111] asked participants to rate their own level of physical attractiveness. This variable affected their mating strategies—but especially for women. Women who rated themselves as unattractive were less likely to "go for" males they met in the process who were of relatively high mate value. This effect was considerably diminished for males, suggesting that males in a speed-dating context may have much more of a go-for-broke attitude.

In a more recent study, Back and associates studied the mating dynamics in a speed-dating situation, applying the social relations perspective.[112] The social relations perspective takes into account both the *individual* level and the *dyadic* level. This allows researchers to investigate different kinds of effects.

Actor effects involve an individual's typical behavior when interacting with multiple people. For instance, perhaps Fred acts shy *on average*, when chatting with lots of different people at first acquaintance. *Partner effects* involve the typical kinds of reactions a person receives from others. In the unfortunate case of Fred, people on average may perceive his shyness as pomposity and may try to avoid him, which of course makes poor Fred even shyer! Finally, *relationship effects* involve how a person treats a particular person, taking into account that person's actor and partner effects. Perhaps Fred opens up like a flower when he gets to know someone and feels comfortable with that person. Therefore, that's why Fred acts like a party animal around his best friend of 30 years, whereas he still has difficulty chatting with strangers.

Adopting this perspective, Mitja Back and associates[113] distinguish between *individual reciprocity* ("Are people who choose many others as potential mates chosen more often by others?") and *dyadic reciprocity* ("Is a person who uniquely chooses a specific other person uniquely chosen by that specific person?"). Prior research has shown a rather low (and sometimes even negative) relation between choosiness and popularity.[114] In other words, people's mate choices are rarely reciprocated!

To get to the bottom of this puzzle, Back and colleagues[115] set up a speed-dating event in Berlin, in which a total of 190 men and 192 women aged 18 to 54 years went on a number of dates lasting 3-minutes each. The speed-daters then selected whom they'd like to see again and also filled out measures of their personality, including a measure of sociosexuality (which measures how much a person has a short-term mating orientation), extraversion, self-perceived mate value, and shyness. The researchers also had other people judge the facial attractiveness of each speed dater as well as rate the extent to which each speed dater flirted with other dates. What did they find?

Even though people expected their choices to be reciprocated, for the most part they were not. The researchers suggest that this (false) assumption of reciprocity may be a form of self-deception that causes greater displays of confidence and self-assured behavior in an ambiguous social environment.[116]

Even though choices were not reciprocal, flirting was, on both an individual and dyadic level. In other words, those who were flirty in general tended to receive flirting in return on average, and those who flirted at a specific dating partner tended to receive a flirtatious response from that partner in return.

Even so, flirting did not predict the actual outcome of the date. This is not the only study to find this; Karl Grammer and colleagues[117] looked at initial heterosexual encounters and found that flirting was only weakly related to actual interest. We apologize to all the flirters out there, but it seems as though flirting doesn't necessarily indicate interest. People can flirt for a number of reasons: to keep interactions running smoothly, to appear more attractive, or to disguise mating interest.

Looking beyond flirting, how did personality play a role? Although extraverted individuals and men with more of a short-term mating orientation flirted more, the most telling correlation was with self-perceived mate value. Those with a higher self-perceived mate value were choosier and also more popular. Men with a higher self-perceived mate value were more flirtatious and were more likely to receive flirtations in response. Shy men tended to be less choosy, flirted less, and were less popular. Also, consistent with other research presented throughout this book, the effects of personality similarities on mate choices were weak.

In addition to individual differences, the researchers also found a very interesting sex difference. The more popular the man, the more choosy he tended to be, but this relation did not hold for women. This finding seems to be a result of the fact that both self-perceived mate value and physical attractiveness are more strongly related to choosiness and popularity in men than in women. This finding is consistent with another recent study that found that when given the opportunity to choose a mate without any constraints, those with a higher self-reported mate value are much more choosy than those with a lower self-reported mate value.[118]

Back and colleagues also found that men with a higher self-perceived mate value tended to flirt with others and tended to receive more flirtations, whereas this relation was not found among women. The researchers suggest that this may be due to the possibility that women react more negatively than men to indicators of low choosiness. Future research should further explore the fascinating effects of self-perceived mate value at both the individual and sex-specific levels. Also, dating interactions across the world should be examined: Germany dating rituals may somehow be a quirk of human nature!

Nonetheless, these data speak to an important variable surrounding human mating—one's own mate value. We admit, getting into the details of measuring and defining mate value is a pretty slippery slope! And rightfully so. One of the points we've tried to make in this book is that there are many diverse tools in the arsenal of human mating—from having a square jaw to being effective at self-deprecating humor. That said, Lars Penke and colleagues got it right in determining self-assessed mate value. For years, psychologists have reliably measured different aspects of the self as filtered through self-assessment measures, and at the very least, such measures *do* provide the researcher with a clear sense of self-perception. So, it's reasonable to think about how one's self-assessed mate value likely affects mating decisions.[119]

As with life history strategy, one's self-assessed mate value is an important contextual variable that affects mating strategies and decisions—that actually resides within the person. Sometimes, changing your self-perception of mate value regardless of your *actual* mate value (a term we admit is rather hazy) can have profound effects on your mating outcomes. We discuss the adaptive benefits of self-deception in the next chapter. Just keep in mind that context is sometimes on the inside.

Physical Attractiveness and Mating Strategy

Even with our emphasis in this book on cognitive and dispositional factors, there is no denying that physical features also play an important role in the mating domain.[120]

One study looked at the role of physical attractiveness in mate selection using the popular website HOTorNOT.com.[121] HOTorNOT.com allows members to rate others on how physical attractive (i.e., "hot") they think they are on a 1 to 10 scale. Each user can also upload his or her own picture for rating by others to rate. There is also an option to engage in the dating component of the site, where members can chat and send messages to others they are interested in. Unsurprisingly, the researchers found that the more physically attractive the person (i.e., highly rated on the website), the more that person preferred dates who also were physically attractive.

Interestingly, one's own rated level of physical attractiveness did not influence the ratings they gave others. In the researchers' words:

> ...the results from analyzing the HOTorNOT.com data imply that whereas less attractive people are willing to accept less attractive others as dating partners, they do not delude themselves into thinking that these less attractive others are, in fact, more physically attractive than they really are. (Lee et al., 2008, p. 675)

The researchers also conducted a study at a speed-dating event in Boston. Before the event, participants filled out a survey in which they indicated their preferences on six dimensions (physical attractiveness, intelligence, sense of humor, kindness, confidence, and extraversion). During the speed-dating event, people went on a series of 4-minute dates where they rated each date on physical attractiveness and how much they were interested in seeing the person again. The researchers found that physically attractive people tended to place more emphasis on the physical attractiveness of others and less emphasis on other traits such as humor. These results are fascinating because they suggest that one's own level of physical attractiveness may be an important variable that predicts mate choice. At the same time, universally evolved mechanisms are still at play here: people, regardless of their individual levels of physical attractiveness, still agree on others' levels of physical attractiveness. As the researchers put it:

> People seem to adapt to the advantages they experience as a result of their physical looks (much as they adapt to many other situations), achieving roughly similar levels of happiness throughout a wide range of attractiveness levels. (Frederick & Loewenstein, 1999, p. 675)

How do people attain such "hedonic adaptation" (their own phrase)? The researchers suggest they do this by "deluding themselves that what is unattainable is not as great as it looks" and by diverting their attention away from attributes that may seem out of reach to options that may be perceived as attainable.

As we discuss later in this book (see Chapters 6 and 8), self-delusion may be adaptive. Perhaps those who *think* they can attain mates out of their reach actually change the probability of attaining that mate. As we pointed out in Chapter 4, through continued interaction, one's perceived levels of physical attractiveness can change quite substantially.[122] Lee and colleagues' study[123] involved only very brief encounters. Finally, we don't know how successful their participants were after they went on their dates. In other words, did their selections actually work out, leading to mating or even relating? We don't know, but we suspect that the more cues one has available, the better the mating choices they will make. Therefore, because physical attractiveness is the most salient characteristic of a person, it may play a larger role during the initial encounter, whereas many of the mating intelligence components we mention in this book increasingly influence attractiveness as interactions continue.

Mate Copying

Simply put: women like men who are liked by women. This makes sense. Sometimes, a potential mate's value is ambiguous. Under these conditions, the opinions of others can heavily influence how that person is perceived. In social psychology, this is referred to as "social proofing."[124] As François de La Rochefoucauld once put it, "Before we set our hearts too much upon anything, let us first examine how happy those are who already possess it."[125]

Evolutionary psychologists call the process by which people choose mates who have been chosen by others *mate copying* and refer to the strategy as a *conformity heuristic*. This phenomenon has been documented in other species, such as birds[126] and fish.[127] In humans, mate copying happens quite frequently[128] and may function as a shortcut for learning about a person's mate value that is not easily attainable on first glance.[129]

Often, people mistakenly believe that they are making decisions about a person based on the information they gleaned from the situation when in fact they are really basing their decisions on how other people reacted to the situation. Mate copying usually occurs in ambiguous situations when someone is observed to be of high mate value or is told that they have high mate value. Indeed, gossip relating to the sexual domain may just be one of the most widespread behaviors of human nature!

Consider the following set of results relating to the prominence of mate copying in human mating and what factors increase the likelihood that a person will use a conformity heuristic in choosing a mate:

- Both men and women can be influenced by social information about a person when choosing both a short-term and long-term mate.[130]
- Female mate copying is influenced by the amount of time spent looking at the partner, whereas male mate copying is influenced by the amount of time looking back and forth between the partner and the mate.[131]
- Women (but not men) show a decrease in interest after watching a date in which the individuals are clearly not interested in each other. Females do show an increase in interest, however, if the individuals look like they are clearly interested in each other.[132]
- Women tend to be more interested in a man as a potential mate if the man is surrounded by other interested females and/or is clearly committed (i.e., married). These cues hardly influence a potential friend or a potential co-worker.[133]
- A women's recommendation can be quite a potent force for other women, sometimes even overriding what women initially consciously think will attract themselves to a man (e.g., looks, age, height, humor).[134]
- Finding out that a potential partner was rejected by his or her last partner negatively affects participants' desire to pursue a romantic relationship with that person.[135]
- Females spend more time looking at a man when he is shown next to an attractive woman compared with when he is shown next to a women lower in attractiveness.[136]
- Sexually experienced women are less likely to use the conformity heuristic.[137] This is presumably because more experienced women have more confidence in what they want in a partner.
- Males tend to show greater mate copying of women whose attractiveness approaches or surpasses their own.[138] This effect does not hold for women.
- Men tend to like another man *less* if he receives a smile from a woman.[139] Presumably, this is because in such cases, men tend to feel threatened by such men.

- The conformity heuristic is stronger for already unattractive men (although this is most likely due to a statistical artifact called regression toward the mean, whereby variables that are extreme on first measurement tend to be closer to the "average" when later measured).[140]
- Those who pay the highest price of the conformity heuristic are undesirable men. So, what's an undesirable man to do? He can try to create conditions in which he appears in demand by many women, perhaps surrounding himself with a lot of female friends.

Age

An important contextual factor that influences a person's mating strategy (particularly women) is age. Think college-aged women are more sexual than older ladies? Think again! Judith Easton, Jaime Confer, Cari Goetz, and David Buss[141] classified more than 800 women taken from a college and community sample into three age groups based on their probable fertility status: ages 18 to 26 years (high-fertility women), 27 to 45 years ("reproduction-expediting" women), and 46 years and older (women close to or at menopause). The researchers found that those aged 27 to 45 thought more about sex, had more sexual fantasies, and were more willing to engage in sexual intercourse after knowing someone for 1 month, 1 week, or 1 night (a finding that even surprised the researchers!) than both of the other age groups. Although not statistically different from menopausal women, those in the 27- to 45-year-old group also reported a higher intensity of sexual fantasies, fantasized more about their current romantic partner or someone else, and engaged in more sexual intercourse compared with the high-fertility age group. These results held even after controlling for the number of children women already had and whether participants consciously desired having another child.

The researchers argue that women who experience a decline in fertility have evolved a "reproduction expediting adaptation designed to capitalize on their remaining fertility by increasing motivation to engage in sexual activity and increasing frequency of actual sexual behavior."[142] This research is also consistent with the work of Schmitt and colleagues,[143] who found that women in their early 30s reported feeling more lustful and seductive and less abstinent than women in other age groups.

Children

Most of the women in Easton and colleagues' study[144] did not have children. Another important factor that may bear on mating strategy (again, particularly for women) is whether the person already has a child or not. Viviana Weekes-Shackelford, Judith Easton, and Emily Stone[145] propose that having children from a previous relationship is a major contextual factor that affects a women's mate preference and strategy. The researchers note the unfortunate finding that the best indicator of child abuse is living with a step-parent,[146] a finding that remains even after controlling for potentially related factors such as socioeconomic status. Weekes-Shackelford and colleagues[147] argue that because of the potential costs to a women who remarry while having children, women with children from a prior mateship might place greater importance on finding a partner who is willing to invest in the woman and her current or future children. The researchers predict that women with children seeking a mate would place a greater emphasis on the ability and willingness to invest in children, good parenting skills, and compatibility and less emphasis on physical size and strength and attractiveness than a women who does not have children. These predictions await further research but provide interesting hypotheses. Another important contextual factor is a woman's ovulatory cycle.

Time of Month Matters, Too—and Not Just for Women

This book would be remiss not to touch on the effects of ovulation on human mating strategies. The cat is out of the bag. Based on a flood of recent research on the psychological effects of ovulation, modern scientists are starting to fully rethink the longstanding belief that, unlike in other primates, ovulation in humans is hidden. Human females are rare in the animal world in that they are open to copulation across the ovulatory cycle. Further, although menstruation has obvious physical markers, it has long been thought that ovulation in humans does not.

Evolutionary psychologists who have examined these issues carefully in the past few years have determined that, at the very least, the story has to change a bit. From the evolutionary perspective, being able to detect ovulation would have huge benefits because a female can only become impregnated within a very short window of time each month (with estimates varying between 6 and 72 hours).[148] So, it makes sense that ovulation-detection mechanisms would be a part of human mating intelligence.

Primatologists are correct in pointing out that ovulation does not have the same physically conspicuous display in humans as in other primates. In chimpanzees, for instance, ovulating females develop bright-red displays on their rumps that they advertise proudly. Until recently, it was thought that no parallels existed in humans. Turns out, we simply weren't looking carefully enough. And it turns out that the outward displays of ovulation in human females are largely behavioral in nature.

Not only is ovulation discernible by males, but it also has significant implications for the behavior of both males and females. Earlier in this chapter, we discussed the relative differences in mating strategy between men and women on average. Looking at ovulatory effects adds a bit more nuance to that idea.

Consider a recent study in the city of Vannes in France.[149] In this study, 506 women between the ages of 18 and 25 years who were walking alone were approached at random in the pedestrian zone by a 20-year-old "hot" guy and told:

> *Hello, My name's Antoine. I just want to say that I think you're really pretty. I have to go to work this afternoon, and I was wondering if you would give me your phone number. I'll phone you later and we can have a drink together someplace.*

The man, who was a part of the research study as a confederate, waited 10 seconds, then gazed and smiled at the participant. Each participant was then debriefed by another experimenter and given a questionnaire, which asked the number of days since the onset of her most recent menses.

The researchers found an ovulatory cycle effect: young women in their fertile phase (and therefore with a higher probability of bearing a child) agreed more favorably to the request than women in their luteal phase or in their menstrual phase.

Interestingly, this effect was only found with women who were not taking birth control pills. The researchers raise the possibility that pill users may be more sexually experienced, which could have led them to view the confederate as less attractive than those taking the pill. In support of this idea, Hess, Brody, Van Der Schalk, and Fischer[150] found that more sexually active women considered men who were strangers as less facially attractive than did women who were less sexually experienced. Nonetheless, this study shows how women's mating strategies are highly contextual, not just in terms of outside influences but also in regard to internal biological changes (see Chapter 2 for ovulatory cycle effects on perceptions of humor and intelligence).

Other effects of ovulation in females include the following:

- More female-initiated sex with partners
- A relatively strong preference for traditionally masculine partners (and a preference for features that indicate a good marriage partner as they move away from their high-fertility window)
- A higher likelihood of sexual infidelity
- A tendency to be more likely to touch males in casual social situations
- A tendency to be attracted to the scent of relatively symmetrical males
- A tendency to be attracted to relatively creative males
- A tendency to take more risks
- A tendency to be interested in erotic movies

- A tendency to wear relatively skimpy clothing
- A tendency to dance relatively dynamically
- A tendency for different body parts, including breasts, to be more symmetrical

And more.[151]

The recent research on this topic strongly supports the assertion that the ovulatory cycle has a substantial effect on the behavior of females. Ovulation in humans is observable—you just have to know what you're looking for.

These effects have significant and measureable outcomes on male behavior, such as the following:

- Males give bigger tips to female strippers who are ovulating.[152]
- Males find the voices of ovulating females relatively attractive.[153]
- Males find the scent of ovulating females relatively attractive.[154]
- Males report finding ovulating females as physically attractive compared with photos of the same women when not ovulating.[155]

And more.

Human mating is not static. A woman's ovulatory cycle is in a state of constant change—and the mating psychology and physiology of both females and males seem to take this important contextual factor into account. Human mating strategies depend importantly on the ovulatory cycle.

Dimensions of Human Mating that Reside Outside the Box

Homosexuality

A common issue people raise regarding evolutionary psychology pertains to the presence of homosexuality. If the human mind and resultant behavioral patterns evolved to facilitate reproduction of an individual's own genes, how on earth does something like homosexual behavior—which is decidedly not procreative—come about? Although we agree that this is a big question worth extensive discussion and scientific inquiry, we think that people who see this as an issue that ameliorates evolutionary theory are overstating things.

Yes, homosexuality exists—and it exists in varying degrees across all cultures that have been studied.[156] Although exclusive homosexuality is more common among males than females,[157] exclusive homosexuality does exist across the sexes in varying degrees—and bisexuality exists, too.

Can we conceptualize homosexual behavioral patterns as mating strategies? And, if so, does it make sense to discuss the evolutionary function and origins of such patterns?

We admit, this book is primarily about heterosexual behavior—and we're not unique—many treatises of mating and relationship behavior share this focus.[158] Nonetheless, homosexual behavior is clearly a form of mating behavior—and the widespread prevalence of homosexuality necessitates that evolutionists pay attention to this important human phenomenon.

To this point, theories that try to explain homosexuality within the confines of evolutionary theory have had limited success. Some theories focus on kin-selection-based explanations of homosexuality, suggesting that homosexuals divert a high proportion of parenting behavior to the offspring of genetic relatives, thereby facilitating their genetic lineage because these genes exist in the bodies of nieces and nephews.[159] Alternatively, homosexual tendencies may come about as an artifact of the relatively complex functioning of the nervous system, which leads to many kinds of nonadaptive outcomes (from an evolutionary perspective), simply as a function of its complexity.[160]

There also may be good reason to scientifically discriminate between male and female homoerotic behavior. When asked about their preferences in group-sex situations, heterosexual males reported that they are more likely to prefer having no other males involved, whereas heterosexual females showed an equal preference for including males or females.[161] These data suggest that homoerotic tendencies may well be sex differentiated, and that females may be naturally more bisexual than males. This fact may result from the highly polygamous nature of ancestral mating systems, which often included harem-like situations. Females under ancestral conditions who were included in harems of dominant males were likely considered lucky in terms of mating success. Further, given the nature of the harem situation, coupled with males' desire for multiple females, females may have become comfortable with group-sex situations that included multiple females. On the other hand, heterosexual males were in a very different situation—and monopolizing the females in a harem for themselves would have had clear fitness benefits. This account may explain why heterosexual women are more likely to show bisexual tendencies than heterosexual men.

In any event, homosexuality is clearly a significant part of human relationships and behavior and clearly warrants more extensive study. Future research on the nature of mating intelligence and mating psychology more generally on this topic should bear many fruits as scholars work to better understand this highly valued aspect of humanity.

Sexual Coercion

Is sexual coercion an evolved mating strategy? This question may well be one of the most controversial questions in all of evolutionary psychology. The issues involved ultimately get to the issue of whether rape is an adaptation—and, if so, if there is something *natural* about rape. You don't have to think too hard to see how contentious this topic is. Right off the bat, we want to note that no research, no matter what it shows, should condone rape. We agree with Buss and Schmitt when they say:

> It should go without saying that rape is illegal, immoral, and terribly destructive to women, and should in no way be condoned, whatever the ultimate causes turn out to be. (Buss & Schmitt, 2011)

With this important point out of the way, there has been some research on this front. In a provocative book on this topic, *A Natural History of Rape: Biological Bases of Sexual Coercion*, Craig Palmer and Randy Thornhill[162] argue that rape is part of a conditional mating strategy—utilized as something of a last resort after alternative strategies fail. Male scorpionflies try to obtain mates by one of three strategies.[163] First, they try to carve out a nice territory on a fresh carcass (*"Look, my pad's got a water view and it's near town!"*). If that doesn't work, they dance in front of the females—showing off their symmetrical bodies. Well, this second strategy really only works if they have symmetrical bodies! A final (and least successful) strategy is used as a last resort—and it is essentially forced copulation.

Are humans like scorpionflies? Do males resort to forms of sexual coercion as a result of the failure of other mating strategies? Is, then, sexual coercion a form of a mating strategy?

This question is a hot topic among evolutionary psychologists—and we believe that it is not directly relevant to the primary goals of this book. But we will say that there are a few broad schools of thought within the evolutionary literature. The idea of forms of sexual coercion as an adaptation has been studied extensively—with data sets that speak to this idea.[164]

Importantly, all mating occurs in a social context, including a broader community. Wilson and colleagues[165] argue that if we're thinking about rape from an evolutionary perspective, we should focus on how such an act affects the whole community. If there's a known rapist in the community, this adversely affects everyone. Being a rapist is not so great for one's reputation. Although a single act of rape may have fitness-enhancing consequences in the short-term, it is likely to have severely negative consequences in the medium- and long-term. Being beaten up or killed by the male kin of a rape victim is not very good for passing on genes. Getting labeled as a rapist in a small community is extremely detrimental for developing strong alliances and social networks. The long-term fitness consequences of acts of sexual coercion are dramatic and negative within normal human communities.

With these ideas in mind, a current research project being conducted in the SUNY New Paltz Evolutionary Psychology Lab seeks to address the question of whether people have specialized abilities to detect convicted rapists. Are people able to discriminate a set of rapists from a set of other convicted (non-rapist) criminals by looking at a series of mug shots? Are women better at this task than are men? Does scoring high on a measure of mating intelligence give people an edge at this task? SUNY New Paltz graduate student Mary Finn is currently leading a project on precisely these questions—looking at how well people can accurately detect whether someone is a rapist.

Something that everyone can agree on is that rape is a very serious problem, one that requires multiple perspectives to fully understand. Griet Vandermassen[166] notes that evolutionary scientists and feminists have been needlessly antagonistic. She criticizes both for not being completely open to each other's scholarly contributions. We believe that multiple perspectives are necessary to come to a deeper understanding of the disturbing phenomenon of rape, including sexual motivations, such as anger, hostility, and hatred toward women, and the role of psychopathy in sexual coercion (see Chapter 8). As Buss and Schmitt[167] note, "scientists from all theoretical perspectives have a responsibility to uncover the actual underlying causes of rape, even if they turn out to be unpalatable or repugnant."

Regardless of whether sexually coercive acts represent evolutionary adaptations per se, mating intelligence may well hold a key to determining who might be most likely to commit such acts. The ability to detect such individuals may well be an important adaptation that is part of human mating intelligence.

Mating Intelligence as Optimal Strategizing

By this point, it is clear that there is not a single mating strategy in humans. Although we are products of organic evolutionary forces, ultimately and largely shaped to increase genetic fitness of our own genetic lineages, the "mate as much as possible" strategy is, actually, very ineffective for pretty much anyone. Optimal mating strategies in humans have been shaped across thousands of generations of human evolution—and they are, importantly, complex and designed to take into account several important environmental and biological factors that surround human mating (e.g., prevailing sex ratio, one's own life history strategy, one's biological sex).

Human mating intelligence is the set of cognitive abilities that underlie mating psychology. Among the mating mechanisms that make up the core of mating intelligence, the ability to calibrate these mechanisms when implementing mating strategies is crucial. Someone with high mating intelligence will modify behavioral strategies as a function of the prevailing ecology. A male with high mating intelligence in an environment flooded with other males would likely utilize long-term mating tactics. He might underscore his kindness. He might advertise himself as fond of children and willing to take time to attend to them. A male in this same situation who is low in mating intelligence might not realize that it's never great to be a jerk—but it's particularly bad to be a jerk in this female-depleted scenario.

As another example, a woman high in mating intelligence might be savvier about ovulation effects than other women. She may realize when she's with her partner that even though she's not at the time of month when she's all fired up, so to speak, this is an effect of this naturally changing cycle. She may allow her cycle to affect her relationship less than if she were not as savvy about such mating-relevant effects of the ovulatory cycle.

For anyone, modifying behaviors as a function of context is often an adaptive process. This is likely especially true when it comes to the mating domain. As we will argue later (see Chapter 9) and throughout this book, we believe that mating intelligence can be increased. We believe that learning about the many variables that affect human mating psychology is a key to this process. Understanding the nature of the human mating strategies and variables that affect them, as described in this chapter—as well as in the broader literature on mating psychology—can have significant and positive effects on the mating lives of modern adults.

"She Totally Wants Me"

In the World of Mating, Biased Perceptions Are Everywhere

> "…if you lived in a group, as humans have always done, per-
> suading others of your own needs and interests would be
> fundamental to your well-being. Sometimes you had to use
> cunning. Clearly, you would be at your most convincing if you
> persuaded yourself first and did not even have to pretend to
> believe what you were saying. The kind of self-deluding indi-
> viduals who tended to do this flourished, as did their genes. So
> it was we squabbled and scrapped, for our unique intelligence
> was always at the service of our special pleading and selective
> blindness to the weakness of our case."
>
> (McEwan, 1997, *p. 112*)

Perceptions of the Social World Are Imperfect

If you're old enough to be reading this book, then you're old enough to know
without question that this subheading, "perceptions of the social world are
imperfect," is necessarily true. How many times have you totally misread a
social situation? Ever go to a party where you didn't know too many people,
fully expecting a dull time—only to be surprised by how friendly everyone was
and how fun the whole experience ended up being?

How many times have you ever misread yourself? Ever use the phrase "I'd
never do that"—only to find that, as life progresses, *doing that* becomes a common part of your behavioral repertoire? When one of the authors of this book
(GG) was a bit younger, he'd primarily drink beer—concluding that he'd "never
become a wine guy—that's just not me." Years later, he rarely drinks beer, and
he can actually discriminate between a shiraz and a merlot with some level of
accuracy. And he can tell the bad box wine from the really bad box wine! But
28-year old GG never would have imagined.

As McEwan's insight at the start of this chapter suggests, an inaccurate,
biased, erroneous, and imperfect cognitive system makes all too much sense as
characterizing a species like ours. Indeed, it's been shown over and over again
that the way we think about abilities in general (e.g., whether they are fixed

or malleable), as well as our self-perceived level of ability, significantly affects success above and beyond our measured ability.[1] Self-belief (or in some cases, self-deception!) is adaptive in domains such as academic achievement, business, sports, and love. Why not the mating domain as well?

And as O'Sullivan's[2] research tells us, self-deception, which often has a significant mating-relevant component, is defining of who we are—and self-deception is an effective tool in solving evolutionarily adaptive problems. For instance, consider a guy who's really pretty average on most physical and behavioral dimensions. Average Joe. Just how adaptive would it be for Average Joe to *see himself* as Average Joe? There'd be some interesting conversations:

> YOUNG WOMAN: So tell me about yourself, Joe.
> JOE: Well, there's not much to tell. I'm pretty average. I'm not really great at anything much. I've always done OK at school, but not much better than OK. People sometimes tell me I'm a nice guy—but I'm not like super-nice—pretty average on that one too, now that I think about it....
> YOUNG WOMAN: Oh! I'm sorry Jim, there's my friend Susie over there...I'll be right back!

Okay, Joe—sometimes honesty can be a self-handicap. In fact, modest levels of self-enhancement (seeing oneself in an overly positive light) seem to be adaptive in both the everyday sense (it helps you cope with who you are on an ongoing basis) and in an evolutionary sense (allowing you to cope well in social situations certainly is beneficial in terms of turning up mating opportunities and holding onto high-quality mates).

Social psychology is the branch of psychology that deals with the psychology of the social world—largely including how people perceive themselves and others. A core theme of social psychology pertains to the study of such social-perceptual biases as self-enhancement. In the next section, we discuss several basic kinds of social-perceptual biases in a way that connects with the mating domain.

Biases and Human Mating

The study of biased attitudes and perceptions has been so extensive in the field of social psychology[3] that, to some extent, this field can be thought of as an area that is largely dedicated to documenting the shortcomings of human social cognition. Although a full list of such biases would be too comprehensive for inclusion here, several major biases that likely bear on issues of human mating follow.

I Think I Know Why I Know What I Know

In a series of studies on the concept of *knowing more than we can know*, Nisbett and Wilson[4] found strong evidence for the fact that people cannot be relied on to give accurate answers when asked for reasons underlying why they have done what they have done. These studies are simple, powerful, and elegant. In one study, two groups of college students watched a movie (same movie over two showings in the same room). During one showing, conditions were normal. During the other, a loud drilling sound emerged from the hallway during the entire movie. People in the "loud drilling sound" condition didn't like the movie nearly as much as participants in the other condition. When asked *why* they didn't like it, they easily gave reasons. It was a poorly thought-out plot. The acting seemed forced. It was predictable. The settings were not well-done. Not a single person said "I think I didn't like it partly because of the annoying loud noise that was present throughout." In other words, with this simple experimental design, the experimenters were able to show (1) that the noise made it so that people did not like the movie and (2) that people were fully unconscious of this fact in thinking about their attitude about the movie.

The idea that we are "strangers to ourselves" (the title of Wilson's 2002 book) has been shown time and time again in a variety of domains, from problem solving to happiness.[5] As a species, we're not that great at describing why we act the way we do, and we're not that great at predicting how we are going to feel in the future.

Does this kind of thing also happen in the mating world? Certainly. For instance, we know what kinds of physical and psychological features make someone attractive to others. It's often the case that someone is attracted to someone else because of some such specific feature (e.g., smooth skin) without realizing the cause of the attraction. Then you could see courtship, dating, and the development of a long-term relationship forming—all because one member of the couple had smooth skin when they first met and this feature was attractive enough to spark the courtship process. When asked years later about how the relationship began, the smooth skin when they first met may well be the kind of detail that gets lost in the retelling—just like the loud noise in the hallway accompanying the movie.

And, of course, in the mating arena, skin texture is just the tip of the iceberg. Researchers have documented a dizzying array of factors that have unconscious influences on attraction, courtship, and relationship maintenance—from things like height, underarm scent, and facial symmetry to appropriate and effective use of self-denigrating humor, displays of kindness, and musical displays.

It is one thing to state mate preferences on a paper-and-pencil questionnaire and quite another thing when we are actually interacting with a flesh-and-blood person. Research does suggest that the traits people select in real life can differ drastically from the "cool," rational state of mind we are in when we are ticking boxes on an experimentally administered checklist.[6] In one study, the strongest predictor of desirability was physical attractiveness, even though women reported that their decisions were based on their desired level of relationship commitment. In reality, this factor was one of the least important factors! Interestingly, the men in their sample accurately indicated that physical attractiveness influenced their ratings. Maybe men deceive themselves less when it comes to what attracts them (at least when it comes to physical attraction), or they are more honest about it.

Either way, our point is this: humans are complex beings, and once you add context, hormones, and emotions into the mix, behaviors become even harder to predict.

This doesn't negate the evolutionary approach to understanding mating; it just means we have to be more nuanced in our predictions. Although people may have evolutionarily evolved ideal preferences, the actual mating marketplace considerably constrains the actual attainment of those preferences. Also, as we've mentioned (see Chapter 5), context affects how people actually act in a given situation. Most of these contextual effects lie outside of our conscious awareness or even access. Although the ways we act in the mating domain may sometimes seem perplexing to others and even to ourselves, a further understanding of the evolutionary rationale for these behaviors may give us insight into why we do what we do. All of these considerations need to be taken into account when applying the mating intelligence concept to understand actual human mating behavior.

People can tell you all about mating in their lives—but given the sophisticated nature of our unconscious processing of so much information, any and all self-reports regarding one's mating history should be taken with a grain of salt. And a course in social psychology.

Other People Do Things Because of Who They Are—I Do Things Because of the Situation

In a classic series of studies in the 1970s, Lee Ross documented a deeply entrenched part of human social psychology—dubbed, infamously, the Fundamental Attribution Error.[7] This bias in social cognition generally corresponds to the tendency to think that social outcomes derive from dispositional, internal sources more than from external causes—especially for people other than oneself. In a classic study of this phenomenon, Ross had undergraduate students engage in a quiz show in which the "questioner" created difficult questions that were then asked of the "contestant" in front of a randomly selected "observer." The roles of questioner and contestant were determined by a coin flip that was done when the observer was present. Subsequent to the coin flip, the questioner proceeded to ask the questions of the contestant. On average, contestants got 40% of the questions correct. Later, the observer was asked to rate the questioner and the contestant in terms of intelligence—and (here's the bottom line) the observers consistently rated the questioners as more intelligent than the contestants (which should not have actually been the case on average because all participants were selected from the same population and were randomly assigned across these two conditions). Short version: observers saw the questioner as more intelligent than the contestant (he had to seem more intelligent; he had all the answers on him!)—and instead of attributing this outcome to the random assignment to conditions, observers demonstrated the fundamental attribution error by overestimating the role of a dispositional trait (intelligence) as the cause of what was observed.

Interestingly, people don't make this same kind of dispositional attribution about their own behavior. After failing a test, people rarely say, "Well, I'm just an idiot"—they are more likely to blame something in the situation:

- It was an unfair test!
- Is this professor kidding us, asking a question about a detail stuck in the middle of the textbook?
- I went to all the lectures and none of the questions were based on the lectures!

And so forth.

For this reason, the fundamental attribution error is now framed in terms of the broader "actor/observer effect" in which people tend to overestimate dispositional causes of the behaviors of others but downplay the importance of dispositional causes of their own behavior.

Does this play out in mating contexts? You bet. Imagine a woman who found herself in a situation with a guy after a party—after several drinks. She thought the guy was cute and doesn't remember too much of what else happened—though she seems to remember sex.

How might this situation play out differently from the perspectives of self versus other? If that woman's you, you're probably feeling a mixture of emotions when you wake up in this guy's room the next morning. Partly, you think *"Wow, this guy's pretty cute"*—perhaps followed by *"This is the second time I've done this with a new guy in a month—I have to stop going to these frat parties"*—perhaps along with *"Kegs shouldn't be allowed at those parties—there was just so much alcohol—I'm just going to slink out of here and go find my friend to talk to."*

The attributions made by another would likely be different and would likely focus less on situational factors. Imagine, for instance, another woman in the same group who's actually had her eye on this same guy. *"She is so promiscuous! Do you know she did this same thing last week with that guy from Theta Xi? I think I heard she's been with half the guys in that frat...."*

Notice that the stories differ slightly in terms of a few things, but they differ particularly in terms of the focus put on dispositional versus situational causes. The woman who woke up with the frat guy blames the alcohol and even the university's broader alcohol policy. The other woman, here presented as an intrasexual rival, sees one clear, glaring, dispositional explanation for this whole thing—that woman's just *promiscuous*. In making this kind of attribution, all situational factors are immediately discounted and deemed irrelevant.

In the world of mating, the actor/observer effect plays a pivotal role.

You Must Be Thinking What I'm Thinking

Extraverts think most other people are extraverts. Christians overestimate the number of other Christians. People with blue eyes overestimate the number of others with blue eyes. People who are "pro-life" overestimate the percentage of others who are actually "pro-life." The false-consensus effect[8] pertains to the fact that we tend to overestimate the degree to which others are like us. And it's easy to see how this bias comes about. You spend 100% of your time in your body, mind, and social world. You spend 0% of your time in the shoes of anyone else. The world looks a certain way to you, and it's always surprising to experience someone seeing some part of it very differently. So we naively overestimate the degree to which others share our traits, dreams, beliefs, attitudes, and even experiences ("*What do you mean you've never been to France? How could a 40-year-old, educated American have never been to France?*").

A particularly problematic instance of the false consensus effect in the mating domain pertains to sex differences in behaviors related to sexual harassment. When asked how bad sexual harassment is, men and women both report that it's bad[9]—but women, whose reproductive futures are more capable of being adversely affected by outcomes associated with harassment (such as rape) hold attitudes about harassment that are relatively negative compared with the attitudes held by males. Owing to the false consensus effect, however, men don't always get this—and this is a major psychological problem with damaging social consequences. It's almost as if men who engage in harassing behavior are thinking, "*Oh it's a little bad, but it's not that bad,*" whereas women who are victimized by such behavior are thinking, "*No, actually, it is really bad.*" The false consensus effect may well be a crucial psychological factor that underlies sexual harassment and aggression (see next chapter for more on the importance of perspective taking).

I Really Am a Much Better Driver than Average—Oh, and Yeah, that Was My Idea!

Modern social psychology has turned up findings that have called many standard issues of mental health into question. For one, Taylor and Brown,[10] along with others,[11] have found strong evidence suggesting that biased (as opposed to accurate) perceptions of the world are actually relatively adaptive. That is, in many cases, being wrong may actually be more associated with mental health than being right.

The two classic examples of phenomena that fall into this category are *self-enhancement*[12] and the tendency for people to *overestimate the degree to which they control situations*.[13] These inter-related biases have something in common—they both speak to errors in perception, but the nature of the errors is positive. Self-enhancement is seeing yourself as better than is warranted (along various dimensions), and overestimating control is seeing yourself as being more powerful, in a very literal sense, than is warranted.

Generally speaking, people tend to engage in self-enhancement, and they tend to overestimate their control over environmental conditions. Although these biases are defined as erroneous, it's not too hard to see how they're also adaptive.

Consider a famous set of psychology experiments from the 1960s in which dogs were exposed to electrical shock emitted through the floor (ouch!). In these famous studies conducted by Martin Seligman and colleagues,[14] half the dogs were given some option that was able to shut the shock off (e.g., jumping over a small fence to another part of the room that had no shock). The other dogs were not given such an option (e.g., going over the fence led to another part of the floor that also emitted shocks). In a later phase of the study, all dogs were put in a condition in which they could remove the shock—but only dogs who had previously been in the condition in which their behavior actually had control over the situation took advantage of this opportunity. Dogs that were previously in the condition in which nothing could be done to ameliorate the shock did not, at this later phase, take action to remove the shock (even though they now could have removed the shock).

The dogs that learn they can control their environment are happier and are more likely to take action in their future to make good decisions for their own well-being. Seligman's research stands as among the most important research in all of psychology. Psychologists are still reaping lessons from this work on *learned helplessness*.

Social psychologists who are interested in the effects of perceived control over environmental conditions have run with Seligman's ideas. We now know that heightened levels of perceptions of control over situations (even if not fully warranted) are adaptive and healthy—as is the tendency to see oneself in a relatively positive light.

With our example of Average Joe, we addressed how self-enhancement can be relevant to mating contexts by helping increase confidence and helping, thus, turn up positive mating opportunities. Here, we consider the potential impact of a heightened sense of control on mating outcomes.

A long-term mateship can easily turn toward a rut. Several standard issues emerge in long-term relationships, including disagreements about money and time investment[15] along with the omnirelevant issue of sex.[16] Such disagreements and resultant difficulties are actually quite normal. Sometimes, such issues lead to separation and divorce, but sometimes they don't. Given the importance of perceived control in social situations, we believe that having a sense of control over a long-term relationship is probably crucial to the success of the relationship. Having both members of a couple share such perceived self-control is particularly beneficial.

If both members of a couple feel zero control over the relationship and everything that goes along with it, then good luck! That scenario is sure to lead to unhappiness and disillusionment. If one member of the couple feels a sense of control more than the other, that could lead to a sense of inequity,[17] which is certainly a negative force for any relationship. If both members of a couple perceive control over the environment that envelops the relationship, it is probably a good thing; the lessons of learned helplessness research suggest that slightly exaggerated perceptions of relationship control may well be the cat's meow when it comes to relationship functioning. Long-term mating intelligence likely serves an important function in helping members of couples realize a healthy sense of relationship control.

Oh, Yeah, That's Exactly What I Meant to Do!
(Cognitive Dissonance Reduction)

In the late 1950s and early 1960s, a major theory of human psychology emerged from the laboratory of Leon Festinger at Stanford University. Through a series of carefully conducted social psychological experiments, Festinger and colleagues[18] demonstrated a variety of ironic effects of large reinforcement. The main finding was that under certain conditions, a large reinforcer for completing some task (e.g., $20), compared with a small reinforcer (e.g., $1), led to relatively negative attitudes about the task. The "trick" here is essentially this: Participants who were given large reinforcers, under certain conditions, attributed their prior work not to anything intrinsically rewarding about the work, but, rather, to the fact that they got this large amount of money.

In this classic study, two groups of participants had engaged in a series of mundane tasks. Members of both groups were then told to tell a subsequent participant that the task was fun. They were told they'd either get $1 or $20 for their participation. Their attitudes about the tasks were then studied separately at the end of the study. The participants who were given $20 reported relatively negative attitudes about the tasks at the end; participants given only $1 reported relatively positive attitudes.

Festinger and his team interpreted these findings in terms of *cognitive dissonance reduction processes*. That is, these researchers believed that a strong force to keep one's thoughts in harmony is at work. It was harder for people to hold a positive attitude about the mundane task if they could justify that they had done the task for a lot of money—this justification is not dissonant with the fact that the person did the mundane tasks. Participants in the other condition could not justify participation in terms of the amount of money, so, as part of a hypothesized universal drive to strive toward cognitive harmony, these people adjusted their attitudes—telling themselves that they liked these tasks. And this is how you can get someone to like doing something for a pittance, if you're so inclined.

In the world of human social perception, cognitive dissonance reduction has important implications. Our thoughts, our attitudes, and our perceptions are partly motivated by a desire for cognitive consistency. And cognitive dissonance plays an important role when it comes to all the different facets of human mating.[19] In fact, cognitive dissonance could be a crucial form of psychological glue for the healthy maintenance of long-term relationships. In a study of nearly 200 adults who were in relationships at the time of the study, participants rated current partners in more positive terms compared with former partners. Current partners were consistently rated as more agreeable, secure, emotionally stable, open-minded, and conscientious compared with past partners. Further, participants who demonstrated the largest discrepancy between their perceptions of current versus former partners were also scored as having the most satisfying relationships in the sample.

These findings went on to suggest that there is a significant physiological cost to *not* holding positive perceptions of one's current partner and negative perceptions of a former partner! In this study, electrodermal activity was measured for more than 60 of the participants. Electrodermal activity is a standard measure of the arousal of the autonomic nervous system as it activates when we perceive a situation as a threat. In one experimental condition, participants were asked to write positive attributes about their most recent former romantic partner—engaging, thereby, in a task predicted to elicit a state of dissonance. Consistent with Festinger's prediction, electrodermal activity was higher for participants in this condition compared with participants in other experimental conditions. As such, our tendency to see our mating world in an optimized, cognitively consonant manner seems strongly connected to our underlying physiology.

What does this mean for the pursuit of a satisfied romantic life? Well, if you're currently committed to a relationship with Fred, and Barney is now in your past, holding Fred in a relatively positive light compared with Barney will reinforce your choices. Imagine the kind of cognitive dissonance that would be created by holding a former partner (Barney, in this case) in a more positive light relative to a current partner (Fred). Based on this study by GG and colleagues, there are, in fact, a sizeable proportion of individuals out there who do, in fact, hold such a perceptual pattern—and, not surprisingly, people who like their former romantic partners more than their current partners are stressed out! When it comes to healthy intimate relationships, a little dissonance reduction—even if it's based on somewhat distorted reasoning—is not always a bad thing.

Evolutionarily Shaped Perceptual Biases

One of the great advances in the behavioral sciences has been the large-scale application of evolutionary principles to understanding human behavior.[20] In recent years, social psychologists have come to apply evolutionary principles to their scholarship more and more.[21] This trend allows us to understand the many social-perceptual biases that have been studied for years by social psychologists in a much broader perspective.

From an evolutionary perspective, it makes good sense that our perceptual systems should have certain biases. Consider, for instance, our visual system, which seems to be hypervigilant to stimuli resembling snakes.[22] There are good reasons to believe that snakes represented a genuine hurdle to survival under ancestral conditions. Snakes represented negatively in samples of human cultures from all corners of the earth.[23] Further, it is particularly noteworthy that approximately 12% of deaths in pre-westernized societies occur from snakebites.[24] Today, as a result of significant evolutionary pressures across many generations, our visual system responds more quickly to snake-like stimuli than to other stimuli, and we are biased toward overperceiving ambiguous stimuli as snakes.[25] Clearly, this perceptual bias has an adaptive function—utilizing our emotion system to keep ourselves clear of these potential killers. Indiana Jones may have seemed a bit irrational in his snake phobia, but he was not alone.

In a significant paper that integrated evolutionary psychology with the social-perception literature, Martie Haselton and David Buss[26] demonstrated evidence for Error Management Theory, or the idea that the human perceptual system is designed, not to be accurate, but, rather, to reduce the likelihood of making costly errors. Drawing on the snake example we cited previously, it seems that our visual system was not designed to accurately perceive snakes but rather was shaped to overperceive snake-like stimuli as snakes in order to reduce the likelihood of getting killed by one. This process surely has saved lives.

Given the centrality of mating in human psychology from the evolutionary perspective, it makes sense that mating-relevant social perceptions should be biased in a way that increases the likelihood of survival and reproduction.

Starting with Haselton and Buss's[27] work on this topic, this is precisely what researchers have found. And, as is true with so many areas of mating, the nature of these biases seems to be different in men and women.

Male-Specific Adaptive Biases

Two significant perceptual biases specific to men nicely include (1) the tendency to oversexualize female stimuli,[28] and (2) the tendency to be particularly sensitive to cues of sexual infidelity.

Since the 1980s, researchers have consistently found that men are more likely than women to see neutral stimuli of women as reflecting sexual desire.[29] In a typical study on this topic, male and female participants are shown photographs of men and women in ambiguous situations. Participants are asked to estimate how much sexual interest each person in the photograph has in the other. Women tend to see the people in such photographs as not sexually involved; men tend to see sexuality—even when it's not there, and particularly if the woman is smiling.

Until the advent of the evolutionarily formed Error Management Theory, this phenomenon was pretty much explained away as, "*Well, men are pigs.*" In light of the power of evolutionary theory, a much more satisfying explanation now exists. The oversexualization of women—that is, the tendency to overestimate sexual interest on the part of women—is likely a bias that increases mating opportunities. Men who tend to think that women are sexually interested are probably more likely to try to court women compared with other men. Given male mating psychology and the evolutionary benefits of increased mating opportunities for males, this bias seems clearly to predict increased mating success. The cost of an error using this strategy—embarrassment at rejection—is offset by the evolutionary benefit of increased mating opportunities.

Hypervigilant sexual jealousy represents another male-specific mating bias with a strong evolutionary foundation.[30] Across multiple contexts—including disparate cultures—males respond strongly to signs of sexual infidelity compared with females.[31] Given the evolutionary reality of paternal uncertainty— the fact that a man can never be fully certain that his wife's offspring are, indeed, his also—males can experience dramatic evolutionary costs if their partner cheats sexually. There is an important asymmetry across the sexes on this issue because females across human evolutionary history were always certain that their offspring were, indeed, theirs.

Accordingly, several adaptive mechanisms have evolved to bias males toward hypervigilance regarding the issue of sexual infidelity.[32] Males are more likely to respond with psychological distress to thoughts of sexual infidelity compared with females,[33] they are more likely to experience physiological distress when thinking about sexual infidelity compared with females,[34] and they are more likely to focus on details relevant to sexual infidelity when assessing social situations compared with females (also see Chapter 5 for an understanding of these findings in terms of attachment theory).[35] These findings all make sense in light of Error Management Theory—the evolutionary benefits for a male to be hypervigilant about sexual infidelity (curtailing a woman from becoming pregnant by another man) outweigh the costs (such as gaining a reputation as a jealous guy or engaging in unhealthy, obsessive jealousy).

Female-Specific Adaptive Biases

Females are not immune from social-perceptual biases, either.

As Haselton and Buss[36] documented, women are *commitment skeptics*—they are more likely than men to be skeptical of statements of commitment compared with men. Rightfully so. Unlike men, women are at risk for getting stuck with the huge evolutionary cost of raising an offspring with no other parental help. This outcome is particularly likely if a woman does not effectively mate with a male who is willing to commit to a long-term relationship. The cost of commitment skepticism, losing out on mating opportunities with males who may actually be good guys, is minor compared with the major evolutionary benefit of this bias, which is to reduce the likelihood of mating with a cad.

Another bias that typifies female psychology is the tendency to think that there just might be someone better out there during the mate-search process.[37] As discussed in Chapter 5, research in a speed-dating context that replicated real-world mate selection found that men tend to settle much more quickly than women do.[38] Given how evolutionarily crucial it is for women to discriminate in choosing a mate, it makes good sense that they would be biased toward checking out a relatively large number of suitors. An understanding of how women make mating decisions is an important step toward understanding human nature.

Mating Intelligence, Bias, and Accuracy

This chapter has focused on biases that permeate human mating psychology. In our own recent study exploring the ability to assess the mating desires of the opposite sex, we found that this kind of assessment is filled with bias—but it also includes a touch of accuracy.[39]

One of the core elements of mating intelligence is the ability to read the thoughts and feelings of potential and actual mates. In a large-scale study designed to examine this ability, nearly 500 young men and women were asked to read through several real personal ads, written by members of their own sex. They were then asked to guess which ads would be most attractive to members of the opposite sex for a long-term relationship—and which ads would be most attractive to members of the opposite sex for a short-term, casual fling.

The ads varied from one another in terms of many dimensions. One particular dimension of interest pertained to sexual content; all ads were coded by two research assistants trained to study the ads for the presence of sexual content.

This research represents some of the first psychological research explicitly designed with the notion of mating intelligence in mind.

Bias in Cross-Sex Mind-Reading

In the initial data analysis, participants' assessments were examined for accuracy: were people good at guessing which ads were most attractive (for both long-term and short-term mateships) to members of the opposite sex?

Participants were not that great at this task. Many errors were made by both males and females. In light of prior work on Error Management Theory, we hypothesized that both males and females would tend to oversexualize the desires of the opposite sex. We predicted males to be likely to overchoose ads that were sexual in nature in guessing what women wanted. Such a tendency would reflect a bias toward oversexualizing the desires of women, consistent with Haselton and Buss's[40] research on Error Management Theory. And this is precisely what we found in our research. When men did err, they tended to err by overestimating the degree to which women desired men who wrote relatively sexual ads.

For instance, for one set of ads, men were faced with three choices given in Table 6.1 (they were asked to guess which ad women would prefer for a short-term mate).

The "correct" answer here was "diversity, cultures, and art..." (option C)—although a large number of males missed the boat, assuming that women prefer "...man in a uniform looking for some fun" (option B). Apparently, men overestimate how interested women are in conspicuous male sexuality—even under conditions that are explicitly framed as bearing on short-term mating!

We also predicted that women would err by overestimating the degree to which men expressed a desire for women who wrote relatively sexual ads. This predicted bias was framed as reflecting commitment skepticism—if a woman overestimates a male's tendency to just want sex, this bias would go hand-in-hand with being skeptical of a man's intentions. Consistent with prior work on Error Management Theory, this is precisely what we found—particularly for women trying to guess the short-term desires of men.

Table 6.1 **Male Short-Term Mating Judgment Example**

	A	B (rated as sexual by trained judges)	C
Item	I'm pretty busy working all week, but that doesn't stop me from having fun, usually out and about a couple nights during the week and always doing something fun and exciting on the weekend.	I've been described as a very energetic individual. I like to think of myself as someone with a lot of positive energy. I'm new to the area, looking to meet new people. **I'm a man in a uniform looking for some fun.**	I'm spontaneous and I like to try new things. **I enjoy diversity, cultures, art,** science, nature, good food and intelligent conversation. I'm happy in the city or the country. I like to draw strange portraits. I believe there is an order to the chaos and vice versa.
Actual male percentages (guessing female choices)	26%	**49%**	25%
Expected percentages (based on actual female choices)	23%	29%	**48%**

*This table was reproduced with permission from Geher's (2009) article published in *Evolutionary Psychology*. For each of the 10 clusters of personal ads, an analysis was computed to determine whether males' guesses regarding what females wanted in short-term mates were significantly discordant from females' actual reported desires.

For instance, in making these judgments, women had to choose which of the ads shown in Table 6.2 was most desirable to a male for a short-term mating.

The results found that not only were women's guesses of men's desires off, but they were off in an interesting way. The promiscuous-flaunting woman of option B is not very popular as a short-term mate among the men (only 24% wanted her), but a majority of women thought that this was the woman whom men most wanted! Whom did men really want? Well, a majority of men wanted the middle-of-the-night sandwich maker! And remember, this is what men wanted in a short-term partner.

Table 6.2 **Female Short-Term Mating Judgment Example**

	A	B (rated as sexual by trained judges)	C
Item	Who said chivalry was dead? Open doors for me, and I will be your mate. I will rub your back when you throw up and listen to you complain about your boss. **I will make your favorite sandwich when you wake up hungry in the night.**	I am searching for a fling of epic proportions, someone to caress my face as we kiss and who will write me love notes and leave them under my door—but will not get upset with me if I decide to kiss another man. **Human beings are not meant to be paired for life, like lobsters.**	I am the kind of girl who loves to sing. **I know all the words to** *Grease*, and I think that love can be a musical. I love to break out into song on a daily basis. I am looking for someone who can make my heart sing.
Actual female percentages (guessing male choices)	35%	**53%**	17%
Expected percentages (based on actual male choices)	**54%**	24%	22%

*This table was reproduced from Geher's (2009) article published in *Evolutionary Psychology*.

For each of the 10 clusters of personal ads, an analysis was computed to determine whether females' guesses regarding what males wanted in short-term mates were significantly discordant from males' actual reported desires.

Apparently there's more to the male psyche than just sex! Interestingly, knowing all the words to *Grease* wasn't very attractive, either.

Taking in the results of this study, it seems that women might be oversexualizing men's desires, whereas men might well be doing the same, at least when assessing women's short-term desires.

But in this data set, there's more to the story.

Mating Intelligence and Accuracy

The fact that so many mating-relevant judgments are biased—and that such bias so often makes evolutionary sense—is something of a conundrum for the concept of mating intelligence. After all, the entire idea of *intelligence* conjures up accurate cognitive processes, doesn't it? And the idea of biased perception seems a bit far from the idea of intelligence.

We agree. For this reason, we believe mating intelligence, steeped in an evolutionary perspective,[41] represents an intelligence that is, in many ways, different from other kinds of intelligence.[42] As a set of evolutionarily adaptive cognitive processes, mating intelligence, in fact, represents a combination of accuracy and bias.

In our own cross-sex mind-reading research described in this chapter, biases were rampant. But recall that men and women were asked to guess both the long-term and short-term desires of members of the opposite sex. In our statistical analysis, we examined *accuracy in judging long-term desires* and *accuracy in judging short-term desires,* and we found a major difference between the sexes. Males were much better than females at guessing the long-term desires of the opposite sex—women were, conversely, much better than males at guessing the short-term desires of the opposite sex. In other words, men are better at knowing what women want in long-term partners, whereas women are better at knowing what men want in short-term partners.

The finding that men are more accurate at knowing women's long-term desires (than women are at knowing men's long-term desires) is interesting because females traditionally score higher than males on myriad areas of social functioning such as emotional intelligence,[43] social intelligence,[44] interpersonal intelligence,[45] nonverbal reading ability,[46] and communication-decoding ability[47]—among others.

Several reasons may account for the sex differences found in this study, but we think two of them, presented here, are the most relevant. First, given the notoriously discriminating nature of females' choices in mate selection (in humans as well as most other sexually reproducing species[48]), there may be particularly strong pressure on males to essentially *get it right.* That is, it should be particularly useful for males (more so than for females) to be accurate in their judgments of the desires of the opposite sex.

Second, many evolutionists who study human mating have focused on asymmetries across the sexes in costs associated with making poor choices in mate selection. Owing to the nature of internal fertilization and the relatively high costs associated with parenting that tax females more than males, female mating psychology should be particularly designed to reduce errors in choosing poorly in the mating domain. In short, it may pay females to overestimate the degree to which "men are all pigs." Males, compared with females, are more likely to demonstrate short-term strategies in mating. For instance, males are more likely to report wanting many sexual partners and are more likely to enter short-term relationships with partners that they judge as less desirable for long-term mating compared with females.[49] Given these features of male mating psychology, females may be more able to rely on a simple heuristic, such as "only cares about sex," compared with males in making opposite-sex judgments.

This tendency to overestimate males' focus on sexuality may be the flip side of the commitment-skepticism bias.[50] This bias is exactly the kind of psychological proclivity that would reduce the likelihood of costly mate-choice errors for females. If females tend to employ this bias very strongly and consistently, it makes sense that their judgments of males' desires are in contrast to males' actual desires. This bias leads to an erroneous overestimation.

In fact, when considering females' patterns of errors in the current study, one might say that they demonstrated a "males are *always* pigs" bias. Regardless of whether they were making judgments of males' long or short-term preferences, they showed a strong tendency to overestimate the degree to which males desired the relatively sexual and promiscuous option (see Tables 6.1 and 6.2). Such a bias is consistent with the idea that women may be employing a simple heuristic suggesting that men "just want sex"—regardless of the temporal context. In other words, women tend to think that men only care about sex for both short-term casual partners *and for long-term partners*. Although this bias may have accounted for the fact that females scored as less accurate than males overall, it may well be an adaptive strategy in the long run—women using such a decision-making rule may be more likely to actually end up with honest, committed, and long-term-relationship-seeking males (an outcome that would be very beneficial for women given the asymmetry in parental investment that typifies our species).[51]

Beyond adaptive biases, mating intelligence includes evolutionarily appropriate processes that are honed for accuracy. To the extent that women are more likely than men on average to be long-term mating strategists,[52] it would be beneficial for men to be particularly attuned to the long-term desires of women. Similarly, to the extent that men are more likely to be short-term strategists on average,[53] it makes sense that women should be particularly astute in cognitive processes connected to the short-term mating psychology of males. So, when it comes to cross-sex mind-reading, male and female strengths match male and female mating psychology—supporting the idea that mating intelligence partly depends on one's sex. This research also shows that an evolutionary perspective is integral to helping us understand the nature of human mating intelligence. The next chapter delves further into the social psychology of mating intelligence—with an eye toward helping us better understand deception in the world of mating.

"I Really Am a Tall Doctor—and
of *Course* I Love You!"

Mind-Reading, Emotional Intelligence, and Deception

What makes us human? Is it our big prefrontal cortex that allows us to inhibit our immediate impulses in the service of longer-term goals?[1] Is it our opposable thumb, which allowed our hominid ancestors to throw stones with better accuracy than any of their predecessors—a fact that allowed for such egalitarian-society-creating acts as public stoning of despicable leaders?[2] Is it that whole group-hunting thing—which required such outcomes as advanced tool use, geographical savvy, and major coordination among group members?[3] Is it language—which is, depending on what book you read, either uniquely human or close to it?[4] How about the fact that cooked foods characterize human diets in cultures around the world—coupled with the fact that all major elements of the human digestive system betray a long history of cooking among our ancestors across thousands of generations?[5]

These are just a few of the hypotheses that have been put forward to explain the uniqueness of humans.[6] Most certainly, there are a number of characteristics that are uniquely developed in humans.[7] In this chapter, we focus on one particular capacity that psychologists have argued takes a more sophisticated flavor in humans compared with other animals: Theory of Mind.[8]

Suppose we're playing poker and I know you as someone who never bluffs— and you put up a $10 bet. I think that you may well have a good hand, that you may well be looking at a pair of aces. I'm not necessarily right, but my ability to make such a mental inference with some level of accuracy is something referred to as Theory of Mind. It involves an individual's ability to understand that others have beliefs, desires, and intentions that are different from his or her own and the ability to take the perspective of another person and imagine what he or she must be thinking and feeling.

Humans are not the only members of the animal kingdom with these abilities. Hints of Theory of Mind have been suggested for all sorts of animals.

For instance, Hare, Call, and Tomasello[9] found that subordinate chimpanzees were keenly able to read the behaviors of dominant chimps in a way that led them to find food hidden by the researchers. The question of whether non-humans genuinely have Theory of Mind abilities is still being hotly debated by animal behavior researchers,[10] but a key to the debate is recognizing that Theory of Mind consists of a variety of skills, some of which are more advanced in humans compared with other species. For example, there is evidence that the ability to read emotions based on facial and bodily cues is different from the ability to employ complex reasoning about the mental states of others.[11] The complex reasoning aspect is most certainly uniquely developed in humans.

Human Theory of Mind is evident not only in our complex social behaviors but also in our anatomy. Among the many species of primates, only humans have white eyes that surround the iris. In step with this seemingly random characteristic of human anatomy is the well-researched and well-accepted concept that we pay attention to where people pay their attention.[12] The white around the eye facilitates this process. We also focus on facial cues in trying to assessment others' feelings,[13] and we make important inferences about what others are thinking based on past experiences and context.[14] Mind-reading (of the non-ESP variety) is a major part of human psychology.

When Theory of Mind is lacking, we see disorders such as Asperger's syndrome and other autism spectrum disorders.[15] People with such disorders generally have difficulty reading others' emotions (i.e., they are "alexithymic"), are bad at reading others in general, and are particularly unable to process sarcasm.

Such disorders that eradicate Theory of Mind abilities dramatically affect the social life of these individuals. Individuals with autism have a hard time fitting into social groups across various contexts,[16] and not surprisingly, they often have difficulty attracting and retaining mates.[17] Even so, people with some autistic-like traits can succeed in the mating domain. To see how this is so, we must step back and review an intriguing new theory.

According to Bernard Crespi and Christopher Badcock's[18] "imprinted brain" theory,[19] autism and psychosis are on opposite ends of a spectrum of mental traits that are heavily dependent on which parent's genes dominated during inheritance. Crespi and Badcock argue that an evolutionary tug of war between the genes coming from the father's sperm and the genes coming from the mother's egg can bias brain development along two different paths.

In particular, they propose that when there is a bias toward the paternal line, the brain develops along the autistic spectrum, which tends to result in the expression of *hypomentalism*: an underactive Theory of Mind, impaired social cognition, and a fascination with details, patterns, and mechanical systems. They propose that when there is a bias toward the maternal line, however, the brain develops along the psychotic spectrum, tending to result in the expression of *hypermentalism*: an overactive Theory of Mind, hypersensitivity to mood (of others and self), megalomania, delusions of grandeur, and erotomania (the delusion that strangers and famous people are in love with you).

Indeed, there is recent brain research suggesting that autism and schizophrenia do display opposite patterns of brain activation—those with autistic-like traits tend to show underactive brain activations in the "default network" that suggest they have an *underdeveloped* Theory of Mind, and those with schizotypy-like traits tend to show overactive brain activations in the same network that suggest they have an *overactive* Theory of Mind.[20] Although the Imprinted Brain Theory is still quite speculative (Crespi and Badcock admit that it is), it does offer intriguing hypotheses and makes testable predictions that could lead to novel insights in a wide range of domains.[21] One of the major insights may be related to the mating domain.

Remember in Chapter 3 when we talked about schizotypy (the milder form of schizophrenia) and its relation to artistic creativity, openness to experience, and short-term mating success? Taking it one step forward, psychologist Daniel Nettle[22] extended Crespi and Badcock's theory to suggest why schizotypy may be attractive to women, particularly in a short-term mating context. According to Nettle, hypermentalizing, psychosis-prone males may be reliably signaling that they have a genotype that is biased toward the maternal line, and therefore their babies will not make excessive demands on their mothers. As Nettle[23] points out, Crespi and Badcock demonstrated that those who are more prone to psychosis do tend to be smaller, grow at a slower rate, and are less demanding as babies, whereas those who are prone to autism tend to be larger, grow at a faster rate, and are more demanding as babies.

Therefore, while the traits and behaviors of the watered-down version of schizophrenia (schizotypy) may be particularly attractive in a short-term mating context, the watered-down version of autism (Asperger's syndrome) may be particularly attractive in a long-term mating context. Extending Nettle's ideas, Marco Del Giudice, Romina Angeleri, Adelina Brizio, and Marco R. Elena[24] have suggested that "both autistic-like and schizotypal traits have an evolutionary history of sexual selection through mate choice," with the former evolving for long-term mating and the latter evolving for shorter-term mating. In support of their theory, they found that whereas people with reduced interpersonal skills tended to display reduced mating effort and no linkage to long-term investment, people who showed more interest in patterns and details tended to display *greater* levels of partner-specific investment and stronger commitment to long-term romantic relationships. Therefore, a major aspect of Asperger's syndrome—attention to detail—may be conducive to long-term relationships. It would be a mistake to count people with autism spectrum disorder out of the mating game!

As we noted in Chapter 3, the meta-trait Stability, which is tied to the serotonin system, may be more conducive to long-term mating, whereas the meta-trait Plasticity, which is tied to the dopaminergic system, may be more conducive to short-term mating. If we look to see where autism and schizophrenia are aligned, there is evidence that autism is primarily related to the serotonin system,[25] whereas there is evidence that schizophrenia is primarily related to the dopaminergic system (although of course both serotonin and dopamine interact).[26] Hence, schizotypy may be more strongly tied to the meta-trait Plasticity and short-term mating, whereas Asperger's may be more strongly tied to the meta-trait Stability and long-term mating. Future research will hopefully test these ideas and potential linkages.

Theory of Mind and Mating

Most of us lie in the moderate range of the autism-psychosis spectrum. Indeed, Crespi and Badcock argue that "normality" represents balanced expression of genes and environmental developmental influences. Moderate levels of Theory of Mind (not extremely overactive or underactive) is a crucial component of the mating intelligence framework. In fact, the entire developmental process involves important elements of Theory of Mind.

And when it comes to mating, Theory of Mind is crucial. *Is he into me? Does he like her more? Does he really like her? How would he react to a forward move on my part?* In trying to attract a mate, there are hundreds if not thousands of Theory of Mind microdecisions that come into play—and that's all before the first kiss!

During courtship, Theory of Mind skills play a paramount role. You know you need to come across as *all that*, but what does *all that* look like to this person? Imagine a guy trying to impress a woman early in the courtship process. He'd better have a great sense of her thought process if he's going to do a halfway decent job. *Does she like the gentleman or the tough guy? I think I should pay for this meal—will she think that's kind? Polite? Or sexist? Was that just a fake, sympathy laugh she made at that joke of mine? Wait, maybe I'm being paranoid . . . .*

Theory of Mind continues to be essential in relationship success across the duration of a relationship. Deep into the throes of a long-term relationship, being able to anticipate a partner's thoughts and feelings is crucial to maintaining a positive, harmonious, and fun relationship.

So, just how good are people in general at judging the romantic interest of others? Skyler Place, Peter Todd, Lars Penke, and Jens Asendorpf[27] set out to answer this question. In their study, they had male and female undergraduates watch short video clips of actual speed-dating sessions. They found that, on average, both men and women watching the videos of the dates were equally able to accurately assess romantic interest at above-chance levels. Interestingly, length of time spent watching the videos had very little effect. Participants were able to predict interest using clips as short as 10 seconds long, although they estimated most accurately when they watched clips at the middle or end of the speed date.

They also found that it was easier for observers to gauge men's intentions than it was to gauge women's intentions. This finding supported the research-er's hypothesis that "women are harder to read, presumably because they mask their true intentions" (p. 26). This may be owing to women's greater choosiness, predicted by parental investment theory. Men may simply face less biological risks by showing their true intentions.

Perhaps most tellingly, though, they found that some observers were better at making judgments than others. In other words, there were individual differ-ences in the ability to be read, even among males and females. In particular, those who indicated they were currently in a relationship did better at predict-ing male interest than those who were single. This suggests that mating expe-rience and the mating intelligence that comes about through this experience may play an important role in this mind-reading ability.

Emotional Intelligence in the Mating World

Emotional intelligence represents a set of important abilities that underlie how well people reason with emotions.[28] Generally, emotional intelligence is the set of cognitive abilities connected to the emotional world. An emotion-ally intelligent person has good Theory of Mind skills and, thus, can read oth-ers' feelings.[29] But emotional intelligence is broader than Theory of Mind and includes many different points of interface between emotional and cognitive processes.[30]

Based on hundreds of published studies on this topic,[31] researchers have found four basic dimensions that underlie emotional intelligence, as follows:

1. Assimilating emotion into thought (e.g., "*I think the Huskies are going to win this game, even though it's tied, because their home-team fans are radiating posi-tive emotions*")
2. Managing emotions in oneself and in others (e.g., "*OK, I just called the host-ess of this party by the wrong name—I feel like an idiot—ahhh!!!!! And her name is Susan—I wasn't even close. AHHH!!! OK—I have to calm down, this is really not a huge deal ...* ")
3. Accurately perceiving emotional stimuli (e.g., "*I said the word 'raise,' and my boss made a pretty clear negative facial expression—it was fast, but it was clear—and unmistakably negative. Let me think about alternative ways to approach this one that will make her less mad and will have the same effect of raising my pay!*")

4. Using emotions for beneficial purposes (e.g., *"If I'm going to get these kids to this dentist today and have all of us get out of there alive, let me see what I can do to at least start with them in a good mood...."*)

And, of course, these skills are all crucial for mating purposes. Let's reconsider the four domains of emotional intelligence in terms of mating:

1. Assimilating emotion into thought (e.g., *"That laugh of hers seemed pretty genuine and pretty strong—OK—I think she's into me...."*)
2. Managing emotions in oneself and in others (e.g., *"Oh no, he is so mad at me because of all that money I spent without even telling him I was going to buy all that stuff—I bet if I buy him a six-pack of his favorite beer, clean this place up, and encourage him to go golfing tomorrow morning while I take the kids out, that'll put a smile on his face!"*)
3. Accurately perceiving emotional stimuli (e.g., *"Hey, I put my arm around her and smiled—and she smiled right back and got closer to me. Win!"*)
4. Using emotions for beneficial purposes (e.g., *"Gosh, he and I are clearly feeling anxious about this latest argument. We should make this anxiety work for us and use it as the impetus to start a new relationship tradition—date night once every 2 weeks—heck, let's even call it sex night for fun! At least let's give that a try."*)

Emotional intelligence and mating intelligence go hand in hand.[32] Emotional intelligence is a plus when it comes to relationships—particularly when it comes to long-term relationships. People who score high in emotional intelligence tend to score higher than others on several indices of success and satisfaction in long-term relationships.

Interestingly, some past research has also addressed what we might call *intracouple emotional intelligence concordance* as it relates to relationship success and satisfaction. This basically refers to the situation in which two members of a couple are matched or not in terms of emotional intelligence. Two primary factors emerge from this research. First, there are relationship benefits to high levels of emotional intelligence. However, there seems to be something of a caveat. If one member of the relationship is low in emotional intelligence, the relationship does not benefit from the other person being high in emotional intelligence. Marc Brackett, Rebecca Warner, and Jennifer Bosco[33] attribute this finding largely to the fact that it is likely very frustrating to be the emotionally intelligent member of such a couple. Generally speaking, higher emotional intelligence tends to correspond with better long-term relationship outcomes, but the concordance in emotional intelligence levels across the members of the couple is an important contextual factor.

Emotional intelligence is vital for understanding mating intelligence in several respects. First, emotional intelligence facilitates relationship success—a couple composed of emotionally intelligent people is likely to be a happy couple.[34] Second, emotional intelligence has a major Theory of Mind component,[35] and mating intelligence, unequivocally, includes the ability to read the thoughts of would-be and actual mates.

The Interplay of Courtship Displays and Psychological Mating Mechanisms

A particularly interesting point of interface between emotional and mating intelligence pertains to the interplay between the two core kinds of processes that underlie mating intelligence—*psychological mating mechanisms* and *courtship displays*.[36] Recall that mating mechanisms are proposed as psychological mechanisms that directly bear on mating-relevant issues (such as trying to figure out whether a potential mate is attracted to a certain look). And courtship displays are processes that are indirectly mating-relevant—they are hypothesized to have evolved for courtship purposes and are attractive in early stages of relationship formation (such as a good sense of humor or creative intelligence; see Chapter 2).

In coming up with this bifurcate conception of mating intelligence, it becomes clear that there are some processes that serve as both mating mechanisms and courtship displays.[37] Emotional intelligence may well be such a psychological concept. Clearly, as delineated previously, emotional intelligence is directly relevant to mating purposes. Emotional intelligence helps people understand the thoughts of would-be and actual mates—it helps people keep their partners happy—and it helps them maintain positive emotions in relationship contexts.[38]

Emotional intelligence is also attractive. Who would you rather marry, a man who was good at knowing your feelings, good at managing his emotions, and good at making others feel good, or a guy who never understands you, blows up at the drop of a pin, and consistently pisses everyone off? All things equal, you will probably find the first guy more attractive. Thus, emotional intelligence may well serve an important display-related function in courtship. This is consistent with research showing that people, in general, are attracted to others who are emotionally stable and who maintain positive moods (see Chapter 3).

Emotional intelligence is important in the mating domain if for no other reason than the fact that it's attractive. The characteristics that go along with emotional intelligence may serve as important signals of the ability to have empathy and provide resources. Displays of emotional intelligence may also partially indicate mental health, which may ultimately signal a healthy nervous system and, perhaps, a relatively small proportion of genetic errors in the genome.[39]

Emotional intelligence, then, may well serve as both a psychological mating mechanism and a fitness indicator. Without question, future research on the topic of mating intelligence will do well to study mating-relevant concepts to see which ones uniquely reflect psychological mating mechanisms, which uniquely reflect mental fitness indicators, and which seem to, like emotional intelligence, overlap across these areas.

Deception in Mating

Communication systems designed to accurately convey information can all be exploited for selfish purposes. Famous examples are rampant in the natural world. Several species of butterflies fool predators into thinking that they are raptors with their wing markings mimicking raptor-like eyes; several nontoxic animals take on the coloration of toxic species; angler fish dangle a biologically sophisticated lure for passersby as they remain hidden and ready to strike—and this is just the tip of the iceberg.[40] The biological world is full of deceptive signals.

Given the centrality of mating to Darwin's bottom line (reproductive success), it makes sense that mating-relevant deception would typify the behavioral arsenal across the spectrum of sexually reproducing animals. And it does. Satellite male sunfish fool larger, dominant males into thinking that they are females—thus allowing the satellites to not get chased away and giving them prime real estate when a female comes to a nest of a dominant male to release her eggs. Satellite males, who come in to blast the eggs with their sperm, have the timing of this deception down to a science. Male praying mantises offer mates *nuptial gifts*—usually small clumps of dead insects[41]—that offer a nice, nutritional snack for the female. But when food is rare, they'll offer deception gifts, clumps of mud that look similar to the insect clumps—sort of like a cubic zirconium instead of a diamond. This deceptive strategy works at some times better than others.

Without question, deception permeates all facets of the human mating domain. People deceive potential mates about their own fitness values. People deceive potential partners about their level of commitment, their tendency toward kindness, their financial status, their social status, their educational background, and so forth.[42] People deceive current mates about such things as levels of love and commitment, attraction to others, infidelity, sexual performance, orgasm, sexual history, whether they cleaned the kitchen sink, and on and on!

And people deceive intrasexual rivals about all kinds of information. Consider the following:

1. Male trying to get another male to stop courting a woman that they both like: *"No dude, Sally's not into you, seriously—I heard that from both Valerie and Kim. She's definitely not into your type."*

2. Female trying to get a guy to stop courting a female rival: *"Really?! You didn't know that about her? And that's hardly the only time she's done that with a guy she met the same night!"*

As the late, great evolutionary psychologist Maureen O'Sullivan tells us:

> ... the mastery of sexual roles within relationships is a crucial aspect of mating intelligence, and a major locus of self-deception. Maintaining the state of being "in love" may take considerable self-monitoring of emotions, selective attention to the lover's positive aspects and willful blindness to their negative ones." (2008, p. 140)

In general terms, self-deception and other-deception in mating have several core features. People use deception to try to attract high-quality mates, to try to beat out intrasexual rivals in securing mates, to try to turn up satisfying sexual opportunities, and to try to form long-term mateships with individuals who are just right for long-term mating.

Like with so many things in the world of mating, a great deal of mating deception is sex specific. A good bit of human mating breaks down differently for males and females—and the nature of mating-relevant deception certainly shares this sex-differentiated nature.

Male-Specific Deception

Males deceive in the mating domain in areas that are highly relevant to successful reproduction as a male. Physically, males deceive about their athletic prowess, their strength, and their height—all physical features that are attractive to potential mates.[43] In terms of psychological traits, males deceive about their levels of kindness, orientation toward children and pets, status with groups, history, and their likely future.

Consider a short, unpopular, fat guy named Ted whose only sport is bowling and who has zero interest in either kids or kittens—and who is still at level 1 after being in his job for 6 years. Ted has a lot to deceive about! He may go to the gym and try to build up that pudgy little body as best he can. He may buy some special shoes that make him look tall along with some black clothes that hide his girth. He may present his career in a way that's semantically attractive (*"I'm an applied physicist working on our company's broad ecology initiative"* as opposed to *"I empty the recycling left near the cubicles ... "*).

None of these tactics makes Ted a horrible person. These kinds of mild tactics, in fact, typify social presentational behaviors in a broad sense. There's a fine line between "spin" and deception.

Do males deceive about these kinds of mating-relevant outcomes? Yes, all the time.[44] In fact, not only do they deceive about these kinds of things to women, but they also deceive about these kinds of things to other males (through intrasexual competition), and they even deceive themselves about these kinds of things.

In males, mating-relevant self-deception can be operationally defined by reporting that you engage in such behaviors as convincing yourself that you have more money than you actually do, convincing yourself that you're good at a particularly demanding sport, or convincing yourself that you've got a kind and humorous personality that others find attractive.

As an example of male-specific mating-relevant deception, consider Daniel Kruger's[45] recent research on sexual outcomes associated with overuse of credit cards and the incurring of credit card debt. On a simple good-bad continuum, I think we'd all agree that running up credit card debt is relatively bad. However, this is not true in all circumstances. Males who run up relatively high amounts of credit card debt are actually more successful than other males in turning up short-term mating success. In Kruger's research, there was a straightforward correspondence between number of sex partners and amount of credit card debt among male college students. Sometimes, deception pays evolutionary dividends.

Another example of such costly and false signaling on the part of males is found in fancy cars. In his work on consumer behavior from an evolutionary perspective, Gad Saad suggests that many of our purchases are ultimately rooted in mate signaling processes. In a study conducted by Saad and his team in the streets of Montreal,[46] young males were given the assignment of driving a Porsche or an old clunker either right through downtown or out toward the strip malls. Their testosterone, a hormone crucially related to mating activities, was measured after the drive. The data were clear: guys driving the Porsche through downtown were all hopped up on testosterone and ready to go. There are few false mating signals quite like a Porsche! Driving a Porsche that you don't own during a psychology experiment doesn't truly make you *all that*—but the lessons are apparent: signaling wealth—regardless of actuality—is a successful (if deceptive) strategy in the arsenal of male mating strategies.

Female-Specific Deception

If you're lucky, you haven't spent too much time in the make-up aisle. Intellectually, the make-up aisle is many things. It is a comment on vanity that permeates the West, a tribute to American consumerism, a lesson in the importance of external presentations, and in terms of evolutionary psychology, it is a window into our ancestral past.

In the mating domain, a major proximate goal for a woman is to appear to be in her peak reproductive years. Given how few ovulations a woman will have in her lifetime,[47] male psychology has been shaped to be very attuned to markers of female ovulation status. Through the use of make-up, a woman can give the impression that she is there (at peak ovulation), even if she's not. And this kind of deception may correspond to either not being at one's peak ovulatory cycle or not being within one's reproductive years. For this latter reason, many women who are postmenopausal use make-up to appear younger. Few, if any, use make-up to appear older.

Lipstick makes lips fuller and richer in color. Creams and lotions reduce the outward effects of wrinkles and help the skin mimic smoothness. Perfume helps a woman smell clean, flowery, and sweet. Hair color helps a woman take on the style of someone who is in the middle of her fecund years, regardless of the purchaser's age.

Women deceive in other ways in the mating world. Female groups are famous as bastions of gossip—women will shred one of their own to eliminate the competition. Research on mating-relevant deception in the world of women bears this out. Compared with men, women are more likely to spend money on products designed to physically enhance their appearance.[48] They are likely to denigrate rivals as promiscuous,[49] and they deceive males about such issues as desire for a long-term relationship (*no, seriously, I'm not interested in that! I'm too young to even think about settling down!*), desire for children, and, early in their relationship, they deceive regarding their own interest in sex[50]—all deceptive tactics designed to get the attention of a high-quality mate.[51]

Deception is a major part of human mating psychology; human mating intelligence is a tool designed partly for cutting through deception to allow people to make informed and accurate mating-relevant decisions.

Evolved Behavioral Sex Differences and a Hotbed of Academic Controversy

All this said, we think it's important to pause and comment on some important controversies in academia.[52] Not everyone appreciates the idea of evolved behavioral sex differences in humans. Critics of the evolutionist perspective on this issue paint it as endorsing some sort of evil genetic determinism, arguing that male-female differences are "natural" and cannot be undone, that sex roles in societies are, thus, immutable, and further, that attempts to change such sex roles through *socially progressive tactics* are pointless and unnatural.

Along with many of our evolutionist sisters and brothers,[53] we have argued that these portraits of the evolutionist approach are misguided and based on straw-man representations of evolutionary psychology and the context-sensitive, flexible nature of genes (see Chapters 3 and 5).

Research on sex differences exists in the midst of a sea of controversy. Scholars who reject the idea of human nature point fully to societal structures as the causal mechanisms that underlie male-female differences. Evolutionists, on the other hand, draw on evolution and human nature as critical in helping us understand these differences. This intellectual war rages—and likely will for years to come.[54] In this context, we believe that the evolutionist approach makes for an intellectually useful framework for understanding the nature of human sex differences—along with much else regarding human social behavior. Human deception is precisely the kind of area that seems to be sex differentiated in a way that is predictable in terms of the evolutionary perspective (of course, we acknowledge that there are differences *within* each sex in the use of deception).

Decoding Deception—Can We Do It?

Maureen O'Sullivan and Paul Ekman's research on *truth wizards* describes the psychology behind expert decoding—how those with exceptional skill separate deceptive from honest signals.[55] Several interesting results have emerged from this research. For one, people are generally not as good at detecting liars relative to how good they think they are. Second, there are a number of kinds of cues through which people reveal deception—however, in trying to detect deception, we often focus on the wrong cues.

Given the huge evolutionary costs associated with being lied to regarding mating-relevant material, the ability to detect mating-relevant deception should be a central part of human mating intelligence.

Let's consider some of Ekman and O'Sullivan's classic work on this topic, and then we can think about how this research paradigm could be adapted to study the nature of mating intelligence explicitly.

In a typical study on deception detection, Ekman and O'Sullivan would have two participants—the *target* and the *judge*. The target is the person who either lies or does not lie. The judge's job is to try to figure out whether the target is telling the truth. There are financial benefits. For instance, the target might go into a room with a briefcase that has a $10 bill in it. The target is instructed to take it or not—and then try to lie about the situation when being interviewed later. Lying would be either saying he did not take it when he actually did, or vice versa. If the lie is successful, the target gets the money (in some conditions, there were particular kinds of lies rewarded with even higher amounts). The judge is asked to determine whether the target is lying. Finally, there is a set of financial reward contingencies for the judge relating to whether he or she catches the liar.

Here's what Ekman and his colleagues[56] learned:

1. People are not really all that great at catching liars. Most people score at about baseline levels (50% accuracy).

2. People in professional positions that require high levels of social perception skills are typically no better at this kind of task than a randomly selected group of college students. Lawyers, judges, psychiatrists, and police officers all do so-so on average.
3. Members of the United States Secret Service, however, have it down—these guys do better on average.
4. We usually focus on the face in looking for a liar—but liars tend to control their facial muscles, only revealing deception via micro-expressions that are very quickly presented and hard to detect.
5. Bodily gestures are more likely to help us detect deception, but people tend to not focus on such gestures as much as they should.
6. Other avenues of communication, such the pitch of one's voice, also are helpful in trying to detect deception.
7. Mismatches between avenues of communication (e.g., *this was a warm physical gesture, but that tone of voice was cold . . .*) are often telling about liars.

When applied to the domain of mating, this research raises several questions. First and foremost: Are people better at lying in mating-relevant scenarios, and, related, are people better at detecting lies in the mating domain (compared with in other life domains)? Given how high the costs can be of getting this wrong, from an evolutionary standpoint, we predict that there have been particular selective pressures for people to be especially effective at lying when it comes to mating-relevant situations, and we expect this ability to go hand in hand with a similar increase in deception-detection ability in the world of mating. This all should be part of human mating intelligence.

We try to uncover deception all the time. Did your daughter really brush her teeth this morning? Was your co-worker late with her proposal because her computer actually broke down? Does your student really have a family emergency on the day of the test? But these are all small potatoes compared with the problem of trying to figure out whether your partner is having a torrid love affair with someone—especially if that someone is a central figure in your small social circle. Research shows: that hurts![57]

You might check your partner's computer history—and research shows that people do this.[58] (Interestingly, women are more likely to check their partners' email and Facebook accounts than men). You might ask your partner questions about whereabouts. You might ask the same questions of the could-be interloper, and you might keep a vigilant eye out, requiring significant cognitive resources, much more than required for the fleeting question about whether your student really did have a family emergency on Thursday.

Deception detection regarding infidelity is just one aspect of costly deception in the mating domain. Mates deceive about sexual interest, they deceive about long-term versus short-term mating goals, and they deceive about their sexual histories. Deception production and deception detection in the mating domain bear directly on Darwin's bottom line of reproductive fitness. Accordingly, the cognitive abilities involved in these tasks should make up a major chunk of human mating intelligence.

What happens when both self-deception and other-deception are taken to the extreme? It should come as no surprise that there are people out there who are extremely selfish and care very little about the emotions of others. Interestingly, these individuals may still benefit in the mating domain—at least in the short-term. In the next chapter, we take up the perennial question, *Do nice guys finish last?*

Do Nice Guys Finish Last?

The Multiple Routes to Mating Success

A wise man once told me, "As a man, you have to die once in order to live." I never fully appreciated his advice, nor did I understand it until I experienced it firsthand. From that time on, I understood the origins of the Jerk vs. Nice Guy battle. Readers may be asking themselves, "What in the world is this guy talking about?" Well, I'm referring to the widely known fact that women habitually date men that are jerks while the "nice" guys are often left twiddling their thumbs in solitaire. Does this sound familiar to anyone? Figuratively speaking, in order for a man to enjoy the company of women and be able to seduce them, his inner nice guy must first die through heartache. It is at this point that his inner bad boy surfaces and goes on the prowl.

(Smith, 2002, as quoted in
Urbaniak & Kilmann, 2006, p. 210).

We all know someone who is the classic *bad boy*: charming, rebellious, self-ish, thrill seeking, impulsive, and with a long list of sexual encounters and heartbreaks left in his path. Such depictions of the edgy guy with women all around him appear widely in popular culture, from James Dean to James Bond. The undeniable mating success of the bad boy has motivated many nice guys throughout the course of human evolution to gel their hair, put on leather jackets, and attempt to change their congenial ways. Today, there exists a wide assortment of dating coaches and "pick-up artists" available to teach the frustrated male how to adopt the attractive traits of the bad boy.[1]

There's no denying that bad boys can be attractive. The traits that bad boys tend to display (at least at first), such as good style, assertiveness, confidence, creativity, humor, charisma, high energy, and good social skills, are all attractive courtship displays. There's no doubt: bad boys exhibit a lot of the crucial aspects of mating intelligence.

But what do women really like about the bad boy? Is it the selfish, aggressive aspects, or the attractive traits that come along for the ride? Do bad boys have more sexual partners because of their higher sex drive, low self-control, aggressiveness, or persistent tactics, or because of their attractive traits? Or is it a bit of a mix of all these qualities? Is it *necessary* for the nice guy to be bad to obtain his mating goals in life? Can he just work on his mating intelligence skills? What does it even mean to be "bad"?

The media loves translating correlations into causation. For instance, *The Independent* reports on a correlation between being bad and number of sexual partners and boldly proclaims in the title: "Why Women Really Do Love Self-Obsessed Psychopaths."[2] Is this right? Do women really love self-obsessed psychopaths? *Really?*

These issues, phrased in a thousand different ways (e.g., *What's the allure of the bad boy? Do jerks finish first? Do nice guys finish last?*), have been debated ever since the dawn of humanity. There is no shortage of speculation coming from all different directions, including peer-reviewed journal articles, magazines, and numerous Internet blogs. This is a topic that intrigues scientists and civilians alike.

We may finally have some answers. Or at the very least, hints. In recent years, a good bit of scientific research has been conducted on this topic, both directly and indirectly. In this chapter, we explore this fascinating topic in a number of ways, drawing on many different literatures.

First, we pinpoint what exactly women mean when they use terms such as "bad boy" and "nice guy." Then we discuss the psychology of individuals who are primarily driven by selfish desires, and how they go about obtaining their mating goals. We go on to discuss the highly related topics of dominance and the attainment of social status. Then, we look at what women actually want. Finally, we present what we think are the most reasonable conclusions based on all of the current evidence. Join us in our search to get to the bottom of this age-old mystery.

How Are "Bad Boys" and "Nice Guys" Perceived?

First things first, let's clarify some terminology. Not all women mean the same thing by the terms "bad boy" and "nice guy." Edward Herold and Robin Milhausen[3] asked 174 female undergraduates enrolled in a first-year course on couple and family relations why they think nice guys are more likely to have fewer sexual partners. The researchers found that there were a number of different explanations for why nice guys are perceived as sexually inexperienced. One reason some women suggested was that nice guys are simply less forward with women. One wrote, *"To me 'nice guys' aren't as persistent or aggressive and don't use sleazy tactics to add another notch to their bedposts."* Another reason was that nice guys want serious relationships and value commitment. Some women wrote that they desired nice guys as friends instead of lovers. As one woman wrote, "*Nice guys are the ones we always see as just friends, and generally aren't seen as potential partners. In general, nice guys are overlooked when it comes to sexual relationships.*" Ouch!

Some women in their sample conceptualized nice guys as needy, weak, predictable, boring, inexperienced, and unattractive. One woman wrote, "*Nice guys often don't provide the drama and adventure women think they want.*" Other women were more flattering in their description of nice guys, viewing them as having positive traits such as a good personality, high standards and morals, and politeness. Nice guys were also considered to be more passive in their interactions with women, lacking confidence and being unsure of themselves. They were also thought to be willing to wait for sex because they cared about their partners and treated them with respect.

In general, nice guys were thought of as less physically attractive. As one woman put it, "*Nice guys are generally not as attractive, and have a great personality to compensate for this shortcoming. Unfortunately, looks, not personality, tend to get a woman into bed.*" Double ouch! No wonder nice guys are frustrated! (We would beg to differ with this woman, though, and refer her to Chapter 3).

Perceptions of bad boys fell into four different categories. One group of women saw bad boys as rebellious, mysterious, daring, arrogant, and dangerous. Another group saw bad boys as macho, strong, and confident. A third group viewed bad boys as fun, adventurous, spontaneous, and outgoing. A fourth group saw the bad boy as sexy, charming, good looking, and sexually experienced.

Women cited many different reasons for why bad boys are sexually experienced. Some women suggested that bad boys use aggressive, dishonest, and manipulative tactics to obtain sex. Others suggested that bad boys are more likely to approach and ask women for sex because of their self-confidence and prior successes with women, which made them less fearful of rejection. Participants reported that the sexual success of bad boys led them to be viewed as more desirable and appealing by women. Bad boys were also considered to be more physically and sexually attractive, approaching relationships more casually, caring more about sex than intimate relationships, and sexually unfaithful.

These are college-aged women, between the ages of 18 and 25 years at one university writing these responses, so the findings must be taken with a grain of salt. Women at different stages of their life and with different life experiences may have different conceptions of (as well as interest in) "bad boys" and "nice guys". Still, this research provides a general idea of how these different kinds of men are perceived.

Taking these results at face value, though, we can see that nice guys are perceived as good people, friends, and marriage partners, but not passionate lovers. Bad boys, on the other hand, are perceived as having more of a mix of positive and negative qualities. On the one hand, bad boys are perceived as having some very attractive traits (e.g., sexy, confident, charming). On the other hand, they are also seen as exhibiting negative behaviors such as aggression and duplicity. Therefore, a number of traits are "bad" in the sense that they are related to highly selfish, exploitative mating strategies.

Although a certain degree of self-deception and other-deception can be adaptive in the mating domain, particularly in the courtship phase (see Chapters 6 and 7), some individuals take deception and selfishness to the extreme, almost completely lacking in the emotional intelligence skills required to respect the feelings of others, let alone form an intimate, meaningful, and committed relationship (not that they necessarily want to).

As we noted in Chapter 3, differences in various personality traits may exist because of the adaptive benefits they may confer on survival and reproductive outcomes. In that chapter, we reviewed research on agreeableness and conscientiousness and demonstrated that individuals high in these two traits show more restraint in many aspects of their lives, behaviors that are conducive to maintaining a long-term relationship. We also mentioned that those with *low* levels of agreeableness and conscientiousness behave in ways that may increase their short-term mating success. A reduction in both of these traits— agreeableness and conscientiousness—is an integral component of a number of personality disorders that are receiving considerable research attention.

In recent years, psychologists have looked at the traits and behaviors of these socially undesirable individuals: those with narcissism, Machiavellianism, and psychopathy. Although they have traditionally been studied only in clinical settings, researchers have started to investigate these traits and behaviors in the general population. Let's zoom in on these people, get into their head, and look at their mating outcomes to get a better sense of how these individuals accomplish their selfish mating goals.

Narcissism

Narcissists display high levels of self-focus, self-importance, and a sense of entitlement while seeking admiration, attention, prestige, and status.[4] This self-focus is even reflected in their brains! People with narcissistic tendencies are quicker at identifying their own picture compared with a picture of a stranger or a friend, and their brains show increased activation in regions associated with self-awareness and representations of the self.[5]

Because enjoying the social scene is a means of boosting status and ego, narcissists are very extraverted and social. According to W. Keith Campbell, "the social scene can be like a drug to them. They get so excited by the social scene that they feel a 'rush.' This rush makes them even more cocky. They feel popular, important, powerful, and desirable."[6] There's no doubt: narcissists are addicted to fleeting ego boosts, and the transient social scene gives them just the boost they crave. Of course, not all extraverts are narcissistic, but narcissists do tend to display extraverted behaviors. They are sensation seekers; they crave excitement and novel experiences. Narcissists aren't interested in just any sort of social scene, though: they intentionally seek out people who will maintain their high positive self-image and intentionally avoid people who may give them a harsh dose of realism.

Unsurprisingly, research shows that narcissists do not tend to do well in long-term relationships and suffer from all sorts of intrapersonal and interpersonal problems.[7] Indeed, their low need for affiliation and high need for power are not conducive to maintaining intimate relationships. Narcissists do report being generally *uninterested* in caring relationships, so they have very few motivations to change. Twenge and Campbell suggest that "this apparent independence on the part of narcissists, however, may veil a deep need for social acceptance—or perhaps for social dominance."[8] It has also been suggested that narcissists may be their own worst enemy because they "lack the self-control necessary to inhibit the behaviors that thwart the attainment of their goals."[9]

Narcissism reaches its peak in adolescence and declines with age. Although part of the reason for this decline may be reduced levels of testosterone, as people get older it also becomes less socially acceptable and increasingly pathetic to display narcissistic traits. "It is one thing to see a twenty-five-year-old with a leased Mercedes lying to a young woman; it is another thing to see a sixty-five-year-old doing the same thing," notes Campbell.[10] There are also sex differences in displays of narcissism.[11] One study, which consisted of face-to-face interviews with 34,653 adults, found that men on average are more narcissistic than women across the life span.[12]

Narcissism can be broken down into various related facets. Robert Emmons[13] distinguishes between *leadership/authority* (those who enjoy being a leader and being seen as an authority), *self-absorption/self-admiration* (those who admire their own physical appearance and personality), *superiority/arrogance* (those who overestimate their own abilities), and *exploitativeness/entitlement* (those who enjoy manipulating and exploiting others and expect favors from others). Even though these four facets are moderately related to one another, there still is a lot of variability amongst narcissists in terms of how they express narcissism. Also, each of these facets lies on a continuum in the general population. In other words, all of us are at least a little bit narcissistic!

All of these facets of narcissism can be quite adaptive to an individual in achieving his or her goals. As we've pointed out repeatedly throughout this book, adaptive does not mean the same thing as socially desirable. Each facet of narcissism can cause great harm to others. Also, some facets may be more adaptive than others. Some researchers have argued that the exploitative-ness/entitlement facet of narcissism may be the most *maladaptive* facet of narcissism.[14]

Narcissists tend to be attracted to the short-term mating scene just as much as they are to the transient social scene. In fact, some researchers have argued that narcissists are so well suited to the short-term mating domain that narcissism may have evolved *for* this purpose!

The Evolution of Narcissism

An emerging hypothesis by Nicholas Holtzman and Michael Strube[15] makes the case that narcissism emerged as a particular form of dominance about 1.5 million years ago when variation in mating strategies emerged. They note that narcissism involves many adaptive traits and that the viability of short-term mating, through the process of evolution, shaped narcissism. In support of their argument, they cite three main links to narcissism.

Attractiveness

First, Holtzman and Strube note that narcissism and attractiveness tend to be associated. To be sure, some studies have suggested that narcissists have positive illusions about themselves that are not always correct.[16] For instance, April Bleske-Rechek, Mark Remiker, and Jonathan Baker[17] found that even though narcissists thought they were hot stuff, outside judges did not rate those high in narcissism any different in physical attractiveness than those lower in narcissism. Still, narcissists will rejoice in the streets when they hear that looking across a great number of studies in total, conducted on more than 1,000 people, there does seem to be a relationship between physical attractiveness and narcissism (although they probably won't be surprised!). Even though the relationship is small, it's still substantial when you consider that the correlation is about as high as what is typically found between other personality traits and attractiveness. Of course, the link here between narcissism and attractiveness doesn't explain *why* narcissists tend to be considered more attractive. Are their bodies more attractive, or is it just all the ornamention?[18]

Recent research suggests it is their "physically attractive veneer" that is attractive, not their unadorned bodies. Consider a study conducted by Simine Vazire, Laura Naumann, Peter Rentfrow, and Samuel Gosling.[19] They found that narcissists put a lot more preparation into their appearance; wore fashionable, stylish, and expensive clothing; appeared cheerful; and were rated as more attractive at first sight compared with those scoring lower in narcissism. They also found effects unique to each gender. Female narcissists applied more make-up, plucked their eyebrows more, and revealed more cleavage than females scoring lower in narcissism, and male narcissists ditched their eye-glasses and pumped up their muscles more compared with the less narcissist males in their study.

The attraction of narcissists is not purely physical. Although narcissists do not fare well in terms of long-term relationships, they can initially be quite striking and attractive as social partners. Del Paulhus[20] found that after the first roughly 2½-hour student work group session, narcissists were rated as *more* agreeable, conscientious, open-minded, competent, entertaining, and well-adjusted by the other members of the group. After the *seventh* session, though, narcissists were rated by the other members of the group as less agree-able, less well adjusted, less warm, and more hostile and arrogant. What a contrast to what the group members thought of the very same narcissistic indi-viduals on the first day!

As S. Mark Young and Drew Pinksy note, narcissists' *"extraverted behavior and desire to be liked can make them enjoyable to work with initially"* because they *"tend to create drama and, thus, are entertaining to watch, especially in competitive situations."* [21] No doubt, narcissists can be fun (if not sometimes excruciating) to watch on reality TV. But what exactly is so attractive about narcissists, at least initially, that explains their popularity? What cues are they broadcasting? Which facets of the narcissist are most related to their popularity, sometimes even celebrity, status?[22]

In a series of four very clever studies, Mitja Back, Stefan Schmukle, and Boris Egloff[23] sought to determine why narcissists are popular at "zero acquain-tance." They propose that narcissists are more popular at first sight because of the cues they produce. They investigated four cues in particular, which they hypothesized, based on prior research,[24] would be related to the popularity of narcissists at first sight. In the researcher's own words:

> ... we assume that narcissism predicts all of the four relevant cue domains—attractiveness, from their flashy and neat attire; interper-sonal warmth, from their charming glances at strangers; competence, from their self-assured behavior; and humor, from their witty verbal expressions. As a result, they thus should enjoy greater initial popu-larity than non-narcissists. (Berscheid & Reis, 1998, p. 134)

Indeed, people often describe narcissists as having a "charismatic air," which usually comprises attractiveness, competence, interpersonal warmth, and humor. Their first study involved 73 freshman psychology students who had never met each other before. At the beginning of an introductory session, each student was randomly assigned a seat number. Then, one by one, students took turns in a round-robin fashion going to a marked spot on the floor and intro-ducing themselves, after which the other freshman evaluated how likeable they found the person and the extent to which they would like to get to know the person. Each introduction was videotaped, and four groups of independent observers rated various physical cues, nonverbal body cues, nonverbal facial cues, and verbal cues of the speaker that were hypothesized by the researchers to relate to attraction. After all the students gave their introductions and the session was over, the students were given a number of surveys to fill out at home, including a self-report narcissism questionnaire.

Narcissists tended to be more liked at first sight, and they exhibited neater and flashier appearances, more charming facial expressions, more self-assured body movement, and more humorous verbal expressions. Perhaps most revealing, though, is that not all facets of narcissism were equally predictive of popularity. In fact, the leadership/authority facet was almost completely unrelated to first impressions. Their most disturbing finding is that the facet that most strongly predicted popularity was the exploitativeness/entitlement facet. Additionally, although all of the facets of narcissism were substantially related to all of the cues that were rated by the observers, the exploitativeness/entitlement facet had more consistent and stronger correlations with the cues than any of the other facets!

In three other studies, the researchers found a striking consistency in this pattern of results. Narcissists with a sense of entitlement and a tendency to exploit others tended to be more popular at first sight for uninvolved perceivers who just watched the video of the introduction and were thus exposed to the full information of the target's behaviors but did not have to actually make an introduction themselves (Study 2), perceivers who were only given physical and nonverbal information of the speaker (no audio condition, Study 3), and perceivers who just had physical information only (body-only condition, Study 4).

In each of these conditions, all the cues that were available were all that were necessary to produce the same pattern of results. For instance, in the body-only condition (Study 4), flashy and neat clothing was all that was needed to show a correlation between the exploitativeness/entitlement facet of narcissism and popularity. In other words, when the only cue was fancy dress, fancy dress predicted popularity, and those with this style of dress tended to score higher in the exploitativeness/entitlement facet of narcissism.

In another study, the same researchers[25] used the Social Relations Lens Model methodology[26] (see Chapter 5) to assess the most popular students in an introductory class in Germany. Each student's self-introduction was evaluated by the rest of the freshman on two dimensions: *liking* ("How likable do you find this person?" "Would you like to get to know this person?") and *meta-perceptions of initial liking* ("How likable will this person find you?" "Will this person like to get to know you?").

Each freshman was also given a packet of questionnaires to complete at home, including measures of personality. Among other personality traits, the personality battery included 35 items related to *self-centered values* (e.g., social power, forgiveness, success, courtesy, ambition), which were combined to form an overall dimension of self-centered versus self-transcendent values. Afterward, all videotapes were coded by independent observers for observable physical, nonverbal, and audible cues.

Those high in neuroticism and low in self-esteem *expected* to be disliked, when in reality neither neuroticism nor self-esteem were related to popularity. It seems, then, that neurotic people and those with low self-esteem have inaccurate perceptions of reality. Extraverts, on the other hand, were *more liked* and were also expected to like others more. In reality though, extraversion was not related to being a liker or expecting to be liked.

Most alarmingly, those who reported more self-centered values were more liked and were also expected to like others more. In reality, self-centered people actually disliked others more, evaluating their peers more negatively! Therefore, although self-centered people may be perceived as more friendly, they are actually less friendly. Why were extraverts and self-centered individuals evaluated more positively? What cues were they broadcasting that influenced their popularity?

Extraversion was related to cues that had a positive effect on popularity: fashionable appearance; speedy, energetic, and self-assured body movements; friendly facial expressions; strong voice; and original self-introductions. Interestingly, those with self-centered values tended to display very similar cues. Prior research has linked the popularity of the extravert to their desire to captivate the attention of others and to their expressive behaviors, verbal humor, and fashionable dress.[27] This study shows that extraverts and self-centered people share similar behavioral cues. These cues appear to be related to emotional expressiveness and social dominance.[28] Extraverts and self-centered people both are signaling these traits, and these traits influence popularity.

People are very quick at detecting extraversion, and a number of narcissists are bound to fall through the cracks with such rapid assessment. Prior research has shown that people accurately perceive extraversion even after being exposed to a face for only 50 milliseconds.[29] Consistent with the study by Back and colleagues,[30] signals such as cheerfulness and positive facial expressions were particularly related to extraversion. Independent of personality, the researchers also found that friendliness of facial expression (amount of smiling) and pleasantness of voice were the best predictors of liking and meta-perceptions. Unsurprisingly, prior research has also found that smiling plays an important role in attraction, especially among women.[31]

Narcissism is also associated with attention-getting behaviors that may specifically excite sexual desire among potential short-term mates. Narcissists do use more sexual language in their everyday life. Nicholas Holtzman, Simine Vazire, and Matthias Mehl[32] set out to find out what happens when you stick audio recorders on a bunch of narcissists in the general population and listen to them naturally go about their day. What do narcissists sound like?

First, the researchers administered a self-report scale of narcissism with items such as "*Everybody likes to hear my stories.*" Then participants wore a small, pocket-sized digital audio recorder for 4 days during their waking hours. Every 12.5 minutes, the recorder recorded 30-second snippets of audio from their environment. Participants had *no clue* as to when the recorder was on.

The researchers then transcribed the audio and submitted the transcriptions to a well-validated psychological text analysis program. They focused their analysis on variables particularly related to narcissism: *extraverted acts* (talking, being in a group, and socializing), *disagreeable acts* (using swear words or anger words), *academic disengagement* (class attendance), and *sexual language use* (e.g., "naked").

The researchers found that narcissism was correlated with extraverted acts, being especially predictive of being in a group, socializing with others, and talking about friends. These correlations were much stronger among female narcissists and remained significant after controlling for extraversion, suggesting that there is something unique about narcissism that predicts extraverted acts above and beyond the personality trait of extraversion (see Chapter 3).

Narcissism was also positively related to engagement in disagreeable behaviors, including arguing, using swear words, and using anger words. For both genders, narcissists high in exploitativeness/entitlement were *the most* disagreeable lot.

As the researchers note, this combination of high extraversion and low agreeableness in narcissists has both benefits and disadvantages:

> Specifically, while most narcissists (especially women in this particular sample) exhibit many extraverted behaviors that are likely to make a good first impression (e.g., socializing, talking about friends), they also exhibit disagreeable behaviors, which probably helps to explain the difficulties they have maintaining favorable reputations over time. (Holtzman, Vazire, & Mehl, 2010, p. 482)

Although the total narcissism composite was not related to class attendance, the exploitativeness/entitlement facet of narcissism was positively related to academic disengagement in both men and women. This link remained after controlling for the personality trait of conscientiousness. This supports the notion that the exploitativeness/entitlement facet is the most maladaptive facet of narcissism. As the researchers put it, this correlation

> ... suggests a mechanism by which self-enhancement is associated with academic disengagement over time...inflated self-importance

may lead to shirking academic obligations, which may potentially contribute to disappointing academic outcomes. (Holtzman, Vazire, & Mehl, 2010, p. 482)

Narcissism was also positively correlated with a greater use of sexual language. As an example, one male narcissist was heard on the audio recorder saying, "Hey we can watch porn on the go. Laptop yes," whereas a female narcissist was much more direct, noting, "I want, like, elaborate sex." This link was strongest among narcissists high in exploitativeness/entitlement and leadership/authority and remained even after controlling for potential overlap with the use of anger and swear words that had sexual connotations. The researchers note that this "impulsive sexual strategy" is "consistent with the view that narcissists tend to be impulsive and seek short-term gains."[33] The use of sexually explicit language may be part of the narcissist's short-term mating strategy. By signaling to everyone his or her strategy, the narcissist makes it crystal clear what he or she is looking for: potential mates who share the same mating strategy (see Chapter 2).

Coercive Tendencies

Narcissists are also more sexually coercive. They have more fantasies about coercion and sadism compared with non-narcissists, and they report actually engaging in coercive and sadistic sexual behaviors.[34] Narcissists tend to look at sexual behavior as chances for manipulation and power over the other person.[35]

Indeed, the language and demeanor of narcissism are often geared toward one objective: to maintain power in an interaction. One study found that "conversational narcissism" involves boasting, refocusing the topic of the conversation on the self, exaggerating hand and body movements, using a loud tone of voice, and showing disinterest by "glazing over" when others speak.[36] In the language of Malamuth's Confluence Model,[37] narcissists tend to have an *antagonistic* sexual and social strategy.[38]

In the sexual realm, promiscuity is a key strategy that allows narcissists to maintain control. Narcissists are keen at employing the *principle of least interest*, in which the partner with the least interest in a relationship has the greatest power. Promiscuity also helps narcissists in being able to always search for a better deal.[39] In fact, when narcissists think their partner is committed, they are more willing to cheat, presumably because they feel as though they are more likely to get away with it.[40] Narcissists get a rush out of getting away with high-risk behaviors such as cheating on their partner or convincing partners to do things they wouldn't normally do, such as engaging in anal sex.[41]

Because narcissists tend to feel so entitled to having mates, they can get quite aggressive when sexually rejected, punishing the person who sexually rejects them.[42] Narcissists also display aggression when socially rejected. This aggression-rejection link was explored by Jean Twenge and W. Keith Campbell[43] in their fascinating paper, "Isn't It Fun to Get the Respect that We're Going to Deserve? Narcissism, Social Rejection, and Aggression." They found across four studies that those scoring higher in narcissism tended to display more anger and aggression after experiencing social rejection, even punishing (i.e., administering a white noise burst) innocent bystanders!

Daniel Jones and Delroy Paulhus[44] found similar results. Those scoring high in narcissism were more likely to punish (i.e., send a white noise burst) to those who gave them negative feedback on an essay (*"This is the worst essay I have ever read!"*). Narcissism was not related to aggression in the positive feedback condition (*"No comments, great essay!"*). Interestingly, the researchers found that those scoring higher on psychopathy were more likely to display aggression in response to physical provocation (receiving a blast of loud white noise) but not personal insult. Therefore, narcissists seem to be particularly likely to show aggression in response to threats to their ego.

Adolescent Peaks

Narcissism peaks in adolescence,[45] and levels of narcissism and entitlement are particularly high among the current generation in individualistic cultures like the United States.[46] But can narcissism in adolescence be adaptive in young adulthood?

In a sample of 807 undergraduates and their family members, Patrick Hill and Brent Roberts[47] found that narcissism and all its components were related to age: the older the participants, the less they reported engaging in narcissistic behaviors. Narcissism was more strongly related to life satisfaction among the students (aged 18 to 25 years) than among their adult participants. Their findings were particularly informative when narcissism was broken down. The relation between life satisfaction and *leadership/authority* and *grandiose exhibitionism* were more positive for younger than older participants. In contrast, *entitlement/exploitativeness* was associated with lower levels of life satisfaction regardless of age.

How were narcissists perceived across the life span? Narcissists weren't seen as very open to new experiences at any age. Those scoring high in leadership/authority and grandiose exhibitionism were perceived as more extraverted across the life span. Adult mothers scoring high in narcissism were perceived as less agreeable and conscientious, and more neurotic, whereas these correlations weren't significant among the students. The differences between the students and mothers were particularly strong when looking at neuroticism.

Therefore, there appear to be developmental periods in which narcissism is more prominent and may provide greater benefits to life satisfaction. An inflated sense of self may be beneficial for the transition to adulthood, as a coping mechanism to get through the rocky period of adolescence when emerging adults are just beginning to form their own, unique identities. Society expects adults, however, to give up their narcissistic grandiosity of the past in order to promote social well-being and become a positive contributor to society. From an evolutionary perspective, Holtzman and Strube[48] argue that adolescent peaks may be an indicator that narcissism may have evolved as a result of reproductive success. Most adolescents have not yet acquired the resources required for high social standing in society; therefore, in adolescence, narcissistic behaviors may be a more direct path to reproductive success.

Narcissism can also be adaptive in adulthood, depending on the career. There is some evidence that rates of narcissism differ depending on the career. Young and Pinksy[49] found that celebrities are significantly more narcissistic than MBA students as well as the general population. Even among celebrities, there are differences in narcissism. Reality television personalities are the most narcissistic, followed by comedians, actors, and musicians. Because Young and Pinsky did not find a relationship between narcissism and the amount of experience in the entertainment industry, it is probable that celebrities have narcissistic tendencies before entering the industry. Therefore, another important line of further research is to investigate individual differences in narcissism and the roles to which different people are attracted.

Can narcissists change? Even though narcissism does show some heritability, the influence of learning and contextual factors in the development of mating strategies is crucial (also see Chapter 3).[50] Also, there are still very active debates in the field about how narcissism develops.[51] An important future line of research will be to investigate both the genetic and societal factors that affect narcissism and the contextual factors that determine whether the traits and behaviors associated with narcissism are more or less likely to display themselves.

Some things are clear: Narcissists possess a number of attractive traits (e.g., verbal intelligence, humor, confidence) and sexually coercive tactics that can increase their chances of short-term mating success but they also possess traits (e.g., aggression, entitlement) that make long-term relationships difficult to maintain. Narcissists are adept at applying many of the principles of mating intelligence. They have style, charm, confidence, humor, and verbal wit. Therefore, even though in the case of narcissists there may be a dark side beneath (especially for those scoring high on exploitativeness/entitlement), there still are benefits of these traits for mating, particularly in short-term social situations.

Solving Longstanding Narcissism Paradoxes

Emmons noted a number of paradoxes of narcissism.[52] More recent findings have helped solve some paradoxes in the field.[53] One paradox concerns the adaptive value of narcissism. How can the most maladaptive facet (exploitative-ness/entitlement) of an already maladaptive interpersonal trait (narcissism) also be the most effective trait in impressing others? Back and colleagues[54] speculated that, paradoxically, the positive feedback that narcissists receive at first acquaintance may confirm their superiority and strengthen their search for similar situations that will allow them to get similar responses. As these researchers noted, "being admired by others is like a drug for narcissists." This behavior often hinders them from sticking with social contexts for a longer period of time, often causing dysfunction in longer-term relationships. Although it may seem like a vicious cycle, this may not be a problem for narcissists, who don't tend to be all that interested in maintaining deep, meaningful, long-term relationships anyhow.

Most narcissists don't care about the long-term (they tend to be more impulsive anyway), but their desire to exploit others and their sense of entitlement *is* adaptive for them in the short-term, even if it hurts others. Indeed, Back and colleagues[55] showed that narcissists scoring high on the exploitativeness/entitlement facet *are* more popular at zero acquaintance. As the researchers noted, considerations of the different facets of narcissism and of the varied situational circumstances that these facets can display (short-term vs. long-term) can be combined to more fully understand the social consequences of narcissism.

Another paradox, which Emmons[56] called the *narcissistic paradox*, is the narcissists' tendency to devalue others while at the same time needing the admiration of others. In their desire for self-affirmation, however, they destroy the very bonds that they crave.[57] Back and colleagues noted that narcissists can "solve" the paradox by only relying on positive feedback from those with zero acquaintance whom they do not have to value: "Because others truly like narcissists at first sight, they contribute to the maintenance of the narcissists' most paradoxical mindset."[58]

Another paradox lies in the *developmental pathway* to narcissism, especially the role of parental reactions. Which type of parent contributes to the narcissistic child: the parent who overvalues the child (as some researchers have speculated) or the parent who undervalues the child (as other researchers have speculated)? A combination of *both* overvaluation and devaluation can contribute to narcissism.[59] The overvaluation-devaluation combination has been suggested by Freud and has received some recent empirical support.[60]

A fourth and final paradox noted by Back and colleagues[61] is the narcissist's lack of insight. These researchers suggest that it is this short-term positive feedback that contributes to the narcissists' lack of self-criticism because they just don't see a need for it. Because they don't get support in the long run, their self is perpetually vulnerable, making immediate admiration even more of a necessity.

Machiavellianism and Psychopathy

Narcissists aren't the only socially undesirable individuals who have recently been studied under the psychologist's microscope. Machiavellian individuals are manipulative and opportunistic, and psychopaths are impulsive, thrill seeking, and prone to lying. Both traits are associated with lower levels of empathy and emotional intelligence.[62] After all, empathy involves "feelings that are more congruent with another's situation than with one's own situation,"[63] and this requires self-sacrifice.

The ability to automatically feel empathy for others is strongly tied to emotional intelligence and is crucial in facilitating harmonious relationships (see Chapter 7). Like narcissism, psychopathy has multiple facets that vary in the general population.[64] A common distinction is made between primary and secondary psychopathy. *Primary psychopathy* consists of the affective and interpersonal aspects of psychopathy, such as callousness, fearlessness, manipulation, lying, high self-esteem (although this may not represent genuine self-esteem, as we discuss later), and social dominance; whereas secondary psychopathy consists of the antisocial aspects of psychopathy, including impulsivity, boredom susceptibility, and aggression. Those with higher levels of secondary psychopathy tend to be more anxious and introverted and tend to display lower levels of self-esteem than those scoring higher in primary psychopathy.

Recent, interesting research examined the question of whether Machiavellianism and psychopathy were related to inappropriate empathic responses to the facial expressions of others in a nonclinical population. Farah Ali, Ines Amorim, and Tomas Chamorro-Premuzic[65] found that those with higher levels of primary psychopathy and Machiavellianism tended to experience more positive affect when looking at sad images. When they presented pictures that were emotionally neutral, however, those with higher levels of secondary psychopathy, Machiavellianism, and anxiety tended to experience more negative affect.

In terms of emotional intelligence, they found that those with higher levels of self-reported emotional intelligence tended to score lower in secondary psychopathy, Machiavellianism, and anxiety and engaged in positive affect in response to the neutral images. Interestingly, there was no significant relation (either positive or negative) between emotional intelligence and primary psychopathy. They also found sex differences: males, in general, had higher scores on primary psychopathy and Machiavellianism than females.

These results are consistent with another recent study on the links among Machiavellianism, emotional intelligence, and Theory of Mind.[66] The researchers studied 109 primary school children and found that Machiavellianism and social and emotional understanding were negatively related to each other.

Further analyses showed that increased levels of emotional and social under-standing did not lead to manipulation in social encounters among the girls in the sample, whereas this was not the case for boys in the sample.

Another recent study conducted by Farah Ali and Tomas Chamorro-Premuzic[67] found that females, on average, show lower levels of primary psychopathy (but not secondary psychopathy) and Machiavellianism compared with males. The researchers also found that females showed reduced levels of short-term mat-ing, consistent with other results reviewed in this book (see Chapter 5). Those scoring higher on Machiavellianism tended to show more of a short-term mat-ing orientation but also tended to score lower in life satisfaction and intimacy.

Primary psychopathy was also positively related to promiscuity, but was not related to life satisfaction (either positively or negatively). Secondary psychopa-thy, on the other hand, was negatively related to intimacy and life satisfaction. Surprisingly, primary psychopathy was *positively* associated with all three com-ponents of Robert Sternberg's theory of love: intimacy, passion, and commit-ment! To explain this very counterintuitive finding, the researchers noted that because people with psychopathic traits are experts at manipulating people, they may report being closer to their partner with the goal of manipulating them better. As psychopathy expert Robert Hare[68] notes, psychopaths "recog-nize and turn to their own advantage the hang-ups and self-doubts that most people have."

Indeed, those scoring higher in psychopathy in the general population are better at perceiving victim vulnerability and most likely use the same set of coercive tactics that narcissists employ. In a study conducted by Sarah Wheeler, Angela Book, and Kimberly Costello,[69] 47 male students watched 12 short video clips of people (8 men and 4 women) walking and provided an esti-mate of each person's vulnerability to being mugged. Those scoring higher on a self-report scale of psychopathy tended to have greater accuracy in assess-ing vulnerability to victimization. The results of Ali and Chamorro-Premuzic's study[70] reinforce the importance of distinguishing primary psychopathy from secondary psychopathy in a nonclinical population.[71] Both primary and sec-ondary psychopathy are associated with coercive behaviors, but individuals with primary psychopathic traits tend to be more extraverted and have higher levels of confidence and self-esteem, a difference that plays out in the mating domain.

Psychopaths are not just opportunistic. They also are highly impulsive. It's important to distinguish between different forms of impulsivity, however. Scott Dickman[72] differentiates between two different forms: functional and dysfunctional impulsivity. *Functional impulsivity* is related to idea generation, enthusiasm, adventurousness, and the ability to make quick decisions. On the other hand, *dysfunctional impulsivity* is related to erratic disorderliness, dis-traction, and inaccurate decision making. In a sample of undergraduates and adults, Daniel Jones and Delroy Paulhus[73] found that both narcissistic and psychopathic individuals tended to show higher levels of overall impulsivity.

More telling, though, were correlations with different types of impulsivity. Psychopathy was primarily associated with dysfunctional impulsivity, whereas narcissism was primarily related to functional impulsivity. Machiavellianism was unrelated to either type of impulsivity. This research is consistent with research showing that psychopaths lack the ability to inhibit their antisocial impulses. The lack of relation between impulsivity and Machiavellianism is interesting and suggests that Machiavellian individuals may have an advantage over psychopaths and narcissists when trying to achieve their selfish goals because their moderate impulsive control may allow them to "refrain from counterproductive behaviors despite their selfish intentions."[74]

This combination of opportunism and dysfunctional impulsivity often leads those scoring high in psychopathy to engage in riskier sexual practices. Risky sexual behaviors are those that are associated with a variety of negative health and social consequences, including sexually transmitted diseases and unplanned pregnancies. Examples include having sex without a condom and having sex while intoxicated. A recent study of college students investigated the relationship between the various components of subclinical psychopathy and engagement in risky sexual behaviors.[75] The researchers distinguished between a *fearless dominance* component of psychopathy (i.e., primary psychopathy) and an *impulsive antisociality* component of psychopathy (i.e., secondary psychopathy). Fearless dominance consists of traits such as social potency, stress immunity, and fearlessness, whereas impulsive antisociality consists of traits such as carefree nonplanfulness, impulsive nonconformity, Machiavellian egocentricity, and blame externalization.

Although the researchers found that impulsive antisociality was associated with risky sexual behaviors for both men and women, fearless dominance was associated with risky sexual behaviors only for the men in the sample. The researchers also administered a self-report measure of sensation seeking and found that when fearless dominance, impulsive antisociality, and sensation seeking were all entered into the same equation, only impulsive antisociality remained a significant predictor of risky sexual behaviors. This suggests that the trait of impulsive antisociality is a key driving force toward engagement in risky sexual behaviors.

These findings are consistent with other research showing that people with lower levels of self-control have greater trouble restraining sexual behavior[76] and with research showing that people with attention deficit disorder (a condition associated with lower levels of self-control) also tend to engage in risky sexual behaviors.[77] These findings are also consistent with those of Jonason and Tost,[78] who found across two studies that psychopathy is associated with multiple measures of self-control, including a tendency to discount future consequences, and high rates of attention deficit disorder. Psychopathy was also related to a fast life history strategy (see Chapter 3). Note that this research doesn't mean that a person with a fast life history strategy or attention deficit disorder is necessarily going to be socially deviant. These are just correlations. Both traits, however, are associated with greater impulsivity, which *permits* such risky behaviors.

Can anything be done to reduce engagement in risky sexual behaviors? Jones and Paulhus[79] suggest that self-regulation exercises, such as practicing using one's nondominant hand for everyday activities,[80] could decrease risky sexual behaviors in men and women high in impulsive antisociality. Such interventions may not be easy among more clinical psychopaths, however. Psychopaths have very low levels of self-control and do not have much of a conscience for their actions.[81] As we've noted before, research suggests that a set of brain areas located in the frontal lobe of humans support self-control processes. These "executive functions" enable humans to plan, inhibit, or delay responding.[82] The extent to which these areas of the brain light up in an individual predicts whether that person is likely to follow the rule norms of society or engage in a wide variety of risky behaviors.[83] Research shows that a lack of positive peer influence, antisocial behavior, deficits in self-control, impulsivity, lack of future orientation, and risk taking all relate to systematic deficits in performance-based measures of executive functioning.[84]

Psychopaths do not just lack self-control, though. They also seem to have emotional deficits that make it difficult for them to empathize with the pain of others (even if they can read others well enough to exploit their weaknesses). This lack of empathy is found among those high in Machiavellianism, narcissism, and psychopathy, partially explaining why these three traits significantly correlate with each other in the general population.

The Dark Triad

Recently, researchers have painted a larger portrait of the collection of traits and behaviors of socially undesirable individuals. This "Dark Triad" includes Machiavellianism, subclinical narcissism, and subclinical psychopathy.[85] Each one of these traits has its own distinctive flavor and social engagement style that is adaptive in certain situations but maladaptive in others.[86] For instance, narcissism is the "lighter cousin" of psychopathy[87] because it involves manipulation tactics oriented more toward social rewards and can involve *soft* tactics such as offering compliments, whereas psychopathy involves more *hard* tactics such as threats.[88] Even though all three Dark Triad traits are partially separable, they are all positively correlated with one another and with low agreeableness and low empathy. Taken together, these three traits represent a social style geared toward exploiting others in short-term social contexts.

In fact, the Dark Triad may have evolved through the course of human evolution as an effective short-term mating strategy.[89] At least, this is what researchers argue in a recent study.[90] In a sample of 224 undergraduates, Peter Jonason, Norman Li, Gregory Webster, and David Schmitt found that the Dark Triad was significantly correlated with various dimensions of short-term mating, such as having more sexual partners and more desire for short-term flings. Consistent with the other research presented in this chapter and with parental investment theory, higher rates of the Dark Triad were found in the males in their sample. This study (along with nearly every other one presented in this chapter) was conducted with college students, so the extent to which this difference between males and females holds across a wider age range remains to be seen.

A number of recent studies have investigated the personality profile of those scoring high on the Dark Triad, including genetic relationships between Big Five personality traits and the Dark Triad.[91] Across two studies, Peter Jonason, Norman Li, and Emily Teicher[92] investigated the psychological profile typical of those scoring high in the Dark Triad traits. In their first study, they found that those scoring high in the Dark Triad traits tended to be more extraverted and open to experience and to have higher self-esteem. They also tended to be less agreeable, less neurotic, and less conscientious. In their second study, they assessed self-reported altruism and had participants allocate dollar amounts to themselves and others across a number of different scenarios. Based on their allocation patterns, participants were identified as either prosocial, a competitor, or an individualist. Unsurprisingly, those scoring high on the Dark Triad tended to be individualistic and competitive.

In another series of recent studies, Peter Jonason, Bryan Koenig, and Jeremy Tost[93] applied life history theory (see Chapter 3) to understanding the Dark Triad. They found across multiple studies that the college-aged men in their sample, on average, tended to have a faster life history strategy than women. They also found that a measure of life history strategy was positively related to a composite measure of the Dark Triad, but this correlation was primarily driven by the psychopathy component of the Dark Triad: the Dark Triad was no longer associated with Machiavellianism, nor narcissism, once psychopathy was taken into account.

This psychopathy link was replicated in another study of theirs in which those higher in psychopathy tended to report engaging in more risk-taking behaviors in their lives, and also engaged in more risk-taking during the actual experiment by choosing a smaller reward that day over a larger one in a year. Two common threads running across all three components of the Dark Triad were confidence in predicting future outcomes and openness to short-term mating. Therefore, the common theme among the three components of the Dark Triad is *opportunism*.

Research also shows that those scoring high in the Dark Triad traits are characterized by a distinct style of love.[94] Researchers have identified six love styles, each one representing a different approach or drive in regard to serious romantic relationships.[95] These styles include *eros* (relating to passionate physical and emotional intimacy), *ludus* (relating to game playing and a motivation for conquest), *pragma* (relating to cerebral, practical concerns such as career goals), *storage* (relating to a relationship as an outgrowth of friendship and similarity), *agape* (relating to selflessness), and *mania* (relating to insecure attachment and obsession). Each of these love styles has been related to relationship satisfaction.[96]

Perhaps unsurprisingly, Peter Jonason and Bryan Kavanagh[97] found that those scoring high on the Dark Triad traits tend to report higher levels of both the ludus and pragma love styles. This suggests that those scoring high on the Dark Triad traits tend to view love as a game and love with their head instead of their heart. This finding is consistent with the emotional, empathic, and Theory of Mind deficits of those higher in narcissism and Machiavellianism that we mentioned earlier. As Jonason and Kavanagh put it, "Individuals who score high on the Dark Triad may not pursue 'love' relationships because of their affections for someone but, instead, the usefulness they see the other person serving."[98] Again, they found in their college sample that men scored higher than women in the Dark Triad traits.

Further analysis localized ludus to the psychopathy component of the Dark Triad. Consistent with the findings of Jonason and Kavanagh, earlier research showed that those with higher levels of psychopathy use more cortical areas of their brain when processing affective stimuli,[99] suggesting that psychopaths do indeed process emotional stimuli with their head rather than their heart. To summarize their findings, the researchers note that the Dark Triad "appears to be characterized by a heartless, game-playing love style."[100] As for why this particular link between ludus and psychopathy exists, the researchers speculated that game playing may be particularly prevalent among those scoring high in psychopathy for a number of reasons, including providing the excitement and sensation they crave and keeping people at arm's length so that they are freer to pursue a short-term mating style.

Additional studies have shed light on how those scoring high in the Dark Triad traits obtain their short-term mating goals. Jonason, Li, and Buss[101] found that scores on the Dark Triad were correlated with rates of poaching (i.e., stealing) mates from others for new relationships and being poached by others for short-term relationships, long-term affairs, and long-term relationships. As the researchers noted, these findings may explain the higher number of sexual partners of high scorers in Dark Triad traits.[102] By being willing to steal partners and leave their own relationships, this opportunism can lead to many new romantic or sexual partners.

Of course, there are costs to scoring high on the Dark Triad. The researchers found that Dark Triad individuals tended to have their own mates stolen by others (presumably by fellow Dark Triad individuals) and that Dark Triad individuals tend to engage in a wide variety of mate-retention tactics (which tend to serve the purpose of manipulating a mate to stay in the current relationship), but most pronounced were tactics characterized by aggression toward others or the partner, appearance enhancements, and resource display.

The Dark Triad and Emotional Intelligence

How can Dark Triad individuals be so successful in a short-term mating context when they have such low emotional intelligence? This paradox is resolved by understanding that there are different components of emotional intelligence, empathy, and Theory of Mind. In a recent paper, Michael Wai and Niko Tiliopoulos[103] looked at the empathic nature of Dark Triad individuals. They distinguished between two types of empathy: *cognitive empathy* and *affective empathy*. Cognitive empathy involves the ability to figure out the emotional states of others without feeling any emotional contagion (i.e., without being able to feel what they are feeling). In contrast, affective empathy involves sharing an emotional reaction in response to others' emotions. This form of empathy facilitates altruistic behaviors. Prior research shows that individuals with high-functioning autism are impaired in cognitive empathy but do not differ from "neurotypical" people in emotional empathy.[104] The exact reverse appears to be true for Dark Triad individuals.

Wai and Tiliopoulos[105] had 139 university students complete personality measures of the Dark Triad, and they also gave them a test of empathy. In the empathy test, they had the students view a series of images of individuals with different facial expressions. For each picture, they were asked to rate how they felt toward the person. This was their measure of affective empathy. They also had people select which emotions they believed each of the images expressed, and their answers were scored on how correctly they identified the emotion that was being expressed. This was their measure of cognitive empathy.

Those scoring high in narcissism, Machiavellianism, and psychopathy all reported a positive feeling when looking at sad faces. They seemed to actually be *happy* when others were sad. Interestingly, only narcissists were accurate at *recognizing* anger. Therefore, out of the three Dark Triad traits, narcissists appear to stand out as having *enhanced* cognitive empathy. This is interesting considering narcissism is tied most heavily to extraversion and a desire to engage in social interactions. Perhaps their enhanced cognitive empathy facilitates superficial, short-term interpersonal interactions and relationships.

Cognitive empathy is only one component of Theory of Mind. The *social-perceptual* component of Theory of Mind involves the ability to determine the mental states of others using immediately available nonverbal cues (e.g., eyes, face, hand gestures). This maps to the cognitive empathy component and is measured by the Reading the Mind in the Eyes test. This component of Theory of Mind shows up earlier in development and is related to the right hemisphere medial temporal and orbitofrontal regions of the brain. In contrast, the *social-cognitive* component of Theory of Mind (not to be confused with cognitive empathy) involves the ability to reason about the mental state of others and to use that reasoning to predict or explain their behavior. This ability involves inferring what others know or believe to be true apart from what you know or believe to be true. This is a later developing skill and is more strongly dependent on linguistic capacities. This component of Theory of Mind draws on left hemisphere circuitry involving medial frontal areas and the temporoparietal junction. Daniel Nettle and Bethany Liddle[106] found a relationship between agreeableness and the social-cognitive component of Theory of Mind, but not the social-perceptual component. It appears that the agreeable, compassionate, altruistic aspect of our human nature is more strongly associated with the higher-level, social-cognitive component of Theory of Mind.

Other research conducted by Elizabeth Austin and her colleagues[107] showed that the *only* element of emotional intelligence Machiavellian individuals aren't impaired on is the *perceiving* dimension, which involves the lower-level, perceptual ability to decipher emotions in faces and pictures. Not only that, but they show a relatively stronger ability to manage the emotions of others than to manage their own emotions. This may be related to their empathy and perspective-taking deficits: they cannot spontaneously feel what others are feeling, but even if they could, they would have difficulty labeling or figuring out what the emotions mean. Additionally, Machiavellian individuals endorse emotionally manipulative behavior. So, according to their own perceptions, they are really good at manipulating others.

Zsofia Esperger and Tamas Bereczkei[108] in Hungary wondered whether Machiavellian individuals mentalize more often than others. Even though their emotional intelligence is impaired, are they still cognitively strategizing, scheming, and trying to infer the intentions of others much more so than those who are less Machiavellian? To measure spontaneous mentalization, they had 112 university students look at 12 pictures depicting everyday situations. The students were asked to write two or three sentences about each picture. The responses were then automatically coded by a computer, which looked for words and sentences that represented mentalization. They found large individual differences in spontaneous mentalization: some people just weren't motivated to constantly try to mentalize the people in the pictures, whereas other just couldn't stop mentalizing! In fact, those scoring high on a measure of Machiavellianism tended to focus more strongly on the mental state of others than those who were less Machiavellian. They concluded that "using spontaneous mentalization, people with an inclination to manipulate others may always try to be one step ahead of the other and gain important knowledge that can later be profitable in deceit and fraud."[109]

Taken together, the evidence points to a clear conclusion: Dark Triad individuals obtain a higher number of sexual partners through a combination of strategies, including enhanced charm and style, ability to read emotional cues from behavior, constant strategizing and mentalization, persistence, opportunism, coercive sexual tactics, and reduced levels of empathy and self-control. Clearly, those scoring high on the Dark Triad are not well suited for maintaining a committed, loving, mutually beneficial long-term relationship. But then again, most of them are not looking for intimacy. Those scoring high on the Dark Triad are well suited to exploitative, short-term social situations.

Are these tactics the only routes to mating success? Many young men may believe that the only way to be successful in the mating domain is to adopt the strategies of the Dark Triad. Let's put these findings in perspective as we make a crucial distinction between dominance and prestige and show how there are multiple paths to mating success.

Dominance Versus Prestige

One striking similarity across all of the studies we've explored here is the sample: *college students*. Most college students have not had the years of expertise that enable them to achieve success in a domain. This is important to keep in mind because the attainment of social status, and the mating benefits that come along with it, can be accomplished through compassion and cooperation just as much (if not more so) than through aggression and intimidation.

Just looking at the social structure of grade school, it's easy to assume that dominance is the only route to social status. It would seem as though Dark Triad bullies who use intimidation, coercion, and fear-inducing tactics are the only ones who rise in the status hierarchy. Unlike other species, however, humans have many alternative routes to high social status that don't rely on dominance.[110] Beyond school, *on the stage of life*, knowledge has societal impact, and those with high prestige tend to be recognized for their skills, success, and knowledge. Also, as a result of family wealth, people can be born into a position of high social status without even having to lift a finger in aggression.

Many scholars across ethnography, ethology, sociology, and sociolinguistics believe that two main routes to social status—dominance and prestige—arose in evolutionary history at different times and for different purposes.[111] Other lines of research support the distinction between dominance and prestige. Self-report measures of dominance and prestige are beginning to be distinguished at both the behavioral level[112] and the hormonal level.[113] Among the

Tsimané (a small-scale Amazonian society), dominance as ranked by peers is positively related to physical size, whereas prestige as ranked by peers is positively associated with hunting ability, generosity, and number of allies.[114]

Of course, the usefulness of employing a dominance or prestige strategy depends on an individual's own set of mental and physical dispositions as well as particular situation. Individuals who possess the physical ability to intimidate others or enforce threats and who live in cultures or environments (e.g., prison) that promote the use of coercive techniques may be more oriented toward dominance. Those who have the mental skills to acquire culturally valued information and skills and find themselves in social situations that don't form dominance hierarchies may be oriented toward prestige.

It would have been too costly for our ancestors to have to consciously figure out in every situation which social status strategy to employ; such a process would be inefficient and error prone, and could easily give rise to self-doubt (how often has your meta-cognitive awareness caused a drop in your ability to accomplish a task smoothly?). Instead, nature would have selected psychological mechanisms that would automatically calculate the relative costs and benefits of employing a given strategy and would only give the result of this complex calculation in the form of powerful emotions. One of the most powerful evolved emotions tied to social status is *pride*. The bulk of the evidence suggests that pride evolved to motivate people to increase social status and to display the traits and behaviors associated with high social status. But just as there are multiple routes to social status, pride also takes multiple forms, and each form may have evolved along a different path.[115]

Hubristic pride is fueled by arrogance and conceit and is associated with antisocial behaviors, rocky relationships, low levels of conscientiousness and high levels of disagreeableness, neuroticism, narcissism, and poor mental health outcomes.[116] Hubristic pride, along with its associated subjective feelings of superiority and arrogance, may facilitate dominance by motivating behaviors such as aggression, hostility, and manipulation. Individuals scoring high on the Dark Triad tend to have a hubristic form of pride.

Authentic pride, on the other hand, is fueled by the emotional rush of accomplishment, confidence, and success and is associated with prosocial and achievement-oriented behaviors, extraversion, agreeableness, conscientiousness, satisfying interpersonal relationships, and positive mental health. Authentic pride is associated with genuine self-esteem, or the aspect of self-esteem that remains after taking narcissism into account. Authentic pride, along with its associated subjective feelings of confidence and accomplishment, may facilitate behaviors that are associated with attaining prestige. People who are confident, agreeable, hard working, energetic, kind, empathic, nondogmatic, and high in genuine self-esteem would draw inspiration from others and would want to be emulated by others.[117] Will Smith is a good example of someone high in authentic pride.

In a recent set of studies of undergraduates and varsity-level athletes, Joey T. Cheng, Jessica Tracy, and Joseph Henrich[118] at the University of British Columbia explored the notion that the two facets of pride involve distinct forms of status. *Self-reported dominance* was associated with lower levels of genuine self-esteem, social acceptance, and agreeableness and with higher levels of self-aggrandizing narcissism, aggression, extraversion, agency, and conscientiousness. Those with higher levels of self-reported dominance were rated by their peers as higher in athleticism and leadership and lower in altruism, cooperativeness, helpfulness, ethicality, and morality.

Self-reported prestige was associated with lower levels of aggression and neuroticism and higher levels of genuine self-esteem, social acceptance, extraversion, agreeableness, conscientiousness, openness to experience, and GPA and was weakly related to self-aggrandizing narcissism. Those with higher levels of self-reported prestige were rated by their peers as being more capable advisors and leaders as well as being more intellectual, athletic, socially skilled, altruistic, cooperative, helpful, ethical, and moral.

The results of the Cheng and colleagues study support the notion that dominance and prestige, along with the distinct sets of emotions and traits associated with each, represent two different paths to attaining and maintaining social status. The distinction between dominance and prestige is important when considering whether nice guys finish last. Perhaps women like the confident, assertive, and ambitious traits of the man high in prestige while disdaining the aggressive and selfish aspects of the man high in dominance.

Enough speculation on what women want. Let's finally dive right into that literature showing what women actually want.

So, What Do Women *Really* Want?

Now that we have examined the traits and behaviors of socially undesirable individuals, and put dominance in its proper perspective (that's right, we dominated dominance!), let's finally look at what women actually want. We know that women around the world report a preference for the nice guy on self-reported surveys. But perhaps they are only stating the socially desirable option. Maybe when it comes right down to it, women *choose* the bad boy.[119]

Recently, researchers have attempted to address this issue by having women in the laboratory make actual decisions about whom they would date with the aim of answering questions like, *Are most women attracted to truly bad men, or are they just attracted to the traits that come along for the ride (assertiveness, extraversion, fearlessness, etc.)? Is it possible to pinpoint exactly what aspects of the bad boy are so appealing?* In reviewing this literature, we'll start with the foundational evidence and move through to the latest research.

In one of the earliest sets of studies conducted on this topic, Edward Sadalla, Douglas Kenrick, and Beth Vershure[120] presented their participants with videotaped and written scenarios depicting two men interacting with each other. They varied on whether the male acted dominant or nondominant. Their idea of nondominance seemed to be one of submissiveness. For instance, here's an excerpt of a scenario in which the male was depicted as dominant:

> John is 5'10" tall, 165 lbs. He has been playing tennis for one year and is currently enrolled in an intermediate tennis class. Despite his limited amount of training he is a very coordinated tennis player, who has won 60% of his matches. His serve is very strong and his returns are extremely powerful. In addition to his physical abilities, he has the mental qualities that lead to success in tennis. He is extremely competitive, refusing to yield against opponents who have been playing much longer. All of his movements tend to communicate dominance and authority. He tends to psychologically dominate his opponents, forcing them off their games and into mental mistakes. (Sadalla, Kenrick, & Vershure, 1987, p. 733)

In contrast, here's an excerpt of a scenario in which the same tennis player is instead depicted as nondominant (the first three lines are the same):

> ... His serve and his returns are consistent and well placed. Although he plays well, he prefers to play for fun rather than to win. He is not particularly competitive and tends to yield to opponents who have been playing tennis much longer. He is easily thrown off his game by opponents who play with great authority. Strong opponents are able to psychologically dominate him, sometimes forcing him off his game. He enjoys the game of tennis but avoids highly competitive situations. (Sadalla, Kenrick, & Vershure, 1987, p. 733)

It probably will come as no surprise, but the researchers found across four studies that, compared with the nondominance scenarios, the dominance scenarios were considered more sexually attractive. (Scenarios that depicted dominant females were not considered more or less sexually attractive than scenarios that depicted nondominant females.)

One of these studies is of particular note because it found that aggressive and domineering tendencies did not increase sexual attractiveness among males or females. Therefore, what the researchers refer to as "dominance" seems to be well aligned with what we described in the previous section as prestige. In sum, the researchers found that men who displayed dominance *in the context of a skilled competition* were considered more sexually attractive than men who were submissive in competition.

We know what you are thinking: *Well, duh! Of course she is going to pick the strong and confident guy over the wimp!* Good point. Jerry Burger and Mica Cosby[121] thought of the same thing and designed a series of experiments with additional experimental conditions, to better pinpoint what is going on here.

In their first study, 118 female undergraduates read the same descriptions of John the tennis player (dominant or wimpy) that Sadalla, Kenrick, and Vershure[122] used, but they also added a control condition in which participants only read the first three sentences of the description (which just gave his height, weight, and experience, mentioned his coordination, and revealed his percentage of wins).

As expected, undergraduate women found dominant John more sexually appealing than wimpy John. However, the John depicted in the control condition had the highest ratings of sexiness of them all. This does not mean that woman actually found the John in the control condition the sexiest, just that they found the John depicted in the other scenarios as *less* sexy.

In their second study, the researchers fiddled with the descriptors of John. In the dominant condition, participants read a short description of John that included some basic information about John (e.g., major, hobbies), and they also read that a recent personality test found that John's five most prominent traits are *aggressive, assertive, confident, demanding,* and *dominant.* Those in the nondominant condition read the same paragraph but were told that John's five most prominent personality characteristics were *easygoing, quiet, sensitive, shy,* and *submissive.* Those in the control condition only read the short paragraph but were not told anything about John's personality.

Participants reading about either a dominant or a nondominant male rated that person as a less desirable date and romantic partner than did women reading about John in the control condition. Also, dominant John was seen as significantly less desirable as a date than nondominant John. However, nondominant John was seen as less sexually attractive than the John depicted in the other two conditions. Ratings of dominant John in terms of sexual attractiveness were essentially the same as ratings of John depicted in the control condition. Therefore, women drew a distinction between the kind of man they find sexually attractive and the kind they would want to date and have as a romantic partner.

In their third and final experiment, they asked participants to indicate which of the adjectives used to describe John are ideal for a date as well as for a romantic partner. They found that only 1 woman out of the 50 undergraduates in their sample identified "dominant" as one of the traits she sought in either an ideal date or a romantic partner. For the rest of the dominant adjectives, the two big winners were *confident* (72% sought this trait for an ideal date, 74% sought this trait for an ideal romantic partner) and *assertive* (48% sought this trait for an ideal date, 36% sought this trait for an ideal romantic partner). Not one woman wanted a demanding male, and only 12% wanted an aggressive person for a date and romantic partner.

In terms of the nondominant adjectives, the big winners were *easygoing* (68% sought this trait for an ideal date, 64% sought this trait for an ideal romantic partner) and *sensitive* (76% sought this trait for an ideal date and ideal romantic partner). Not one woman wanted a submissive male for either a date or romance. Other low-ranked nondominant adjectives were *shy* (2% for dating, 0% for romantic) and *quiet* (4% for ideal, 2% for romantic).

The Ideal Man

Considering the results of these studies in total, it seems like the ideal man (for a date or romantic partner) is one who is assertive, confident, easygoing, and sensitive, without being aggressive, demanding, dominant, quiet, shy, or submissive. Again, this fits the profile of the prestigious man, as described in the last section.

Other research findings are all variations of the same basic theme. Lauri Jensen-Campbell, William Graziano, and Stephen West[123] found across three studies that it wasn't dominance *alone*, but rather the interaction of dominance and prosocial behaviors, that women reported were particularly sexually attractive. In other words, dominance only increased sexual attraction when the person was already high in agreeableness and altruism.

The same was found in a more recent study. Jeffrey Snyder, Lee Kirkpatrick, and Clark Barrett[124] reported that although male dominance was attractive to females (for both a short-term affair and a long-term relationship) in the context of male-male competitions (athletics), women did not find men attractive who used dominance (force or threat of force) while competing for leadership in informal decision making among peers. According to the researchers, this suggests that women are attuned to cues that suggest that the male will direct his aggression toward her, with dominance toward competitors considered more attractive than dominance toward friends or coalition members.

What can we conclude from these studies? It seems that women do not like "jerks" per se, but instead they like men who are strong and confident. Dominant men who show their displays of dominance within a context of competition are considered attractive, but flat-out jerks who signal that they might use aggression and dominance toward peers in situations in which it's important to work together are considered unattractive. Kindness is not the opposite of assertiveness: both traits can exist in the same person.

In fact, it appears that those with both assertiveness and kindness are considered the sexiest for both a short-term and long-term affair. Thus, it seems that a prestigious man, not a dominant man, is a woman's dream. Although there is some overlap between dominant and prestigious men (prestigious men, like dominant men, tend to be confident, achievement oriented, and extraverted), prestigious men also are self-assured, caring, helpful, and genuinely high in self-esteem.

Many popular male sex symbols are prestigious, including the actor George Clooney and the R & B singer Maxwell. SBK went to a Maxwell concert recently at Madison Square Garden, and women were literally throwing their panties on stage as he confidently and genuinely professed his love and caring for the women in the audience. Or take one of our favorite superheroes: Superman. The Man of Steel is the epitome of the prestigious man, whereas his arch nemesis, Lex Luther, is the epitome of the dominant man. Superman isn't loud and obnoxious, but rather has a quiet confidence about him. He is also assertive, talented, and prosocial. In contrast, Luther is a fast talker and is domineering, aggressive, and scrupulous. He's also not very prosocial: his goal is the destruction of the planet. Who gets the most sexual offers and ultimately ends up dating the highest-quality woman? Hint: It's not Lex Luther.

Are Nice Guys *Too* Nice?

> Let's get something straight: The polar opposite of a bad boy is not a nice guy, but an overly-nice guy. The difference is in the desperation. Nice guys call when they say they will. Overly-nice guys call every 20 minutes. "to thank you for just being you, Kristin." ("My name is Kristine," their prey corrects.) Going out with an overly-nice guy is like being beaten to death with a Hallmark card.
>
> —*Advice Goddess Amy Alkon (2000)*

A clear picture is starting to emerge here. When women say they like "bad boys," they seem to mean they like men who are physically attractive, exciting, assertive, and funny. As an example, consider this vignette:

> Not long ago, I watched my friend Laney, an assistant county prosecutor who spends her days putting criminals behind bars, try to choose between a sweet guy who sent her poems and flowers and petted her cats, and a guy who wore sunglasses indoors and found a way to hit on every woman who came his way. Laney fell madly in love with the second guy.
>
> "But the first guy adores you," I said. "I don't even think the second guy even likes you very much."

"Sorry," she said, "but the first guy is dull."
(Hollandsworth, 1994, p. 121, as cited in Urbaniak & Kilmann, 2003)

In contrast, when women refer to "nice guys," they seem to really mean *overly* nice guys. Recent research suggests that jerks are just as disliked as those who are too nice. In one study, participants took part in a computerized public goods game.[125] They were then given fake information about each of the group members and given the option of expelling group members from an upcoming round of the same game. Not only were people expelled when they contributed less than they consumed, but also, to the researcher's surprise, those who contributed more than they consumed were the most likely ones to be voted out of the group.

Why did the generous folks receive such harsh treatment? The researchers suggest it may have been because they were being *overly* generous. In particular, additional studies suggested two main reasons why unselfish contributors were also unpopular. One reason is how unselfish contributors made others feel. When people contributed too much, others felt pressure to do the same, and this comparison incited feelings of inferiority. Another reason is that the generous folks were seen as "rule breakers" who were not following the "appropriate norms" set up by the public-good context. The reasoning behind expelling the generous was different from the reasoning behind expelling the free riders. The free riders were expelled because they were thought of as being asocial and "destructive."

These researchers' findings may be applicable to the mating domain. Perhaps the woman higher in self-esteem and maturity is not as affected by the overly nice guy, whereas the woman who is less secure may be more prone to feel inferior by the overly nice guy. Perhaps she does not even feel worthy of such attention.

Certainly, reasonable levels of altruism can increase social status,[126] and kindness can even increase physical attractiveness (also see Chapter 4).[127] At the same time, the Parks and Stone (2010) study is consistent with other research showing that people in general are not too fond of those who are extremely competent,[128] those who offer too much help,[129] and those who stick too strongly to a moral position.[130]

In fact, there may just be an optimal level of assertiveness for most people, what psychologist Daniel Ames[131] refers to as the "right touch." Ames defines interpersonal assertiveness as the extent to which a person speaks up, defends, and pursues his or her personal interests. In Ames's review of the literature,[132] he shows a link between interpersonal assertiveness and effectiveness. For instance, there are few great leaders and managers who have extreme levels of assertiveness, whereas bad leaders and managers are well represented among both the low and high ends of the assertiveness spectrum.

Given these findings, why do people continue to display extremely low and high levels of interpersonal assertiveness? Some researchers argue that people just have little interest in changing.[133] As Ames notes,

> ... highly assertive people push hard, this logic goes, because they habitually want to win and they care less about others; unassertive people yield because they typically just want to get along. (Ames, 2008a, p. 383)

But Ames suggests another reason: *lack of self-awareness*. Perhaps people just are not aware how they are being perceived by others because they are not receiving the critical feedback necessary to change. In support of this idea, Ames showed that "assertiveness expectancies"—or how pessimistic or optimistic people are about the impact of being assertive—plays a crucial role in determining their assertiveness levels.

In the mating domain, the "right touch" may be just as difficult to reach, but this balancing act seems well worth the effort. As Ames notes, a person's level of assertiveness is likely to cut across multiple domains in their life, with important consequences:

> ... when individuals strike the wrong balance, they are likely to do so across contexts and may often be unaware that their behavior is seen as wide of the mark. (2008a, p. 384)

Is there any hope for the jerks and the overly nice guys out there? Perhaps. We think Ames's recommendations are just as apropos to the mating domain. He suggested that it's possible to calibrate your assertiveness levels by constantly testing and revising your expectancies, which can lead to more appropriate and adaptive responses. For instance, those very high in assertiveness could try to curb their enthusiasm about the consequences of their aggression, whereas those very low in assertiveness can work on achievement and sense of worth.

Another reason overly nice guys may be considered less attractive to women is because that they may appear *too* available. As Amy Alkon wrote:

> To fully understand bad boy allure (beyond the ever-present element of surprise), open your economics book to page one: "Supply And Demand." Bad boys are in demand because they make themselves scarce, thus driving up their value. They're like half-naked people. Half-naked people are generally sexier than totally naked people because the suggestion of what could be is usually better than what actually is. Truth be told, if a woman ever got as much of a bad boy as

she thought she wanted, it would be only moments before she stopped sitting by the phone waiting for him not to call. (Alkon, 2000)

Bad boys may be attractive because their aloof, nonchalance air signals that they have many other options to consider. In support of this idea, Christine Stanik, Robert Kurzban, and Phoebe Ellsworth[134] found that women's ratings of men's attractiveness *increased* after they were told that the men had rejected their previous partner (no such effect was found among men). Other data back up this point, such as Back and colleagues' 2011 study, we mentioned in Chapter 5, in which shy men in a speed-dating context tended to be less choosy, flirted less, and were less popular. Therefore, assertiveness may also signal choosiness.

Short-Term Versus Long-Term Mating Strategies

Throughout this book, we've noted the importance of distinguishing short-term and long-term mating strategies. Perhaps women who are looking for a short-term affair are just looking for a good time and care less about traits that signal good parenting skills. Instead, we'd expect woman with short-term mating goals to be particularly attracted to cues of good genes. Indeed, the women in the Burger and Cosby[135] study made a distinction between the traits they found sexually attractive and the traits they sought in a date and romantic partner.

Geoffrey Urbaniak and Peter Kilmann[136] attempted to get to the bottom of this. Across two studies, female undergraduates read a story about a woman named Susan who was participating in a game show that was similar to the TV show "The Dating Game." Susan is presented with two potential mates: Todd or Michael. In the "Nice Todd" condition, Todd gave responses that signaled that he is a nice guy: kind, attentive, and emotionally expressive. For instance, in one response, Todd said, "A real man is someone who is in touch with his feelings and those of his partner." In the "Middle Todd" condition, Todd gave neutral responses, such as, "A real man knows what he wants and he knows how to get it. Someone who works hard and plays hard, and is good to the women he loves." In the "Jerk Todd" condition, Todd gave answers that were insensitive, self-absorbed, and macho, such as, "Someone who knows who he is, but keeps other people guessing and on their toes—he doesn't go in for all that touchy-feely stuff." In all three conditions, Todd is competing against Michael, whose responses are always neutral.

In their first study, they found that Nice Todd was chosen the most frequently, followed by Middle Todd, followed by Jerk Todd. This pattern was the same when the women were asked whom they would choose for themselves. Nice Todd was considered as more desirable as a marriage partner, steady boyfriend, platonic friend, and sexual partner and was perceived as more intelligent, kind, and considerate and less assertive.

Niceness had no relation to being perceived as exciting, easygoing, sincere, or funny—mating intelligence skills that most likely signal good genes. Indeed, the perceived traits of exciting, easygoing, and funny tended to go together and were more important for those in the neutral condition. Also, when Todd was portrayed as more physically attractive, he was also perceived as having an exciting personality, being easygoing, and being funny. Therefore, a "halo effect" in terms of other good-genes qualities was exhibited for those depicted as physically attractive.

In their second study, participants could now *see* Todd and Michael. The investigators presented the same scenarios, and the female undergraduates viewed photographs of both Todd and Michael and manipulated their levels of physical attractiveness. Even though niceness and attractiveness independently affected the participants' choices, niceness was the strongest factor. The same pattern was found when the participants were asked whom they would choose for themselves. Physical attractiveness had an additional effect, in that if the man was attractive *and* nice, he was considered more desirable (duh!). Interestingly, though, physical attractiveness did not help Jerk Todd. Neutral but lesser attractive Mike was picked more than physically attractive but Jerk Todd. Also, niceness was the strongest predictor when it came to desirability for more serious relationships, whereas physical attractiveness was more important when it came to desirability for more casual, sexual relationships.

The same researchers conducted a follow-up study and found in a sample of 191 male college students that those who reported lower levels of agreeableness tended to have more casual, sexual relationships, but the effect weakened when it came to committed and romantic relationships.[137] Regan and Berscheid[138] also found that although sensitivity, honesty, and kindness are preferred characteristics in a marriage partner, physical attractiveness is the most desired trait in a sexual partner, with nice-guy traits having much less importance.

These studies are quite consistent with evolutionary theory, which predicts that indicators of good genes (e.g., assertive, funny, physically attractive) are more attractive in a short-term mating context, whereas signs of good parenting potential (e.g., kind, considerate) are more valued in a long-term mating context. Of course, if the guy has *both* good genes and good parenting skills, all the better. But if the physically attractive jerk is pitted against the homely nice guy, *niceness wins*. In neither a short-term nor long-term mating context does it help to be an all-out jerk.

What Do *Some* Women Want?

Bad boys appeal to three types of women: Thrill-seeker girls, girls who can't commit, and "Near Zeros"—girls who aren't operating on a full tank of self-esteem. (Alkon, 2000)

Another crucial component of understanding mating intelligence is individual differences. From this perspective, the pertinent question is not "What do women want?" but "What do *some* women want"?

For *most* of the participants in the Urbaniak and Kilmann study,[139] niceness was the most important factor in the participants' decisions. However, a minority of the participants reported they would choose the less nice guy for themselves even though they thought that Susan should choose the nice guy. Some women even chose the less nice guy for both Susan *and* themselves.

Here are two reports from actual women in the study:

- *"[Susan should choose Michael because . . .] He seems like a nice guy who would be there if she needed him. [But I would choose Neutral Todd for myself] because I always go for the wilder type of guy."*
- *"The only reason why I choose [Jerk] Todd is because I am always attracted to the men that are leaders, secure, and I hate the mushy stuff. I felt that Michael was more the nice guy, which is great . . . but, I am just not attracted to that personality to the extreme."*

Other studies have found meaningful individual differences in a preference for a nice guy versus a bad boy. A study conducted by Herold and Milhausen in 1999 found that 56% of the 165 university women in the sample reported that they knew of other women who had the choice of dating the nice but sexually inexperienced guy but chose to date the sexually experienced but not so nice guy instead. In their own sample, although 54% of the women chose John, an inexperienced, nice, but somewhat shy guy, over Mike, an attractive, fun guy who had sex with 10 women, that number was far from 100%. In fact, there were common patterns among the women who preferred the bad boy. Women who preferred Mike over John tended to place more emphasis on the importance of sex, had more sexual partners in total, and were more accepting of men who had many sexual partners. Herold and Milhausen suggested that bad boys may do particularly well with highly sexually experienced women looking for casual, short-term flings. Therefore, a person's level of sociosexuality matters in terms of their mate preferences (see Chapter 3). In contrast, although nice guys may have a lower total number of sexual partners, they do tend to be preferred for friendships and deep, intimate connections. As the researchers note, "In this context, nice guys do not always finish last."[140]

Sexism is another key factor. According to Ambivalent Sexism Theory,[141] there are two distinct forms of sexism: hostile sexism (HS) and benevolent sexism (BS). Hostile sexism involves negative attitudes toward women and explicit desire to maintain male privilege in the face of threats to patriarchal power. In contrast, benevolent sexism is more chivalrous and paternalistic, seemingly more positive but in reality perpetuating traditional gender roles. Various studies have found that sexism does play a role in mate preferences.[142]

In a recent study, Jeffrey Hall and Melanie Canterberry[143] came up with a measure of "assertive strategies" by combing through two popular books written by "speed-seduction gurus" (*The Game* and *The Pickup Artist*). Based on their own interpretation of the techniques, they came up with a 14-item scale assessing three particular "assertive courtship strategies": *competition* (e.g., "compete with other men who are interested in her/you"), *teasing* or *"negging"* (e.g., "picks on her/your appearance or behavior"), and *isolation* (e.g., "try to get her/you alone"). They found that sociosexuality was associated with a preference for assertive strategies. In particular, men high in sociosexuality were more likely to employ assertive strategies, and women high in sociosexuality were more likely to be receptive to assertive strategies.

Sexism also mattered. In both the college and adult samples, women scoring high in hostile and benevolent sexism traits were more receptive to assertive courtship strategies. Among college students, there was an interaction: women with a combination of high sociosexuality and high hostile sexism preferred men's dominant courtship strategy the most. Only in the adult sample, however, was male sexism related to the *use* of assertive strategies, with a positive association between hostile sexism and assertive strategy use. The researchers suggest that assertive courtship strategies may be a form of mutual identification of similarly sexist attitudes, with people preferring courtship strategies that match their same "courtship script." The study also highlights the importance of sociosexuality in mate preferences, and the importance of looking at different age groups (college vs. adults) when studying courtship strategies. Many of these assertive courtship behaviors may be more prevalent in college, lowering the variation in courtship strategies and making it more difficult for researchers to find an effect. It would also be interesting to see the effect of assertive courtship strategy use by females.

Both sociosexuality and sexism are tied to a nexus of other individual difference variables that we have been discussing throughout this book, such as life history strategy and attachment style (see Chapter 3). Those with a fast life history strategy and an insecure attachment style tend to have higher levels of sociosexuality. In general, those living the fast life tend to mate with those living the fast life, and those living a slower life tend to mate with those living the slower life.[144] Although life history strategy predicts relationship satisfaction, the influence of life history strategy decreases over the duration of the relationship, when other variables become more important.

In regard to attachment style, unsurprisingly, securely attached people tend to go well together.[145] Among insecurely attached individuals, even though a dismissive-avoidant/anxious-preoccupied pairing tends to get off to a rocky start, these kinds of relationships do tend to be surprisingly stable over

3 years.[146] This dismissive-anxious pairing seems to a do a better job predicting relationship satisfaction than anxious-anxious or avoidant-avoidant pairings (which are very rare pairings). The picture of the detached, avoidant, "cool" James Dean and the anxiously attached Marilyn Monroe perfectly captures this research finding.

Other individual differences may be at play here and should be explored in future research. Such variables could include a *care-taking personality* (perhaps nurturing women are particularly susceptible to bad boys because they think they can change their bad ways), *self-esteem* (perhaps women with low levels of self-esteem are also particularly susceptible to bad boys because bad boys are good at exploiting their insecurities), and *sensation seeking* (perhaps two people high in sensation seeking go well together because the relationship provides the excitement both partners crave). As you may recall in Chapter 5, Meston and Buss[147] found that women have sex for many different reasons, including darker reasons (e.g., "*I wanted to be used or degraded*"). Perhaps some of these individual differences variables can help explain some of those varied reasons. We suspect that many of these variables are related to each other, and with preferences for a more dominant versus agreeable partner. An exciting future line of research will be to pinpoint which factors are more important than others by including all of the relevant traits in the same study.

What Do Women Want Some of the Time?

In addition to individual differences, another major theme of this book is contextual factors (see Chapter 5). Whether a woman is attracted to nice-guy traits or bad-boy traits may depend on where she is in her ovulatory cycle. Gangestad and co-workers[148] had 237 normally ovulating women watch 1-minute videotapes of men compete for a potential lunch date. Women then rated each man's level of attractiveness for a short-term and a long-term mate. They found that displays of *social presence* (consisting of composure, presentation as athletic, eye contact, lack of self-deprecation, lack of downward gaze, and lack of nice-guy self-presentation) and *direct intrasexual competitiveness* (consisting of derogation of competitor, direct intrasexual competitive tactics, lack of laughing, and lack of mentioning a nice personality) increased on high-fertility days relative to low-fertility days, but only in a short-term (not long-term) mating context.

Another important contextual factor is age. If you recall (see Chapter 5), women between the ages of 27 and 45 years have more of a sex drive than any other age group. Therefore, it would be interesting to test whether women within this age group also are particularly in search of bad boys with good genes, as evolutionary theory would predict.

Although there are sex differences in preference for a nice guy versus bad boy, there are also important individual differences as well as contextual factors. All of these levels of analysis are crucial aspects of mating intelligence.

Nice Guys Finish Last—Where It *Really* Counts

Although this book isn't about the actual act of intercourse (see *The Guide to Getting It On!* by Paul Joannides, 2009, for an excellent guide in this department), we would be remiss if we didn't note that when it comes to sex, nice guys may actually finish last—in a good way! Galinsky and Sonenstein[149] analyzed 3,200 students, aged 18 to 26 years, who had taken part in the third wave of the National Longitudinal Study of Adolescent Health. Overall, they found that men were more likely than women to report having had orgasms during sex (87% of men compared with 47% of women). Men, on average, were also more likely to enjoy giving oral sex than women were. Therefore, men might not be as selfish in bed as stereotypes might have it.

In terms of individual differences though, high self-esteem, autonomy, and empathy were associated with greater total sexual pleasure (frequency of orgasm, enjoyment level for giving and receiving oral sex) in females, whereas only empathy was associated with total sexual pleasure among the men in the study. Among men, autonomy was positively correlated to the frequency of orgasm, whereas self-esteem was linked to the enjoyment of giving oral sex. The researchers suggest that those with higher levels of empathy are more responsive to their partner's needs, and their partner is thus more responsive in return. Therefore, it seems as though nice guys may finish last where it really counts—in the bedroom.

Do Nice Guys Really Finish Last?

Based on all of the evidence, we can make some reasonable conclusions. As a first pass, we can say this: If you define success in terms of sheer number of sexual partners, jerks do finish first, but if you define success in terms of relationship quality, nice guys have the clear advantage. With that said, there are a number of qualifications.

Just because bad boys have a higher number of sexual partners, it does not prove that women are attracted to the aggressive and manipulative aspects of bad boys. Correlation doesn't equal causation. We have demonstrated that there are a number of reasons why the correlation may exist:

1. Bad boys are more interested in short-term encounters so pursue them more frequently.

2. Bad boys use sexually coercive techniques to acquire mates.
3. Bad boys tend to display traits and behaviors (e.g., confidence, assertiveness, exciting and unpredictable personality) that are attractive at first sight.

Taken together, the research studies suggest that women are in fact not attracted to these aggressive and manipulative characteristics. When women say they like the bad boy, they tend to mean his exciting, unpredictable personality. On the other hand, when women refer to *nice guys*, they tend to mean traits relating to being overly nice and submissive (e.g., neediness, desperation, lack of self-confidence). Niceness is not the opposite of assertiveness. Both can coexist in the same person.

Individual differences and contextual factors are at play, however. Women with higher levels of sociosexuality are less interested in cues of "good dad" (e.g., agreeableness) and are more interested in cues of "good genes." Women at peak fertility during their ovulatory cycle are more interested in cues of assertiveness and less interested in agreeableness. Women with a long-term mating strategy do want a man who has it all but tend to value kindness and understanding above all else. In no cases, though, are women attracted to aggression and hostility. Assertiveness can be distinguished from aggression.

Finally, there are multiple paths to mating success. In fact, guys who strike the right balance of assertiveness and agreeableness—who display high levels of mating intelligence, skill, creativity, and prosocial behaviors—are *most* attractive for both short-term and long-term relationships.

Advice

Based on all the evidence, we think we can give some sensible advice to both men and women.

For Women

If you are looking for a good man but find yourself constantly ending up with narcissists, here are some tips:

- *Understand the narcissistic mindset*. Narcissists are easy to spot and easy to avoid. Once you understand the narcissists' mindset and what drives them, you realize just how predictable they really are. Beware of:
  - Men who talk about themselves, name drop, or spend more time in the mirror than you do.
  - Men who put others down, especially inferiors and strangers.

- Men who always need to be the center of attention and outshine you.
- Men who react too harshly to criticism and see criticism where it doesn't even exist.
- Men who act entitled to you.

- *Slow down.* Relationships with narcissists start off with a bang (literally) but fizzle out fast. Relationships with good guys may take more time to develop but may ultimately be more satisfying and exciting. If you're looking for a long-term relationship, don't put so much stock in your initial attraction, and be open-minded to guys who may not be as flashy.
- *Assess him in multiple contexts.* Sometimes extraverts can be very hard to distinguish from narcissists at first encounter. If you are attracted to a guy at first encounter, assess him in multiple contexts before getting in too deep.
- *Ask for a dating resume.* If he has had a lot of failed relationships, or has no balls because they have been cut off by a prior mate, that's not a good sign.
- *Listen to your friends.* If your friends stopped hanging out with you because they don't want to go anywhere near your new boyfriend, that's an important sign. If everyone else thinks you are dating a self-absorbed narcissist, you probably are.
- *Look at where you are going to find a mate.* If you frequent bars and clubs, you are more likely to encounter narcissists on the prowl. Avoid breeding grounds for narcissists.
- *Give nice guys a chance.* Stable and secure guys don't tend to wear flashy, neon lights on their shirts. If a guy looks like he's genuinely interested in you and is being nice, don't automatically assume the guy is "weak." Some of the most self-assured and cocky guys are the most narcissistic, and many guys with the worst "game" make for the most satisfying and exciting relationship partners.
- *Examine why you are attracted to narcissists.* "If you are searching for an ambitious and exciting man who is not 'too nice,' you are likely to be drawn to many narcissists. Also, if you are always looking for excitement rather than emotional closeness you are more likely to be drawn to narcissists," notes psychologist W. Keith Campbell.[150] What narcissistic need of yours do narcissists exploit? Understanding why you date narcissistic men will help you make significant changes to your life.
- *Examine why bad boys tend to be attracted to you.* A body of research suggests that there are certain body language cues that are more prominent among those vulnerable to victimization.[151] For instance, Grayson and Stein[152] found that potential victims differed from nonvictims with respect to five motion cues: longer or shorter strides, nonlateral weight shifts, gestured versus postural movements, and foot movement (potential victims tended to lift their feet higher while walking). A key factor in victimization seems to be nonverbal cues of dominance versus submissiveness.[153]

Can anything be done? Prison psychologist Mariso Mauro, who deals with criminals and people with psychopathic traits, notes that: "besides one's walk, individuals can purposefully project dominance thereby potentially decreasing perceived vulnerability by increasing eye contact, decreasing the use of small body movements of the hand and feet, and increasing large body movements or changes in postural positioning."[154]

- *Don't let narcissists get into your head.* Narcissists are really good at exploiting people's emotional weaknesses and insecurities. If you find yourself constantly questioning yourself and feeling guilty for things your partners really should be guilty for doing, this is a sign the narcissist's tactics have succeeded. Recognize this, and don't let his mind games get into your head.

- *Get out as soon as you can.* If you do find yourself in a relationship with a narcissist, don't try to change him. Remember, he *enjoys* being a narcissist. Be prepared to cut off the relationship swiftly and abruptly. The more emotionally attached you get, the harder it will be to leave the relationship and the easier it will be for the narcissistic to manipulate you.

- *Take responsibility for your situation.* "Understand the situation you are in does not reflect your personality, and you can change your circumstance," notes Campbell.[155] "Responsibility is the ability to respond."

For Men

If you aren't getting the mating results you want, hold off on becoming a card-carrying narcissist. You may only need to make some minor adjustments. Here are some tips:

- *Dial-down your eagerness.* Hold your horses, cowboy. Women want quality men, and quality men don't act desperate. It is simple supply and demand: the more a guy acts like he's in short supply, the more women will demand him.

- *Be more playful.* You may be boring dates and scaring women away because you are too serious and anxious. Try watching some comedy before going out to get yourself in a playful frame of mind.

- *Be more assertive.* If you are constantly being put into the "friend zone," perhaps you are not being assertive enough about what you want. There is a difference between dominance and assertiveness. Get out of your comfort zone by making bold romantic gestures. They won't always work out, but at least it gives the girl a chance to see you in the way you want her to see you. If you are nervous, remember: women find honesty sexy.

- **Be authentic.** Don't try to be the kind of man you think women want, but play up your own unique strengths. A healthy dose of self-promotion is okay. *Own yourself.* Women can tell when you are trying to be someone you aren't. Jerks don't try to be nice guys, so why should nice guys try to be jerks?
- **Get out of your head.** Instead of worrying about following a set of rules that puts you too much in your own head and creates unnecessary anxiety, direct your attention to the external world. Ask a woman questions and genuinely care about her answers. Women like to be understood and will appreciate that you care about what they have to say. Too much self-focus will come across as unattractive.
- **Do good things for others.** Smile at strangers. Help grannies cross the street. Volunteer at a homeless shelter. Do *Habitat for Humanity.* Learn a culturally valued skill and become really good at it. Instead of trying to *manufacture* attraction, work on genuinely becoming the type of man women want. Then attraction will come naturally as a result.
- **Be flexible.** There are aspects of the Dark Triad that the nice guy can learn, without being a bad person. It is possible to have multiple social strategies at your disposal, one *agentic* and measured by the Dark Triad, and one *prosocial*, measured with altruistic behavior, agreeableness, and conscientiousness.[156] There certainly are times when an altruistic, cooperative orientation is essential (e.g., when forming meaningful reciprocal relationships and developing a skill that helps humanity) and times when you may want to adopt an agentic social strategy (e.g., when you want to hold your ground on your beliefs and maintain your self-respect, or in quickly bouncing back from rejection).

Advice for Bad Boys

- If you are tired of the fast life, dial down the signals that you are looking for a short-term affair (e.g., sexual language, approaching every woman in sight) and work on your empathy and relationship skills. Also, try acquiring socially valuable skills that help others.

We do not purport to have settled all these issues once and for all. At the very least, we hope we brought you closer to understanding the truth and opened up further avenues for research. *Do assholes really finish first?* Because it's such a complicated question, with so many caveats, this question will no doubt continue to be debated and argued for the rest of humanity. Nonetheless, based on all the evidence, the most reasonable conclusion is that, yes, assholes may finish first, but prestigious men stay there.

|| 9 ||

Mating Intelligence Saves the World

In a world in which extraordinary competition exists everywhere you look, doing what you can to give yourself an advantage is not a bad idea. That said, think about modern human sexuality and its impact on the nature of the social world. Mating-relevant factors are arguably responsible for some of the world's greatest creations (e.g., the song "Let it Be") as well as some of the social world's notable disasters (e.g., Ted Bundy's murderous rampage). The motivations to mate can even affect levels of physical injury by leading to risk-taking behavior and physical conflict during courtship.[1] And recent research shows that being shut out of a local mating market has potential to lead to behavior that can be detrimental to oneself or to others—specifically, males who are at risk for being shut out of mating are at increased risk for both suicide and homicide.[2]

Mating systems drive the nature of the local economy.[3] Mating patterns may well hold the secret to the origins of war in our species—with the idea that men form all-male coalitions to launch wars—and that women are often "the spoils of war." This depiction of war is remarkably consistent across human history and human cultures.[4] In short, mating matters. And in a world in which mating matters, improved mating intelligence can help us better understand ourselves and others in our social worlds. Perhaps, for instance, understanding mating's role in war can help us better understand the roots of war—and how to circumvent war in the future.

A current line of research into mating intelligence pertains to a potential overhaul of modern sex education in the United States. To date, sex education in public schools has focused on details regarding reproductive anatomy, contraception, and sexually transmitted diseases (STDs).[5] Without question, these are important issues that need to be taken seriously. However, we believe that current curricula on these topics fall short in terms of context. Sure, it's important to know how to put a condom on a penis, and it's important to know why doing so is likely to reduce the probability of unwanted pregnancy and the probability of contracting chronic disease. But shouldn't there be some context?

Mating Intelligence in High School Curricula

In an early interview regarding mating intelligence, Geoffrey Miller[6] spoke of an important implication of mating intelligence. To the extent that increasing mating intelligence is beneficial for life as an adult, Miller said, people should be schooled in the skills that make up mating intelligence. Sex education in schools should not be exclusively about the details of copulation. At the end of the day, that's actually quite boring. What's exciting, interesting, and important is the fact that human sexuality comprises a set of physiological and behavioral processes that sit at the heart of our nature as evolved organisms. Understanding sex without understanding human mating, along with its social and evolutionary origins, is comparable to understanding how a bicycle tire works without realizing why a bike was made and what its ultimate purpose is (to get people from here to there, if you're curious).

Given the centrality of mating from an evolutionary perspective in all aspects of human life,[7] we believe that *sex education* for adolescents should shift to *mating education*. A curriculum for such an educational experience could—and should—include the same elements that typify current sex education curricula—including information on anatomy, contraception, and STDs. However, we believe that it would be beneficial to add content to the curriculum to address such issues as the following:

1. The distinction between long-term and short-term mating
2. Factors sought in potential mates
3. Mating qualities desired by both men and women
4. Mating features that are particularly important to men
5. Mating features that are particularly important to women
6. Personality trade-offs in the mating domain
7. The relevance of paternal uncertainty in driving several elements of the mating process
8. The importance of *female choice*—and sexual selection generally—to human mating
9. The interface of the mating domain with the parenting domain
10. Sex-differentiated mating processes—including the use of relatively risky strategies by males during courtship
11. The importance and nature of courtship in human mating
12. The importance of kindness and love as central to mating preferences across cultures and sexes
13. Cross-sex mind-reading—parameters of accuracy and biases
14. The evolutionary psychology of sexual harassment and rape—why these processes exert such high evolutionary costs on females and what can be done to prevent these acts

With the help of funding from the National Science Foundation, we are in the process of conducting a study that will develop, implement, and test a newly created sex education curriculum designed with this very reasoning in mind. This mating-relevant curriculum will include the standard features of the New York State sex educational experience along with content that addresses the mating-relevant issues described herein. This curriculum is designed with the following goals:

1. To put sex education in the broader context of evolved human mating psychology
2. To make high school students aware of similarities between the sexes in terms of many features of mating psychology
3. To inform high school students about important psychological differences between the sexes in the area of mating psychology
4. To provide context for understanding issues such as contraception and STDs
5. To develop awareness of gender-specific mating psychology with the goals of creating empathy in mating—which we believe should be a key feature in reducing such adverse outcomes as sexual harassment and rape.

This research will succeed to the extent that we can demonstrate significant effects of the curriculum on important outcomes. The specific outcomes we are studying include: (a) standard measures of knowledge of sexuality, (b) measures of understanding details of human mating psychology and its broad, evolutionary context, and (c) measures of social attitudinal variables such as the "attitude toward women" scale[8] and measures of the "sexual objectification" that women often experience.[9] Finally, (d) we are including a modified version of the Mating Intelligence Scale[10] (see the Epilogue) designed to be appropriate for an adolescent audience.

Our expectation is that students who are exposed to the mating-relevant curriculum will score as well as students who take the standard curriculum on standard measures of knowledge of sexual issues such as STDs and contraception, but should score higher in knowledge of mating psychology and mating intelligence. Further, we expect that students given the enhanced curriculum should demonstrate relatively positive attitudes toward women, less likelihood to objectify women, less likelihood to hold sex-based stereotypes, and less likelihood to hold attitudes that would predispose one toward sexual harassment (these final predictions are particularly relevant for males in the sample).

Although this research on the beneficial effects of a mating intelligence-based sex education curriculum is ongoing, think about the possibilities. This applied research may well improve dramatically the understanding of the social world that young adults find themselves immersed in. Armed with the unmatched explanatory power of evolutionary theory as a set of basic principles, we hope that young adults who learn this curriculum will develop clearer and more informed perspectives on who they are, what their goals are, why sexuality exists, why competition in so many domains exists, why being "nice" has both long-term and short-term benefits, and why long-term mating is the dominant form of mating in our species. Students given standard sex education curricula today simply do not get this experience.

Mating Intelligence, Evolutionary Psychology, and Psychotherapy

Psychology applied in educational settings, in terms of our current research on a high school health curriculum based on mating intelligence theory, exemplifies scholarship in action that is of broad social value. In fact, applied psychology has many faces beyond educational psychology. Other applied fields of psychology include health psychology (psychology applied to health and medical settings), industrial and organizational psychology (psychology applied to the work world), and sports psychology (psychology applied to issues of athletics and recreation). That said, the most conspicuous form of applied psychology—applied psychology sine qua none—is psychotherapy.

Psychotherapy (a term used here to subsume both *clinical* and *counseling psychology*) is pretty much what most people think of when they think of psychology writ large. Sometimes people develop major pathologies that interfere with functioning at all levels, and sometimes people develop anxieties or stress responses that are specific to some particular situation. Everyone has problems at some point.

Can the idea of mating intelligence help lead to improvements in the field of psychotherapy? Before asking this question, it's useful to think of a more general question: Can evolutionary psychology lead to improvements in psychotherapy? A large and growing group of scholars believe the answer to this broader question is a resounding "YES." The recently formed Applied Evolutionary Psychology Society (AEPS—yes, from APES TO AEPS!) takes this charge seriously—and is based on the idea that evolutionary psychology is crucial to understanding all aspects of human behavior and is, accordingly, crucial to coming up with solutions to personal and social problems.

To think about how evolutionary psychology can lead to fresh and useful new approaches to psychotherapy, consider the following example: Michael is a young male in his senior year of college. He's majoring in history and, like many 22-year-olds, has little idea where his career (specifically) and life (generally) are headed. He's also someone who's always felt uncomfortable in social situations and who has a difficult time dealing with ambiguity of any sort. Michael is finding this particular life stage extremely stressful.

Always nervous to venture into unchartered territory, Michael has lived at home during college and hasn't developed much of a social network as a young adult. In regard to romance—forget it—Michael, who is sure of his heterosexuality, has never been with a woman in an intimate way.

Michael's parents are encouraging him to move out on his own, to start a career, and to go ahead and make something of himself. Michael hasn't the foggiest idea where to start—the stress of the situation has led him to finally seek out therapy for guidance.

Several fields of psychotherapy have been honed over the past several decades to address Michael's issues, and there is clearly some merit to the different approaches that are out there. A cognitive behavioristically trained therapist might get Michael to develop a list of specific stimuli that make him feel stressed and develop responses to these stimuli that are incompatible with stress. A humanistic therapist might work with Michael over several sessions, getting him to develop a self-identity that is positive and optimistic in scope. A psychoanalyst trained in the Freudian tradition might work with Michael to delve deeply into his past to find how early experiences with his parents are at the core of his current state of stress. The point of this section is not to disparage existing approaches to therapy—when done with high-quality training, existing approaches can have positive effects.[11] Rather, the point here is to present the fresh angle on therapy offered by an approach that's informed by evolutionary psychology—and rooted in the ideas of mating intelligence.

A therapist taking the mating intelligence approach considers Michael's situation in evolutionary context. Michael is a young adult male. He exists because his ancestors possessed a battery of adaptations that facilitated reproductive success. Ultimately, Michael is stressed out by the lack of mating success to this point. He has yet to succeed in the following mating-relevant domains:

- Courtship
- Infatuation
- Love
- Foreplay
- Copulation
- Dating
- Having someone commit to being with him for the long-term

Not only has Michael failed as of yet to succeed in these clearly relevant mating domains, but he also has yet to succeed in many crucial life domains that surround mating.

Michael has yet to:

- Become a core member of an all-male coalition
- Develop a reliable and broad social network beyond his kin network
- Dazzle anyone—demonstrating some outstanding abilities in some behavioral area (e.g., artistic ability, musical ability, oratory skills)
- Develop an opportunity to demonstrate to others that he is a kind, other-oriented, good soul

That's okay—Michael's 22—he's young yet! Michael's highly skilled and evolutionarily oriented therapist sees the problem and the solution. She realizes that stress responses are usually not a mark of *psychopathology*. Rather, Michael's stress response here seems like an adaptive response to a situation that is evolutionarily threatening. From this perspective, the human emotion system was shaped by millennia of selection forces to send signals to individuals when it would be adaptive to alter their situations.[12] Male ancestors of Michael who were in circumstances similar to his but who were perfectly content in such circumstances likely failed to reproduce, and failed to pass on genes coding for a lack of emotional reactivity during mating-shutout conditions.

To become less stressed about his lot, Michael needs to take steps that will increase mating prospects. Increasing the cognitive skills that underlie the mating domain should go a long way toward helping Michael in his situation.

Michael needs to develop some kind of courtship-display abilities by demonstrating expertise in some area. As shown earlier in this book and in other recent books,[13] courtship display in humans can take many forms. Michael did well as a history student in college. He can join one of the many history-related social groups out there—demonstrating his skills to interested others—and expand his social group, an outcome that always correlates positively with mating-relevant outcomes. Michael also can work on his personality. He can work on his humor, work on his social skills, work on things that will make him more exciting and interesting to potential mates.

Thinking about Michael's situation in terms of mating intelligence has two beneficial qualities. First, this approach places Michael and his emotional state squarely in an evolutionary context, allowing the light of evolutionary theory, which sheds on phenomena across all academic areas,[14] to illuminate Michael's world and possible futures. Further, mating intelligence theory has a clear set of concepts, such as mental courtship display, attractive personality traits, and optimistic attitudes about oneself, that provide a clear toolbox for a therapist working with clients across demographic groups. To the extent that mating is relevant to an individual (and it always is), mating intelligence theory provides a useful set of solutions. Just ask Michael, whose future could hold in store presidency of the Podunk Historical Society and a happy marriage to another quirky history buff!

Mating Intelligence and Social Problems Near and Far

In this chapter, we are exploring the ways mating intelligence theory can be used to solve practical social and personal problems. Here, we discuss six broad-scale societal problems that can be informed by mating intelligence. Specifically, we'll focus on:

1. Violence toward women
2. Hooking-up miscommunication
3. Runaway spending
4. Young male syndrome[15]
5. Social class and mortality
6. Educational disparities

Reducing Violence Toward Women

The literature in evolutionary psychology is clear: violence toward women is a subset of relational and familial violence, the most species-typical form of human violence, and one that can be illuminated with an understanding of evolutionary psychology.

The most common forms of violence toward women are highly related to mating, including reactions to suspected infidelity,[16] reactions to relationship breakups,[17] reactions to the withholding of sex within the confines of an intimate relationship,[18] and reactions that take place when paternity is in question.[19] Violence toward women is related to our evolutionary heritage. Understanding our evolutionary origins, thus, holds a key to helping solve this important social problem.

High mating intelligence is partly characterized as accurately knowing the mating psychology of the opposite sex. Helping individuals of both genders to increase this skill will help them better empathize with members of the other sex. Sexual harassment and aggression, both core elements of violence toward women, are seen as stressful by both sexes—but males consistently underestimate how costly such actions are in the eyes of women.[20] Increasing awareness of this kind of issue (through such programs as the health education initiative, outlined in a prior section of this chapter) should help males to become better able to empathize with female psychology and less likely to engage in violent acts toward women.

High levels of mating intelligence correspond to high levels of empathy toward the opposite sex. We predict that future research will demonstrate that males high in mating intelligence are less likely to engage in sexually harassing behaviors, less likely to rape women, and less likely to engage in violence toward

women. This prediction rests on two ideas. First, males high in mating intelligence should, by definition, empathize with women better than other males
do. Second, being high in mating intelligence is attractive. As such, men high
in mating intelligence should more easily start relationships with women and
should find relationships relatively smooth—thus facing less mating-relevant
conflict compared with men who are low in mating intelligence.

Imagine a guy who is out on the dating scene armed with a clear awareness
of the evolutionary psychology of sex differences in sexual harassment. And, as
a bonus, he's been educated both implicitly and explicitly on the importance of
keeping a reputation as a good, helpful guy who's always a plus in the community. Now picture him out on a date with a woman who's just not as interested
in the same things he is interested in. Armed with his education on issues tied
to mating, and resultant high mating intelligence, he's going to be much more
likely to treat her respectfully and move on compared with a similar guy who
just doesn't have the skills or education in this area.

Further, in terms of courtship signaling, mating intelligence theory tells
us that behaviors that reveal relatively high levels of creativity and particularly high levels of other-oriented behavior are attractive to potential mates.
Although aggression and violence do have their attractive sides under some
rare mating contexts,[21] creative, funny, and kind eventually win the race (see
Chapter 8).

Increasing awareness of these facts may well go a long way toward reducing a
culture of violence. Educational programs such as the health education program
described earlier have potential to educate adolescents on these issues early in
their mating-relevant years. Increasing mating intelligence in such individuals
early on should serve as a key to reducing so many social problems, such as violence toward women, that have issues of human mating at their core.

Hooking-Up Miscommunication

Human mating operates on a continuum, from "hook-ups" and "booty-calls"
on one end[22] to "open relationships" and committed sexual relationships on
the other. Hooking-up behaviors, in particular, have become widespread across
college campuses throughout North America, replacing the traditional "dating
scene" of prior generations.[23] Studies show that 65% to 80% of undergraduates
report engaging in hook-up behaviors at least once in their college careers.[24]
What is causing such an increase?

Garcia and Reiber[25] make a compelling case that pluralistic ignorance (PI)
plays an important role. PI happens when people behave in accordance with
perceived beliefs about their own groups while ignoring their own beliefs.
Unfortunately, PI can lead people to act in ways that they aren't really comfortable with. To test how PI may play a role in the prevalence of hook-up behaviors,

Garcia and Reiber administered a variety of survey questions to 507 undergraduate students (55% female, 45% male) at a mid-sized public university. They found that 81% of their participants reported having engaged in some form of sexual hook-up behavior, and consistent with prior research, men reported higher comfort levels engaging in all sexual behaviors compared with women. Men also overestimated women's comfort levels with oral sex and intercourse, behaviors that potentially pose higher physical and mental health risks, such as STDs, unintended pregnancy, and psychological injury.

The researchers also found PI effects. For all sexual behaviors, both genders attributed to others of the same gender higher comfort levels than they, themselves, felt. Although women reported moderate discomfort with intercourse during a hook-up, 32% of women and 35% of men reported having engaged in intercourse during a hook-up. Over one third of the women reported engaging in oral sex even though their comfort levels were generally negative about engaging in this act. The researchers suggest that:

> The pressure to act in accordance with these false perceived norms may be leading people to engage in behaviors in which they are uncomfortable, a state of affairs that poses potential risks in terms of sexually transmitted diseases, pregnancy, and psychological trauma. (Garcia & Reiber, 2010, p. 399)

As the researchers note, these three factors—men's higher comfort, men's overestimation of women's comfort, and women's overestimation of other women's comfort—may work together and increase the chances for sexual assault. As we discussed in Chapter 6, men in general tend to overperceive a women's sexual intent. This effect, paired with the PI effect, can lead to dangerous sexual activity in which partners have differing and misinformed perceptions of their engagement.

Women also were found to attribute higher comfort levels to other women than they themselves felt. This suggests that women were viewing other women as competitors for mates and is consistent with Garcia and Reiber's earlier study,[26] which found that more than half of both men and women did not hold out any expectations that the hook-up would lead to a relationship, whereas 51% of men and women reported that the desire to engage in a relationship did motivate their choice to engage in a hook-up. Clearly, individual differences play a role here. "String-free" hooking up may not be as string free for everyone.

So, what can be done to reduce potential for misunderstanding between men and women? Garcia and Reiber suggest adopting *social norms marketing*—or the idea that people can benefit from knowing what other people really do (as opposed to what they are led to think that others do by media and other biased forms of communication). Such techniques have been useful in dealing with alcohol use on campuses. The authors propose applying the same technique to hook-up behaviors by continuing to survey trends on an ongoing basis and developing and implementing an educational campaign that, in collaboration with the campus counseling center, the student life office, and the student health service, will disseminate accurate information about hook-up attitudes and behavior on campus. It is hoped that such techniques will prove useful in reducing negative outcomes. We think their conclusion is very sensible and worthy:

> We neither condemn nor condone sexual activity, but rather, we endorse the need for young adults to be aware of, honestly communicate, and act in accordance with, their own comfort levels and those of their partner(s) during engagement in sexual activity. (Garcia & Reiber, 2010 p. 401)

Spending More than You Can Afford

In case you haven't noticed, the United States has a problem. People spend more than they can afford. This trend has increased rapidly in the past few decades and has come to a head with the recent mortgage meltdown that has ravaged our nation's economy.

Budgeting is really not that complicated. If someone has $100 and a pair of shoes costs $120 plus tax—the shoes are out of budget. But given the full range of personal finance in modern societies (such as credit cards), this simple reasoning is lost on millions. The lifeblood of the financial credit industry, which is foundational in countries such as the United States, is helping people purchase things they cannot afford. In fact, to own a house, purchasing something that you cannot afford is usually the only possible means.

Spending more than you can afford allows you to appear to have all kinds of qualities that you may not actually have. In a recent study on the evolutionary psychology of credit card debt, Kruger[27] found that, controlling for income levels, males who were more likely to overspend and build up balances that they could not afford were more likely than other males to have multiple sex partners. Overspending may act as a false signal of wealth, and although it is a false signal, sometimes this deception is effective. In fact, given how core deception is in human mating, it seems clear that overspending has become a modern form of false signaling, or mating deception.

In his recent book on the evolutionary psychology of modern spending patterns and consumerism, *Spent*, Geoffrey Miller[28] argues that modern-day materialism is the result of runaway selection and false courtship signaling. If every other guy is driving a Mercedes and I'm on a scooter, I must not have something that they all have. And the "thing" that they all "have" may be more than just a better vehicle. In making social judgments of others, we infer all kinds of things from people's belongings. We infer personality traits, social status, familial background, and intelligence levels, and ultimately, Miller argues, we unconsciously infer genetic quality. And this analysis is fully consistent with Gad Saad and John Vongas's[29] analysis of young adult males whose testosterone levels increase as a function of driving a Porsche downtown.

According to Robert Frank,[30] people also seem to spend a lot of money on positional goods, goods that have little utilitarian impact on survival but that signal our relative position in our local social circle. How many square feet is *your* house? Oh, you live on *how* many acres? How many cars fit in your garage? What kind of wood is *your* deck made out of? Which landscape company did *your* landscaping? Granite counters, of course, I assume?

Sound like a conversation you might have in modern America?

It truly is nicer to chop onions on a granite counter than on a laminate counter. But let us ask you this: Don't you chop your onions on a cutting board anyway? Oh, did you get that cutting board from France when you were in Europe?...but we digress.

Positional goods abound. The proportion of money that Americans spend on positional goods so as to (usually unconsciously) keep up with or beat out the Joneses is in the billions of dollars each year.[31] Welcome to America.

Using the evolutionary perspective on mating, spending is a form of courtship signaling. Not rich? But want to *appear* rich to potential mates? Get a credit card! (And watch MTV to know what to wear.) Then go to the mall with a smile and inhibit your mathematical skills.

But mating does not end after courtship. And mating does not end after the initial formation of a long-term mateship. We're pretty monogamous as a species (see Chapter 3).

As relationships progress toward long-term mateship, there are still plenty of bad reasons to spend money on stuff you don't need. For the sake of your relationship and your family, you may find yourself spending money on items that, on superficial reflection, are luxuries—commodities that come with mating-relevant signals. Yes, the kids each have their own Nintendo DSi. Yes, they each have two pairs of Crocs. Of course the boy has a Star Wars lunchbox—and we might get a separate one for the little one's snacks. Oh, we don't mind you asking at all, the paved driveway cost $6,000—but you know he went with the best pavers in town. Positional goods. A high proportion of our dialog with one another is all about positional goods.

Working to keep your status at levels that are acceptable or above seems a basic part of human nature.[32] And any mating psychologist will tell you that status and mating success are inextricably linked.

But as Geoffrey Miller tells us, even though commodities that signal quality and status of individuals *do* serve mating functions, these signals are often *false signals*. And someone with high mating intelligence should be better able than others to pick this out. Sure, Joe may have a BMW, but this is not because he's a higher-quality person than Tom (who drives a Kia). In fact, they make the same salary. Joe is simply more willing to utilize false signaling in his courtship strategy compared with Tom. Oh, that's not really very attractive when you put it that way!

An understanding of mating intelligence has a lot to offer in our attempts to understand broad spending patterns, especially in modern societies. And high levels of mating intelligence should go a long way in helping people tease apart genuine from false courtship signals.

Why Are Our Adolescent Males Dying?

One of the largest, most socially relevant, and thought-provoking areas of research to be illuminated by modern evolutionary psychology context pertains to male-female differences in the domain of death and injury. Think that evolutionary psychology somehow presents a biased view of the social world that favors men? Apparently, a lot of people do hold this opinion.[33] Well, think again. First off, evolutionary psychology is a scientific explanatory framework, rather than a moral code replete with *oughts*.[34] Regardless, even the most cursory look at the research on sex differences in injury and death paint a clear picture that is not particularly warming to hearts of men like ourselves.

In short, compared with females, males are more likely to:

- Die as a result of spontaneous abortion in utero[35]
- Die of some accident in the first year of life[36]
- Die of an accident in childhood—including falling, bicycle accidents, and even automobile accidents[37]
- Die of a wound as a function of a physical altercation[38]
- Die as a result of adverse effects of drugs and alcohol misuse[39]
- Die during midlife at the hands of other males during postmarriage reentry into the mating market[40]
- Suffer injuries during childhood that are likely to lead to concussion, stitches, casts, and hospital visits[41]

Is this portrait of a relatively difficult male world not clear enough? Then you should consider the fact that in virtually every culture that's ever been studied, males have significantly lower life expectancies than females. Further, consider the *male-to-female mortality ratio*. This ratio (see Fig. 9.1) speaks to how much more likely males are to die (at a given age) than females (of that

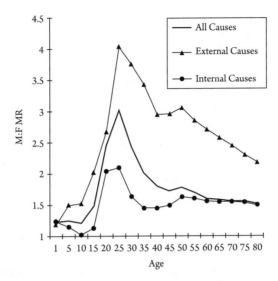

Figure 9.1: 2001 U.S. male-to-female mortality ratio for all causes, external causes, and internal causes of death. (Kruger & Nesse, 2007).

same age group). If the male-to-female mortality ratio = 1.0, that means that the proportion of males who die at a given age in life equals the proportion for females. As the number increases (e.g., male-to-female mortality ratio = 2.0), males are more likely than females to die at a particular life stage.

In a series of high-profile studies on this topic, Dan Kruger and Randolph Nesse[42] have documented that the male-to-female mortality ratio is particularly pronounced between the ages of 15 and 25 years, the years that largely correspond to courtship in our species. Humans are animals, and mate selection is competitive. Further, standard evolutionary biology tells us that if one sex invests a lot into parenting relative to the other sex, that high-investing sex will become relatively choosy in mate selection, and members of the other sex will compete more fiercely for access to mates. In humans, females invest more in offspring, females are more discriminating when it comes to mating,[43] and men compete fiercely with one another for access to mates.

We may think that this idea of males competing fiercely with one another characterizes nature documentaries (imagine two bull elk with antlers right about…now…) or non-Western societies, such as the Yanomami of South America, where males engage in public fights trying to injure or kill their opponents with clubs or spears. Yeah, that's fierce. But head to an emergency room in any North American city late on a Saturday night, and you'll see that we're not much different than the Yanomami culture. The proportion of physical injuries as a result of competitive fights at bars and parties is extremely sex biased, with young adult males much more likely than young adult females to show up at the emergency room after a scuffle, often over status or a woman, or something that likely ultimately relates to status or a woman.

Consider the Children

Maria Peclet and colleagues[44] conducted an analysis of sex differences in injuries in children in a sample of 3,472 cases of Massachusetts residents over a 34-month period. All the individuals in this sample were children. Injuries were coded in terms of several categories—injuries from a fall, automobile crash, and so forth. The sex bias, which parallels the trend found across studies of this kind, is clear. More than 60% of injuries documented were found in boys.

That's the world we live in—injury and death are integrally tied to whether one is male or female. And an evolutionarily informed perspective tells us why. From our perspective, understanding our behavior in evolutionary context by understanding *why* injury and death are so strongly connected to biological sex can help reduce risks for premature death and injury from accidents. Understanding our evolutionary roots—and the nature of human mating intelligence and where it comes from—may well help us understand issues such as injury rates in terms of their ultimate causes, thereby allowing us to create better informed solutions to the problems that permeate society.

Social Class and Mortality

Throughout this book, we have discussed the important effects of context on mating behaviors (see Chapter 3). Evolutionary psychology and behavioral ecology offer us new ways of understanding and explaining behavioral patterns seen in conditions of low socioeconomic status.[45] The combination of these approaches allows us to nonjudgmentally understand the cause of behaviors of people all around the world living under different conditions. The main tenet of behavioral ecology is that all animals exhibit the potential for behavioral flexibility and they use this flexibility to do the best they can in terms of survival and reproductive success given the context in which they find themselves.[46]

Behavioral ecology has proved quite useful in explaining human behavior. Humans behave very differently depending on their socioeconomic status. To make sense of why people behave the way they do, it's important to take into account factors that differ widely from one environment to the next. As we mentioned in Chapter 3, one major factor associated with socioeconomic status is the rate of mortality present in the environment. Mortality rates differ quite a bit from one neighborhood to the next and have a dramatic impact on people's life expectancy.

As one demonstration of this, Madhavi Bajekal,[47] head of the United Kingdom government's *Morbidity and Healthcare* team, looked at all of the electoral wards in Britain and assessed the relationship between the length of time expected to be alive and healthy and the level of social deprivation. The difference in life expectancy between the most deprived areas of Britain and the least deprived areas is as much as two decades (50 vs. 70 years)!

Such differences in life expectancy can have dramatic effects on people's psychology and behavior. Daniel Nettle[48] examined 8,660 families in Britain and found that in the most deprived neighborhoods, the age at first birth is younger, birth weights are lower, and breastfeeding duration is shorter than in the most affluent neighborhoods. In the poorest areas, women have babies at about the age of 20 years, compared with the age of 30 years in the richest areas. There is also indirect evidence that reproductive rates are higher in the poorest areas. In other words, when people expect to die young, they live fast, adopting a fast life history strategy (see Chapter 3).

This pattern is not just found in Britain. Across a set of small-scale subsistence societies, one study[49] found that for every 10% decline in the infant survival rate, there is a 1-year decrease in mothers' age at first birth, whereas another study[50] found that all across the world, the shorter the life expectancy, the earlier women reproduced. This pattern holds not just among humans but also across a large number of mammalian species.[51] Both within humans and across species, we tend to find that the higher the mortality rate, the earlier the onset of sexual reproduction in females and among males, the higher the mating effort and male-male competition.

Looking through a mating intelligence lens, informed by evolutionary psychology and behavioral ecology, we can start to make sense of these behaviors. When mortality is low, it would be evolutionarily adaptive for a female to have a small number of offspring and invest in each one. But in ecologies where mortality is high, that same strategy would leave the female with a high probability of having no offspring at all surviving to adulthood. Indeed, Arline Geronimus[52] found in Harlem, New York that the infant mortality rate of babies born to teenagers is half as great as the infant mortality rate of babies born to mothers in their 20s. Of course, the term *adaptive* as used here does not necessarily mean the same thing as socially desirable. Adaptive strictly refers to the likelihood that certain (conscious or unconscious) behaviors maximize survival and reproductive success. Still, the evolutionary approach allows us to explain widespread behavioral patterns that might seem random.

In general, the behavioral ecology approach views low socioeconomic behaviors as adaptive within harsh and unpredictable environments.[53] This approach can explain seeming puzzles, such as why those living in harsh and unpredictable environments, who have the most need to take care of themselves, are the least likely to do so.[54] Some of the evolutionary predictions made by behavioral ecologies even go against common intuition. For instance, one might think that low birth weight or early life stress would cause females' reproductive development to slow down, but instead these factors actually speed up women's sexual development (see Chapter 3).

Although mortality is a major determinant of the harshness of an environment, there are different types of mortality. Behavioral ecologists differentiate between extrinsic and intrinsic mortality. *Extrinsic* forms of mortality, such as the level of pollution in the air, is relatively unaffected by people's behavior. *Intrinsic* mortality, on the other hand, is affected by people's decisions, such as ignoring medical advice or choosing foods with poor nutrition. People can make a choice to reduce intrinsic mortality by trying to take care of themselves, but making that choice is a form of investment that takes up time and energy, an investment some people living in harsh environments may not view as worth it. Indeed, as the rate of extrinsic mortality goes up, the return in the investment of taking care of one's health does go down.[55] As Nettle notes,

> Who would spend money on regularly servicing a car in an environment where most cars were stolen each year anyway? (2009b, p. 936)

Still, we remain optimistic that we can use our understanding of the deep evolutionary logic of these behaviors to influence public policy and have a real effect on the well-being of those living in the harshest of environments. Certainly, epidemiologists have done a remarkable job describing the extent to which separate behaviors, such as sexual behavior, drugs, and violence, are related to the total rate of mortality in a society. A major limitation of their approach, however, is that they tend to treat these behaviors as unrelated. The evolutionary perspective suggests instead that these behaviors cluster together in nonrandom ways for evolutionarily adaptive reasons.

Neither biology nor environmental circumstances are destiny. But that does not mean change is going to be easy. Many factors at many different levels play a crucial role in shaping the fast life. A person's individual traits and the family, neighborhood, peers, and norms of conduct of that society each play crucial roles. To make large-scale changes you can't just change one particular trait, behavior, or aspect of the environment. Large-scale changes will require large-scale interventions that address many aspects of the system at once. A lot needs to happen in the harshest of environments to convince people and their genes that investing in their health will have a long-term payoff. As Nettle notes,

> We should not be surprised that social gradients in diet, breast-feeding or teenage pregnancy have failed to diminish, since the underlying inequality of our society has not diminished either.... Actually reducing poverty in the most deprived areas is far more likely to be influential than superficial education or awareness-raising schemes. (2009b, p. 937)

Against this advice, the U.K. government attempted to reduce the teenage pregnancy rate by educating young people about reproduction and contraception.[56] These programs have shown to be ineffective. From an evolutionary perspective, ignorance is not the issue. In fact, it may be ignorant for educators to think ignorance is the issue! Younger women in low socioeconomic status areas tend to reproduce at younger ages owing to the circumstances of their environment. In fact, they are actually taking an informed risk based on their life expectancy. As social scientist Lisa Arai at the University of London argued,

> ...policymakers find it hard to believe that young women, often in the least auspicious circumstances, might actually want to be mothers (Arai, 2003, p. 212).

As another example, many social interventionists think that adding basketball courts in low-socioeconomic neighborhoods will help redirect aggressive energies into friendly neighborhood games. The thinking is that by diverting such energies away from gang-related violence to cooperative play, gang violence will dissipate. This approach has failed. Increasing the basketball efficiency of inner-city youths has had no observable effect on the rate of violent crime.[57] Changing more than just one aspect of the interconnected web of life history factors is required.

Significant changes are possible, though. For example, the royalties that came from building a casino in a poor U.S. neighborhood led to an unexpected reduction in psychopathology and antisocial behaviors.[58] Additionally, there was a considerable decline in teenage birth rates in the United States in the 1990s, particularly among African Americans, which was probably owing to a better economy and increase in employment opportunities for black women during this time.[59] As *the New Scientist* reports, however, teen birth rates among African Americans are rising again, most likely a result of the relatively recent economic decline.

There is tremendous potential for the behavioral ecology perspective to inform public policy, but we agree with Nettle[60] that there is a great need for social scientists and evolutionary theorists to unite in a common cause and go beyond misconceptions about what it really means for something to have an evolutionary basis: "evolved" is not the opposite of "learned," and "evolutionary causes" are not the opposite of "social causes." As Nettle eloquently wrote,

> Evolutionary thinking in the human sciences is nothing more or less than the holistic, integrative understanding that we, like other animals, respond to our social and developmental environment in non-arbitrary ways. (2009b, p. 937)

Educating Those in the Fast Lane

We see opportunity for the mating intelligence perspective to be integrated with educational psychology, particularly when it comes to developing creativity. The mating intelligence framework, informed by life history theory, gives us greater insight into the mechanisms by which students adapt to their environments inside *and outside* the classroom. Many students with extraordinary potential for making socially valuable contributions see their potential squandered because their energies are directed toward other concerns involving survival and reproduction.

Note that although life history strategy is directly related to brain-based executive functions that may get in the way of school performance (e.g., emotional regulation skills), life history strategy is *not* directly related to IQ. The processes evoked when taking an IQ test are related but are not exactly the same as the processes evoked on tests of executive functioning, and not all executive functions are equally related to intelligence.[61] Life history strategy is less directly tied to IQ and more related to the self-control and emotional self-regulation executive functions, skills that have a significant impact in a classroom environment.[62] It is important to keep in mind that fast life strategists are not stupid. In fact, if you define intelligence as the ability to adapt to the environment (as many intelligence researchers define the term), then fast-life strategists are, in certain environments, *very* intelligent from an evolutionary perspective.

Many fast-life strategists are reprimanded in school for displaying social problems that are adaptive in their environment outside the classroom but may not be adaptive inside the classroom. Indeed, Robert J. Sternberg has long-argued that "practical intelligence" is a form of intelligence just as important as the type of analytical skills measured by IQ tests.[63]

Although intelligence theorists rarely peer through an evolutionary lens (a state of affairs we find unfortunate), we think that looking at the entire suite of human strategies from an evolutionarily informed perspective offers potential for helping teachers better understand the evolutionary logic behind many of the traits and behaviors they see in their classrooms. We think teachers may get more out of their students by really getting into their students' heads and attempting to understand the evolutionary logic behind many of their students' classroom behaviors. Such an understanding can potentially help students boost their self-regulation skills[64] and channel their life history strategies toward socially acceptable creative and productive pursuits, which in the long run is conducive to mating success much more so than aggression and dominance.

In our view, there is no need to throw out the baby with the bathwater; some fast life traits such as risk-taking, questioning of authority, and rebelliousness can be quite conducive to creativity. Don't we want to teach our students to question authority, and not blindly follow other people's rules? Unfortunately, most displays of creativity and spontaneity are not highly valued in most class-rooms—even though recent research has found that creative activities improve the brain's ability to process information.[65]

Thankfully, there's some exciting work being done looking at education from an evolutionarily informed perspective. We highly recommend checking out Peter Gray's work on the topic.[66] At the end of the day, the key to dealing with life's many demands seems to be the ability to strategically activate or deactivate executive functions depending on the context. This kind of flexibility is not taught in schools, but why not?

Another key to educating those in the fast lane is to convince them that there is a reason for them to invest in creativity—that their investments will pay off. Many living the fast life really do perceive their future as dire. The life history framework predicts that in order to have long-lasting changes on students who are living the fast life, you have to change their harsh and unpre-dictable contexts. This is the most likely way their strategies will change from seeking short-term gains to seeing a purpose for longer-term planning (see previous section).

Although the mating intelligence perspective, informed by life history the-ory, certainly does not explain *everything*, we think there is a lot of untapped potential to inform educational structure and practices. Many students may not be well adapted to a structured classroom environment, but that does not mean they cannot harness their particular way of thinking and behaving in a way that that is highly innovative as well as socially and culturally valued.

Coda

Throughout this book, we have presented the new idea of mating intelligence. Rooted in an evolutionary perspective on human nature, Mating Intelligence Theory has the capacity to illuminate many areas of human life. Both inside and outside the walls of academia, scholars are often asked how their ideas are useful. What are the practical applications? How can this all benefit society? Why should I care?

In this chapter, we discussed several ways that mating intelligence has the capacity to help people at the individual and societal levels. The sex education approach described here has the capacity to help educate adolescents by putting sexuality in the contexts of society and human evolution. This approach, rooted in the core ideas of Mating Intelligence Theory, has potential to help young adults better understand why sexuality is so central to human social behaviors and how to make informed, adaptive, and other-oriented decisions regarding sex.

The applications to psychotherapy described in this chapter have the capacity to revolutionize psychotherapy writ large. Whether people like it or not, evolutionary psychology is seeping into all aspects of the behavioral sciences.[67] Evolutionary psychology is shedding light on all aspects of humanity as a result. Using the insights of evolutionary psychology to inform approaches to psychotherapy seems, to us, to be the only reasonable way for therapists to progress in their efforts to help others. Mating Intelligence Theory is a specific set of ideas, informed both by evolutionary psychology and individual differences research on intelligence and personality, with the potential to help therapists get to core issues of human mating that lead to such psychological issues as stress and depression.

This chapter also addressed the major societal problems of violence toward women, runaway spending, male injury, mortality, and implications of mating intelligence in the classroom. Future work in the area of applied psychology will benefit from the insights of Mating Intelligence Theory as social scientists and policy makers battle these important social issues.

Life is not easy. And mating is not easy. An understanding of mating intelligence, the cognitive processes that underlie human mating, can help.

EPILOGUE

A Brief History of the Mating Intelligence Scale

For mating intelligence to be a useful psychological idea, a valid measure was needed. Fortunately, we got the phone call from *Psychology Today* that provided the encouragement to develop a way for people to test themselves. In 2006, Kaja Perina, Editor-in-Chief of *Psychology Today*, contacted us about our work on mating intelligence. She indicated that she was planning to write a cover story all about mating intelligence.[1] Along with the article, Kaja thought it would be good to include some measure of mating intelligence that readers of the magazine could take so as to better understand where they stacked up. "Yes, absolutely!" we responded. This sounded like fun!

So the Mating Intelligence Scale[2] was initially designed as a fun scale made for a popular magazine—not created with an academic agenda. However, as two psychometrically trained research psychologists, we created the scale using the same kind of reasoning that would go into any scale we were creating for research purposes.

Facets of the Mating Intelligence Scale

In creating the scale, we first considered the core aspects of mating intelligence. By this point in the book, you shouldn't be surprised by the concepts we include as *facets* (or subscales) of the main scale. These facets include processes that we consider core to our understanding of mating intelligence. Below is a description of each facet along with an example item from the True-or-False Mating Intelligence Scale that corresponds to that facet:

1. **Accurate Cross-Sex Mind-Reading** (this facet addresses how well you can read the mating-relevant thoughts of the opposite sex)

Sample item: *I can tell when a man is being genuine and sincere in his affections toward me.*

2. **Adaptive Self-Deception in the Mating Domain** (this facet addresses the tendency to inflate your value as a mate in your understanding of yourself)

Sample item: *I look younger than most women my age.*

3. **Adaptive Mate-Deception** (this facet addresses how well you can deceive mates in a way that may be evolutionarily adaptive)

Sample item: *If I wanted to make my current guy jealous, I could easily get the attention of other guys.*

4. **Effective Behavioral Courtship Display** (this facet addresses your abilities related to creative intelligence, which are attractive to potential mates)

Sample item: *I'm definitely more creative than most people.*

5. **Adaptive Perceptual Bias** (this facet is sex differentiated; for males, items that tap this facet address the tendency toward oversexualizing females; for females, items that tap this facet reflect *commitment skepticism*)

Sample female item: *Most guys who are nice to me are just trying to get into my pants.* Sample male item: *Women tend to flirt with me pretty regularly.*

6. **Self-Reported Mating Success** (this facet is something of an outcome hypothesized to follow from mating intelligence—how successful are you in the mating domain?)

Sample item: *I attract many wealthy, successful men.*

Therein lies the reasoning underlying the structure of the Mating Intelligence Scale.[3] Later in this chapter, we include the full test (both the male and female versions) along with a scoring key and commentary on how to interpret results. We also include comments on specific people who have scored at different levels of the range on this scale.

Mating Success: A Critical Outcome Associated with Mating Intelligence

Whenever we talk about mating intelligence, we have to keep in mind Darwin's bottom line. Remember, Darwin described adaptations as producers of evolutionary forces that facilitate the reproductive success of an organism. Typically, biologists will study the number of offspring produced by an organism as a measure of that organism's fitness. We can't do that very easily with modern humans. Modern humans have plentiful forms of birth control that did not exist during the lion's share of human evolutionary history. A person with all the hallmarks of an evolutionary success story might just be dynamite at using condoms properly—and leave no descendants.

As scientists studying human psychology from an evolutionary perspective, the best we can do, then, really, is to approximate reproductive success. Work along these lines has begun in evolutionary psychology labs around the world.[4] In measuring mating success, we essentially need to think about tapping outcomes that *would have been associated with ultimate reproductive fitness* under ancestral conditions. In light of Trivers'[5] parental investment theory, we realized that any index of mating success must be sex differentiated because, for example, a male who copulates at high frequencies will gain fitness benefits while a female will not gain any fitness benefits from such a strategy. Work on creating optimal measures of mating success is still in progress and will likely never fully approach the elusive variable of reproductive success in postcontraceptive human societies. But given the cards in our hand, measuring indices of mating success is currently the best way to examine the validity of any tests designed to measure mating intelligence.

Scientific Validation of the Mating Intelligence Scale

Initially, the scale was created for fun, and although we put some good thought into the creation of this scale, scientific validation was not on our initial radar. Still, the scale took on something of a life of its own. The issue of *Psychology Today* that published the scale, we were told, ended up being one of the best-selling issues in the magazine's history. The article was picked up by several other media outlets—*Arts and Letters Daily, The New Scientist, The Washington Times*, and more. Not to mention the hundreds of blogs and OK Cupid.

At some point, several researchers affiliated with Binghamton University's world-renowned evolutionary studies program, directed by David Sloan Wilson, became interested in this scale. Dan O'Brien, then a PhD student in Biology with a concentration in evolutionary studies at Binghamton, asked us if he could include this scale (along with other evolutionarily relevant scales) to administer to undergraduate students at Binghamton. We were delighted.

A few months later, we got an intriguing email from Dan. Were we aware that our Mating Intelligence Scale better predicted several sexual outcomes than any of the other scales used in their study? This suggested that the scale must have some scientific validity and significant predictive validity. Considering the humble origins of the scale, this was exciting news.

Since then, several studies have been conducted (and published) on the scientific merit of the Mating Intelligence Scale.[6] This first study, done in conjunction with Dan O'Brien, Andy Gallup, and Justin Garcia at SUNY Binghamton, examined the reliability, validity, and predictive utility of the Mating Intelligence Scale. It was administered to more than 100 undergraduate males and females—along with several measures of sexual activity, including (1) age at first sexual intercourse, (2) number of sex partners in the past year, and (3) number of lifetime sex partners.

In this study,[7] the Mating Intelligence Scale was psychometrically examined in two important ways. First, an analysis was conducted to see whether the different subscales are "internally reliable" and "distinct"—that is, do the statistics bear out our prediction that the facets of mating intelligence that we built into the scale really are distinct and reliable facets of this concept? Short answer: not necessarily—the subscales generally showed relatively *low internal reliability*. That is, this initial analysis did not provide strong evidence that this measure scientifically breaks down into these facets. However, we then conducted a reliability analysis on the full scales—for both the male and female versions—and found the full scales did, indeed, demonstrate strong internal reliability. So we essentially found that the full scales are reliable scales—and we could make the case that we are measuring overall *mating intelligence* (while not necessarily measuring each facet of mating intelligence). At least we had evidence that we had strong and psychometrically verified full scales of mating intelligence for each of the sexes.

We then go on to our research questions to address the validity of mating intelligence: Does mating intelligence predict sexual behavior for males and females—and does it do so in a way that makes evolutionary sense?

Things played out a bit differently for each of the sexes. As such, analyses were conducted separately for men and women. For males, high mating intelligence corresponded to having sex relatively early in life, having a relatively high number of lifetime sexual partners, and having a relatively high number of partners in the past year. Consistent with much past research on male mating psychology from an evolutionary perspective,[8] success in the mating domain for males corresponds to a relatively high number of sexual partners.

Mating psychologists have consistently shown that mating psychology is often highly sex differentiated.[9] For mating intelligence to be valid within this sphere of academia, it makes sense, then, that the Mating Intelligence Scale would predict outcomes in a sex-differentiated manner that are consistent with the large body of past work in this area. Female mating psychology tends to be more complex, on average, than male mating psychology,[10] and a good measure on mating psychology should catch this important nuance.

Sure enough, in predicting these basic sexual outcomes, the Mating Intelligence Scale does exactly this. Females who scored high on the Mating Intelligence Scale showed a slightly different pattern from males who scored high on this scale—and a pattern that makes good evolutionary sense. Females who scored high (1) had sex relatively early in their lives and (2) had a higher number of lifetime sex partners compared with females who scored low. Importantly, this second outcome, having more lifetime sexual partners, is explainable as a statistical artifact that follows from having a longer lifetime sexual history. Importantly, females who scored high on the Mating Intelligence Scale did *not* report more sexual partners in the past year compared with other females. This pattern is different from what was found with males (which was simply, more mating intelligence, more partners), and it reflects the complexities of female sexuality. For a female, high mating intelligence may well increase with early sexual experiences, but it may also ultimately shape a behavioral pattern that is highly discriminating in mate selection.

In a more recent study that we are conducting with our colleagues Ben Crosier and James C. Kaufman, we gave out the Mating Intelligence Scale to hundreds of young men and women in an ethnically diverse sample of students in California. Along with the Mating Intelligence Scale, participants in this study completed a measure of general intelligence,[11] and measures of the most scientifically accepted personality traits there are—the Big Five personality traits of neuroticism, extraversion, openness, agreeableness, and conscientiousness. Decades of intensive research on the nature of the basic personality traits has led to the determination that these five trait dimensions reflect significant aspects of people that discriminate individuals from one another. From a scientific perspective, these are considered the five most robust personality traits. With the addition of general intelligence, which is also, clearly, a major dimension of human variation, psychologist Geoffrey Miller[12] refers to these dimensions as the *Central Six* (the Big 5 plus general intelligence).

In our study, a measure of mating success, including items related to short-term mating success (such as being able to turn up short-term partners easily) and long-term mating success (such as currently being in a satisfying long-term relationship), was also presented to participants.

We hope that this study represents a crucial step in terms of the validation of mating intelligence. If the Mating Intelligence Scale has *predictive validity*, then it should predict this evolutionarily important outcome (mating success) in a way (1) that is distinct from the ability of the Central Six to predict mating success and (2) that leads to *predictions of significant amounts of variability in mating success*. In short, this all means that scores on the Mating Intelligence Scale should be related to scores on the mating success scale, and if the Mating Intelligence Scale is valid, scores on this scale should be more related to mating success than scores on the general intelligence measure or scores on the Big 5 personality traits.

After a series of advanced statistical analyses (including a process called *multiple regression*) conducted by the formidable Ben Crosier as part of his master's thesis, the data were clear: the Mating Intelligence Scale emerged as the single best predictor of mating success for both males and females.

From an evolutionary perspective, this finding is, actually, quite enormous. Darwin's bottom line is clear. Organisms are in natural competition for reproduction into subsequent generations. From a Darwinian perspective, the ultimate outcome variable is reproductive success. As we've discussed earlier in this book, reproductive success (number of offspring and grand-offspring) cannot be tapped in a meaningful way in modern societies owing to the large-scale use of contraception. The best that we can do to approximate reproductive success in modern humans is to measure mating success, which should include outcomes and behaviors that would have led to increased reproductive success under ancestral conditions.[13] We believe that predicting mating success is crucial for any psychological variable posited to have evolutionary relevance. And compared with general intelligence and the Big 5—representing, in composite, the most intensively studied and validated constructs in all of personality psychology—mating intelligence best predicts mating success.

Since this large-scale validation study, several advanced students in the SUNY New Paltz Evolutionary Psychology Lab have found in their own studies that the Mating Intelligence Scale continues to predict important life outcomes. Haley Dillon examined mating intelligence as it relates to narcissism and found that there is a slight positive correlation between narcissism and mating intelligence for both sexes (although females score higher on narcissism than do males). This capacity may entail a bit of self-absorption, but not too much.

Ashley Peterson, another graduate student in the SUNY New Paltz Evolutionary Psychology Lab, gave the Mating Intelligence Scale to undergraduate students along with measures of the Big Five personality traits, and asked participants for their degrees of preference for various sexual acts. Interestingly, mating intelligence was positively related to preferences for several acts but was mostly predictive of a preference for vaginal intercourse over oral or anal intercourse; this finding was pronounced for females in the sample.[14] Mating intelligence also tended to correspond to being relatively extraverted, which we know from Chapter 3 is associated with a proclivity toward sexual variety (although introverts can certainly score high in mating intelligence and have an active sex life).

Mating Intelligence as a Predictor of Casual Hook-Ups

In another recent study conducted by Daniel O'Brien and his colleagues,[15] the Mating Intelligence Scale was shown to play an important predictive role regarding a common and socially relevant class of modern mating behavior: hook-ups. Hook-ups are defined as casual mating experiences with no expectations of the creation of long-term bonds.[16] Among college students, hook-up experiences are quite common. Although statistics vary from study to study and school to school, generally, it seems that a majority of college students report having engaged in some hook-up behaviors.

With an explicit focus on short-term mating, hook-up behaviors seem a bit evolutionarily strange in a relatively monogamous species such as ours. With this thought in mind, Justin Garcia and Chris Reiber[17] conducted a study to explore the motivations underlying hook-up experiences. They came to find that most females who engage in hook-ups do, actually, hope that hook-up experiences will lead to long-term relationships. Interestingly, a majority of males who were included in this study reported the same thing! Contrary to what a lot of people think, males often expect and hope (probably privately) that hook-up experiences will lead to long-term relationships. Hook-up experiences and the emotions driving them are more complex than they might seem.

In a follow-up to Garcia and Reiber's study,[18] we explored the role of mating intelligence as it relates to hook-ups. At the suggestion of our colleague Melanie Hill, we decided to break hook-up experiences into three categories—because not all hook-ups are the same.

In this research, hook-up experiences were broken down as follows:

A. Type I: hook-up with a total stranger
B. Type II: hook-up with an acquaintance
C. Type III: hook-up with a friend

In this study, the Mating Intelligence Scale was given to a sample including about 200 male and female college students. Participants were also asked to report if they had engaged in any Type I, Type II, or Type III hook-ups.

Consistent with the study that predicted sexual activity from mating intelligence, two important general themes emerged. First, mating intelligence significantly predicted the outcome variables, providing further evidence that mating intelligence is strongly related to mating-relevant outcomes. Additionally, the pattern of relationship between mating intelligence and hook-up behaviors played out differently for males and females, in a way that makes sense in light of what we know about evolutionary psychology.

For males, the story remains the same. Males who had experienced any of the three kinds of hook-ups generally scored higher on the Mating Intelligence Scale than males who had not experienced the different kinds of hook-ups. For females, the results were much more nuanced. Females who had engaged in type I hook-ups (hook-ups with total strangers) were no different from other females in their Mating Intelligence Scale scores. Similarly, females who had engaged in type III hook-ups (hook-ups with "friends") were no different from other females in their Mating Intelligence Scale scores. But females who had engaged in type II hook-ups (hook-ups with "acquaintances") did score higher than other females on the Mating Intelligence Scale.

These findings speak to the kind of complexity underlying female sexuality that evolutionary psychologists have documented extensively.[19] A female engaging in too many short-term flings, with no chance of commitment, is taking on an evolutionarily questionable strategy because she is at risk for being abandoned and facing exorbitant parental costs. It makes sense, then, that a female who is high in mating intelligence is not necessarily a female who is engaging in many short-term flings because such behavior would not be "intelligent" from a female mating perspective.

Further, based on published research regarding opposite-sex friendships,[20] it makes sense that females would not be hooking up with men whom they assess as friends. Females are much more likely than males to see opposite-sex friends in nonsexual terms and to expect a circle of male friends to serve nonsexual benefits, such as providing a broader social network and protection. Once a female has designated a male as having *friend status* in her mind, a hook-up with that male would defeat much of the evolutionary purpose of that friendship. So, it might not make sense for a woman with high mating intelligence to have sex with her male friends.

A man defined as an *acquaintance*, however, might be precisely at a level that would be evolutionarily reasonable to hook-up with—particularly if hook-ups in females are *really* part of a strategy of turning up a high-quality long-term mate.[21] And females with relatively high mating intelligence *are* more likely than other females to engage in these kinds of hook-ups.

All of these findings together suggest that the Mating Intelligence Scale has the potential to chart not only personality traits but also important mating-relevant life outcomes.

Mating Intelligence as a Window into Optimal Mating

When the idea of mating intelligence first hit the streets, we'll admit, there were some skeptics. Rightfully so. Any idea framed as a fresh new theory in the field of psychology should be met with a good bit of skepticism. Psychology has seen plenty of wheel reinventing in its history, and newly invented wheels aren't often useful.

A common criticism that we heard echoes the most common criticism lobbed at emotional intelligence[22] when it first emerged. What's new here?

At this point in the book, we hope the reader will agree that there is actually quite a lot new here. Mating intelligence is not just "mating psychology" repackaged. Here, we'd like to draw attention to a particular innovation that follows from the idea of mating intelligence. In the past, mating researchers spent considerable time and energy trying to understand mating processes as optimized by evolutionary forces. Males show preference for females with a particular tone of voice[23]; women sort through a relatively high number of suitors before settling on a particular mate[24]; male jealousy responses are particularly sensitive to sexual prompts[25]; and so forth.

As we attempt to understand human nature, this research is illuminating. However, this past research all has a limitation that can actually be addressed by the idea of mating intelligence. Saying that some behaviors and processes are part of "human nature" does not speak to all the differences found among humans in these behaviors and processes. Sometimes, it's more informative to look at the effects of different levels that exist among humans in order to come to a deeper understanding of a phenomenon.

As an example, consider *commitment skepticism*, documented by Martie Haselton and David Buss,[26] defined as the evolutionarily adaptive tendency for females to be particularly skeptical of a man's faithfulness or long-term intentions. Sure, this process typifies female mating psychology, and we have even documented it in our own research.[27] But thinking about this process as a species-typical process says nothing about individual differences in this tendency.

It may well be the case that women in general are commitment skeptics, but consider the following issues:

1. Some women may be more commitment skeptical than others.
2. There may be an optimal amount of commitment skepticism for most effective mating success.

and

3. Having an optimal amount of commitment skepticism may go along with other psychological mating tendencies that are relatively intelligent (e.g., the ability to read effectively the behaviors, thoughts, and intentions of potential suitors).

A woman who is high in mating intelligence may well be a solid exemplar of commitment skepticism, just as a woman who is high in mating intelligence

may well be an exemplar of strategic and optimized hook-up behavior and strategic and optimized sexual activity more generally.[28]

Future research on mating-relevant adaptations may do well to see whether
high mating intelligence tends to correspond to a "relatively adaptive response."
In this way, mating intelligence scores may actually be used as a barometer of
sorts, measuring whether a proposed mating-relevant adaptation is, indeed,
something that typifies how mating experts behave.

Deconstructing the Mating Intelligence Scale

Until this point, we've been trying to make the case that the Mating Intelligence
Scale is pretty much the best thing since color TV. In reality, as is true with any
scientific measure, this scale could benefit from some improvement. In this
section, we'll talk about the pros and cons of the scale as well as the future of
psychometric work in this area.

Remember, the Mating Intelligence Scale was designed with a general audience in mind; we needed to then substantiate it scientifically. With that said,
strong psychometric work has been published on this scale,[29] and several studies have now demonstrated its ability to predict the kinds of mating outcomes
that should be predicted by a measure of mating intelligence.[30]

But a great deal of work still needs to be done. First and foremost, the Mating
Intelligence Scale has primarily been administered to college students. As we
have repeatedly pointed out in this book, mating behaviors are very contextual,
and age is an important factor in determining mating-relevant outcomes. Much
more research needs to be conducted on how mating intelligence operates across
the life span. It may eventually turn out that we need to have separate scales,
one for young adulthood and another for adulthood. Or perhaps even more differentiated scales, such as one for senior citizens. Our grandparents are probably up to a lot more hooking-up behavior than we realize (or care to realize)!

Second, it seems that the Scale acts best as a total scale rather than as a set
of facets or subscales. More research needs to be done to properly measure the
various components of mating intelligence. This will require coming up with
new items and getting rid of some of the older ones.

Third, the male and female versions are different. On the one hand, this
makes sense given that male and female mating psychology is not the same. On
the other hand, it makes for a classic apples-and-oranges problem. Because the
two scales have largely different content, it is unclear whether they are tapping
the same underlying concepts. Although our preliminary work in validating
the scale suggests that the two versions do seem to behave similarly, this is still
a point that researchers need to keep in mind.

Fourth, even though the Mating Intelligence Scale has been shown to be a
valid and effective initial measure of mating intelligence, we believe that it just

scratches the surface of the measurement of mating intelligence. The history of the measurement of emotional intelligence is complex,[31] and we expect mating intelligence to go through a similar development. With emotional intelligence, two kinds of measures have been created—*trait measures* and *ability measures*.[32] Trait measures include self-reports of emotional intelligence,[33] whereas ability-based measures tap actual abilities in terms of dealing with emotions (such as the ability to guess which emotion best characterizes a particular response illustrated by an actor in a video).[34]

In terms of this *trait/ability measure* distinction, the Mating Intelligence Scale would be considered a trait measure. Research on emotional intelligence has often been critical of trait measures, suggesting that such measures are tapping personality traits as opposed to any kind of intelligence.[35] Might this same kind of criticism make sense in terms of mating intelligence? Quite possibly—and this is certainly an important issue for future research on mating intelligence to take on.

In fact, in thinking about future research on mating intelligence, it becomes clear that developing valid ability-based indices of this construct sits at the forefront of future scientific work in this field. As examples, it would be great to be able to measure people's actual abilities to successfully guess the mating-relevant thoughts of the opposite sex. Similarly, an ability-based measure of mating intelligence could examine individual differences in mating-relevant deception—are some people simply better at this skill than others? Can we operationally define differences in how well people can make a potential mate feel comfortable in a social setting? Can we measure how people differ in their abilities to convince a potential mate to go on a date? Can we measure individual differences in the ability to smooth things over during a moment of conflict within a long-term mateship using a combination of cognitive and emotional skills?

We believe that the Mating Intelligence Scale has proved very useful in paving the way for empirical research on this topic—but creating genuine ability-based measures of the different elements of mating intelligence certainly will lead to more insights into human nature and its many variations, in the future.[36]

A final concept to consider in deconstructing the Mating Intelligence Scale pertains to *scoring low versus high*. After this scale was published, you might imagine that we were busy having pretty much everyone we knew take the test. Scott's Grandma took it—and scored off the charts. Glenn's grandmother-in-law also scored in the upper echelon. A high-level administrator at SUNY New Paltz took it, but he came out as a bit *mating challenged*. Glenn's brothers took it and scored pretty low. Glenn's son Andrew scored slightly above the mean—Andrew is currently 7 years old! And so on . . .

Although we are confident in this scale having strong science behind it and being a great tool for research purposes, its usefulness in everyday life is still open for discussion. So take this scale with a grain of salt! But, with that said . . .

Take the Test!

In this final section of this chapter, you'll find the Mating Intelligence Scale (in full) along with a scoring key and a breakdown of which items go with which facets of mating intelligence. Have fun!

FOR MEN

1. ___ I think most women just like me as a friend.
2. ___ I have slept with many beautiful women.
3. ___ I'm pretty good at knowing if a woman is attracted to me.
4. ___ I'm definitely not the best at taking care of kids.
5. ___ I'm good at saying the right things to women I flirt with.
6. ___ I haven't had as many sexual partners compared with other guys I know (who are my age).
7. ___ I have a difficult time expressing complex ideas to others.
8. ___ I am good at picking up signals of interest from women.
9. ___ I'm definitely near the top of the status totem pole in my social circles.
10. ___ I doubt that I'll ever be a huge financial success.
11. ___ If I wanted to, I could convince a woman that I'm really a prince from some little-known European country.
12. ___ Honestly, I don't get women at all!
13. ___ Women tend to flirt with me pretty regularly.
14. ___ If a woman doesn't seem interested in me, I figure she doesn't know what she's missing!
15. ___ Women definitely find me attractive.
16. ___ I've dated many intelligent women.
17. ___ People tell me that I have a great sense of humor.
18. ___ When I lie to women, I always get caught!
19. ___ I am usually wrong about who is interested in me romantically.
20. ___ It's hard for me to get women to see my virtues.
21. ___ At parties, I tend to tell stories that catch the attention of women.
22. ___ I'm not very talented in the arts.
23. ___ I can attract women, but they rarely end up interested in me sexually.
24. ___ When a woman smiles at me, I assume she's just being friendly.

FOR WOMEN

1. ___ I can tell when a man is being genuine and sincere in his affections toward me.
2. ___ I doubt I could ever pull off cheating on my beau.
3. ___ I look younger than most women my age.
4. ___ When a guy doesn't seem interested in me, I take it personally and assume something is wrong with me.
5. ___ Good-looking guys never seem into me.
6. ___ I have a sense of style and wear clothes that make me look sexy.
7. ___ I attract many wealthy, successful men.
8. ___ Honestly, I don't think I understand men at all!
9. ___ With me, a guy gets what he sees—no pretenses here.
10. ___ If I wanted to make my current guy jealous, I could easily get the attention of other guys.
11. ___ Men don't tend to be interested in my mind.
12. ___ I'm definitely more creative than most people.
13. ___ I hardly ever know when a guy likes me romantically.
14. ___ I laugh a lot at men's jokes.
15. ___ If a guy doesn't want to date me, I figure he doesn't know what he's missing!
16. ___ I am not very artistic.
17. ___ My current beau spends a lot of money on material items for me (such as jewelry).
18. ___ I am usually right on the money about a man's intentions toward me.
19. ___ I really don't have a great body compared with other women I know.
20. ___ Intelligent guys never seem interested in dating me.
21. ___ I believe that most men are actually more interested in long-term relationships than they're given credit for.
22. ___ Most guys who are nice to me are just trying to get into my pants.
23. ___ When it comes down to it, I think most men want to get married and have children.
24. ___ If I have sex with a man too soon, I know he will leave me.

How high is your mating intelligence? The Mating Intelligence Scale included here was created by us for a *Psychology Today* article on mating intelligence, published a few years ago. There are two versions, one for heterosexual males and one for heterosexual females. Each test is designed to provide a rough guide to your relationship effectiveness—not a definitive statement about individual character. To take the test, simply answer True or False for each of the 24 items under the test that pertains to you. Scroll to the end for scoring—and note that however you score, mating intelligence is a malleable dimension of human psychology!

How to Tally your Mating Intelligence Score

FOR MALES

Give yourself one point for every T answer to questions 2, 3, 5, 8, 9, 11, 13, 14, 15, 16, 17, and 21. Add one point for every F answer to items 1, 4, 6, 7, 10, 12, 18, 19, 20, 22, 23, and 24.

FOR FEMALES

Give yourself one point for every T answer to questions 1, 3, 6, 7, 10, 12, 14, 15, 17, 18, 22, and 24. Add one point for every F answer to items 2, 4, 5, 8, 9, 11, 13, 16, 19, 20, 21, and 23.

Based on a recent study (O'Brien et al., 2010), male scores tend to average about 12.3, whereas the female average is about 10.5. And there is a lot of variability in scores within each sex.

Mating Intelligence Facet	Male Version	Female Version
Accurate Cross-Sex Mind-Reading (this facet addresses how well you can read the mating-relevant thoughts of the opposite sex)	Items 3, 8, **12**, **19**	Items 1, **8**, **13**, 18
Adaptive Self-Deception in Mating Domain (this facet addresses the tendency to inflate your value as a mate in your understanding of yourself)	Items **4**, 9, **10**, 14	Items 3, **4**, 15, **19**
Adaptive Mate-Deception (this facet addresses how well you can deceive mates in a way that may be adaptive)	Items 5, 11, **18**, **20**	Items **2**, 6, **9**, 10
Effective Behavioral Courtship Display (this facet addresses your abilities related to creative intelligence, which are attractive to potential mates)	Items **7**, 17, 21, **22**	Items **11**, 12, 14, **16**
Adaptive Bias (for males, this facet speaks to oversexualizing women; for females, this facet speaks to commitment skepticism)	Items 1, 13, 15, **24**	Items **21**, 22, **23**, 24

Self-Reported Mating Success (this facet is something of an outcome hypothesized to follow from mating intelligence—how successful are you in the mating game?)	Items 2, **6**, 16, **23**	Items **5**, 7, 17, **20**
	Boldfaced Items are "reversed"—thought about as reflecting "low mating intelligence"	Boldfaced Items are "reversed"— thought about as reflecting "low mating intelligence"

Note that this scale and these instructions were published in *Psychology Today* (January, 2007). The re-publication here was done with the written consent of *Psychology Today*.

NOTES

Chapter 1

1. See Buss, 1994; Flam, 2008; and Ridley, 2003.
2. See Mayr, 1963.
3. See Dugatkin, 2009.
4. See Cunningham, 1986.
5. Evolutionary psychologists do recognize that there can be cross-cultural differences and individual differences in the characteristics associated with physical attractiveness. Nonetheless, they argue that such differences aren't *infinitely* variable but rather are constrained to some degree by evolutionary selection pressures.
6. See Spearman, 1904.
7. See Chabris, 2007.
8. See Kaufman, DeYoung, Gray, Brown, & Mackintosh, 2009; Sternberg & Kaufman, 2011; and van der Maas et al., 2006.
9. See Deary, Strand, Smith, & Fernandes, 2007; Hunt, 2011; Mackintosh, 2011; Naglieri & Bornstein, 2003; and Kaufman, Liu, McGrew, & Kaufman, 2010.
10. See Gottfredson, 1997.
11. See Deary & Batty, 2011.
12. See Flam, 2008; Mystery, 2007, 2010; Strauss, 2005; and Thorn, 2011.
13. See Keller & Miller, 2006.
14. See Arden et al., 2008; Banks, Batcheor, & McDaniel, 2010; Bates, 2007; Calvin et al., 2010; Deary & Batty, 2011; Furlow et al., 1997; Prokosch, Yeo, & Miller, 2005; Silventoinen, Posthuma, van Beijsterveldt, Bartels, & Boomsma, 2006; and Sundet, Tambs, Harris, Magnus, & Torjussen, 2005.
15. See, for example, Johnson, Segal, & Bouchard, 2008.
16. See Moore, 2002; Shenk, 2010; and Ridley, 2003.
17. See Mandelman & Grigorenko, 2011.
18. See Deary, Penke, & Johnson, 2010; and Gray & Thompson, 2004.
19. See Johnson, 2010; and Johnson, Turkheimer, Gottesman, & Bouchard, 2009.
20. For good reviews on the many environmental influences on intelligence, see Ceci, 1996; and Nisbett, 2010.
21. See Hasson, 2006.
22. See Fisher, 2004; and Sternberg & Weis, 2008.
23. See Zebrowitz & Rhodes, 2004.
24. See Johnson, Ahern, & Cole, 1980.
25. See Baer & Kaufman, 2005; Kaufman, 2009a; Kaufman & Sternberg, 2010; Kim, 2005; and Kim, Crammond, & VanTassel-Baska.
26. See DeYoung, 2011.

27. See Shamosh & Gray, 2008; Shamosh et al., 2008; Chiappe & MacDonald, 2005; Eastwick, 2009; Geary, 2004; Gabora & Kaufman, 2010; and Stanovich, 2005.

28. See Miyake et al., 2000; and Miyake & Friedman, 2012.

29. See Wilhelm et al., 2008.

30. See Pronk et al., 2011.

31. See Pinker, 1999.

32. Although it may seem so, modules aren't incompatible with the *g* factor (see Kaufman, DeYoung, Reis, & Gray, 2011). Each module may show important sources of variability among *Homo sapiens*, but all of the modules may be reliant on the same process or set of processes. For instance, working memory may contribute to successful problem solving by many modules, or deleterious mutations may affect many modules at once, resulting in a very low total IQ score (Furlow et al., 1997).

33. See Gardner, 1983, 1993.

34. See Gardner, 2006.

35. See Feist, 2008; Gelman, 2009; and Gelman & Brenneman, 1994.

36. See Ceci, 1996; and Sternberg, 1997.

37. See Goleman, 2006.

38. See Gardner, 2006.

39. See Sternberg, 1997, 2011.

40. Sternberg also discusses the importance of appreciating *creative intelligence*, a topic we take up in much more detail in the next chapter.

41. See Mayer, Salovey, Caruso, & Cherkasskiy, 2011.

42. See Schulte, Ree, & Carretta, 2004.

43. See Mayer, Salovey, & Caruso, 2008; Mayer, Salovey, Caruso, & Cherkasskiy, 2011; and Mayer, Roberts, & Barsade, 2008.

44. See Baumeister et al., 1998; Baumeister & Tierney, 2012; Schmeichel, Vohs, & Baumeister, 2003.

45. See Karremans et al., 2009.

46. See Ritter, Karremans, & van Schie , 2010.

47. See Vohs & Ciarocco, 2004.

48. See Ciarocco, Echevarria, & Lewandowski, 2012.

49. See Gailliot & Baumeister, 2007.

50. See Lenton & Francesconi, 2010.

51. See Miller, 1997; and Miller & Todd, 1998.

52. See Epstein, 1994, 2003; Evans, 2008, 2010; Evans & Frankish, 2009; Kahneman, 2011; Kahneman & Frederick, 2002, 2005; Lieberman, 2003, 2007; Stanovich, 2005, 2009, 2011; Stanovich & Toplak, 2012; Stanovich & West, 2000; Strack & Deutsch, 2004; Kaufman, 2009a, 2011. For criticisms of dual-process theory, see Osman, 2004; Keren & Schul, 2009; and Kruglanski & Gigerenzer, 2011.

53. See Gigerenzer, 2008; and Wilson, 2002.

54. See Davidson, 2011; Kaufman, 2009a; and Kaufman, 2011.

55. See Buss & Haselton, 2005.

56. See Kanazawa, 2010; Kaufman, DeYoung, Reis, & Gray, 2011; Penke, 2010; and Penke et al., 2011.

Chapter 2

1. See Fisher, Cox, & Gordon, 2009.

2. See Griskevicius, Cialdini, & Kenrick, 2006.

3. See Trivers, 1972.

4. See Campbell, Kaufman, & Gau, 2010.

5. See Van den Bergh, Dewitte, & Warlop, 2008.

6. See Wilson & Daly, 2004.

7. See Ronay & von Hippel, 2010.

8. See Dreber, Gerdes, & Gransmark, 2010.

9. See, for example, Ariely & Loewenstein, 2005.
10. Although the focus of this book is on mating, it should be noted that Miller's theory is only one among many that attempts to explain the evolution of uniquely human forms of creativity. The range of explanations is quite vast, from the argument that music is just "auditory cheesecake" (Pinker, 1999), to the notion that music and language combine both evolutionarily new and old traits (Marcus, 2004, 2009, 2012), to the argument that art evolved for purposes of social bonding (Dissanayake, 1990, 1995, 2012), to the hypothesis that cultural evolution played the primary role in the evolution of uniquely human forms of creativity (Gabora, 2008; Gabora & Kaufman, 2010; Changizi, 2011). Liane Gabora and SBK even go so far as to argue that the cultural flourishing of creativity found at the onset of the Upper Paleolithic era between 60,000 and 30,000 years ago came about because of our ability to transcend biology, to evolve from the realm of "what is" to the realm of "what could be." According to this account, the drive to create is at least partially separable from the drive to procreate.
11. See Nettle, 2009a.
12. See Miller, 2000.
13. See Buss, 1989.
14. See Rowatt, Delue, Strickhouser, & Gonzalez, 2001.
15. See Nettle & Clegg, 2006.
16. See Clegg, Nettle, & Miell, 2011.
17. See Kaufman & Kaufman, 2007.
18. See, for example, Buss, 1989; and Buss & Barnes, 1986.
19. See Bressler, Martin, & Balshine, 2006.
20. See Provine, 2000.
21. See Bressler & Balshine, 2006.
22. See Chapell et al., 2002; and McAdams, Jackson, & Kirschnit, 1984.
23. See Chapman & Foot, 1976.
24. See Grammer & Eibl-Eibesfeldt, 1990.
25. See Azim, Mobbs, Booil, Menon, & Reiss, 2005.
26. See Hay, 2000.
27. See Kotthoff, 2000.
28. See Kaufman, Kozbelt, Bromley, & Miller, 2008.
29. See Feingold & Mazella, 1991; Greengross, 2009; Howrigan & McDonald, 2008; and Masten, 1986.
30. See Greengross & Miller, 2011.
31. Kaufman, Erickson, Ramesh, Kozbelt, Magee, & Kaufman, 2010.
32. See Kozbelt & Nishioka, 2010.
33. See O'Quin & Derks, 1997; and Ziv, 1980.
34. See Greengross & Miller, 2009; and Howrigan & McDonald, 2008.
35. See Howrigan & McDonald, 2008.
36. See Gueguen, 2010.
37. See Martin, 2006; and Shiota, Campos, Keltner, & Hertenstein, 2004.
38. See Li et al., 2009.
39. See Greengross, 2008.
40. See Martin, 2006.
41. See Campbell, Martin, & Ward, 2008.
42. See Buss, 1988; and Kaufman et al., 2008.
43. See Cunningham, 1989.
44. See Baumeister et al., 1998; Baumeister & Tierney, 2012; and Schmeichel et al., 2003.
45. See Lewandowski et al., 2012.
46. See Brunswick, 1956.
47. See Cunningham, 1989.
48. See Li et al., 2002; and Li, 2008.
49. See Cunningham & Barbee, 2008.
50. See Senko & Fyffe, 2010.

51. See Bale, Morrison, & Caryl, 2006.
52. See Walle, 1976.
53. See Cooper et al., 2007.
54. See Cunningham & Barbee, 2008.
55. See Cooper et al., 2007.
56. See Shaver & Mikulincer, 2006.
57. See Mikulincer & Horesh, 1999.
58. See Cooper et al., 2007.
59. See Wade, Butrie, & Hoffman, 2009.
60. See Grammer, Kruck, Juette, & Finke, 2000.
61. See Feist, 2001.
62. See Kaufman, Kozbelt, Bromley, & Miller, 2008.
63. Similar lines of thought can be found in Dissanayake (1990, 1995, 2012), who argues that art serves as a crucial social bonding experience, and Mithen (2007), who presents evidence that the musicality of our ancestors and relatives may have been a valuable means of communicating emotions, intentions, and information and of facilitating cooperation.
64. See Eskine, 2011.
65. See Kaufman, Erickson, Huang, Ramesh, & Thompson, et al., 2009.
66. Future research should also try to determine the particular characteristics of various mental displays that are sexually attractive. Various forms of creativity (e.g., artistic) may be considered more attractive than other forms (e.g., scientific), not because of indications of general intelligence (indeed, scientific forms of creativity are probably more g-loaded than artistic forms of creativity), but because of indications of kindness, emotional expressivity, and so forth. Future research should continue to assess the importance of individual differences in preferences for a wide-range of mental courtship displays.
67. See Haselton & Miller, 2006.
68. See Gangestad et al., 2004.
69. See Gangestad et al., 2004.
70. See Miller & Caruthers, 2003.
71. See Kaufman, Erickson, et al., 2009.

Chapter 3

1. See Buss & Barnes, 1986.
2. See MacDonald, 1995; Nettle, 2006, 2008; and Penke, Denissen, & Miller, 2007.
3. See Nettle & Clegg, 2008.
4. See Penke, Denissen, & Miller, 2007.
5. See Smith, 1998.
6. See Figueredo et al., 2005.
7. See Hrdy, 1999.
8. See Figueredo et al., 2008; and Hrdy, 1999.
9. See Ellis et al., 2009, to learn more about all the different ways various environmental factors can combine to produce different life history strategies.
10. See Figueredo et al., 2005.
11. See Figueredo et al., 2004.
12. See Brumbach, Figueredo, & Ellis, 2009.
13. See Flinn & Ward, 2005.
14. See Belsky et al., 2007; Ellis & Essex, 2007; and Tither & Ellis, 2008.
15. See Figueredo et al., 2008; and Sefcek et al., 2006.
16. See Ellis, 2004.
17. See Belsky et al., 1991.
18. See Chisholm, 1993.
19. See Chisholm, 1999.
20. See Belsky et al., 1991.
21. See Chilsholm, 1993.

22. See Del Giudice, 2010.
23. Also see West-Eberhard, 2003.
24. See Barry, Kochanska, & Philibert, 2008; Comings et al., 2002; and Khron & Bogan, 2001.
25. See Belsky, 1997, 2005; Belsky & Pluess, 2009; Boyce & Ellis, 2005; and Wolf, van Doorn, & Weissing, 2008.
26. See Del Giudice & Belsky, 2010; and West-Eberhard, 2003.
27. See Cassidy & Shaver, 2008.
28. See Bakermans-Kraneburg & Van IJzendoorn, 2006; Barry, Kochanska, & Philibert, 2008; Bradley & Corwyn, 2008; and Caspi et al., 2002.
29. See Belsky et al., 1991.
30. See Chilsholm, 1993.
31. See Figueredo et al., 2008.
32. See Costa & McCrae, 1985, 1992; and Digman, 1990.
33. See DeYoung, 2006; DeYoung, Peterson, & Higgins, 2002; Digman, 1997; Olson, 2005; and Hirsh, DeYoung, & Peterson, 2009.
34. See Carver, Johnson, & Joormann, 2009.
35. See Hirsh, DeYoung, & Peterson, 2009.
36. See Botwin, Buss, & Shackelford, 1997; Buss et al., 1990a; and Buss & Barnes, 1986.
37. See Figueredo, Sefcek, & Jones, 2006.
38. See Nettle & Clegg, 2008.
39. See Haselton & Nettle, 2006.
40. See Dyrenforth, Kashy, Donnellan, & Lucas, 2010.
41. See Nettle & Clegg, 2008.
42. See Hirsh, 2008.
43. See DeYoung & Gray, 2009.
44. See DeYoung et al., 2010.
45. See MacDonald, 1995; and Nettle, 2006.
46. See Hirsh et al., 2009.
47. See Claridge & Davis, 2001; and Neeleman, Sytema, & Wadsworth, 2002.
48. See Barelds, 2005; Davila, Karney, Hall, & Bradbury, 2003; Heaven, Smith, Prabhakar, Abraham, & Mete, 2006; Karney & Bradbury, 1997; Kelly & Conley, 1987; and Watson, Hubbard, & Wiese, 2000.
49. See Nettle & Clegg, 2008, p. 125.
50. See Mathews, Mackintosh, & Fulcher, 1997.
51. See Nettle & Clegg, 2008.
52. See McKenzie, Taghavi-Knosary, & Tindell, 2000; and Ross, Stewart, Mugge, & Fultz, 2001.
53. Also see Nettle & Clegg, 2008.
54. See Nettle & Clegg, 2008.
55. See Schmitt, 2004.
56. See Nettle, 2006.
57. See Hirsh et al., 2008.
58. See Friedman et al., 1995.
59. See Austin & Deary, 2000; and Claridge & Davis, 2003.
60. See Sternberg, 1998.
61. See Ahmetoglu, Swami, & Chamorro-Premuzic, 2009; and Engel, Olson, & Patrick, 2002.
62. See Engel, Olson, & Patrick, 2002.
63. See Nettle & Clegg, 2008.
64. See Schmitt, 2004.
65. See Heaven, 1996; Miller et al., 2004; Schmitt, 2004; and Schmitt & Buss, 2000.
66. See Nettle & Clegg, 2008.
67. See Baron-Cohen & Wheelwright, 2004; and Nettle, 2007.
68. See Hirsh et al., 2008.
69. See Costa, Terraciano, & McCrae, 2001.
70. See Dyrenforth, Kashy, Donnellan, & Lucas, 2010; and Jensen-Campbell, Knack, & Gomez, 2010.

71. See Byrne & Whiten, 1988; Dunbar, 1996; and Humphrey, 1976.
72. See Ahmetoglu, Swami, & Chamorro-Premuzic, 2009.
73. See Caprara, Bararanelli, & Zimbardo, 1996; Graziano, Jensen-Campbell, & Hair, 1996; Heaven, 1996; Jensen-Campbell & Graziano, 2001; Jensen-Campbell, Knack, & Gomez, 2010; and Suls, Martin, & David, 1998.
74. See Schmitt, 2004; and Schmitt & Buss, 2001.
75. See Urbaniak & Kilmann, 2006.
76. See Boudreau, Boswell, & Judge, 2001; although note that altruistic and generous behaviors can increase social status in environments where contributions to the group are public—see Hardy & Van Vugt, 2006.
77. See Nettle, 2006.
78. See, for example, Hardy & Van Vugt, 2006.
79. See Chen et al., 1999; and Kircaldy, 1982.
80. See Kenrick et al., 1993.
81. See Luo & Zhang, 2009.
82. See Eysenck, 1976; Heaven, Fitzpatrick, Craig, Kelly, & Sebar, 2000; Nettle, 2006; and Schmitt, 2004.
83. See Nettle, 2005.
84. See Schmitt & Buss, 2001.
85. See Luo & Zhang, 2009.
86. See Buss & Barnes, 1986; and Goodwin, 1990.
87. See Botwin, Buss, & Shackelford, 1997; and Goodwin, 1990.
88. See Nettle & Clegg, 2008.
89. See Ahmetoglu, Swami, & Chamorro-Premuzic, 2009; Buchanan, Johnson, & Goldberg, 2005; Franken, Gibson, & Mohan, 1990; and Watson, Hubbard, & Wiese, 2000.
90. See Hirsh et al., 2008.
91. See Nettle, 2005.
92. See Ellis, 1987; and Samuels et al., 2004.
93. See Nettle, 2005.
94. See Johnson, 1994.
95. See Hirsh et al., 2008.
96. See Saucier, 1992.
97. See DeYoung, Quility, & Peterson, 2007.
98. See Goldberg, 1999.
99. See DeYoung, Shamosh, Green, Braver, & Gray, 2009.
100. See DeYoung, Grazioplene, & Peterson, 2011.
101. See Kaufman et al., 2010.
102. See Kaufman, 2009a, 2009b; Peterson & Carson, 2000; and Peterson, Smith, & Carson, 2002.
103. See Kaufman, 2009a; McCrae & Costa, 1997; Miller & Tal, 2007; Nelson & Rawlings, 2010; Nusbaum & Silvia, 2011; and Silvia et al., 2009.
104. See Martindale, 1999.
105. See Green & Williams, 1999; Lubow & Gerwritz, 1995; Lubow & Weiner, 2010; Miller & Tal, 2007; Nelson & Rawlings, 2010; and Woody & Claridge, 1977.
106. See Mason, Claridge, & Jackson, 1995; Nelson & Rawlings, 2010; Nettle, 2001; Rawlings & Freeman, 1997; and McCreery & Claridge, 2002.
107. See Nettle & Clegg, 2006.
108. See Beaussart, Kaufman, & Kaufman, in press.
109. See Del Giudice, Angeleri, Brizio, & Elena, 2010.
110. See Miller & Tal, 2007.
111. See Carson, Peterson, & Higgins, 2003; Kaufman, 2009b.
112. See Shaner, Miller, & Mintz, 2008.
113. See, for example, Avila, Thaker, & Adami, 2001; Nowakowska, Strong, Santosa, Wang, & Ketter, 2005; and Shaner, Miller, & Mintz, 2004, 2008.
114. See Clegg, Nettle, & Miell, 2011; Nettle, 2001; and Nettle & Clegg, 2006.

115. See Sunnafrank & Ramirez, 2004.
116. See Geher & Miller, 2008.
117. See Garver-Apgar et al., 2006; Thornhill et al., 2003; and Wedekind et al., 1995, 2007.
118. See, for example, Back, Stopfer, et al., 2010; Borkenau, Brecke, Mottig, & Paelecke, 2009; Gosling, Ko, Mannarelli, & Morris, 2002; Levesque & Kenny, 1993; and Watson, 1989.
119. See Fisher et al., 2009; Fisher, Island, Rich, Marchalik, & Brown, submitted; Fisher, Rich, Island, Marcalika, & Brown, submitted.
120. See Rodrigues et al., 2009.
121. Available at http://www.Chemistry.com.
122. See Fisher, Rich, Island, Marcalika, & Brown, submitted.
123. See Roney, Mahler, & Maestripieri, 2003.
124. See Mazur & Michalek, 1998.
125. See Ahmetoglu, Swami, & Chamorro-Premuzic, 2009.
126. See Ahmetoglu, Swami, & Chamorro-Premuzic, 2009.

Chapter 4

1. See Judge, Hurst, & Simon, 2009.
2. See Bono & Judge, 2004.
3. See Dion, Berscheid, & Walster, 1972.
4. See Przygodzki-Lionet, Olivier, & Desrumaux, 2010.
5. See Snyder, Tanke, & Berscheid, 1977.
6. See Hatfield, 1986.
7. Some of you may not have to imagine this.
8. See Swami & Furnham, 2007; and Swami & Tovee (2012).
9. See Buss, 2003.
10. These comments are probabilistic in nature—but that's how evolution works. In its effort to shape organisms that are most likely to be able to reproduce, natural forces select individuals who tend to make decisions that would be, on average, most likely to lead to reproductive success.
11. See Schaich Borg, Lieberman, & Kiehl, 2008.
12. See Cunningham, 1986.
13 See Buss, 2003.
14. See Swami, Furnham, & Joshi, 2008.
15. See Swami & Furnham, 2007.
16. See Buss, 2011; Platek & Singh, 2010; and Singh & Singh, 2011.
17. See Garver-Apgar, Gangestad, & Thornhill, 2008.
18. See Buss, 1989; and Marlowe, 2004.
19. See Cunningham, 1986.
20. See Buss & Schmitt, 2011; and Sugiyama, 2005.
21. See Buss, 1996; Singh & Singh, 2011; Vandermassen, 2005; and Wolf, 1991.
22. See Buss, 2003; Buss & Schmitt, 2011; and Schmitt & Buss, 1996.
23. See Miller, Tybur, & Jordan, 2007.
24. See Buss & Schmitt, 1993.
25. See Pennebaker, 1979.
26. See Garcia & Reiber, 2008.
27. See Buss, 1989.
28. See Buss, 2003.
29. See Gangestad, Thornhill, & Carver-Apgar, 2005.
30. See Gangestad & Simpson, 2000.
31. See Buss, 2003.
32. See Scheib, 1994.
33. See Kruger, Fisher, & Jobling, 2003.
34. See Shoup & Gallup, 2008.
35. See Garver-Apgar, Gangestad, & Thornhill, 2008.

36. See Gangestad & Thornhill, 2003.
37. See Buss, 2003.
38. See Frederick & Haselton, 2007.
39. See Shoup & Gallup, 2008.
40. See Pipitone & Gallup, 2008.
41. See Kruger, Fisher, & Jobling, 2003.
42. See Gangestad & Simpson, 2000.
43. See Buss, 2003.
44. See Kniffin & Wilson, 2004.
45. See Buss, 1989.
46. See Townsend, 1998.
47. See DeBruine et al., 2010, for a comprehensive review.
48. See Penton-Voak et al., 1999.
49. Also described in Penton-Voak et al., 1999.
50. See Buss & Schmitt, 2011; Buss & Shackelford, 2008; and Roney et al., 2010.
51. See Buss & Shackelford, 2008.
52. See Roney, Simmons, & Gray, 2011.
53. See Geher & Miller, 2008; and Miller, 2000.
54. See Kniffin & Wilson, 2004.
55. See Griskevicius, Cialdini, & Kenrick, 2006.
56. See Miller, 2000.
57. See Geher & Miller, 2008.
58. See Christie & Geis, 1970.
59. See Greene, 2003.
60. See Fisher, Cox, & Gordon, 2009.
61. See Geher, Camargo, & O'Rourke, 2008.
62. See Geher & Miller, 2008; and Miller, 2000.
63. See Miller, 2000.
64. See Andrews & Carroll, 2010; and Gottschall & Wilson, 2005.
65. See Miller & Todd, 1998.
66. See Brunswik, 1956.
67. See Miller & Todd, 1998.
68. See Simon, 1957; also see Gigerenzer & Goldstein, 1996.
69. See Kenrick, Sadalla, Groth, & Trost, 1990.
70. See Asendorpf, Penke, & Back, 2011.
71. See Penke et al., 2007.

Chapter 5

1. See, for example, Shoup & Gallup, 2008.
2. See O'Sullivan, 2008.
3. See Volk & Atkinson, 2008.
4. See Fisher et al., 2009.
5. See Duntley & Buss, 2005.
6. See Buss, 2003.
7. See Krebs & Davies, 1997; and Nettle, 2009b, 2009c.
8. See Buss, 2005a.
9. See Buss & Schmitt, 1993.
10. See Buss, 2006; Buss & Schmitt, 2011; Gangestad & Buss, 1993; Gangestad & Simpson, 2000; Gangestad et al., 2006; Lippa, 2009; and Schmitt, 2005.
11. See Buss, 2003.
12. See Geher, 2009.
13. See Kennair, Schmitt, Fjeldavli, & Harlem, 2009.
14. See Trivers, 1972.

15. See Geher & Gambacorta, 2010.
16. See Gangestad & Simpson, 2000.
17. Not all; see Trivers, 1985, for important exceptions.
18. See Volk & Atkinson, 2008.
19. See Euler & Weitzel, 1996.
20. See Buss et al., 1990.
21. See Li, 2002, 2008.
22. See Li, 2002, 2008.
23. See Penke, Todd, Lenton, & Fasolo, 2008.
24. See Buss, 2003.
25. See Trivers, 1985.
26. See Buss, 2003.
27. See Blumstein & Schwartz, 1983.
28. See Buss et al., 1999.
29. See Penke et al., 2008.
30. See Clark & Hatfield, 1989.
31. See Clark, 1990.
32. See Hald & Hogh-Olesen, 2010.
33. See Clark & Hatfield, 1989.
34. See Hamilton & Zuk, 1982.
35. See Clark & Hatfield, 1989.
36. See Clark, 1990.
37. Adapted from Buss & Schmitt, 2011.
38. See Schmitt, 2005.
39. See Lippa, 2009.
40. See Penke, Todd, Lenton, & Fasolo, 2008,
41. See Schmitt, Coudon, & Baker, 2001.
42. See Meston & Buss, 2007.
43. See Atkins et al., 2001; Glass & Wright, 1985; Oliver & Hyde, 1993; Petersen & Hyde, 2010; Thompson, 1983; and Wiederman, 1997.
44. See Blumstein & Schwartz, 1983; Brand et al., 2007; Hansen, 1987; Laumann et al., 1994; Lawson & Samson, 1988; and Spanier & Margolis, 1983.
45. See Davies et al., 2007; Jonason et al., 2009; Parker & Burkley, 2009; Schmitt et al., 2004; and Schmitt & Buss, 2001.
46. See Ehrlichman & Eichenstein, 1992; Ellis & Symons, 1990; Jones & Barlow, 1990; Leitenberg & Henning, 1995; and Rokach, 1990.
47. See Burley & Symanski, 1981; Mitchell & Latimer, 2009; and Symons, 1979.
48. See Hald, 2006; Koukounas & McCabe, 1997; Malamuth, 1996; Murnen & Stockton, 1997; Salmon & Symons, 2001; and Youn, 2006.
49. See Bereczkei & Csanaky, 1996; Betzig, 1986; Jokela et al., 2010; Perusse, 1993; Stone et al., 2005; and Zerjal et al., 2003.
50. See Fenigstein & Preston, 2007; McBurney et al., 2005; Njus & Bane, 2009; Rowatt & Schmitt, 2003; Schmitt et al., 2003; and Wilcox, 2003.
51. See Herold & Mewhinney, 1993; and Spanier & Margolis, 1983.
52. See Cohen & Shotland, 1996; McCabe, 1987; Njus & Bane, 2009; Rowatt & Schmitt, 2003; and Schmitt et al., 2003.
53. See Clark, 1990; Clark & Hatfield, 1989; Greitemeyer, 2005; Hald & Høgh-Olesen, 2010; Schützwohl et al., 2009; and Voracek et al., 2005, 2006.
54. See Baumeister et al., 2001; Laumann et al., 1994; and Purnine et al., 1994.
55. See Hendrick et al., 1985; Laumann et al., 1994; Oliver & Hyde, 1993; and Petersen & Hyde, 2010.
56. See Bradshaw et al., 2010; Campbell, 2008; de Graaf & Sandfort, 2004; Garcia & Reiber, 2008; Paul & Hayes, 2002; Reiber & Garcia, 2010; Roese et al., 2006; and Townsend et al., 1995.
57. See Clark, 2006; Lippa, 2009; Penke & Asendorf, 2008; Schmitt, 2005a; Schmitt et al., 2001; and Simpson & Gangestad, 1991.

58. See Kenrick et al., 1990; Kenrick et al., 1993; Li et al., 2002; Li & Kenrick, 2006; Regan, 1998a, 1998b; Regan & Berscheid, 1997; Regan et al., 2000; Simpson & Gangestad, 1992; Stewart et al., 2000; and Wiederman & Dubois, 1998.
59. See Abbey, 1982; Haselton & Buss, 2000; Henningsen et al., 2006; and Sigal et al., 1988.
60. See Gouveia-Iliverira & Pederson, 2009.
61. Buss & Schmitt, 2011, p. 2.
62. See Buss, 2003.
63. See Mecklinger & Ullsperger, 1995.
64. See Clark & Hatfield, 1989.
65. See Meston & Buss, 2007.
66. Meston & Buss, 2007, p. 500.
67. Stephenson, Ahrold, & Meston, 2010.
68. See Pederson, Putcha-Bhagavatula, & Miller, in press.
69. See Conley, 2011.
70. Conley, 2011, p. 2.
71. See Gustafson's (1998) gendered risk perception theory for related ideas.
72. See Buss & Schmitt, 2011.
73. Conley, 2011, p. 18.
74. See Abramson & Pinkerton, 2002.
75. See Buss & Schmitt, 2011.
76. See Armstrong et al., 2010.
77. See Schützwohl et al., 2009. 78 See Regan, 1998c.
79. See Buss et al., 1990b.
80. See Fisher et al., 2009.
81. See Hill & Preston, 1996; and Meston & Buss, 2007; 2009.
82. See Meston & Buss, 2007.
83. See Sternberg, 1999; and Sternberg & Weis, 2008.
84. See Stanik & Ellsworth, 2010.
85. See Fisher, Moore, & Pittenger, 2011.
86. See Bowlby, 1969.
87. Still, there is an emerging consensus among neurobiologists and social-personality psychologists that both parent-infant bonds and long-term couple relationships draw on the *same* attachment motivational system (Del Giudice & Belsky, 2010). The behavioral and psychological displays of adult bond formation, separation, and loss show striking similarities with the same displays in children (Feeney, 1999), and neurobiological studies also show substantial overlap in the neurochemical and neuroanatomical substrates involved in both types of relationships (e.g., Pedersen et al., 2005).
88. See Diamond & Hicks, 2005.
89. See Belsky, 1997.
90. See Buss, Larsen, & Westen, 1996; and Buss, Larsen, Westen, & Semmelroth, 1992.
91. See Levy & Kelly, 2010.
92. See Del Giudice, 2011.
93. See Birnbaum, 2007.
94. See Allen & Baucom, 2004.
95. See Del Giudice, 2009.
96. See Sroufe et al., 1993.
97. See Del Giudice, 2009.
98. Meston & Buss, 2007, p. 502.
99. See Figueredo et al., 2008.
100. See Figueredo et al., 2008.
101. See Giosan, 2006.
102. See Kruger, Reischl, & Zimmerman, 2008.
103. See Schmitt, 2005.
104. See Simon, 1957.
105. See Eastwick & Finkel, 2008; and Todd, Penke, Fasolo, & Lenton, 2007.

106. See Miller & Todd, 1998.
107. See Johnstone, 1997; Miller & Todd, 1998; and Todd & Miller, 2000.
108. See Todd & Miller, 1999.
109. See Gutierres, Kenrick, & Partch, 1999.
110. See Regan, 1998.
111. See Penke et al., 2008.
112. See Back & Kenny, 2010; and Back, Schmukle, & Egloff, 2010.
113. See Back et al., 2011.
114. See Eastwick, Finkel, Mochon, & Ariely, 2007; Kurzban & Weeden, 2005; and Luo & Zhang, 2009.
115. See Back et al., 2011.
116. Also see von Hippel & Trivers, 2011.
117. See Grammer et al., 2000.
118. See Edlund & Sagarin, 2010.
119. See Hill & Buss, 2008.
120. See Back et al., 2011; Feingold, 1990; Kurzban & Weeden, 2005; Langlois et al., 2000; Penke, Todd, Lenton, & Fasolo, 2008; Luo & Zhang, 2009; Rhodes & Simmons, 2007; Swami & Furnham, 2007; and Todd et al., 2007.
121. See Lee, Loewenstein, Ariely, Hong, & Young, 2008.
122. See Kniffin & Wilson, 2004.
123. See Lee et al., 2008.
124. See Cialdini, 1993.
125. See de La Rochefoucauld, 2007, p. 354.
126. See Freed-Brown & White, 2009.
127. See Dugatkin, 1992; and Pruett-Jones, 1992.
128. See Eva & Wood, 2006; Gilbert, Killingsworth, Eyre, & Wilson, 2009; Jones et al., 2007; Place, Todd, Penke, & Asendorf, 2010; Stanik, Kurzban, & Ellsworth, 2010; Waynforth, 2007; and Yorzinski & Platt, 2010.
129. See Hill & Ryan, 2006; Little et al., 2008; and Place, Todd, Penke, & Asendorf, 2009.
130. See Place, Todd, Penke, & Asendorpf, 2010.
131. See Yorzinski & Platt, 2010.
132. See Place, Todd, Penke, & Asendorpf, 2010.
133. See Eva & Wood, 2006.
134. See Gilbert, Killingsworth, Eyre, & Wilson, 2009.
135. See Stanik, Kurzban, & Ellsworth, 2010.
136. See Yorzinski & Platt, 2010.
137. See Waynforth, 2007.
138. See Place, Todd, Penke, & Asendorpf, 2010.
139. See Jones et al., 2007.
140. See Waynforth, 2007.
141. See Easton, Confer, Goetz, & Buss, 2010.
142. Easton et al., 2010, pp. 518–519.
143. See Schmitt et al., 2002.
144. See Easton et al., 2010.
145. See Weekes-Shackelford, Easton, & Stone, 2008.
146. See Daly & Wilson, 1988.
147. See Weekes-Shackelford et al., 2008.
148. See Gallup, Burch, & Berens Mitchell, 2006.
149. See Gueguen, 2009.
150. See Hess, Brody, Van Der Schalk, & Fischer, 2007.
151. See Gangestad, Thornhill, & Garver-Apgar (2005) for a summary of this growing body of research.
152. See Miller, Tybur, & Jordan, 2007.
153. See Pipitone & Gallup, 2008.
154. See Gangestad, Thornhill, & Garver-Apgar, 2005.

155. See Haselton, Pillsworth, Bleske-Recheck, & Frederick, 2007.
156. See Muscarella, 2000.
157. See Hughes et al., 2004.
158. See, for example, Buss, 2003; and Miller, 2000.
159. See Muscarella, 2000.
160. See Keller & Miller, 2006.
161. See Hughes et al., 2004.
162. See Palmer & Thornhill, 2001.
163. See Thornhill, 1981.
164. For a great summary of this work, including critiques of the Thornhill and Palmer book, we suggest you check out Malamuth, Huppin, and Bryant's (2005) chapter from David Buss' *Handbook of Evolutionary Psychology*, which provide an extensive treatment of research on sexual coercion.
165. See Wilson et al., 2003.
166. See Vandermassen, 2010.
167. Buss & Schmitt, 2011, p. 780.

Chapter 6

1. See Bandura, 1977; Dweck, 2007; Greven et al., 2009.
2. See O'Sullivan, 2008.
3. See Ross & Nisbett, 1991.
4. See Nisbett & Wilson, 1977.
5. See Gigerenzer, 2008; Gilbert, 2007; and Wilson, 2002.
6. See Eastwick & Finkel, 2008.
7. See Ross, 1977.
8. See Bauman & Geher, 2003; and Ross, Greene, & House; 1977.
9. See Muehlenhard & Linton, 1987.
10. See Taylor & Brown,1988.
11. For example, Langer, 1975.
12. See Robins & Beer, 2001.
13. See Langer, 1975.
14. See Seligman & Maier, 1967.
15. See Zahavi, 1977.
16. See Byers & Lewis, 1988.
17. See Walster, Walster, & Berscheid, 1978.
18. See Festinger & Carlsmith, 1959.
19. See Geher, Bloodworth, Mason, & Stoaks, 2005.
20. See Wilson, Geher, & Waldo, 2009.
21. See Webster, 2007.
22. See Marks, 1987.
23. See Marks, 1987.
24. See Hill & Hurtado, 1996.
25. See Marks, 1987.
26. See Haselton & Buss, 2000.
27. See Haselton & Buss, 2000.
28. See Haselton & Buss, 2000.
29. See Abbey, 1982.
30. See Buss, Larsen, Westen, & Semmelroth, 1992.
31. See Buss et al., 1999.
32. See Hughes, Harrison, & Gallup, 2004.
33. See Buss et al., 1999.
34. See Buss et al., 1992.
35. See Buss & Haselton, 2005.
36. See Haselton & Buss[36] 2000.

37. See Penke et al., 2008.
38. See Buss, 2003.
39. See Geher, 2009.
40. See Haselton & Buss, 2000.
41. See Geher, Miller, & Murphy, 2008.
42. See Geher & Kaufman, 2011.
43. See Mayer, Salovey, & Caruso, 1999.
44. See Connellan, Baron-Cohen, Wheelwright, Batkia, & Ahluwalia, 2000.
45. See Rammstedt & Rammsayer, 2000.
46. See Nowicki & Duke, 1994.
47. See Noller, 1986.
48. See Trivers, 1985.
49. See Penke, Todd, Lenton, & Fasolo, 2008; and Schmitt, 2005.
50. See Haselton & Buss, 2000.
51. These findings dovetail nicely with two other current studies on mating-relevant cross-sex mind-reading that also found, using varied methodological approaches, that males are generally more accurate at knowing the desires of the opposite sex than are females (DeBacker, Braeckman, & Farinpour, 2008).
52. See Gangestad & Simpson, 2000.
53. See Gangestad & Simpson, 2000.

Chapter 7

1. See Coolidge & Wynn, 2009.
2. See Bingham, 1999.
3. See Tiger, 1987.
4. See Pinker, 2007; and Marcus, 2004, 2009.
5. See Wrangham, 2009.
6. See Coolidge & Wynn, 2009; Feist, 2008; Gabora, & Kaufman, 2010; Geary, 2004; Marcus, 2004, 2009; and Mithen, 1999; 2007.
7. See Evans, 2008, for use of the term "uniquely developed."
8. See Baron-Cohen, Wheelwright, Skinner, Martin, & Clubley, 2001.
9. See Hare, Call, & Tomasello, 2001.
10. See Heyes, 1998, for a review.
11. See Nettle & Liddle, 2008.
12. See Tomasello, Carpenter, Call, Behne, & Moll, 2005.
13. See Ekman & Friesen, 1968.
14. See Ross & Nisbett, 1991.
15. See Shaner, Mintz, & Miller, 2008.
16. See Weiss & Harris, 2001.
17. See Shaner et al., 2008.
18. See Crespi & Badcock, 2008.
19. See Buckner, Andrews-Hanna, & Schacter, 2008.
20. See Crespi & Badcock, 2008; Badcock, 2009.
21. See Cook & Leventhal, 1996.
22. See Nettle, 2008.
23. See Nettle, 2008.
24. See Del Giudice, Angeleri, Brizio, & Elena, 2010.
25. See Lubow & Weiner, 2010.
26. See Mayer, Salovey, Caruso, & Cherkasskiy, in press; Salovey & Mayer, 1990.
27. See Place, Todd, Penke, & Asendorpf, 2009.
28. See Barlow, Qualter, & Stylianou, 2010.
29. See Geher, 2004.
30. See, for example,, Mayer & Geher, 1996.
31. See, for example,, Casey, Garrett, Brackett, & Rivers, 2008.

32. See Casey et al., 2008.
33. See Brackett, Warner, & Bosco, 2005.
34. See Mayer et al., 2000.
35. See Geher & Miller, 2008.
36. See Geher, Camargo, & O'Rourke, 2008.
37. See Casey et al., 2008.
38. See Keller, 2008.
39. See Dawkins, 1989.
40. See O'Sullivan, 2008.
41. See Dugatkin, 2003.
42. See O'Sullivan, 2008.
43. See O'Sullivan, 2008.
44. See Saad & Vongas, 2008.
45. See Kruger, 2008.
46. See Saad, 2011.
47. See Reiber, 2010.
48. See Buss, 2003.
49. See Buss & Schmitt, 1996.
50. See Haselton, Buss, Oubaid, & Angleitner, 2005.
51. See O'Sullivan, 2008.
52. See Geher & Gambacorta, 2010; and Geher, 2006.
53. See, for example, Kurzban & Haselton, 2006; Pinker, 2002.
54. See Geher & Gambacorta, 2010.
55. See Ekman, 2009.
56. See Ekman, O'Sullivan, & Frank, 1999.
57. See Fisher, et al., 2009.
58. See Demarest, Snee, & Correa, 2008.

Chapter 8

1. See Flam, 2008; Mystery, 2007, 2010; Strauss, 2005; and Thorn, 2011.
2. See Connor, 2008.
3. See Herald & Mishausen, 1999.
4. See Twenge & Campbell, 2009.
5. See Kramer et al., under review; and Sheng, Gheytanchi, & Aziz-Zadeh, 2010.
6. Campbell, 2005, p. 24.
7. See Morf & Rhodewalt, 2001; and Rhodewalt & Morf, 1995.
8. Twenge & Campbell, 2003, p. 270.
9. Vazire & Funder, 2006, p. 154.
10. See Campbell, 2005.
11. See Foster, Campbell, & Twenge, 2003; and Stinson et al., 2008.
12. See Stinson et al., 2008.
13. See Emmons, 1984.
14. See Raskin & Novacek, 1989.
15. See Holtzman & Strube, 2011.
16. See, for example, Bleske-Rechek, Remiker, & Baker, 2008; and Gabriel, Critelli, & Ee, 1994.
17. See Bleske-Rechek, Remiker, & Baker, 2008.
18. See Holtzman & Strube (in press); and Vazire, Nauman, Rentfrow, & Gosling, 2008.
19. See Vazire, Naumann, Rentfrow, & Gosling, 2008.
20. See Del Paulhus, 1998.
21. See Young & Pinksy, 2006, pp. 464, 470.
22. See, for example, Pinsky & Young, 2009; and Young & Pinsky, 2006.
23. See Back, Schmukle, &Egloff, 2010a.
24. See Berscheid & Reis, 1998.

25. See Back, Schmukle, & Egloff, 2010b.
26. See Back & Kenny, in press.
27. See Ashton, Lee, & Paunonen, 2002; Borkenau & Liebler, 1992; Riggio & Riggio, 2002; and Scherer, 1986.
28. See Butler et al., 2003; DePaulo, 1992; and Grammer, Keki, Striebel, Atzmuller, & Fink, 2003.
29. See Borkenau, Brecke, Möttig, & Paelecke, 2009.
30. See Back et al., 2010a.
31. See Friedman, Riggio, & Casella, 1988; and Gueguen, 2008.
32. See Holtzman, Vazire, & Mehl, 2010.
33. Holtzman, Vazire, & Mehl, 2010, p. 482.
34. See Williams, Cooper, Howell, Yuille, & Paulhus, 2009.
35. See Foster, Shira, & Campbell, 2006.
36. See Vangelisti, 1990.
37. See Malamuth, 1996.
38. Also see Figueredo & Jacobs, 2010.
39. See Campbell & Foster, 2002; Campbell, Foster, & Finkel, 2002; and Foster, Shira, & Campbell, 2006.
40. See Foster & Campbell, 2005.
41. See Max, 2005.
42. See Bushman et al., 2003.
43. See Twenge & Campbell, 2003.
44. See Jones & Paulhus, 2010.
45. See Carlson & Gjerde, 2009; and Hill & Roberts, 2011.
46. See Foster, Campbell, & Twenge, 2003; Twenge, 2007; and Twenge, Konrath, Foster, Campbell, & Bushman, 2008a, 2008b.
47. See Hill & Roberts, 2011.
48. See Holtzman & Strube, 2011.
49. See Young & Pinksy, 2006.
50. See Belsky, Steinberg, & Draper, 1991; Gangestad, Haselton, & Buss, 2006; Gangestad & Simpson, 2000; Kurzban & Aktipis, 2007; and Vernon et al., 2008.
51. See Barry, Kerig, Stellwagen, & Barry, 2010; Morf & Rhodewall, 2001; and Otway & Vignoles, 2006.
52. See Emmons, 1984.
53. See Back, Schmukle, & Egloff, 2010a.
54. See Back et al., 2010a.
55. See Back et al., 2010a.
56. See Emmons, 1984.
57. See Morf & Rhodewalt, 2001.
58. Back et al., 2010a, p. 143.
59. See Back et al., 2010a.
60. See Otway & Vignoles, 2006.
61. See Back et al., 2010a.
62. See Austin, Farrelly, Black, & Moore, 2007; and Malterer, Glass, & Newman, 2008.
63. Hoffman, 2000, p. 30.
64. See Del Gaizo & Falkenbach, 2008; Fowles & Dindo, 2006; Harpur, Hare, & Hakstian, 1989; Levenson, Kiehl, & Fitzpatrick, 1995; Mahmut, Homewood, & Stevenson, 2008; Mealey, 1995; and Williams, Paulhus, & Hare, 2007.
65. See Ali, Amorim, & Chamorro-Premuzic, 2009.
66. See Barlow, Qualter, & Stylianou, 2010.
67. See Ali & Chamorro-Premuzic, 2010.
68. See Hare, 1999.
69. See Wheeler, Book, & Costello, 2009.
70. See Ali & Chamorro-Premuzic, 2010.
71. See Jakobwitz & Egan, 2006.
72. See Dickman, 1990.

73. See Jones & Paulhus, 2011.
74. Jones & Paulhus, 2010, p. 682.
75. See Fulton, Marcus, & Payne, 2010.
76. See Gailliot & Baumeister, 2007.
77. See Flory, Molina, Pelham, Gnagy, & Smith, 2006.
78. See Jonason & Tost, 2010.
79. See Jones & Paulhus, 2010
80. See Baumeister, Gailliot, DeWall, & Oaten, 2006.
81. See Hare, 1999.
82. See Miyake et al., 2000.
83. See Figueredo & Jacobs, 2010.
84. See Figueredo et al., 2005.
85. See Jonason, Li, Webster, & Schmitt, 2009; and Paulhus & Williams, 2002.
86. See Jones & Paulhus, 2011.
87. From Jonason, personal communication.
88. See Jonason, Slomski, & Partyka, 2012; and Jonason & Webster, 2011.
89. See Holtzman & Strube, 2011; and Jonason, Li, Webster, & Schmitt, 2009.
90. Note similarities with Holtzman and Straube's (in press) emerging hypothesis of narcissism.
91. See Jakobwitz & Egan, 2006; Jonason, Li, & Teicher, 2010; and Vernon, Villani, Vickers, & Harris, 2008.
92. See Jonason, Li, & Teicher, 2010.
93. See Jonason, Koenig, &Tost, 2010.
94. See Jonason & Kavanagh, 2010.
95. See, for example, Dion & Dion, 1988.
96. See, for example, Davis & Latty-Mann, 1987.
97. See Jonason & Kavanagh, 2010.
98. Jonason & Kavanagh, 2010, p. 609.
99. See Kiehl et al., 2001; and Munro et al., 2007.
100. Jonason & Kavanagh, 2010, p. 610.
101. See Jonason, Li, & Buss, 2010.
102. See, for example, Jonason, Li, Webster, & Schmitt, 2009.
103. See Wai & Tiliopoulos, 2012.
104. See Dziobek et al., 2008.
105. See Wai & Tiliopoulos, 2012.
106. See Nettle & Liddle, 2008.
107. See Austin et al., 2007.
108. See Esperger & Bereczkei, 2011.
109. Esperger & Bereczkei, 2011, p. 6.
110. See Kemper, 1990; and Josephs, Sellers, Newman, & Mehta, 2006.
111. See Henrich & Gil-White, 2001.
112. See Buttermore, 2006; and Cheng, Tracy, & Henrich, in press.
113. See Johnson, Burk, & Kirkpatrick, 2007; Josephs, Sellers, Newman, & Mehta, 2006; Kemper, 1990; and Mehta & Josephs, 2010.
114. See Reyes-Garcia et al., 2008; and von Rueden, Gurven, & Kaplan, 2008.
115. See Cheng, Tracy, & Henrich, in press.
116. See Tracy, Cheng, Robins, & Trzesniewski, 2009.
117. See Cheng, Tracy, & Henrich, in press.
118. See Cheng, Tracy, & Henrich, 2010.
119. See Urbaniak & Kilmann, 2003.
120. See Sadalla, Kenrick, & Vershure, 1987.
121. See Burger & Cosby, 1999.
122. See Sadalla, Kenrick, & Vershure, 1987.
123. See Jensen-Campbell, Graziano, & West, 1995.
124. See Snyder, Kirkpatrick, & Barrett, 2008.

125. See Parks & Stone, 2010.
126. See, for example, Hardy & Van Vugt, 2006.
127. See, for example, Kniffin & Wilson, 2004.
128. See Exline & Lobel, 1999.
129. See Fisher, Nadler, & Whitcher-Alagna, 1982.
130. See Monin, Sawyer, & Marquez, 2008.
131. See Ames, 2008a.
132. See Ames, 2008a; 2009.
133. See Carnevale & De Dreu, 2006.
134. See Stanik, Kurzban, & Ellsworth, 2010.
135. See Burger & Cosby, 1999.
136. See Urbaniak & Kilmann, 2003.
137. See Urbaniak & Kilmann, 2006.
138. See Regan & Berscheid, 1997.
139. See Urbaniak & Kilmann, 2003.
140. Herold & Milhausen, 1999, p. 342.
141. See Glick & Fiske, 1996, 2001.
142. See Bohner et al., 2010; Chapleau et al., 2007; Hall & Canterberry, 2011; Johannesen-Schmidt & Eagly, 2002; Lee et al., 2010; and Travaglia et al., 2009.
143. See Hall & Canterberry, 2011.
144. See Olderbak & Figueredo, 2010; and Olderbak & Figueredo, in preparation.
145. See Kirkpatrick & Davis, 1994.
146. See Kirkpatrick & Davis, 1994.
147. See Meston & Buss, 2009.
148. See Gangestad et al., 2004.
149. See Galinsky & Sorenstein, 2011.
150. Campbell, 2005, p. 213.
151. See Grayson & Stein, 1981; Murzynski & Degelman, 1996; and Sakaguchi & Hasegawa, 2006.
152. See Grayson and Stein, 1981.
153. See Book, Quinsey, & Langford, 2007; Gunns, Johnston, & Hudson, 2002; Hall, Coats, & Smith-Le Beau, 2005; Montepare & Zebrowitz-McArthur, 1988; and Richards, Rollerson, & Phillips, 1991.
154. Mauro, 2010.
155. Campbell, 2005, p. 215.
156. See Hawley, 1999; Jonason, Li, Webster, & Schmitt, 2009; and Lievens, Chasteen, Day, & Christensen, 2006.

Chapter 9

1. See, for example, Kruger & Nesse, 2007.
2. See Kruger, 2010.
3. See, for example, Chagnon, 1968.
4. See Smith, 2007.
5. See Kirby, Lepore, & Ryan, 2005.
6. In Perina, 2007.
7. See Geher & Miller, 2008.
8. See Spence & Helmreich, 1972.
9. See Hill & Fischer, 2008.
10. See Geher & Kaufman, 2007.
11. See Comer, 2003.
12. See Nesse, 2005.
13. See Geher & Miller, 2008; and Miller, 2000.
14. See Wilson, Geher, & Waldo, 2009.
15. See Daly & Wilson, 1985.

16. See Daly, Wilson, & Weighorst, 1982.
17. See Buss, 2005b.
18. See Buss, 2003.
19. See Burch & Gallup, 2004.
20. See Muelenhard & Linton, 1987.
21. See, for example, Burch & Gallup, 2004.
22. See Jonason, Li, & Richardson, 2010.
23. See Reitman, 2006.
24. See England, Shafter, & Fogarty, 2007; Garcia & Reiber, 2008; Lambert, Kahn, & Apple, 2003; Paul & Hayes, 2002; and Paul, McManus, & Hayes, 2000.
25. See Garcia & Reiber, 2010.
26. See Garcia & Reiber, 2008.
27. See Kruger, 2008.
28. See Miller, 2009.
29. See Saad & Vongas, 2008.
30. See Frank, 2004.
31. See Frank, 2004.
32. See Frank, 2004.
33. See Geher & Gambacorta, 2010.
34. See Geher, 2006; and Pinker, 2002.
35. See Kruger & Nesse, 2007.
36. See Kruger & Nesse, 2007.
37. See Peclet et al., 1990.
38. See Daly & Wilson, 1988.
39. See Kruger & Nesse, 2007.
40. See Johnsen & Geher, 2010.
41. See Giordano, Johnsen, & Geher, 2010.
42. See Kruger, 2010; and Kruger & Nesse, 2006, 2007.
43. See Clark & Hatfield, 1989.
44. See Maria Peclet et al., 1990.
45. See Krebs & Davies, 1997; and Nettle, 2009b, 2009c.
46. See Krebs & Davies, 1997; and Nettle, 2009b, 2009c.
47. See Bajekal, 2005.
48. See Nettle, 2010.
49. See Walker et al., 2006.
50. See Low, Hazel, Parker, & Welch, 2008.
51. See Promislow & Harvey, 1990.
52. See Geronimus, 1997.
53. See Nettle, 2009b, 2009c.
54. See Nettle, 2009b.
55. See Robson & Kaplan, 2003.
56. See Nettle, 2009b.
57. See Figueredo & Jacobs, 2010.
58. See Costello, Compton, Keeler, & Angold, 2003.
59. See Geronimus, Bound, & Waidmann, 1999.
60. See Nettle, 2009b.
61. See Blair, 2006; Friedman et al., 2006; Friedman et al., 2008; Garlick & Sejnowski, 2006; Heitz et al., 2006; and Kane & Engle, 2002.
62. See Howse, Calkins, Anastopoulos, Keane, & Shelton, 2003; McClelland et al., 2007; Rueda, Posner, & Rothbart, 2005; and Ponitz, McClelland, Matthews, & Morrison, 2009.
63. See Sternberg, 1997, 2011. The importance of looking at context in making sense of a wide range of intelligent behaviors has also been made quite convincingly by Ceci (1996).
64. See Diamond, Barnett, Thomas, & Munro, 2007, for an example of an intervention.
65. See Thompson-Schill, Ramscar, & Chrysikou, 2009.

66. Consult his *Psychology Today* blog "Freedom to Learn": http://www.psychologytoday.com/blog/freedom-learn.
67. See Wilson, 2007.

Epilogue

1.   See Perina, 2007.
2.   See Geher & Kaufman, 2007.
3.   See Geher & Kaufman, 2007.
4.   See Geher, Camargo, & O'Rourke, 2008.
5.   See Trivers, 1972.
6.   See Geher & Kaufman, 2007.
7.   See O'Brien, Geher, Gallup, Kaufman, & Garcia, 2010.
8.   See, for example, Buss, 2003.
9.   See Gangestad & Simpson, 2000.
10. See Thornhill & Gangestad, 2008.
11. See Raven's Progressive Matrices; Raven, Raven, & Court, 2003.
12. See Miller, 2009.
13. See Geher, Camargo, & O'Rourke, 2008.
14. See Peterson, Geher, & Kaufman, 2011.
15. See O'Brien et al., 2010.
16. See Garcia & Reiber, 2008.
17. See Garcia & Reiber, 2008.
18. See Garcia & Reiber, 2008.
19. See Thornhill & Gangestad, 2008.
20. See Bleske-Recheck & Buss, 2001.
21. See Garcia & Reiber, 2008.
22. See Salovey & Mayer, 1990.
23. See Pipitone & Gallup, 2008.
24. See Penke et al., 2008.
25. See Landolfi, Geher, & Andrews, 2007.
26. See Haselton & Buss, 2000.
27. See Geher, 2009.
28. See O'Brien et al., 2010.
29. See O'Brien et al., 2010.
30. See O'Brien et al., 2010; and Crosier et al., in preparation.
31. See Geher, 2004.
32. See Mayer et al., 2000.
33. See Geher, 2004.
34. See Geher, Warner, & Brown, 2001.
35. See Bracket & Salovey, 2004.
36. If you are a young scholar in the behavioral sciences looking for an important research topic, might we suggest that you consider working on the development of psychometric indices of the cognitive mechanisms, personality traits, and abilities that underlie mating intelligence?

REFERENCES

Abbey, A. (1982). Sex differences in attributions for friendly behavior: Do males misperceive females' friendliness? *Journal of Personality and Social Psychology, 42,* 830–838.Abramson, P. R., & Pinkerton, S. D. (2002). *With pleasure: Thoughts on the nature of human sexuality.* New York, NY: Oxford University Press.

Ahmetoglu, G., Swami, V., & Chamorro-Premuzic, T. (2009). The relationship between dimensions of love, personality, and relationship length. *Archives of Sexual Behavior, 39,* 1181–1190.

Ali, F., Amorim, I. S., & Chamorro-Premuzic, T. (2009). Empathy deficits and trait emotional intelligence in psychopathy and Machiavellianism. *Personality and Individual Differences, 47,* 758–762.

Ali, F., Chamorro-Premuzic, T. (2010). The dark side of love and life satisfaction: Associations with intimate relationships, psychopathy and Machiavellianism. *Personality and Individual Differences, 48,* 228–233.

Alkon, A. (2000). *Nice guys are from Uranus?* Retrieved November 7th, 2010, from http://www. advicegoddess.com/columns/column18.html.

Allen, E. S., & Baucom, D. H. (2004). Adult attachment and patterns of extradyadic involvement. *Family Process, 43,* 467–488.

Ames, D. R. (2008a). In search of the right touch: Interpersonal assertiveness in organizational life. *Current Directions in Psychological Science, 17,* 381–385.

Ames, D. R. (2008b). Assertiveness expectancies: How hard people push depends on the consequences they predict. *Journal of Personality and Social Psychology, 95,* 1541–1557.

Ames, D. R. (2009). Pushing up to a point: Assertiveness and effectiveness in leadership and interpersonal dynamics. *Research in Organizational Behavior, 29,* 111–133.

Andrews, A., & Carroll, J. (2010). *The Evolutionary Review.* New York, NY: SUNY Press.

Arai, L. (2003). Low expectations, sexual attitudes and knowledge: Explaining teenage pregnancy and fertility in English communities. *Sociological Review, 51,* 199–217.

Arden, R., Gottfredson, L. S., Miller, G., & Pierce, A. (2008). Intelligence and semen quality are positively correlated. *Intelligence, 37,* 277–282.

Ariely, D., & Loewenstein, G. (2005). The heat of the moment: The effect of sexual arousal on sexual decision making. *Journal of Behavioral Decision Making, 19,* 87–98.

Armstrong, E. A., England, P., & Fogarty, A. C. K. (2012). Accounting for women's orgasm and sexual enjoyment in college hookups and relationships. *American Sociological Review, 77,* 435–462.

Asendorpf, J. B., Penke, L., & Back, M. D. (2011). From dating to mating and relating: Predictors of initial and long-term outcomes of speed-dating in a community sample. *European Journal of Personality, 25,* 16–30.

Ashton, M. C., Lee, K., & Paunonen, S. V. (2002). What is the central feature of extraversion? Social attention versus reward sensitivity. *Journal of Personality and Social Psychology, 83,* 245–252.

Atkins, D. C., Baucom, D. H., & Jacobson, N. S. (2001). Understanding infidelity: Correlates in a national random sample. *Journal of Family Psychology, 15*, 735–749.

Austin, E. J., & Deary, I. J. (2000). The four "A"s: A common framework for normal and abnormal personality? *Personality and Individual Differences, 28*, 977–995.

Austin, E. J., Farrelly, D., Black, C., & Moore, H. (2007). Emotional intelligence, Machiavellianism and emotional manipulation: Does EI have a dark side? *Personality and Individual Differences, 43*, 179–189.

Avila, M., Thaker, G., & Adami, H. (2001). Genetic epidemiology and schizophrenia: A study of reproductive fitness. *Schizophrenia Research, 47*, 233–241.

Azim, E., Mobbs, D., Booil, J., Menon, V., & Reiss, A. L. (2005). Sex differences in brain activation elicited by humor. *Proceedings of the National Academy of Sciences of the United States of America, 102*, 16496–16501.

Back, M. D. & Kenny, D. A. (2010). The Social Relations Model: How to understand dyadic processes. *Social and Personality Psychology Compass, 4*, 855–870.

Back, M. D., Penke, L., Schmuckle, S. C., Sachse, K., Borkenau, P., & Asendorpf, J. B. (2011). Why mate choices are not as reciprocal as we assume: The role of personality, flirting, and physical attractiveness. *European Journal of Personality, 25*, 120–132.

Back, M. D., Schmukle, S. C. & Egloff, B. (2010). A closer look at first sight: Social relations lens model analyses of personality and interpersonal attraction at zero acquaintance. *European Journal of Personality, 25*, 225–238.

Back, M. D., Schmukle, S. C., & Egloff, B. (2010a). Why are narcissists so charming at first sight? Decoding the narcissism-popularity link at zero acquaintance. *Journal of Personality and Social Psychology, 98*, 132–145.

Back, M. D., Schmukle, S. C., & Egloff, B. (2010b). A closer look at first sight: Social relations lens model analysis of personality and interpersonal attraction at zero acquaintance. *European Journal of Personality. 3*, 225–238.

Back, M. D., Stopfer, J. M., Vazire, S., Gaddis, S., Schmukle, S. C., & Egloff, B., et al. (2010). Facebook profiles reflect actual personality not self-idealization. *Psychological Science, 21*, 372–374.

Badcock, C. (2009). *The imprinted brain: How genes set the balance of the mind between autism and psychosis.* London, UK: Jessica Kingsley Publishers.

Baer, J., & Kaufman, J.C. (2005). Bridging generality and specificity: The Amusement Park Theoretical (APT) Model of Creativity. *Roeper Review, 27*, 158–163.

Bajekal, M. (2005). Healthy life expectancy by area deprivation: Magnitude and trends in England, 1994–9. *Health Statistics Quarterly, 25*, 18–27.

Bakermans-Kranenburg, M. J., & van Ijzendoorn, M. H. (2006). Gene-environment interaction of the dopamine D4 receptor (DRD4) and observed maternal insensitivity predicting externalizing behavior in preschoolers. *Developmental Psychobiology, 48*, 406–409.

Bale, C., Morrison, R., & Caryl, P. G. (2006). Chat-up lines as male sexual displays. *Personality and Individual Differences, 40*, 655–664.

Bandura, A. (1977). Self-efficacy: Toward a unifying theory of behavioral change. *Psychological Review, 84*, 191–215.

Banks, G. C., Batchelor, J. H., & McDaniel, M. A. (2010). Smarter people are (a bit) more symmetrical: A meta-analysis of the relationship between intelligence and fluctuating asymmetry. *Intelligence, 4*, 393–401.

Barelds, D. P. H. (2005). Self and partner personality in intimate relationships. *European Journal of Personality, 19*, 501–518.

Barlow, A., Qualter, P., & Sylianou, M. (2010). Relationships between Machiavellianism, emotional intelligence and theory of mind in children. *Personality and Individual Differences, 48*, 78–82.

Baron-Cohen, S., & Wheelwright, S. (2004). The empathy quotient: An investigation of adults with Asperger syndrome or high functioning autism, and normal sex differences. *Journal of Autism and Developmental Disorders, 34*, 163–175.

Baron-Cohen, S., Wheelwright, S., Skinner, R., Martin, J., & Clubley, E. (2001). The Autism-spectrum Quotient (AQ): Evidence from Asperger syndrome/high-functioning autism, males and females, scientists and mathematicians. *Journal of Autism and Developmental Disorders, 31*, 5–17.

Barry, C. T., Kerig, P. K., Stellwagen, K. K., & Barry, T. D. (2010). *Narcissism and Machiavellianism in youth: Implications for the development of adaptive and maladaptive behavior.* Washington, D.C.: American Psychological Association.

Barry, R. A., Kochanska, G., & Philibert, R. A. (2008). G X E interactions in the organization of attachment: mother's responsiveness as a moderator of children's genotypes. *The Journal of Child Psychology and Psychiatry, 12*, 1313–1320.

Bates, T. C. (2007). Fluctuating asymmetry and intelligence. *Intelligence, 35*, 41–46.

Bauman, K. P., & Geher, G. (2003). The role of perceived social norms on attitudes and behavior: An examination of the false consensus effect. *Current Psychology: Developmental, Learning, Personality, Social, 21*, 293–318.

Baumeister, R.F., Bratslavsky, E., Muraven, M., & Tice, D.M. (1998). Ego depletion: Is the active self a limited resource? *Journal of Personality and Social Psychology, 74*, 1252–1265.

Baumeister, R.F., & Tierney, J. (2012). *Willpower: Rediscovering the greatest human strength.* New York, NY: Penguin Books.

Baumeister, R. F., Catanese, K. R., & Vohs, K. D. (2001). Are there gender differences in strength of sex drive? Theoretical views, conceptual distinctions, and a review of relevant evidence. *Personality and Social Psychology Review, 5*, 242–273.

Baumeister, R. F., Gailliot, M., DeWall, C. N., & Oaten, M. (2006). Self-regulation and personality: How interventions increase regulatory success, and how depletion moderates the effects of traits on behavior. *Journal of Personality, 74*, 1773–1801.

Beaussart, M., Kaufman, S.B., & Kaufman, J.C. (in press). Creative activity, personality, mental illness, and short-term mating success. *Journal of Creative Behavior.*

Belsky, J. (1997). Attachment, mating and parenting: An evolutionary interpretation. *Human Nature, 8*, 361–381.

Belsky, J. (2005). Differential susceptibility to rearing influence: an evolutionary hypothesis and some evidence. In B. Ellis & D. Bjorklund (Eds.), *Origins of the social mind: evolutionary psychology and child development* (pp. 139–163). New York, NY: Guildford.

Belsky, J., Steinberg, L., Houts, R., Friedman, S., DeHart, G., Cauffman, E., Roisman, G., et al. (2007). Family reading antecedent of pubertal timing. *Child Development, 78*, 1302–1321.

Belsky, J., & Pluess, M. (2009). The nature (and nurture?) of plasticity in early human development. *Perspectives in Psychological Science, 4*, 345–351.

Belsky, J., Steinberg, L., & Draper, P. (1991). Childhood experience, interpersonal development, and reproductive strategy: An evolutionary theory of socialization. *Child Development, 62*, 647–670.

Bereczkei, T., & Csanaky, A. (1996). Mate choice, marital success, and reproduction in a modern society. *Ethology and Sociobiology, 17*, 17–35.

Berscheid, E., & Reis, H. T. (1998). Attraction and close relationships. In D. T. Gilbert, S. T. Fiske, & G. Lindzey (Eds.), *The handbook of social psychology* (4th ed., Vol. 2, pp. 193–281). New York, NY: McGraw-Hill.

Betzig, L. (1986). *Despotism and differential reproduction: A Darwinian view of history.* New York, NY: Aldine.

Bingham, P. M. (1999). Human uniqueness: A general theory. *Quarterly Review of Biology, 73*, 3–49.

Birnbaum, G. E. (2007). Beyond the borders of reality: Attachment orientations and sexual fantasies. *Personal Relationships, 14*, 321–342.

Blair, C. (2006). How similar are fluid cognition and general intelligence? A developmental neuroscience perspective on fluid cognition as an aspect of human cognitive ability. *Behavioral and Brain Sciences, 29*, 109–125.

Bleske-Recheck, A. L., & Buss, D. M. (2001). Opposite-sex friendship: Sex differences and similarities in initiation, selection, and dissolution. *Personality and Social Psychology Bulletin, 27*, 1310–1327.

Bleske-Rechek, A., Remiker, & Baker, J. P. (2008). Narcissistic men and women think they are so hot—But they are not. *Personality and Individual Differences, 45*, 420–424

Blumstein, P., & Schwartz, P. (1983). *American couples*. New York, NY: William Morrow.

Bohner, G., Ahlborn, K., & Steiner, R. (2010). How sexy are sexist men? Women's perception of male response profiles in the ambivalent sexism inventory. *Sex Roles, 62*, 568–582.

Bono, J. E., & Judge, T. A. (2004). Personality and transformational and transactional leadership: A meta-analysis. *Journal of Applied Psychology, 89*, 901–910.

Book, A. S., Quinsey, V. L., & Langford, D. (2007). Psychopathy and the perception of affect and vulnerability. *Criminal Justice and Behavior, 34*, 531–544.

Borkenau, P., Brecke, S., Mottig, C., & Paelecke, M. (2009). Extraversion is accurately perceived after a 50-ms exposure to a face. *Journal of Research in Personality, 43*, 703–706.

Borkenau, P., & Liebler, A. (1992). Trait inferences: Sources of validity at zero acquaintance. *Journal of Personality and Social Psychology, 62*, 645–657.

Botwin, M. D., Buss, D. M., & Shackelford, T. K. (1997). Personality and mate preferences: Five factors in mate selection and marital satisfaction. *Journal of Personality, 65*, 107–136

Boudreau, J. W., Boswell, W. R., & Judge, T. A. (2001). Effects of personality on executive career success in the United States and Europe. *Journal of Vocational Behavior, 58*, 53–58.

Bowlby, J. (1969/1982). *Attachment and loss: Vol. 1. Attachment*. New York, NY: Basic Books.

Boyce, W. T., & Ellis, B. J. (2005). Biological sensitivity to context: I. An evolutionary-developmental theory of the origins and functions of stress reactivity. *Development and Psychopathology, 17*, 271–301.

Brackett, M. A., & Salovey, P. (2004). Measuring emotional intelligence as a mental ability with the Mayer-Salovey-Caruso Emotional Intelligence Test. In G. Geher (Ed.), *Measurement of emotional intelligence* (pp. 179–194). Hauppauge, NY: Nova Science Publishers.

Brackett, M. A., Warner, R. M., & Bosco, J. (2005). Emotional intelligence and relationship quality among couples. *Personal Relationships, 12*, 197–212.

Bradley, R. H., & Corwyn, R. F. (2008). Infant temperament, parenting, and externalizing behavior in first grade: a test of the differential susceptibility hypothesis. *Journal of Child Psychology and Psychiatry and Allied Disciplines, 49*, 124–131.

Bradshaw, C., Kahn, A. S., & Saville, B. K. (2010). To hook up or date: Which gender benefits? *Sex Roles, 62*, 661–669.

Brand, R. J., Markey, C. M., & Hodges, S. D. (2007). Sex differences in self-reported infidelity and its correlates. *Sex Roles, 57*, 101–109.

Bressler, E. R., & Balshine, S. (2006). The influence of humor on desirability. *Evolution and Human Behavior, 27*, 29–39.

Bressler, E. R., Martin, R. A., & Balshine, S. (2006). Production and appreciation of humor as sexually selected traits. *Evolution and Human Behavior, 27*, 121–130.

Brumbach, B. H., Figueredo, A. J., & Ellis, B. J. (2009). Effects of harsh and unpredictable environments in adolescence on development of life history strategies. *Human Nature, 20*, 25–51.

Brunswik, E. (1956) *Perception and the Representative Design of Psychological Experiments* (2nd ed.), Berkeley, CA: University of California Press.

Buchanan, T., Johnson, J. A., & Goldberg, L. R. (2005). Implementing a five-factor personality inventory for use on the internet. *European Journal of Psychological Assessment, 21*, 115–127.

Buckner, R. L., Andrews-J. R., & Schacter, D. L. (2008). The brain's default network: Anatomy, function, and relevance to disease. *Annals of the New York Academy of Sciences, 1124*, 1–38.

Burch, R. L., & Gallup, G. G. (2004). Is pregnancy a stimulus for domestic violence? *Journal of Family Violence, 19*(4), 243–247.

Burger, J. M., & Cosby, M. (1999). Do women prefer dominant men? The case of the missing control condition. *Journal of Research in Personality, 33*, 358–368.

Burley, N., & Symanski, R. (1981). Women without: An evolutionary and cross-cultural perspective on prostitution. In R. Symanski (Ed.), *The immoral landscape: Female prostitution in Western societies* (pp. 239–274). Toronto, Canada: Butterworth.

Bushman, B. J., Bonacci, A. M., van Dijk, M., & Baumeister, R. F. (2003). Narcissism, sexual refusal, and aggression: Testing a narcissistic reactance model of sexual coercion. *Journal of Personality and Social Psychology, 84*, 1027–1040.

Buss, D. M. (1988). The evolution of human intrasexual competition: Tactics of mate attraction. *Journal of Personality & Social Psychology, 54*, 616–628.

Buss, D. M. (1989). Sex differences in human mate preferences: Evolutionary hypotheses tested in 37 cultures. *Behavioral and Brain Sciences, 12*, 1–49.

Buss, D. M. (1994/2003) *The evolution of desire: Strategies of human mating*, New York, NY: Basic Books.

Buss, D. M. (1996). Sexual conflict: Evolutionary insights into feminism and the "battle of the sexes." In D. M. Buss & N. Malamuth (Eds.), *Sex, power, conflict: Evolutionary and feminist perspectives* (pp. 296–318). New York, NY: Oxford University Press.

Buss, D. M. (1999). Human nature and individual differences: The evolution of human personality. In L. A. Pervin & O. P. John (Eds.), *Handbook of personality: Theory and research* (2nd ed.) (pp. 31–56). New York, NY: Guilford.

Buss, D. M. (2005a), *The handbook of evolutionary psychology*. New York, NY: Wiley.

Buss, D. M. (2005b). *The murderer next door: Why the mind is designed to kill*. New York, NY: Penguin.

Buss, D. M. (2006). The evolution of love. In R. J. Sternberg & K. Weis (Eds.), *The new psychology of love* (pp. 65–86). New Haven, CT: Yale University Press.

Buss, D. M. (2011). *Evolutionary psychology: The new science of the mind* (4th ed.). Needham Heights, MA: Allyn & Bacon.

Buss, D. M., Abbott, M., Angleitner, A., Ashherian, A., Biaggio, A., & et al. (1990a). International preferences in selecting mates: A study of 37 cultures. *Journal of Cross-Cultural Psychology, 21*, 5–47.

Buss, D. M., Abbott, M., Angleitner, A., Biaggio, A., Blanco-Villasenor, A., Bruchon Schweitzer, M., [& 45 additional authors]. (1990b). International preferences in selecting mates: A study of 37 societies. *Journal of Cross Cultural Psychology, 21*, 5–47.

Buss, D. M., & Barnes, M. (1986). Preferences in human mate selection. *Journal of Personality and Social Psychology, 50*, 559–570.

Buss, D. M., & Haselton, M. G. (2005). The evolution of jealousy: A reply to Buller. *Trends in Cognitive Science, 9*, 506–507.

Buss, D. M., Larsen, R. J., Westen, D., & Semmelroth, J. (1992). Sex differences in jealousy: Evolution, physiology and psychology. *Psychological Science, 3*, 251–255.

Buss, D. M., Larsen, R. J., & Westen, D. (1996). Sex differences in jealousy: Not gone, not forgotten, and not explained by alternative hypotheses. *Psychological Science, 7*, 373–375.

Buss, D. M., & Schmitt, D. P. (1993). Sexual Strategies Theory: An evolutionary perspective on human mating. *Psychological Review, 100*, 204–232.

Buss, D.M. & Schmitt, D. P. (1996). Strategic Self-Promotion and Competition Derogation: Sex and Conflict Effects on Perceived Effectiveness of Mate Attraction Tactics. *Journal of Personality and Social Psychology, 70*, 6, 1185–1204.

Buss, D. M., & Schmitt, D. P. (2011). Evolutionary psychology and feminism. *Sex Roles, 64*, 768–787.

Buss, D. M., & Shackelford, T. K. (2008). Attractive women want it all: Good genes, economic investment, parenting proclivities, and emotional commitment. *Evolutionary Psychology, 6*, 134–146.

Buss, D. M., Shackelford, T. K., Kirkpatrick, L. A., Chloe, J., Hasegawa, M., Hasegawa, T., & Bennett, K. (1999). Jealousy and beliefs about infidelity: Tests of competing hypotheses in the United States, Korea, and Japan. *Personal Relationships, 6*, 125–150.

Butler, E. A., Egloff, B., Wilhelm, F. H., Smith, N. C., Erickson, E. A., & Gross, J. J. (2003). The social consequences of expressive suppression. *Emotion, 3*, 48–67.

Buttermore, N. (2006). *Distinguishing dominance and prestige: Validation of a self-report scale. Poster presented at the Human Behavior and Evolution Society's 18th Annual Meeting.* Philadelphia, PA.

Byers, E. S., & Lewis, K. (1988). Dating couples' disagreements over desired levels of intimacy. *Journal of Sex Research, 23*, 12–22.

Byrne, R. W., & Whiten, A. (Eds.). (1988). *Machiavellian intelligence: Social expertise and the evolution of intelligence in monkeys and apes.* New York, NY: Oxford University Press.

Calvin, C. M., Deary, I. J., Fenton, C., Roberts, B. A., Der, G., Leckenby, N., & Batty, G. D. (2010). Intelligence in youth and all-cause-mortality: Systematic review with meta-analysis. *International Journal of Epidemiology. 40*, 626–644.

Campbell, A. (2008). The morning after the night before: Affective reactions to one-night stands among mated and unmated women and men. *Human Nature, 19*, 157–173.

Campbell, K., Kaufman, J. C., & Gau, J. M. (2010, August). *Creativity: Does being in-love matter?* Paper presented at the annual meeting of the *American Psychological Association*, San Diego, CA.

Campbell, L., Martin, R. A., & Ward, J. A. (2008). An observational study of humor use during a conflict discussion. *Personal Relationships, 15*, 41–55.

Campbell, W. K. (2005). *When you love a man who loves himself.* Naperville, IL: Sourcebooks.

Campbell, W. K., & Foster, C. A. (2002). Narcissism commitment in romantic relationships: An Investment Model analysis. *Personality and Social Psychology Bulletin, 28*, 484–495.

Campbell, W. K., Foster, C. A., & Finkel, E. J. (2002). Does self-love lead to love for others? A story of narcissistic game playing. *Journal of Personality and Social Psychology, 83*, 340–354.

Caprara, G. V., Barbaranelli, C., & Zimbardo, P. (1996). Understanding the complexity of human aggression: Affective, cognitive and social dimensions of individual differences. *European Journal of Personality, 10*, 133–155.

Carlson, K. S., & Gjerde, P. F. (2009). Preschool personality antecedents of narcissism in adolescence and young adulthood: A 20-year longitudinal study. *Journal of Research in Personality, 43*, 570–578.

Carnevale, P. J., & De Dreu, C. K. W. (2006). Motive: The negotiator's raison d'être. In L. Thompson (Ed.), *Frontiers of social psychology: Negotiation theory and research* (pp. 55–76). New York, NY: Psychology Press.

Carson, S. H., Peterson, J. B., & Higgins, D. M. (2003). Decreased latent inhibition is associated with increased creative achievement in high-functioning individuals. *Journal of Personality and Social Psychology, 85*, 499–506.

Carver, C. S., Johnson, S. L., & Joormann, J. (2009). Two-mode models of self-regulation as a tool for conceptualizing effects of the serotonin system in normal behavior and diverse disorders. *Current Directions in Psychological Science, 18*, 195–199.

Casey, J. J., Garrett, J., Brackett, M. A., & Rivers, S. (2008). Emotional intelligence, relationship quality, and partner selection. In G. Geher & G. F. Miller, (Eds.) *Mating intelligence: Sex, relationships, and the mind's reproduction system.* Mahwah, NJ: Lawrence Erlbaum.

Caspi, A., McClay, J., Moffitt, T. E., Mill, J., Martin, J., Craig, I. W., et al. (2002). Role of genotype in the cycle of violence in maltreated children. *Science, 297*, 851–854.

Cassidy, J., & Shaver, P. R. (Eds.). (2008). *Handbook of attachment: Theory, research and clinical applications* (2nd ed.). New York, NY: Guilford.

Ceci, S. (1996). *On intelligence...more or less: A biological treatise on intellectual development.* Cambridge, MA: Harvard University Press.

Chabris, C. F. (2007). Cognitive and neurobiological mechanisms of the Law of General Intelligence. In M. J. Roberts (Ed.), *Integrating the mind: Domain general vs. domain specific processes in higher cognition* (pp. 449–491). New York, NY: Psychology Press.

Chagnon, N. A. (1968). *Yanomamo: The Fierce People.* Canada: Holt, Rinehart & Winston.

Changizi, M. (2011). *Harnessed: How language and music mimicked nature and transformed ape to man.* Dallas, TX: BenBella Books.

Chapell, M., Batten, M., Brown, J., Gonzalez, E., Herquet, G., Massar, C., & Pedroche, B. (2002). Frequency of public laughter in relation to sex, age, ethnicity, and social context. *Perceptual and Motor Skills, 95*, 746.

Chapleau, K. M., Oswald, D. L., & Russell, B. L. (2007). How ambivalent sexism toward women and men support rape myth acceptance. *Sex Roles, 57*, 131–136.

Chapman, A. J., & Foot, H. C. (1976). *Humor and laughter: Theory, research, and applications.* London: Wiley.

Chen, C., Burton, M., Greenberger, E., & Dmitrieva, J. (1999). Population migration and the variation of dopamine D4 receptor (DRD4) allele frequencies around the globe. *Evolution and Human Behavior, 20,* 309–324.

Cheng, J. T., Tracy, J. L., & Henrich, J. (2010). Pride, personality, and the evolutionary foundations of human social status. *Evolution and Human Behavior, 31,* 334–347.

Chiappe, D., & McDonald, K. (2005). The evolution of domain-general mechanisms in intelligence and learning. *Journal of General Psychology, 132,* 5–40.

Chisholm, J. S. (1993). Death, hope, and sex: Life-history theory and the development of reproductive strategies. *Current Anthropology, 34,* 1–24.

Chisholm, J. S. (1999). *Death, hope and sex: Steps to an evolutionary ecology of mind and morality.* New York, NY: Cambridge University Press.

Christie, R., & Geis, F. (1970) *Studies in Machiavellianism.* New York, NY: Academic Press.

Cialdini, R. (1993) *Influence: Science and practice* (3rd ed.), New York, NY: HarperCollins.

Ciarocco, N.J., Echevarria, J., & Lewandowski, G.W. (2012). Hungry for love: The influence of self-regulation on infidelity. *The Journal of Social Psychology, 152,* 61–74.

Claridge, G., & Davis, C. (2001). What's the use of neuroticism? *Personality and Individual Differences, 31,* 383–400.

Claridge, G., & Davis, C. (2003). *Personality and psychological disorders.* London, UK: Arnold.

Clark, A. P. (2006). Are the correlates of sociosexuality different for men and women? *Personality and Individual Differences, 41,* 1321–1327.

Clark, R. D. (1990). The impact of AIDS on gender differences in willingness to engage in casual sex. *Journal of Applied Social Psychology, 20,* 771–782.

Clark, R. D., & Hatfield, E. (1989). Gender differences in receptivity to sexual offers. *Journal of Psychology and Human Sexuality, 2,* 39–55.

Clegg, H., Nettle, D., & Miell, D. (2011). Status and mating success amongst visual artists. *Frontiers in psychology, 2,* 310.

Cohen, L. L., & Shotland, R. L. (1996). Timing of first sexual intercourse in a relationship: Expectations, experiences, and perceptions of others. *Journal of Sex Research, 33,* 291–299.

Comer, R. J. (2003). *Abnormal psychology.* New York, NY: Worth.

Comings, D. E., Muhlemann, D., Johnson, J. P. & Mac Murray, J. P. (2002). Parent-daughter transmission of the androgen receptor gene as an explanation of the effect of father absence on age of menarche. *Child Development, 73,* 1046–10451.

Conley, T. D. (2011). Perceived proposer personality characteristics and gender differences in acceptance of casual sex offers. *Journal of Personality and Social Psychology, 100,* 309–329.

Connellan, J., Baron-Cohen, S., Wheelwright, S., Batki, A., & Ahluwalia, J. (2000). Sex differences in human neonatal social perception. *Infant Behavior and Development, 23,* 113–118.

Connor, S. (2008). *Why women really do love self-obsessed psychopaths.* Retrieved December 15th, 2010, from http://www.independent.co.uk/news/science/why-women-really-do-love-selfobsessed-psychopaths-850007.html. Retrieved December 15th, 2010.

Cook, E. H., & Leventhal, B. L. (1996). The serotonin system in autism. *Current Opinions in Pediatrics, 8,* 348–354.

Coolidge, F.L., & Wynn, T. (2009). *The rise of Homo sapiens: The evolution of modern thinking.* New York, NY: Wiley-Blackwell.

Cooper, M., O'Donnell, D., Caryl, P. G., Morrison, R., & Bale, C. (2007). Chat-up lines as male displays: Effects of content, sex, and personality. *Personality and Individual Differences, 43,* 1075–1085.

Costa, P. T., Jr., & McCrae, R. R. (1985). *The NEO Personality Inventory Manual.* Odessa, FL: Psychological Assessment Resources.

Costa, P. T., Jr., & McCrae, R. R. (1992). Four ways five factors are basic. *Personality and Individual Differences, 13,* 653–665.

Costa, R., Terraciano, A., & McCrae, R. (2001). Gender differences in personality traits across cultures: Robust and surprising findings. *Journal of Personality and Social Psychology, 81,* 322–331.

Costello, E. J., Compton, S. N., Keeler, G., & Angold, A. (2003). Relationships between poverty and psychopathology. *Journal of the American Medical Association, 290,* 2023–2029.

Crespi, B., & Badcock, C. (2008). Psychosis and autism as diametrical disorders of the social brain. *Behavior and Brain Sciences, 31,* 241–320.

Crosier, B., Geher, G., Kaufman, S.B, & Kaufman, J.C. (in preparation). The structure, reliability and predictive validity of mating intelligence.

Cunningham, M. R. (1986). Measuring the physical in physical attractiveness: Quasi-experiments on the sociobiology of female facial beauty. *Journal of Personality and Social Psychology, 50,* 925–935.

Cunningham, M.R. (1989). Reactions to heterosexual opening gambits: Female selectivity and male responsiveness. *Personality and Social Psychology Bulletin, 15,* 27–41.

Cunningham, M.R., & Barbee, A.P. (2008). Prelude to a kiss: Nonverbal flirting, opening gambits, and other communication dynamics in the initiation of romantic relationships. In S. Sprecher, A. Wenzel, & J. Harvey (Eds.), *Handbook of relationship initiation* (pp. 97–120). New York, NY: Psychology Press.

Daly, M., Wilson, M. I. (1988). *Homicide.* New York, NY: Aldine de Gruyter.

Daly, M., Wilson, M. I., & Weghorst, S. J. (1982). Male sexual jealousy. *Ethology and Sociobiology, 3,* 11–27.

Darwin, C. (1871). *The descent of man, and selection in relation to sex* (2 vols.). London, UK: John Murray.

Davies, A. P. C., Shackelford, T. K., & Hass, R. G. (2007). When a "poach" is not a poach: Re-defining human mate poaching and re- estimating its frequency. *Archives of Sexual Behavior, 36,* 702–716.

Davila, J., Karney, B. R., Hall, T. W., & Bradbury, T. N. (2003). Depressive symptoms and marital satisfaction: Within-subject associations and the moderating effects of gender and neuroticism. *Journal of Family Psychology, 17,* 557–570.

Davis, K. E., & Latty-Mann, H. (1987). Love styles and relationship quality: Contribution to validation. *Journal of Social and Personal Relationships, 4,* 409–428

Dawkins, R. (1989). *The selfish gene.* Oxford, UK: Oxford University Press.

Deary, I. J., & Batty, G. D. (2011). Intelligence as a predictor of health, illness, and death. In R. J. Sternberg & S. B. Kaufman (Eds.), *The Cambridge handbook of intelligence.* New York, NY: Cambridge University Press.

Deary, I. J., De Fruyt F., & Ostendorf, F. (Eds.), *Personality psychology in Europe* (Vol. 7, pp. 7–28). Tilburg, the Netherlands: Tilburg University Press.

Deary, I. J., Penke, L., & Johnson, W. (2010). The neuroscience of human intelligence differences. *Nature Reviews Neuroscience, 11,* 201–211.

Deary, I., Strand, S., Smith, P., & Fernandes, C. (2007). Intelligence and educational achievement. *Intelligence, 35,* 13–21.

DeBacker, C., Braeckman, J., & Farinpour, L. (2008). Mating intelligence in personal ads: Do people care about mental traits, and do self-advertised traits match opposite-sex preferences? In G. Geher & G. F. Miller (Eds.), *Mating intelligence: Sex, relationships, and the mind's reproductive system.* Mahwah, NJ: Lawrence Erlbaum.

DeBruine, L., Jones, B. C., Frederick, D. A., Haselton, M. G., Penton-Voak, I. S., & Perrett, D. I. (2010). Evidence for menstrual cycle shifts in women's preferences for masculinity: A response to Harris (in press) "Menstrual Cycle and Facial Preferences Reconsidered." *Evolutionary Psychology, 8,* 768–775.

de Graaf, H., & Sandfort, T. G. M. (2004). Gender differences in affective responses to sexual rejection. *Archives of Sexual Behavior, 33,* 395–403.

de La Rochefoucauld, F. (2007). *Collected maxims and other reflections.* Oxford, UK: Oxford University Press.

Del Gaizo, A. L., & Falkenbach, D. M. (2008). Primary and secondary psychopathic traits and their relationship to perception and experience of emotion. *Personality and Individual Differences, 45,* 206–212.

Del Giudice, M. (2011). Sex differences in romantic attachment: A meta-analysis. *Personality and Social Psychology Bulletin, 37,* 193–214.

Del Giudice, M. (2010). The development of life history strategies: Toward a multi-stage theory. In D. M. Buss & P. H. Hawley (Eds.), *The evolution of personality and individual differences*, New York, NY: Oxford University Press.

Del Giudice, M. (2009). Sex, attachment, and the development of reproductive strategies. *Behavioral and Brain Sciences, 32*, 1–67.

Del Giudice, M., Angeleri, R., Brizio, A., & Elena, M. R. (2010). The evolution of autistic-like and schizotypal traits: a sexual selection hypothesis. *Frontiers in Psychology, 1*, 1–18.

Del Giudice, M. D., & Belsky, J. (2010). Sex differences in attachment emerge in middle child-hood: An evolutionary hypothesis. *Child Development Perspectives, 4*, 97–105.

Demarest, J., Snee, J., Correa, V. (2008). *Sex differences in spying on your Mate: Female ovulation status and other factors*. Presentation given at meeting of the NorthEastern Annual Psychology Society, May. Manchester, NH.

DePaulo, B. M. (1992). Nonverbal behavior and self-presentation. *Psychological Bulletin, 111*, 203–243.

DeYoung, C. G. (2006). Higher-order factors of the Big Five in a multi-informant sample. *Journal of Personality and Social Psychology, 91*, 1138–1151.

DeYoung, C. G. (2011). Intelligence and personality. In R. J. Sternberg & S. B. Kaufman (Eds.), *The Cambridge handbook of intelligence*. New York, NY: Cambridge University Press.

DeYoung, C. G., & Gray, J. R. (2009). Personality neuroscience: Explaining individual differ-ences in affect, behavior, and cognition. In P. J. Corr & G. Matthews (Eds.), *The Cambridge handbook of personality psychology* (pp. 323–346). New York, NY: Cambridge University Press.

DeYoung, C. G., Grazioplene, R. G., & Peterson, J. B. (2011). From madness to genius: The Openness/Intellect trait domain as a paradoxical simplex. *Journal of Research in Personality, 46*, 63–78.

DeYoung, C. G., Hirsh, J. B., Shane, M. S., Papademetris, X., Rajeevan, N., & Gray, J. R. (2010). Testing predictions from personality neuroscience: Brain structure and the Big Five. *Psychological Science, 21*, 820–828.

DeYoung, C. G., Peterson, J. B., & Higgins, D. M. (2002). Higher-order factors of the Big Five predict conformity: Are there neuroses of health? *Personality and Individual Differences, 33*, 533–552.

DeYoung, C. G., Quilty, L. C., & Peterson, J. B. (2007). Between facets and domains: Ten aspects of the Big Five. *Journal of Personality and Social Psychology, 93*, 880–896.

DeYoung, C. G., Shamosh, N. A., Green, A. E., Braver, T. S., & Gray, J. R. (2009). Intellect as distinct from openness: Differences revealed by fMRI of working memory. *Journal of Personality and Social Psychology, 97*, 883–892.

Diamond, A., Barnett, W. S., Thomas, J., & Munro, S. (2007). Preschool program improves cog-nitive control. *Science, 318*, 1387–1388.

Diamond, L. M., & Hicks, A. M. (2005). Attachment style, current relationship security, and negative emotions: the mediating role of physiological regulation. *Journal of Social and Personal Relationships, 22*, 499–518.

Dickman, S. (1990). Functional and dysfunctional impulsivity: personality and cognitive cor-relates. *Journal of Personality and Social Psychology, 58*, 95–102.

Digman, J. M. (1990). Personality structure: Emergence of the five-factor model. *Annual Review of Psychology, 41*, 417–440.

Digman, J. M. (1990). Functional and dysfunctional impulsivity: Personality and cognitive correlates. *Journal of Personality and Social Psychology, 58*, 95–102.

Digman, J. M. (1997). Higher-order factors of the Big Five. *Journal of Personality and Social Psychology, 73*, 1246–1256.

Dion, K., Berscheid, E., & Walster, E. (1972). What is beautiful is good. *Journal of Personality and Social Psychology, 24*, 285–290.

Dion, K. L., & Dion, K. K. (1988). Romantic love: Individual and cultural perspectives. In R. J. Sternberg & M. L. Barnes (Eds.), *The psychology of love* (pp. 264–289). New Haven, CT: Yale University Press.

Dissanayake, E. (1990). *What is art for?* Seattle, WA: University of Washington Press.

Dissanayake, E. (1995). *Homo aestheticus: Where art comes from and why.* Seattle, WA: University of Washington Press.

Dissanayake, E. (2012). *Art and intimacy: How the arts began.* University of Seattle, WA: University of Washington Press.

Dreber, A., Gerdes, C., & Gransmark, P. (2010). *Beauty queens and battling knights: Risk taking and attractiveness in chess.* Working paper.

Dugatkin, L. (2003). *Principles of animal behavior.* New York, NY: Norton.

Dugatkin, L. (1992) Sexual selection and imitation: females copy the mate choice of others *American Naturalist, 139,* 1384–1389.

Dugatkin, L. A. (2009). *Principles of animal behavior* (2nd ed.), New York, NY: Norton.

Dunbar, R. I. M. (1996). *Grooming, gossip and the evolution of language.* London, UK: Faber.

Duntley, J. D. & Buss, D. M. (2005). The plausibility of adaptations for homicide. In P. Carruthers, S. Laurence, & S. Stich (Eds.), *The Innate Mind: Structure and Contents* (pp. 291–304). New York, NY: Oxford University Press.

Dweck, C. (2007). *Mindset: The new psychology of success.* New York, NY: Ballantine.

Dyrenforth, P. S., Kashy, D. A., Donnellan, M. B., & Lucas, R. E. (2010). Predicting relationship and life satisfaction from personality in nationally representative samples from three countries: The relative importance of actor, partner, and similarity effects. *Journal of Personality and Social Psychology, 4,* 690–720.

Dziobek, I., Rogers, K., Fleck, S., Bahnemann, M., Heekeren, H. R., Wolf, O. T., & Convit, A. (2008). Dissociation of cognitive and emotional empathy in adults with Asperger syndrome using the Multifaceted Empathy Test (MET). *Journal of Autism and Developmental Disorders, 38,* 464–473.

Easton, J. A., Confer, J. C., Goetz, C. D., & Buss, D. M. (2010). Reproduction expediting: Sexual motivations, fantasies, and the ticking biological clock. *Personality and Individual Differences, 49,* 516–520.

Eastwick, P. W. (2009). Beyond the Pleistocene: Using phylogeny and constraint to inform the evolutionary psychology of human mating. *Psychological Bulletin, 135,* 794–821.

Eastwick, P. W., Finkel, E. J., Mochon, D., & Ariely, D. (2007). Selective versus unselective romantic desire: Not all reciprocity is created equal. *Psychological Science, 18,* 317–319.

Eastwick, P. W., & Finkel, E. J. (2008). Sex differences in mate preferences revisited: Do people know what they initially desire in a romantic partner? *Journal of Personality and Social Psychology, 94,* 245–264.

Edlund, J. E., & Sagarin, B. J. (2010). Mate value and mate preferences: An investigation into decisions made with and without constraints. *Personality and Individual Differences, 49,* 835–839.

Ehrlichman, H., & Eichenstein, R. (1992). Private wishes: Gender similarities and differences. *Sex Roles, 26,* 399–422.

Ekman, P. (2009). *Telling lies: Clues to deceit in the marketplace, politics, and marriage.* New York, NY: Norton.

Ekman, P., & Friesen, W. V. (1968). Nonverbal behavior in psychotherapy research. In J. Shlien (Ed.), *Research in psychotherapy* (Vol. 3, pp. 179–216). Washington, DC: American Psychological Association.

Ekman, P., O'Sullivan, M., Frank, M. (1999). A few can catch a liar. *Psychological Science, 10,* 263–266.

Ellis, B. J. (2004). Timing of pubertal maturation in girls: an integrated life history approach. *Psychological Bulletin, 130,* 920–958.

Ellis, B. J., & Essex, M. J. (2007). Family environments, adrenarche, and sexual maturation: A longitudinal test of a life history model. *Child Development, 78,* 1799–1817.

Ellis, B. J., Figueredo, A. J., Brumbach, B. H., Schlomer, G. L. (2009). Fundamental dimensions of environmental risk: The impact of harsh versus unpredictable environments on the evolution and development of life history strategies. *Human Nature, 20,* 204–268.

Ellis, B. J., & Symons, D. (1990). Sex differences in sexual fantasy: An evolutionary psychological approach. *Journal of Sex Research, 27,* 527–556.

Ellis, L. (1987). Relationships of criminality and psychopathy with eight other apparent manifestations of sub-optimal arousal. *Personality and Individual Differences, 8*, 905–925.

Emmons, R. A. (1984). Factor analysis and construct validity of the Narcissistic Personality Inventory. *Journal of Personality Assessment, 48*, 291–300.

Engel, G., Olson, K. R., & Patrick, C. (2002). The personality of love: Fundamental motives and traits related to components of love. *Personality and Individual Differences, 32*, 839–853.

England, P., Shafer, E. F., and Fogarty, A. C. K. (2007). Hooking up and forming romantic relationships on today's college campuses. In M. S. Kimmel & A. Aronson (Eds.), *The gendered society reader* (3rd ed., pp. 531–547). New York, NY: Oxford University Press.

Epstein, S. (1994). Integration of the cognitive and the psychodynamic unconscious. *American Psychologist, 49*, 709–724.

Epstein, S. (2003). Cognitive-experiential self-theory of personality. In T. Millon & M. J. Lerner (Eds.), *Comprehensive handbook of psychology* (Vol. 5, pp. 159–184). Personality and social psychology. Hoboken, NJ: Wiley.

Eskine, K. E. (2011). *On the propagation of musicality: Taking cues from sexual selection. Unpublished doctoral dissertation*, The Graduate Center of the City University of New York, New York, NY.

Esperger, Z., & Bereczkei, T. (2011). Machiavellianism and spontaneous mentalization: One step ahead of others. *European Journal of Personality*, doi: 10.1002/per.859.

Euler, H. A., & Weitzel, B. (1996). Discriminative grandparental solicitude as reproductive strategy. *Human Nature, 7*, 39–59.

Eva, K. W., & Wood, T. J. (2006). Are all the taken men good? *Canadian Medical Association Journal, 175*, 1573–74.

Evans, J. St. B. T. (2008). Dual-processing accounts of reasoning, judgment, and social cognition. *Annual Review of Psychology, 59*, 255–278.

Evans, J. St. B. T. (2010). *Thinking twice: Two minds in one brain*. Oxford, UK: Oxford University Press.

Evans, J. S. B. T., & Frankish, K. (2009). *In two minds: Dual-processses and beyond*. New York, NY: Oxford University Press.

Exline, J. J., & Lobel, M. (1999). The perils of outperformance: Sensitivity about being the target of a threatening upward social comparison. *Psychological Bulletin, 125*, 307–337.

Eysenck, H. K. (1976). *Sex and personality*. London, UK: Open Books.

Farah, A., & Chamorro-Premuzic, T. (2010). The dark side of love and life satisfaction: Associations with intimate relationships, psychopathy and Machiavellianism. *Personality and Individual Differences, 48*, 228–233.

Feeney, J. A. (1999). Adult romantic attachment and couple relationships. In J. Cassidy & P. R. Shaver (Eds.), *Handbook of attachment: Theory, research and clinical applications* (pp. 355–377). New York, NY: Guilford.

Feingold, A. (1990). Gender differences in effects of physical attractiveness on romantic attraction: A comparison across five research paradigms. *Journal of Personality and Social Psychology, 59*, 981–993.

Feingold, A., & Mazzella, R. (1991). Psychometric intelligence and verbal humor ability. *Personality and Individual Differences, 12*, 427–435.

Feist, G. (2001). Natural and sexual selection in the evolutionary of creativity. *Bulletin of Psychology and the Arts, 2*, 11–16.

Feist, G. (2008). *The psychology of science and the origins of the scientific mind*. New Haven, CT: Yale University Press.

Festinger, L., & Carlsmith, J. M. (1959). Cognitive consequences of forced compliance. *Journal of Abnormal and Social Psychology, 58*, 203–210.

Fenigstein, A., & Preston, M. (2007). The desired number of sexual partners as a function of gender, sexual risks, and the meaning of "ideal." *Journal of Sex Research, 44*, 89–95.

Figueredo, A. J., Brumbach, B. H., Jones, D. N., Sefcek, J. A., Vasquez, G., & Jacobs, W. J. (2008). Ecological constraints on mating tactics. In G. Geher & G. Miller (Eds.), *Mating intelligence: Sex, relationships, and the mind's reproductive system* (pp. 337–365). Mahwah, NJ: Lawrence Erlbaum.

Figueredo, A. J., & Jacobs, W. J. (2010). Aggression, risk-taking, and alternative life history strategies: The behavioral ecology of social deviance. In M. Frias-Armenta & V. Corral-Verdugo (Eds.), *Biopsychosocial perspectives on interpersonal violence*. Hauppauge, NY: Nova Science.

Figueredo, A. J., Sefcek, J. A., & Jones, D. N. (2006). The ideal romantic partner personality. *Personality and Individual Differences, 41*, 431–441.

Figueredo, A. J., Vásquez, G., Brumbach, B. H., & Schneider, S. M. R. (2004). The heritability of life history strategy: The K-factor, covitality, and personality. *Social Biology, 51*, 121–143.

Figueredo, A. J., Vásquez, G., Brumbach, B. H., Sefcek, J. A., Kirsner, B. R., & Jacobs, W. J. (2005). The K-Factor: Individual differences in life history strategy. *Personality and Individual Differences, 39*, 1349–1360.

Fisher, J. D., Nadler, A., & Whitcher-Alagna, S. (1982). Recipient reactions to aid. *Psychological Bulletin, 91*, 27–54.

Fisher, H. (2004). *Why we love: The nature and chemistry of romantic love*. New York, NY: Holt.

Fisher, H. E. (2009). *Why him? Why her?* New York, NY: Henry Holt.

Fisher, H. E., Island, H.D., Rich, J., Marchalik, D., & Brown, L.L. (in preparation). Four primary structures of temperament: Characteristics, further correlational analyses and comparisons with the Big Five.

Fisher, H. E., Rich, J., Island, H. D., Marchalik, D., & Brown, L.L. (in preparation). The role of four temperament dimensions in the initial attraction phase of mate choice.

Fisher, M., Cox, A., & Gordon, F. (2009). Deciding between competition derogation and self-promotion. *Journal of Evolutionary Psychology, 7*, 287–308.

Fisher, M. L., Geher, G., Cox, A., Tran, U. S., Hoben, A., Arrabaca, A., et al. (2009). Impact of relational proximity on distress from infidelity. *Evolutionary Psychology, 7*, 560–580.

Fisher, T. D., Moore, Z. T., & Pittenger, M. J. (2011). Sex on the brain? An examination of frequency of sexual cognitions as a function of gender, erotophilia, and social desirability. *Journal of Sex Research, 0*, 1–9.

Flam, F. (2008). *The score: How the quest for sex has shaped the modern man*. New York, NY: Avery.

Flinn, M. V., & Ward, C. V. (2005). Ontogeny and evolution of the social child. In B. J. Ellis & D. F. Bjorklund (Eds.), *Origins of the social mind: Evolutionary psychology and child development* (pp. 19–44). New York, NY: Guilford.

Flory, K., Molina, B. S. G., Pelham, W. E., Gnagy, E., & Smith, B. (2006). Childhood ADHD predicts risky sexual behavior in young adulthood. *Journal of Clinical Child and Adolescent Psychology, 35*, 571–577.

Foster, J. D., & Campbell, W. K. (2005). Narcissism and resistance to doubts about romantic partners. *Journal of Research in Personality, 39*, 550–557.

Foster, J. D., Campbell, W. K., & Twenge, J. M. (2003). Individual differences in narcissism: Inflated self-views across the lifespan and around the world. *Journal of Research in Personality, 37*, 469–486.

Foster, J. D., Shrira, I., & Campbell, W. K. (2006). Theoretical models of narcissism, sexuality, and relationship commitment. *Journal of Social and Personal Relationships, 23*(3), 367–386.

Fowles, D. C., & Dindo, L. (2006). A dual-deficit model of psychopathy. In C. J. Patrick (Ed.), *Handbook of the psychopathy* (pp. 14–34). New York, NY: Guilford.

Frank, R. H. (2004). Human nature and economic policy: Lessons for the transition economies. *Journal of Socio-Economics, 33*, 679–694.

Franken, R. E., Gibson, K. J., & Mohan, P. (1990). Sensation seeking and disclosure to close and casual friends. *Personality and Individual Differences, 11*, 829–832.

Frederick, D. A., & Haselton, M. G. (2007). Why is muscularity sexy? Tests of the fitness-indicator hypothesis. *Personality and Social Psychology Bulletin, 33*, 1167–1183.

Frederick, S., & Loewenstein, G. (1999). Hedonic adaptation. In D. Kahneman, E. Diener, & N. Schwarz (Eds.), *Well-being: The foundations of hedonic psychology* (pp. 302–329). New York, NY: Russell Sage Foundation.

Freed-Brown, G., & White, D. J. (2009). Acoustic mate copying: Female cowbirds attend to other females' vocalizations to modify their song preferences. *Proceedings of the Royal Society B: Biological Sciences, 276,* 3319–3325.

Friedman, H. S., Riggio, R. E., & Casella, D. F. (1988). Nonverbal skill, personal charisma, and initial attraction. *Personality and Social Psychology Bulletin, 14,* 203–211.

Friedman, H. S., Tucker, J. S., Schwartz, J. E., Martin, L. R., Tomlinsonkeasey, C., Wingard, D. L., & Criqui, M. H. (1995). Childhood conscientiousness and longevity: Health behaviors and cause of death. *Journal of Personality and Social Psychology, 68,* 696–703.

Friedman, N. P., Miyake, A., Corley, R. P., Young, S. E., DeFries, J. C., & Hewitt, J. K. (2006). Not all executive functions are related to intelligence. *Psychological Science, 17,* 172–179.

Friedman, N. P., Miyake, A., Young, S. E., DeFries, J. C., Corley, R. P., & Hewitt, J. K. (2008). Individual differences in executive functions are almost entirely genetic in origin. *Journal of Experimental Psychology: General, 137,* 201–225

Fulton, J. J., Marcus, D. K., & Payne, K. T. (2010). Psychopathic personality traits and risky sexual behavior in college students. *Personality and Individual Differences, 49,* 29–33.

Furlow, F. B., Armijo-Prewitt, T., Gangestad, S. W., & Thornhill, R. (1997). Fluctuating asymmetry and psychometric intelligence. *Proceedings of the Society of London, Series B, 264,* 823–829.

Gabora, L. (2008). Mind. In R. A. Bentley, H. D. G. Maschner, & C. Chippindale (Eds.), *Handbook of archaeological theories* (pp. 283–296). Walnut Creek CA: Altamira Press.

Gabora, L., & Kaufman, S.B. (2010). Evolutionary approaches to creativity. In R. J. Sternberg & J. C. Kaufman (Eds.), *The Cambridge handbook of creativity* (pp. 279–301). Cambridge, UK: Cambridge University Press.

Gabriel, M. T., Critelli, J. W., & Ee, J. S. (1994). Narcissistic illusions in self Evaluations of intelligence and attractiveness. *Journal of Personality, 62,* 143–155.

Gailliot, M. T., & Baumeister, R. F. (2007). Self-regulation and sexual restraint: Dispositionally and temporarily poor self-regulatory abilities contribute to failures at restraining sexual behavior. *Personality and Social Psychology Bulletin, 33,* 173–186.

Galinsky, A., & Sonenstein, F. L. (2011). The association between developmental assets and sexual enjoyment among emerging adults. *Journal of Adolescent Health, 48,* 610–615.

Gallup, G. G., Jr., Burch, R. L., & Berens Mitchell, T. J. (2006). Semen displacement as a sperm competition strategy: Multiple mating, self-semen displacement, and timing in-pair copulations. *Human Nature, 17,* 253–264.

Gangestad, S. W., & Buss, D. M. (1993). Pathogen prevalence and human mate preferences. *Ethology and Sociobiology, 14,* 89–96.

Gangestad, S. W., Haselton, M. G., & Buss, D. M. (2006). Evolutionary foundations of cultural variation: Evoked culture and mate preferences. *Psychological Inquiry, 17,* 75–95.

Gangestad, S. W., & Simpson, J. A. (2000). The evolution of human mating: Trade-offs and strategic pluralism. *Behavioral and Brain Sciences, 23,* 573–587.

Gangestad, S. W, Simpson, J. A., Cousins, A. J., Garver-Apgar, C. E., & Christensen, P. N. (2004). Women's preferences for male behavioral displays change across the menstrual cycle. *Psychological Science, 15,* 203–207.

Gangestad, S. W., & Thornhill, R. (2003). Facial masculinity and bodily fluctuating asymmetry. *Evolution and Human Behavior, 24,* 231–241.

Gangestad, S.W., Thornhill, R., & Garver-Apgar, C.E. (2005). Adaptations to ovulation: implications for sexual and social behavior. *Current Directions in Psychological Science, 14,* 312–316.

Garcia, J. R., MacKillop, J. Aller, E. L., Merriwether, A. M., Wilson, D. S., & Lum, J. K. (2010). Associations between dopamine D4 receptor gene variation with both infidelity and sexual promiscuity. *PLoS One, 11,* e14162.

Garcia, J. R., & Reiber, C. (2008). Hook-up behavior: A biopsychosocial perspective. *Journal of Social, Evolutionary, and Cultural Psychology, 2,* 192–208.

Garcia, J.R., & Reiber, C. (2010). Hooking up: Gender differences, evolution, and pluralistic ignorance. *Evolutionary Psychology, 8,* 390–404.

Gardner, H. (1983). *Frames of mind: The theory of multiple intelligences.* New York, NY: Basic Books.

Gardner, H. (1993). *Frames of mind: The theory of multiple intelligences* (2nd ed.). New York, NY: Basic Books.

Gardner, H. (2006). *Multiple intelligences: New horizons in theory and practice.* New York, NY: Basic Books.

Garlick, D., & Sejnowski, T. J. (2006). There is more to fluid intelligence than working memory capacity and executive function. *Behavior and Brain Sciences, 29,* 134–135.

Garver-Apgar, C. E., Gangestad, S. W., & Thornhill, R. (2008). Hormonal correlates of women's mid-cycle preference for the scent of symmetry. *Evolution and Human Behavior, 49,* 509–518.

Garver-Apgar, C. E., Gangestad, S. W., Thornhill, R., Miller, R. D., & Olp, J. J. (2006). Major histocompatibility complex alleles, sexual responsivity, and unfaithfulness in romantic couples. *Psychological Science, 17,* 830–835.

Geary, D. (2004). *The origin of mind: Evolution of brain, cognition, and general intelligence.* Washington, DC: American Psychological Association.

Geher, G. (Ed.). (2004). *Measuring emotional intelligence: Common ground and controversy.* New York, NY: Nova Science.

Geher, G. (2006). Evolutionary psychology is not evil...and here's why ... *Psihologijske Teme (Psychological Topics); Special Issue on Evolutionary Psychology, 15,* 181–202.

Geher, G. (2009). Accuracy and oversexualization in cross-sex mind-reading: An adaptationist approach. *Evolutionary Psychology, 7,* 331–347.

Geher, G., Bloodworth, R., Mason, J, Downey, H. J., Renstrom, K. L., & Romero, J. F. (2005). Motivational underpinnings of romantic partner perceptions: Psychological and physiological evidence. *Journal of Personal and Social Relationships, 22,* 255–281.

Geher, G., Camargo, M. A., & O'Rourke, S., (2008). Future directions in research on mating intelligence. In G. Geher & G. F. Miller (Eds.), *Mating intelligence: Sex, relationships, and the mind's reproductive system.* Mahwah, NJ: Lawrence Erlbaum.

Geher, G., & Gambacorta, D. (2010). Evolution is not relevant to sex differences in humans because I want it that way! Evidence for the politicization of human evolutionary psychology. *EvoS Journal: The Journal of the Evolutionary Studies Consortium, 2*(1), 32–47.

Geher, G., & Kaufman, S. B. (2007). The mating intelligence scale. *Psychology Today, 40,* 78–79.

Geher, G., & Kaufman, S. B. (2011). Mating intelligence. In R. Sternberg, & S. B. Kaufman (Eds.), *Cambridge handbook of intelligence.* Cambridge, UK: Cambridge University Press.

Geher, G., & Miller, G. F. (Eds.) (2008). *Mating intelligence: Sex, relationships, and the mind's reproductive system.* Mahwah, NJ: Lawrence Erlbaum.

Geher, G., Murphy, J., & Miller, G. F. (2008). Mating intelligence: Toward an evolutionarily informed construct. In G. Geher & G. F. Miller (Eds.), *Mating intelligence: Sex, relationships, and the mind's reproduction system.* Mahwah, NJ: Lawrence Erlbaum.

Geher, G., Warner, R. M., & Brown, A. (2001). Predictive validity of the Emotional Accuracy Research Scale. *Intelligence, 29,* 373–388.

Gelman, R. (2009). Learning in core and noncore domains. In Tommasi, L., Peterson, M. A., Nadel, L. (Eds.), *Cognitive biology: Evolutionary and development perspectives on mind, brain, and behavior* (pp. 247–260). Cambridge, MA: MIT Press.

Gelman, R., & Brenneman, L. (1994). First principles can support both universal and culture specific learning about number and music. In L. A. Hirschfeld & S. A. Gelman (Eds.), *Mapping the mind: Domain specificity in cognition and culture* (pp. 369–391). New York, NY: Cambridge University Press.

Geronimus, A. T. (1997). Teenage childbearing and personal responsibility. *Political Science Quarterly, 112,* 405–430.

Geronimus, A. T., Bound, J., & Waidmann, T. A. (1999). Health inequality and population variation in fertility timing. *Social Science and Medicine, 49,* 1623–1636.

Gigerenzer, G. (2008). *Gut feelings: The intelligence of the unconscious.* New York, NY: Penguin.

Gigerenzer, G., & Goldstein, D. (1996) Reasoning the fast and frugal way: models of bounded rationality *Psychological Review, 103,* 650–669.

Gilbert, D. T. (2007). *Stumbling on happiness*. New York, NY: Vintage.

Gilbert, D. T., Killingsworth, M. A., Eyre, R. N., & Wilson, T. D. (2009). The surprising power of neighborly advice. *Science, 323*, 1617–1619.

Giosan, C. (2006). High-K Strategy Scale: A measure of the high-K independent criterion of fitness. *Evolutionary Psychology, 4*, 394–405.

Glass, S. P., & Wright, T. L. (1985). Sex differences in type of extramarital involvement and marital dissatisfaction. *Sex Roles, 12*, 1101–1120.

Glick, P., & Fiske, S. T. (1996). The ambivalent sexism inventory: Differentiating hostile and benevolent sexism. *Journal of Personality and Social Psychology, 70*, 491–512.

Glick, P., & Fiske, S. T. (2001). An ambivalent alliance: Hostile and benevolent sexism as complementary justifications for gender inequality. *American Psychologist, 56*, 109–118.

Goldberg, L. R. (1999). A broad-bandwidth, public domain, personality inventory measuring the lower-level facets of several five-factor models. In I. Mervielde, I. Deary, F. De Fruyt, & F. Ostendorf (Eds.), *Personality psychology in Europe* (Vol. 7, pp. 7–28). Tilburg, The Netherlands: Tilburg University Press.

Goleman, D. (1997). *Emotional intelligence: Why it can matter more than IQ*. New York, NY: Bantam.

Goleman, D. (2006). *Social intelligence: The new science of human relationships*. New York, NY: Bantam.

Goodwin, R. (1990). Sex differences among partner preferences: Are the sexes really very similar. *Sex Roles, 23*, 501–513.

Gosling, S. D., Ko, S. J., Mannarelli, T., & Morris, M. E. (2002). A room with a cue: Personality judgments based on offices and bedrooms. *Journal of Personality and Social Psychology, 82*, 379–398.

Gottfredson, L. S. (1997). Why *g* matters: The complexity of everyday life. *Intelligence, 24*, 79–132.

Gottschall, J., & Wilson, D. S. (Eds.) (2005). *The literary animal: Evolution and the nature of narrative*. Evanston, IL: Northwestern University Press.

Gouveia-Oliveira, R., & Pedersen, A. G. (2009). Higher variability in the number of sexual partners in males can contribute to a higher prevalence of sexually transmitted diseases in females. *Journal of Theoretical Biology, 261*, 100–106.

Grammer, K., & Eibl-Eibesfeldt, I. (1990). *The ritualisation of laughter*. Bochum, Germany: Brockmeyer.

Grammer, K., Keki, V., Striebel, B., Atzmüller, M., & Fink, B. (2003). Bodies in motion: A window to the soul. In E. Vol, & K. Grammer (Eds.), *Evolutionary aesthetics* (pp. 295–324). New York, NY: Springer.

Grammer, K., Kruck, K., Juette, A., & Fink, B. (2000). Non-verbal behavior as courtship signals: The role of control and choice in selecting partners. *Evolution and Human Behavior, 21*, 371–390.

Gray, J., & Thompson, P. M. (2004). Neurobiology of intelligence: science and ethics. *Nature Reviews Neuroscience, 5*, 471–482.

Grayson, B., & Stein, M. I. (1981). Attracting assault: Victims' nonverbal cues. *Journal of Communication, 31*, 68–75.

Graziano, W. G., Jensen-Campbell, L. A., & Hair, E. C. (1996). Perceiving interpersonal conflict and reacting to it: The case for agreeableness. *Journal of Personality and Social Psychology, 70*, 820–835.

Green, M. J., & Williams, L. M. (1999). Schizotypy and creativity as effects of reduced cognitive inhibition. *Personality and Individual Differences, 27*, 263–276.

Greene, R. (2003). *The art of seduction*. New York, NY: Penguin Books.

Greengross, G. (2008). Dissing oneself versus dissing rivals: Effects of status, personality, and sex on the short-term and long-term attractiveness of self-deprecating and other-deprecating humor. *Evolutionary Psychology, 6*, 393–408.

Greengross, G., & Miller, G. F. (2009). The big five personality traits of professional comedians compared to amateur comedians, comedy writers, and college students. *Personality and Individual Differences, 47*, 79–83.

Greengross, G., & Miller, G. F. (2011). Humor ability reveals intelligence, predicts mating success, and is higher in males. *Intelligence, 39,* 188–192.

Greitemeyer, T. (2005). Receptivity to sexual offers as a function of sex, socioeconomic status, physical attractiveness, and intimacy of the offer. *Personal Relationships, 12,* 373–386.

Greven, C. U., Harlaar, N., Kovas, Y., Chamorro-Premuzic, T., & Plomin, R. (2009). More than just IQ: School achievement is predicted by self-perceived abilities—but for genetic rather than environmental reasons. *Psychological Science, 20,* 753–762.

Griskevicius, V., Cialdini, R. B., & Kenrick, D. T. (2006). Picasso, and parental investment: The effects of romantic motives on creativity. *Journal of Personality and Social Psychology, 91,* 63–76.

Gueguen, N. (2008). The effect of a woman's smile on men's courtship behavior. *Social Behavior and Personality: an International Journal, 36,* 1233–1236.

Gueguen, N. (2009). The receptivity of women to courtship solicitation across the menstrual cycle: A field experiment. *Biological Psychology, 80,* 321–324.

Gueguen, N. (2010). Men's sense of humor and women's responses to courtship solicitations: An experimental field study. *Psychological Reports, 107,* 145–156.

Gunns, R. E., Johnston, L., & Hudson, S. M. (2002). Victim selection and kinematics: A point-light investigation of vulnerability to attack. *Journal of Nonverbal Behavior, 26,* 129–158.

Gustafson, P. E. (1998). Gender differences in risk perception: Theoretical and methodological approaches. *Risk Analysis, 18,* 805–811.

Gutierres, S. E., Kenrick, D. T., & Partch, J. J. (1999). Beauty, dominance, and the mating game: Contrast effects in self-assessment reflect gender differences in mate selection. *Personality and Social Psychology Bulletin, 25,* 1126–1134.

Hald, G. M. (2006). Gender differences in pornography consumption among young heterosexual Danish adults. *Archives of Sexual Behavior, 35,* 577–585.

Hald, G. M., & Hogh-Olesen, H. (2010). Receptivity to sexual invitations from strangers of the opposite gender. *Evolution and Human Behavior, 31,* 453 458.

Hall, J. A., & Canterberry, M. (2011). Sexism and assertive courtship strategies. *Sex Roles, 65,* 840–853.

Hall, J. A., Coats, E. J., & Smith-Le Beau, L. (2005). Nonverbal behaviour and the vertical dimension of social relations: A meta-analysis. *Psychological Bulletin, 131,* 898–924.

Hamilton, W. D., & Zuk, M. (1982). Heritable true fitness and bright birds: A role for parasites? *Science, 218,* 384–387.

Hansen, G. L. (1987). Extradyadic relations during courtship. *Journal of Sex Research, 23,* 382–390.

Hardy, C. L., & Van Vugt, M. (2006). Nice guys finish first: The competitive altruism hypothesis. *Personality and Social Psychology Bulletin, 32,* 1402–1413.

Hare, B., Call, J., & Tomasello, M. (2001). Do chimpanzees know what conspecifics know and do not know? *Animal Behavior, 61,* 139–151.

Hare, R. (1999). *Without conscience: The disturbing world of the psychopaths among us.* New York, NY: Guilford.

Harpur, T. J., Hare, R. D., & Hakstian, A. R. (1989). Two-factor conceptualization of psychopathy: Construct validity and assessment implications. *Psychological Assessment, 1,* 6–17.

Haselton, M. G. & Buss, D. M. (2000). Error management theory: A new perspective on biases in cross-sex mind reading. *Journal of Personality and Social Psychology, 78,* 81–91.

Haselton, M. G., & Miller, G. F. (2006). Women's fertility across the cycle increases the short-term attractiveness of creative intelligence compared to wealth. *Human Nature, 17,* 50–73.

Haselton, M. G., & Nettle, D. (2006). The paranoid optimist: An integrative evolutionary model of cognitive biases. *Personality and Social Psychological Review, 10,* 47–66.

Haselton, M. G., Buss, D. M., Oubaid, V., & Angleitner, A. (2005). Sex, lies, and strategic interference: The psychology of deception between the sexes. *Personality and Social Psychology Bulletin, 31,* 3–23.

Haselton, M. G., Mortezaie, M., Pillsworth, E. G., Bleske-Recheck, A. E., & Frederick, D. A. (2007). Ovulation and human female ornamentation: Near ovulation, women dress to impress. *Hormones and Behavior, 51,* 40–45.

Hasson, O. (2006). The role of amplifiers in sexual selection: An integration of the amplifying and the Fisherian mechanisms. *Evolutionary Ecology, 4,* 277–289.

Hatfield, E. (1986). *Mirror, mirror: The importance of looks in everyday life.* New York, NY: State University of New York Press.

Hawley, P. H. (1999). The ontogenesis of social dominance: A strategy-based evolutionary perspective. *Developmental Review, 19,* 97–132.

Hay, J. (2000). Functions of humor in the conversations of men and women. *Journal of Pragmatics, 32,* 709–742.

Heaven, P. L. (1996). Personality and self-reported delinquency: Analysis of the "Big Five" personality dimensions. *Personality and Individual Differences, 20,* 47–54.

Heaven, P. L., Fitzpatrick, J., Craig, F. L., Kelly, P., & Sebar, G. (2000). Five personality factors and sex: Preliminary findings. *Personality and Individual Differences, 28,* 1133–1141.

Heaven, P. C. L., Smith, L., Prabhakar, S. M., Abraham, J., & Mete, M.E. (2006). Personality and conflict communication patterns in cohabiting couples. *Journal of Research in Personality, 40,* 829–840.

Heitz, R. P., Redick, T. S., Hambrick, D. Z., Kane, M. J., Conway, A. R. A., & Engle, R. W. (2006). WM, EF, and gF are not the same. *Behavioral and Brain Sciences, 29,* 135–136.

Hendrick, S., Hendrick, C., Slapion-Foote, M. J., & Foote, F. H. (1985). Gender differences in sexual attitudes. *Journal of Personality and Social Psychology, 48,* 1630–1642.

Henningsen, D. D., Henningsen, M. L. M., & Valde, K. S. (2006). Gender differences in perceptions of women's sexual interest during cross-sex interactions: An application and extension of cognitive valence theory. *Sex Roles, 54,* 821–829.

Henrich, J., & Gil-White, F. J. (2001). The evolution of prestige: Freely conferred deference as a mechanism for enhancing the benefits of cultural transmission. *Evolution and Human Behavior, 22,* 165–196.

Herold, E. S., & Mewhinney, D. M. K. (1993). Gender differences in casual sex and AIDS prevention: A survey of dating bars. *Journal of Sex Research, 30,* 36–42.

Herold, E. S., & Milhausen, R. R. (1999). Dating preferences of university women: An analysis of the nice guy stereotype. *Journal of Sex and Marital Therapy, 25,* 333–343.

Hess, U., Brody, S., Van Der Schalk, J., & Fischer, A. H. (2007). Sexual activity is inversely related to women's perceptions of the facial attractiveness of unknown men. *Personality and Individual Differences, 43,* 1991–1997.

Heyes, C. M. (1998). Theory of mind in non-human primates. *Behavioral and Brain Sciences, 21,* 101–148.

Hill, C. A., & Preston, L. K. (1996). Individual differences in the experience of sexual motivation: Theory and measurement of dispositional sexual motives. *Journal of Sex Research, 33,* 27–45.

Hill, P. L., & Roberts, B. W. (2011). Narcissism, well-being, and observer-rated personality across the lifespan. *Social Psychological and Personality Science, 3,* 216–223.

Hill, K., & Hurtado, A. M. (1996). *Ache life history.* New York, NY: Aldine De Gruyter.

Hill, M. S., & Fischer, A. R. (2008). Examining objectification theory: Sexual objectification's link with self-objectification and moderation by sexual orientation and age in White women. *The Counseling Psychologist, 36,* 745–776.

Hill, S. E., & Buss, D. M. (2008) The evolution of self-esteem. In M. Kernis (Ed.) *Self-esteem issues and answers: A source book of current perspectives.* New York, NY: Guilford.

Hill, S. E., & Ryan, M. (2006). The role of model female quality in the mate choice copying behaviour of sailfin mollies. *Biology Letters, 2,* 203–205.

Hirsh, J. B., DeYoung, C. G., & Peterson, J. B. (2009). Metatraits of the big five differentially predict engagement and restraint of behavior. *Journal of Personality, 77,* 1–17.

Hoffman, M. L. (2000). *Empathy and moral development: Implications for caring and justice.* New York, NY: Cambridge University Press.

Hollandsworth, S. (1994, October). What you don't know about nice guys. *Mademoiselle* (pp. 120–123).

Holtzman, N.S. & Strube, M. J (in press). People with dark personalities tend to create a physically attractive veneer. *Social Psychological and Personality Science*.

Holtzman, N. S., & Strube, M. J. (2010). Narcissism and attractiveness. *Journal of Research in Personality*, 44, 133–136.

Holtzman, N. S., & Strube, M. J. (2011). The intertwined evolution of narcissism and short-term mating: An emerging hypothesis. In W. K. Campbell & J. D. Miller (Eds.), *The handbook of narcissism and narcissistic personality disorders: Theoretical approaches, empirical findings, and treatments* (pp. 210–220). Hoboken, NJ: Wiley.

Holtzman, N. S., Vazire, S., & Mehl, M. R. (2010). Sounds like a narcissist: Behavioral manifestations of narcissism in everyday life. *Journal of Research in Personality*, 44, 478–484.

Howrigan, D. P., & MacDonald, K. B. (2008). Humor as a mental fitness indicator. *Evolutionary Psychology*, 6, 625–666.

Howse, R. B., Calkins, S. D., Anastopoulos, A. D., Keane, S. P., & Shelton, T. L. (2003). Regulatory contributors to children's kindergarten achievement. *Early Education and Development*, 14, 101–119.

Hrdy, S. B. (1999). *Mother nature: Maternal instincts and how they shape the human species*. New York, NY: Ballantine Books.

Hughes, S., Harrison, M., & Gallup, G. (2004). Sex differences in mating and multiple concurrent sex partners *Sexualities, Evolution, and Gender*, 6, 3–13.

Humphrey, N. K. (1976). The social function of intellect. In R. A. Hinde (Ed.), *Growing points in ethology* (pp. 303–317). Cambridge, UK: Cambridge University Press.

Hunt, E. (2011). *Human intelligence*. New York, NY: Cambridge University Press.

Jakobwitz, S., & Egan, V. (2006). The dark triad and normal personality traits. *Personality and Individual Differences*, 40, 331–339.

Jensen-Campbell, L. A., & Graziano, W. G. (2001). Agreeableness as a moderator of interpersonal conflict. *Journal of Personality*, 69, 323–362.

Jensen-Campbell, L. A., Graziano, W. G., & West, S. (1995) Dominance, prosocial orientation, and female preferences: do nice guys really finish last? *Journal of Personality and Social Psychology*, 68, 427–440.

Jensen-Campbell, L.A., Knack, J.M., & Gomez, H.L. (2010). The psychology of nice people. *Social and Personality Compass*, 4, 1042–1056.

Joannides, P. (2009). *The guide to getting it on*. Saline, MI: Goofy Foot Press.

Johannesen-Schmidt, M. C., & Eagly, A. H. (2002). Another look at sex differences in preferred mate characteristics: The effects of endorsing the traditional female gender role. *Psychology of Women Quarterly*, 26, 322–328.

Johnsen, L., & Geher, G. (2010). *Divorce patterns and the male-to-female mortality ratio: Is midlife crisis the death of men?* Presentation given at the meeting of the NorthEastern Evolutionary Psychology Society (NEEPS), March, New Paltz, NY.

Johnsen, L., Giordano, N., & Geher, G. (2010). *Patterns of childhood injury: A life history analysis*. Presentation given at the meeting of the NorthEastern Evolutionary Psychology Society (NEEPS), March, New Paltz, NY.

Johnson, J.A. (1994). Clarification of Factor Five with the help of the AB5C Model. *European Journal of Personality*, 8, 311–334.

Johnson, R. C., Ahern, F. M., & Cole, R. F. (1980). Secular change in degree of assortative mating for ability? *Behavior Genetics*, 10,1–8.

Johnson, R. T., Burk, J. A., & Kirkpatrick, L. A. (2007). Dominance and prestige as differential predictors of aggression and testosterone levels in men. *Evolution and Human Behavior*, 28, 345–351.

Johnson, W. (2010). Understanding the genetics of intelligence: Can height help? Can corn oil? *Current directions in psychological science*, 19, 177–182.

Johnson, W., Segal, N. L., & Bouchard, T. J. (2008). Fluctuating asymmetry and general intelligence: No genetic of phenotypic association. *Intelligence*, 36, 279–288.

Johnson, W., Turkheimer, E., Gottesman, I. I., & Bouchard, T. J. (2009). Beyond heritability: Twin studies in behavioral research. *Current Directions in Psychological Science*, 18, 217–220.

Johnstone, R. A. (1997) The tactics of mutual mate choice and competitive search. *Behavioral Ecology and Sociobiology, 40,* 51–59.

Jokela, M., Rotkirch, A., Rickard, I. J., Pettay, J., & Lummaa, V. (2010). Serial monogamy increases reproductive success in men but not in women. *Behavioral Ecology, 21,* 906–912.

Jonason, P. K., & Kavanagh, P. (2010). The dark side of love: The Dark Triad and love styles. *Personality and Individual Differences, 49,* 606–610.

Jonason, P.K., Koenig, B., & Tost, J. (2010). Living a fast life: The Dark Triad and Life History Theory. *Human Nature, 21,* 428–442.

Jonason, P. K., Li, N. P., & Buss, D. M. (2010). The costs and benefits of the Dark Triad: Implications for mate poaching and mate retention tactics. *Personality and Individual Differences, 48,* 373–378.

Jonason, P. K., Li, N. P., & Richardson, J. (2010). Positioning the booty-call on the spectrum of relationships: Sexual but more emotional than one-night stands. *Journal of Sex Research, 47,* 1–10.

Jonason, P. K., Li, N. P., & Teicher, E. A. (2010). Who is James Bond? The Dark Triad as an agentic social style. *Individual Differences Research, 8,* 111–120.

Jonason, P. K., Li, N. P., Webster, G. W., Schmitt, D. P. (2009). The Dark Triad: Facilitating short-term mating in men. *European Journal of Personality, 23,* 5–18.

Jonason, P. K., Slomski, S., & Partyka, J. (2012). The Dark Triad at work: How toxic employees get their way, *Personality and Individual Differences, 52,* 449–453.

Jonason, P. K., & Tost, J. (2010). I just cannot control myself: The Dark Triad and self-control. *Personality and Individual Differences, 49,* 611–615.

Jonason, P. K., & Webster, G. D. (2011). A protean approach to social influence: Dark Triad personalities and social influence tactics. *Personality and Individual Differences, 52,* 521–526.

Jones, B. C., DeBruine, L. M., Little, A. C., Burriss, R. P., & Feinberg, D. R. (2007). Social transmission of face preferences among humans. *Proceedings of the Royal Society: B, 274,* 899–903.

Jones, D. N., & Paulhus, D. L. (2010). Different provocations trigger aggression in narcissists and psychopaths. *Social Psychological and Personality Science, 1,* 12–18.

Jones, D. N., & Paulhus, D. L. (2011). The role of impulsivity in the Dark Triad of personality. *Personality and Individual Differences, 51,* 679–682.

Jones, J. C., & Barlow, D. H. (1990). Self-reported frequency of sexual urges, fantasies and masturbatory fantasies in heterosexual males and females. *Archives of Sexual Behavior, 19,* 269–279.

Josephs, R. A., Sellers, J. G., Newman, M. L., & Mehta, P. H. (2006). The mismatch effect: When testosterone and status are at odds. *Journal of Personality and Social Psychology, 90,* 999–1013.

Judge, T. A., Hurst, C., & Simon, L. S. (2009). Does it pay to be smart, attractive, or confident (or all three)? Relationships among general mental ability, physical attractiveness, core self-evaluations, and income. *Journal of Applied Psychology, 94,* 742–755.

Kahneman, D. (2011). *Thinking, fast and slow.* New York, NY: Farrar, Straus, and Giroux.

Kahneman, D. & Frederick, S. (2002). Representativeness revisited: Attribute substitution in intuitive judgment. In T. Gilovich, D. Griffin, & D. Kahneman (Eds.), *Heuristics and biases: The psychology of intuitive judgment* (pp. 49–81). New York, NY: Cambridge University Press.

Kahneman, D., & Frederick, S. (2005). A model of heuristic judgment. In K. J. Holyoak & R.G. Morrison (Eds.), *The Cambridge Handbook of Thinking and Reasoning* (pp. 267–293). New York, NY: Cambridge University Press.

Kanazawa, S. (2010). Evolutionary psychology and intelligence research. *American Psychologist, 65,* 279–289.

Kane, M. J., & Engle, R. W. (2002). The role of prefrontal cortex in working-memory capacity, executive attention, and general fluid intelligence: An individual-differences perspective. *Psychonomic Bulletin & Review, 9,* 637–671.

Karney, B. R., & Bradbury, T. N. (1997). Neuroticism, marital interaction, and the trajectory of marital satisfaction. *Journal of Personality and Social Psychology, 72*, 1075–1092.

Karremans, J. C., Verwijmeren, T., Pronk, T. M., & Reitsma, M. (2009). Interacting with women can impair men's cognitive functioning. *Journal of Experimental Social Psychology, 45*, 1041–1044.

Kaufman, J. C., & Plucker, J. A. (2011). Intelligence and creativity. In R. J. Sternberg & S. B. Kaufman (Eds.), *The Cambridge handbook of intelligence*. New York, NY: Cambridge University Press.

Kaufman, J.C., & Sternberg, R.J. (Eds.) (2010). *The Cambridge handbook of creativity*. New York, NY: Cambridge University Press.

Kaufman, S. B. (2009a). *Beyond general intelligence: The dual-process theory of human intelligence (Doctoral dissertation)*. New Haven, CT: Yale University Press.

Kaufman, S. B. (2009b). Faith in intuition is associated with decreased latent inhibition in a sample of high achieving adolescents. *Psychology of Aesthetics, Creativity, and the Arts, 3*, 28–34.

Kaufman, S. B. (2011). Intelligence and the cognitive unconscious. In R. J. Sternberg & S. B. Kaufman (Eds.), *The Cambridge handbook of intelligence*. New York, NY: Cambridge University Press.

Kaufman, S.B. (2013). *Ungifted: Intelligence redefined*. New York, NY: Basic Books.

Kaufman, S. B., DeYoung, C. G., Gray, J. R., Brown, J., & Mackintosh, N. (2009). Associative learning predicts intelligence above and beyond working memory and processing speed. *Intelligence, 37*, 374–382.

Kaufman, S. B., DeYoung, C. G., Gray, J. R., Jimenez, L., Brown, J. B., & Mackinosh, N. (2010). Implicit learning as an ability, *Cognition, 116*, 321–340.

Kaufman, S. B., DeYoung, C. G., Reis, D. L., & Gray, J. R. (2011). General intelligence predicts reasoning ability even for evolutionarily familiar content. *Intelligence, 39*, 311–322.

Kaufman, S. B., Erickson, J. E., Huang, J. Y., Ramesh, S., Thompson, S., Kozbelt, A., Paul, E., & Kaufman, J. C. (2009, July). Art as an aphrodisiac. Oswego, NY: *Northeastern Evolutionary Psychology Society*.

Kaufman, S. B., Erickson, J., Ramesh, S., Kozbelt, A., Magee, M., & Kaufman, J. C. (2010). *What are funny people like?* Paper presented at the *Annual Meeting of the Human Behavior and Evolution Society* (HBES), Eugene, OR.

Kaufman, S. B., & Kaufman, J. C. (2007). Ten years to expertise, ten more to greatness: An investigation of modern writers, *Journal of Creative Behavior, 41*, 114–124.

Kaufman, S. B., Kozbelt, A., Bromley, M. L., & Miller, G. F. (2008). The role of creativity and humor in human mate selection. In G. Geher & G. Miller (Eds.), *Mating intelligence: Sex, relationships, and the mind's reproductive system*. Mahwah, NJ: Lawrence Erlbaum.

Kaufman, S.B., Reynolds, M.R., Liu, X., Kaufman, A.S., McGrew, K.S. (2012). Are cognitive g and academic achievement g one and the same g? An exploration on the Woodcock-Johnson and Kaufman tests. *Intelligence, 40*, 123–138.

Keller, M. C. (2008). The role of mutation in mating intelligence. In G. Geher & G. F. Miller (Eds.), *Mating intelligence: Sex, relationships, and the mind's reproduction system*. Mahwah, NJ: Lawrence Erlbaum.

Keller, M., & Miller, G. F. (2006). Which evolutionary genetic models best explain the persistence of common, harmful, heritable mental disorders? *Behavioral and Brain Sciences, 29*, 385–404.

Kelly, E., & Conley, J. (1987). Personality and compatibility: A prospective analysis of marital stability and marital satisfaction. *Journal of Personality and Social Psychology, 52*, 27–40.

Kemper, T. D. (1990). *Social structure and testosterone: Explorations of the socio-bio-social chain*. New Brunswick, NJ: Rutgers University Press.

Kennair, L. E. O., Schmitt, D. P., Fjeldavli, Y. L., & Harlem, S. K. (2009). Sex differences in sexual desires and attitudes in Norwegian samples. *Interpersona, 3*, 1–32.

Kenrick, D. T., Sadalla, E. K., Groth, G., & Trost, M. R. (1990) Evolution, traits, and the stages of human courtship: qualifying the parental investment model. *Journal of Personality, 58*, 97–116.

Kenrick, D. T., Groth, G. E., Trost, M. R., & Sadalla, E. K. (1993). Integrating evolutionary and social exchange perspectives on relationships: Effects of gender, self-appraisal, and involvement level on mate selection criteria. *Journal of Personality and Social Psychology, 64*, 951–969.

Keren, G., & Schul, Y. (2009). Two is not always better than one: A critical evaluation of two-system theories. *Perspective on Psychological Science, 4*, 533–550.

Khron, F. B., & Bogan, Z. (2001). The effects absent fathers have on female development and college attendance. *College Student Journal, 35*, 598–608.

Kiehl, K. A., Smith, A. M., Hare, R. D., Mendrek, A., Forster, B. B., Brink, J., et al. (2001). Limbic abnormalities in affective processing by criminal psychopaths as revealed by functional magnetic resonance imaging. *Biological Psychiatry, 50*, 677–684.

Kihlstrom, J. F. (2011). Social intelligence. In R. J. Sternberg & S. B. Kaufman (Eds.), *The Cambridge handbook of intelligence*. New York, NY: Cambridge University Press.

Kim, K. H. (2005). Can only intelligent people be creative? *Journal of Secondary Gifted Education, 16*, 57–66.

Kim, K.H., Crammond, B., & VanTassel-Baska, J. (2011). The relationship between creativity and intelligence. In J.C. Kaufman & R.J. Sternberg (Eds), *The Cambridge Handbook of Creativity*. New York, NY: Cambridge University Press.

Kirby, D., Lepore, G., & Ryan, J. (2005). *Sexual risk and protective factors: Factors affecting teen sexual behavior, pregnancy, childbearing and sexually transmitted disease: Which are important? Which can you change?* Washington, DC: National Campaign to Prevent Teen Pregnancy.

Kircaldy, B. D. (1982). Personality profiles at various levels of athletic participation. *Personality and Individual Differences, 3*, 321–326.

Kirkpatrick, L. A., & Davis, K. E. (1994) Attachment style, gender and relationship stability: A longitudinal analysis. *Journal of Personality and Social Psychology, 66*, 502–512.

Kleinke, C., Meeker, F., & Staneski, R. (1986). Preference for opening lines: Comparing ratings by men and women. *Sex Roles, 15*, 585–600.

Kniffin, K. M., & Wilson, D. S. (2004). The effect of nonphysical traits on the perception of physical attractiveness: Three naturalistic studies. *Evolution and Human Behavior, 25*, 88–101.

Kotthoff, H. (2000). Gender and joking: On the complexities of women's image politics in humorous narratives. *Journal of Pragmatics, 32*, 55–80.

Koukounas, E., & McCabe, M. (1997). Sexual and emotional variables influencing sexual response to erotica. *Behaviour Research and Therapy, 35*, 221–230.

Kozbelt, A., & Nishioka, K. (2010). Humor comprehension, humor production and insight: An exploratory study. *Humor: International Journal of Humor Research, 23*, 375–401.

Kramer, R., Jordan, K., Mantulenko, M., Soder, H., Amati, F., and Keenan, J.P. (under review). The special brain: Narcissism and self-face recognition and the right medial frontal gyrus. *Social Cognitive and Affective Neuroscience.*

Krebs, J. R., & Davies, N. B. (1997). *Behavioural ecology: An evolutionary approach* (4th ed.). Oxford, UK: Blackwell.

Kruger, D. J. (2008). Male financial consumption is associated with higher mating intentions and mating success. *Evolutionary Psychology, 6*, 603–612.

Kruger, D. J. (2010). Socio-demographic factors intensifying male mating competition exacerbate male mortality rates. *Evolutionary Psychology, 8*, 194–204.

Kruger, D. J., Fisher, M., & Jobling, I. (2003). Proper and dark heroes as dads and cads: Alternative mating strategies in British Romantic literature. *Human Nature, 14*, 305–317.

Kruger, D. J., & Nesse, R. M. (2007). Economic transition, male competition, and sex differences in Mortality Rates. *Evolutionary Psychology, 5*, 411–427.

Kruger, D. J., Reischl, T., & Zimmerman, M. A. (2008). Time perspective as a mechanism for functional developmental adaptation. *Journal of Social, Evolutionary and Cultural Psychology, 2*, 1–22.

Kruglanski, A., & Gigerenzer, G. (2011). Intuitive and deliberate judgments are based on common principles. *Psychological Review, 118*, 97–109.

Kurzban, R., & Aktipis, C. A. (2007). Modularity and the social mind: Are psychologists too self-ish? *Personality and Social Psychology Review, 11*, 131–149.

Kurzban, R., & Haselton, M. G. (2006). Making hay out of straw: Real and imagined debates in evolutionary psychology. In J. Barkow (Ed.), *Missing the revolution: Evolutionary perspectives on culture and society*. New York, NY: Oxford University Press.

Kurzban, R., & Weeden, J. (2005). HurryDate: Mate preferences in action. *Evolution and Human Behavior, 26*, 227–244.

Lambert, T. A., Kahn, A. S., and Apple, K. J. (2003). Pluralistic ignorance and hooking up. *Journal of Sex Research, 40*, 129–133.

Landolfi, J., Geher, G., & Andrews, A. (2007). The role of stimulus-specificity on infidelity reactions: Seeing is disturbing. *Current Psychology: Developmental, Learning, Personality, Social, 26*, 45–59.

Langer, E. J. (1975). The illusion of control. *Journal of Personality and Social Psychology, 32*, 311–328.

Langlois, J. H., Kalakanis, L., Rubenstein, A. J., Larson, A., Hallam, M., & Smoot, M. (2000). Maxims or myths of beauty? A meta-analytic and theoretical review. *Psychological Bulletin, 126*, 390–423.

Laumann, E. O., Gagnon, J. H., Michael, R. T., & Michaels, S. (1994). *The social organization of sexuality*. Chicago, IL: University of Chicago Press.

Lawson, A., & Samson, C. (1988). Age, gender and adultery. *British Journal of Sociology, 39*, 409–440.

Lee, L., Loewenstein, G., Ariely, D., Hong, J., & Young, J. (2008). Hot or not? Physical-attractiveness evaluations and dating preferences as a function of one's own attractiveness. *Psychological Science, 19*, 669–677.

Lee, T. L., Fiske, S. T., Glick, P., & Chen, Z. X. (2010). Ambivalent sexism in close relationships: (Hostile) power and (benevolent) romance shape relationship ideals. *Sex Roles, 62*, 583–601.

Leitenberg, H., & Henning, K. (1995). Sexual fantasy. *Psychological Bulletin, 117*, 469–496.

Lenton, A. P., & Francesconi, M. (2010). How humans cognitively manage an abundance of mate options. *Psychological Science, 21*, 528–533.

Levy, K. N., & Kelly, K. M. (2010). Sex differences in jealousy: A contribution from attachment theory. *Psychological Science, 21*, 168–173.

Levenson, M. R., Kiehl, K. A., & Fitzpatrick, C. M. (1995). Assessing psychopathic attributes in a noninstitutionalised population. *Journal of Personality and Social Psychology, 68*, 151–158.

Levesque, M. J., & Kenny, D. A. (1993). Accuracy of behavioral predictions at zero acquaintance: A social relations analysis. *Journal of Personality and Social Psychology, 65*, 1178–1187.

Lewanowski, G.W., Ciarocco, N.J., Pettenato, M., & Stephan, J. (2012). Pick me up: Ego depletion and receptivity to relationship initiation. *Journal of Social and Personal Relationships*, doi: 10.1177/0265407512449401.

Li, N. P. (2008). Intelligent priorities. In G. Geher & G. F. Miller (Eds.), *Mating intelligence: Sex, relationships, and the mind's reproduction system*. Mahwah, NJ: Lawrence Erlbaum.

Li, N. P., Bailey, M. J., Kenrick, D. T., & Linsenmeier, J. A. (2002). The necessities and luxuries of mate preferences: Testing the tradeoffs. *Journal of Personality and Social Psychology, 82*, 947–955.

Li, N. P., Griskevicius, V., Durante, K. M., Jonason, P. K., Pasisz, D. J., & Aumer, K. (2009). An evolutionary perspective on humor: Sexual selection or interest indication? *Personality and Social Psychology Bulletin, 35*, 923–936.

Li, N. P., & Kenrick, D. T. (2006). Sex similarities and differences in preferences for short-term mates: What, whether, and why. *Journal of Personality and Social Psychology, 90*, 468–489.

Lieberman, M.D. (2003). Reflexive and reflective judgment processes: A social cognitive neuroscience approach. In J.P. Forgas, K.R. Williams, & W. von Hippel (Eds.), *Social judgments: Implicit and explicit processes* (pp. 44–67). New York, NY: Cambridge University Press.

Lieberman, M.D. (2007). Social cognitive neuroscience: A review of core processes. *Annual Review of Psychology, 58*, 259–289.

Lievens, F., Chasteen, C. S., Day, E. A., & Christensen, N. D. (2006). Large-scale investigation of the role of trait activation theory for understanding assessment center convergent and discriminant validity. *Journal of Applied Psychology, 91*, 247–258.

Lippa, R. A. (2009). Sex differences in sex drive, sociosexuality, and height across 53 nations: Testing evolutionary and social structural theories. *Archives of Sexual Behavior, 38*, 631–651.

Little, A., Burriss, R. P., Jones, B. C., DeBruine, L. M., & Caldwell, C. A. (2008). Social influence in human face preference: Men and women are influenced more for long-term than short-term attractiveness decisions. *Evolution and Human Behavior, 29*, 140–146.

Low, B. S., Hazel, A., Parker, N., & Welch, K. (2008). Influences of women's reproductive lives: Unexpected ecological underpinnings. *Cross-Cultural Research, 42*, 201–219.

Lubow, R. E., & Gewirtz, J. C. (1995). Latent inhibition in humans: Data, theory, and implications for schizophrenia. *Psychological Bulletin, 117*, 87–103.

Lubow, R., & Weiner, I. (Eds.) (2010). *Latent inhibition: Cognition, neuroscience and applications to schizophrenia*. Cambridge, UK: Cambridge University Press.

Luo, S., & Zhang, G. (2009). What leads to romantic attraction: Similarity, reciprocity, security, or beauty? Evidence from a speed-dating study. *Journal of Personality, 77*, 933–964.

Lynch, J. W., Davey Smith, G., Kaplan, G. A., & House, J. S. (2000). Income inequality and mortality. *British Medical Journal, 320*, 1200–1204.

MacDonald, K. B. (1995). Evolution, the five factor model, and levels of personality. *Journal of Personality, 63*, 525–567.

Mackintosh, N. J. (2011). *IQ and human intelligence* (2nd Ed.). Oxford, UK: Oxford University Press.

Macleod, M. (2010). Die young, live fast: The evolution of an underclass. *New Scientist, 2769*, 40–43.

Mahmut, M. K., Homewood, J., & Stevenson, R. J. (2008). The characteristics of noncriminals with high psychopathy traits: Are they similar to criminal psychopaths? *Journal of Research in Personality, 42*, 679–692.

Malamuth, N. M. (1996). The confluence model of sexual aggression: Feminist and evolutionary perspectives. In Buss, D. M., & Malamuth, N. M., (Eds.), *Sex, power, conflict: Evolutionary and feminist perspectives* (pp. 269–295). New York, NY: Oxford University Press.

Malamuth, N. M. (1996). Sexually explicit media, gender differences, and evolutionary theory. *Journal of Communication, 46*, 8–31.

Malamuth, N. M., Huppin, M., & Bryant, P. (2005). Sexual coercion. In D. M. Buss (Ed.), *The handbook of evolutionary psychology*. New York, NY: Wiley.

Malterer, M. B., Glass, S. J., & Newman, J. P. (2008). Psychopathy and trait emotional intelligence. *Personality and Individual Differences, 44*, 735–745.

Mandelman, S. D., & Grigorenko, E. L. (2011). Intelligence: genes, environments, and their interactions. In R. J. Sternberg & S. B. Kaufman (Eds.), *The Cambridge handbook of intelligence*. New York, NY: Cambridge University Press.

Marcus, G. (2004). *The birth of the mind: How a tiny number of genes create the complexities of human thought*. New York, NY: Basic Books.

Marcus, G. (2009). *Kluge: The haphazard evolution of the human mind*. New York, NY: Mariner Books.

Marcus, G. (2012). *Guitar zero: The new musician and the science of learning*. New York, NY: Penguin.

Martin, R.A. (2006). *The psychology of humor: An integrative approach*. New York, NY: Academic Press.

Marks, I. (1987). *Fears, phobias, and rituals: Panic, anxiety, and their disorders*. New York, NY: Oxford University Press.

Marlowe, F. W. (2004). Mate preferences among Hadza hunter gatherers. *Human Nature, 15*, 365–376.

Martindale, C. (1999). 7 Biological bases of creativity. In R. J. Sternberg (Ed.), *Handbook of creativity*. New York, NY: Cambridge University Press.

Mascie-Taylor, C.G.N. (1989). Spouse similarity for IQ and personality and convergence. *Behavior Genetics, 19*, 223–227.∂

Mascie-Taylor, C.G.N., & Vandenberg, S.G. (1988). Assortative mating for IQ and personality due to propinquity and personal performance. *Behavior Genetics*, *18*, 339–345.

Mason, O., Claridge, G., & Jackson, M. (1995). New scales for the assessment of schizotypy. *Personality and Individual Differences*, *1*, 7–13.

Masten, A. S. (1986). Humor and competence in school-aged children. *Child Development*, *57*, 461–473.

Mathews, A., Mackintosh, B., & Fulcher, E. P. (1997). Cognitive biases in anxiety and attention to threat. *Trends in Cognitive Sciences*, *1*, 340–345.

Mauro, M. (2010). *Vulnerability and other prey of psychopaths*. Retrieved December 16, 2010, from http://www.psychologytoday.com/blog/take-all-prisoners/201001/vulnerability-and-other-prey-psychopaths.

Max, T. (2005). *I hope they serve beer in hell*. Citadel Press.

Mayer, J. D., & Geher, G. (1996). Emotional intelligence and the identification of emotion. *Intelligence*, *22*, 89–113.

Mayer, J. D., Roberts, R. D., & Barsade, S. G. (2008). Human abilities: Emotional intelligence. *Annual Review of Psychology*, *59*, 507–536.

Mayer, J. D., Salovey, P., & Caruso, D. (1999). Emotional intelligence meets traditional standards for an intelligence. *Intelligence*, *27*, 267–298.

Mayer, J. D., Salovey, P., & Caruso, D. R. (2000) Models of emotional intelligence. In R. J. Sternberg (Ed.). *Handbook of Intelligence (pp. 396–420)*. Cambridge, England: Cambridge University Press.

Mayer, J. D., Salovey, P., & Caruso, D. R. (2008). Emotional intelligence: New ability or eclectic traits? *American Psychologist*, *63*, 503–517.

Mayer, J. D., Salovey, P., Caruso, D., & Cherkasskiy, L. (2011). Emotional intelligence. In R. J. Sternberg & S. B. Kaufman (Eds.), *The Cambridge handbook of intelligence*. New York, NY: Cambridge University Press.

Mayr, E. (1963). *Animal species and evolution*. Cambridge, MA: Belknap Press of Harvard University Press.

Mazur, A., & Michalek, J. (1998). Marriage, divorce, and Male testosterone. *Social Forces 77*, 315–330.

McAdams, D. P., Jackson, R. J., & Kirshnit, C. (1984). Looking, laughing, and smiling in dyads as a function of intimacy motivation and reciprocity. *Journal of Personality*, *52*, 261–273.

McBurney, D. H., Zapp, D. J., & Streeter, S. A. (2005). Preferred number of sexual partners: Tails of distributions and tales of mating systems. *Evolution and Human Behavior*, *26*, 271–278.

McCabe, M. P. (1987). Desired and experienced levels of premarital affection and sexual intercourse during dating. *Journal of Sex Research*, *23*, 23–33.

McClelland, M. M., Cameron, C. E., Connor, C. M., Farris, C. L., Jewkes, A. M., & Morrison, F. J. (2007). Links between behavioral regulation and preschoolers' literacy, vocabulary, and math skills. *Developmental Psychology*, *43*, 947–959.

McCrae, R. R., & Costa, P. T. (1997). Conceptions and correlates of Openness to Experience. In R. Hogan, J. Johnson, & S. Briggs (Eds.), *Handbook of personality psychology* (pp. 825–847). Boston, MA: Academic Press.

McCreery, C., & Claridge, G. (2002). Healthy schizotypy: The case of out-of-the-body experiences. *Personality and Individual Differences*, *32*, 141–154.

McEwan, I. (1997). *Enduring Love*. London: Jonathan Cape.

McKenzie, J., Taghavi-Knosary, M., & Tindell, G. (2000). Neuroticism and academic achievement: The Furneaux factor as a measure of academic rigour. *Personality and Individual Differences*, *29*, 3–11.

Mealey, L. (1995). The sociobiology of sociopathy: An integrated evolutionary model. *Behavioral and Brain Sciences*, *18*, 523–599.

Mecklinger, A., & Ullsperger, P. (1995). The P300 to novel and target events: A spatiotemporal dipole model analysis. *NeuroReport*, *7*, 241–245.

Mehta, P. H., & Josephs, R. A. (2010). Testosterone and cortisol jointly regulate dominance: Evidence for a dual-hormone hypothesis. *Hormones and Behavior*, *58*, 898–906.

Meston, C. M., & Buss, D. M. (2007). Why humans have sex. *Archives of Sexual Behavior, 36,* 477–507.

Meston, C. M., & Buss, D. M. (2009). *Why women have sex: Understanding sexual motivation from adventure to revenge (and everything in between).* New York, NY: Times Books.

Mikulincer, M., & Horesh, N. (1999). Adult attachment style and the perception of others: The role of projective mechanisms. *Journal of Personality and Social Psychology, 76,* 1022–1034.

Miller, G. (2000). *The mating mind.* New York, NY: Anchor.

Miller, G. F. (1997) Mate choice: From sexual cues to cognitive adaptations. In *Characterizing human psychological adaptations: Ciba Foundation Symposium* (pp. 71–82). New York, NY: Wiley.

Miller, G. F. (2009). *Spent: Sex, evolution, and consumer behavior.* New York, NY: Viking.

Miller, G. F., & Caruthers, D. (2003). *A great sense of humor is a good genes indicator: Ovulatory cycle effects on the sexual attractiveness of male humor ability.* Paper presented at the Human Behavior and Evolution Society 15th Annual Meeting, Nebraska.

Miller, G. F., Tybur, J., & Jordan, B. (2007). Ovulatory cycle effects on tip earnings by lap-dancers: Economic evidence for human estrus? *Evolution and Human Behavior, 28,* 375–381.

Miller, G. F., & Tal, I. (2007). Schizotypy versus intelligence and openness as predictors of creativity. *Schizophrenia Research, 93,* 317–324.

Miller, G. F., & Todd, P. M. (1998). Mate choice turns cognitive. *Trends in Cognitive Sciences, 2,* 190–198.

Miller, J. D., Lynam, D., Zimmerman, R. S., Logan, T. K., Leukfeld, C., & Clayton, R. (2004). The utility of the five factor model in understanding risky sexual behavior. *Personality and Individual Differences, 36,* 1611–1626.

Mitchell, M. M., & Latimer, W. W. (2009). Gender differences in high risk sexual behaviors and injection practices associated with perceived HIV risk among injection drug users. *AIDS Education and Prevention, 21,* 384–394.

Mithen, S. (1999). *The prehistory of the mind: The cognitive origins of art, religion and science.* New York, NY: Thames & Hudson.

Mithen, S. (2007). *The singing Neanderthals: The origins of music, language, mind, and body.* Boston, MA: Harvard University Press.

Miyake, A., & Friedman, N. P. (2012). The nature and organization of individual differences in executive functions: Four general conclusions. *Current Directions in Psychological Science, 21,* 8–14.

Miyake, A., Friedman, N. P., Emerson, M. J., Witzki, A. H., Howerter, A., & Wager, T. (2000). The unity and diversity of executive functions and their contributions to complex "Frontal Lobe" tasks: A latent variable analysis. *Cognitive Psychology, 41,* 49–100.

Monin, B., Sawyer, P. J., & Marquez, M. J. (2008). The rejection of moral rebels: Resenting those who do the right thing. *Journal of Personality and Social Psychology, 95,* 76–93.

Montepare, J. M., & Zebrowitz-McArthur, L. A. (1998). Impressions of people created by age-related qualities of their gaits. *Journal of Personality and Social Psychology, 55,* 547–556.

Moore, D. S. (2002). *The dependent gene.* New York, NY: Times Books/Henry Holt.

Morf, C. C., & Rhodewalt, F. (2001). Unraveling the paradoxes of narcissism: A dynamic self-regulatory processing model. *Psychological Inquiry, 12,* 177–196.

Muehlenhard, C. L., & Linton, M. A. (1987). Date rape and sexual aggression in dating situations: Incidence and risk factors. *Journal of Counseling Psychology, 2,* 186–196.

Munro, G. E., Dywan, J., Harris, G. T., McKee, S., Unsal, A., & Segalowitz, S. J. (2007). ERN varies with degree of psychopathy in emotion discrimination task. *Biological Psychology, 76,* 31–42.

Murnen, S. K., & Stockton, M. (1997). Gender and self-reported sexual arousal in response to sexual stimuli: A meta-analytic review. *Sex Roles, 37,* 135–153.

Murzynski, J., & Degelman, D. (1996). Body language of women and judgments of vulnerability to sexual assault. *Journal of Applied Social Psychology, 26,* 1617–1626.

Muscarella, F. (2000). The evolution of homoerotic behavior in humans. *Journal of Homosexuality, 40,* 51–78.

Mystery. (2007). *The mystery method: How to get beautiful women into bed*. New York, NY: St. Martin's Press.

Mystery. (2010). *The pickup artist: The new and improved art of seduction*. Villard.

Naglieri, J. A., & Bornstein, B. T. (2003). Intelligence and achievement: Just how correlated are they? *Journal of Psychoeducational Assessment, 21*, 244–260.

Neeleman, J., Sytema, S., & Wadsworth, M. (2002). Propensity to psychiatric and somatic ill-health: Evidence from a birth cohort. *Psychological Medicine, 32*, 793–803.

Nelson, B., & Rawlings, D. (2010). Relating schizotypy and personality to the phenomenology of creativity. *Schizophrenia Bulletin, 36*, 388–399.

Nesse, R. (2005). Twelve crucial points about emotions, evolution and mental disorders. *Psychological Review, 11*, 12–14.

Nettle, D. (2001). *Strong imagination: Madness, creativity and human nature*. Oxford, UK: Oxford University Press.

Nettle, D. (2005). An evolutionary approach to the extraversion continuum. *Evolution and Human Behavior, 26*, 363–373.

Nettle, D. (2006). The evolution of personality variation in humans and other animals. *American Psychologist, 61*, 622–631.

Nettle, D. (2007). Empathizing and systemizing: What are they, and what do they contribute to our understanding of psychological sex differences? *British Journal of Psychology, 98*, 237–255.

Nettle, D. (2008). Why is creativity attractive in a potential mate? *Behavioral and Brain Science, 31*, 275–276.

Nettle, D. (2009a). The evolution of creative writing. In S. B. Kaufman & J. C. Kaufman (Eds.), *The psychology of creative writing* (pp. 101–117). Cambridge, UK: Cambridge University Press.

Nettle, D. (2009b). Social class through the evolutionary lens. *The Psychologist, 22*, 934–937.

Nettle, D. (2009c). Beyond nature versus culture: Cultural variation as an evolved characteristic. *Journal of the Royal Anthropological Institute, 15*, 223–240.

Nettle, D. (2010). Dying young and living fast: variation in life history across English neighborhoods. *Behavioral Ecology, 21*, 387–395.

Nettle, D., & Clegg, H. (2006). Schizotypy, creativity and mating success in humans. *Proceedings of the Royal Society: B, 273*, 611–615.

Nettle, D., & Clegg, H. (2008). Personality, mating strategies, and mating intelligence. In G. Geher & G. Miller (Eds.), *Mating intelligence: Sex, relationships, and the mind's reproductive system* (pp. 121–135). New York, NY: Lawrence Erlbaum.

Nettle, D., & Liddle, B. (2008). Agreeableness is related to social-cognitive, but not social-perceptual, theory of mind. *European Journal of Personality, 22*, 323–335.

Nisbett, R. E., & Wilson, T. (1977). Telling more than we can know: Verbal reports on mental processes. *Psychological Review, 84*, 231–259.

Nisbett, R. E. (2010). *Intelligence and how to get it: Why schools and cultures count*. New York, NY: Norton.

Njus, D. M., & Bane, C. M. H. (2009). Religious identification as a moderator of evolved sexual strategies of men and women. *Journal of Sex Research, 46*, 546–557.

Noller, P. (1986). Sex differences in nonverbal communication: Advantage lost or supremacy regained? *Australian Journal of Psychology, 38*, 23–32.

Nowakowska, C., Strong, C. M., Santosa, C. M., Wang, P. W., & Ketter, T. A. (2005). Temperamental commonalities and differences in euthymic mood disorder patients, creative controls, and healthy controls. *Journal of Affective Disorders, 85*, 207–215.

Nowicki, S., & Duke, M. P. (1994). Individual differences in the nonverbal communication of affect: The Diagnostic Analysis of Nonverbal Accuracy Scale. *Journal of Nonverbal Behavior, Special Issue: Development of Nonverbal Behavior: II. Social Development and Nonverbal Behavior, 18*, 9–35.

Nusbaum, E.C., & Silvia, P.J. (2011). Are openness and intellect distinct aspects of openness to experience? A test of the O/I model. *Personality and Individual Differences, 51*, 571–574.

O'Brien, D.T., Geher, G., Gallup, A.C., Garcia, J.R. & Kaufman, S.B. (2010). Self-perceived mating intelligence predicts sexual behavior in college students: Empirical validation of a theoretical construct. *Imagination, Cognition, and Personality, 29,* 341–362.

Olderbak, S. G., & Figueredo, A. J. (2010). Life history strategy as a longitudinal predictor of relationship satisfaction and dissolution. *Personality and Individual Differences, 49,* 234–239.

Olderbak, S. G., & Figueredo, A.J. (2012). Shared life history strategy as strong predictors of romantic relationship satisfaction. *Journal of Social, Evolutionary and Cultural Psychology, 6,* 111–131.

Oliver, M. B., & Hyde, J. S. (1993). Gender differences in sexuality: A meta-analysis. *Psychological Bulletin, 114,* 29–51.

Olson, K. R. (2005). Engagement and self-control: Superordinate dimensions of Big Five traits. *Personality and Individual Differences, 38,* 1689–1700.

Osman, M. (2004). An evaluation of dual-process theories of reasoning. *Psychonomic Bulletin & Review, 11,* 988–1010.

Otway, L. J., & Vignoles, V. L. (2006). Narcissism and childhood recollections: A quantitative test of psychoanalytic predictions. *Personality and Social Psychology Bulletin, 32,* 104–116.

O'Quin, K., & Derks, P. (1997). Humor and creativity: A review of the empirical literature. In M. Runco (Ed.), *Creativity research handbook* (Vol. 1, pp. 227–256). Cresskill, NJ: Hampton Press.

O'Sullivan, M. (2008). Deception and self-deception as strategies in short and long-term mating. In G. Geher & G. F. Miller (Eds.), *Mating intelligence: Sex, relationships, and the mind's reproduction system.* Mahwah, NJ: Lawrence Erlbaum.

Parker, J., & Burkley, M. (2009). Who's chasing whom? The impact of gender and relationship status on mate poaching. *Journal of Experimental Social Psychology, 45,* 1016–1019.

Parks, C.D., & Stone, A.B. (2010). The desire to expel unselfish members from the group. *Journal of Personality and Social Psychology, 99,* 303–310.

Paul, E. L., and Hayes, A. (2002). The casualties of "casual" sex: A qualitative exploration of the phenomenology of college students' hookups. *Journal of Social and Personal Relationships, 19,* 639–661.

Paul, E. L., McManus, B., and Hayes, A. (2000). "Hook-ups": Characteristics and correlates of college students' spontaneous and anonymous sexual experiences. *The Journal of Sex Research, 37,* 76–88.

Paulhus, D. L. (1998). Interpersonal and intrapsychic adaptiveness of trait self-enhancement: A mixed blessing. *Journal of Personality and SocialPsychology, 74,* 1197–1208.

Paulhus, D. L., & Williams, K. M. (2002). The Dark Triad of personality: Narcissism, Machiavellianism, and psychopathy. *Journal of Research in Personality, 36,* 556–563.

Peclet, M. H., Newman, K. D., Eichelberger, M. R., Gotschall, C. S., Guzzetta, P. C., Anderson, K. D., et al. (1990). Patterns of injury in children. *Pediatric Surgery, 25,* 85–91.

Pedersen, W. C., Putcha-Bhagavatula, A., & Miller, L. C. (2011). Are men and women really that different? Examining some of sexual strategies theory (SST)'s key assumptions about sex-distinct mating mechanisms. *Sex Roles, 64,* 629–643.

Pedersen, C. A., Ahnert, L., Anzenberger, G., Belsky, J., Draper, P., Fleming, A. S., et al. (2005). Beyond infant attachment: The origins of bonding in later life. In C. S. Carter, L. Ahnert, K. E. Grossmann, S. B. Hrdy, M. E. Lamb, S. W. Porges, & N. Sachser (Eds.), *Attachment and bonding: A new synthesis* (pp. 385–428). Cambridge, MA: MIT Press.

Penke, L. (2010). Bridging the gap between modern evolutionary psychology and the study of individual differences. In D. M. Buss & P. H. Hawley (Eds.), *The evolution of personality and individual differences.* New York, NY: Oxford University Press.

Penke, L., & Asendorpf, J. B. (2008). Beyond global sociosexual orientations: A more differentiated look at sociosexuality and its effects on courtship and romantic relationships. *Journal of Personality and Social Psychology, 95,* 1113–1135.

Penke, L., Borsboom, D., Johnson, W., Kievit, R. A., Ploeger, A., & Wicherts, J. M. (2011). Evolutionary psychology and intelligence research cannot be integrated the way Kanazawa (2010) suggested. *American Psychologist, 66,* 916–917.

Penke, L., Denissen, J. J. A., & Miller, G. F. (2007). The evolutionary genetics of personality. *European Journal of Personality, 21,* 549–587.

Penke, L., Todd, P. M., Lenton, A., & Fasolo, B. (2008). How self-assessments can guide human mating decisions. In G. Geher, & G. F. Miller (Eds.), *Mating intelligence: Sex, relationships, and the mind's reproductive system* (pp. 37–75). Mahwah, NJ: Lawrence Erlbaum.

Pennebaker, J. W. (1979). Don't the girls get prettier at closing time: A country and western application to psychology. *Personality and Social Psychology Bulletin, 5,* 122–125.

Penton-Voak, I. S., Perrett, D. I., Castles, D. L., Kobaysashi, T., Burt, D. M., Murray, L. K., & Minamisawa, R. (1999). Menstrual cycle alters face preference. *Nature, 399,* 741–742.

Perina, K. (2007, February). Love's loopy logic. *Psychology Today.*

Perusse, D. (1993). Cultural and reproductive success in industrial societies: Testing the relationship at the proximate and ultimate levels. *Behavioral and Brain Sciences, 16,* 267–322.

Petersen, J. L., & Hyde, J. S. (2010). A meta-analytic review of research on gender differences in sexuality, 1993–2007. *Psychological Bulletin, 136,* 21–38.

Peterson, A., Geher, G., & Kaufman, S. B. (2011). Predicting preferences for sex acts: Which traits matter most, and why?" *Evolutionary Psychology, 9,* 371–389.

Peterson, J. B., & Carson, S. (2000). Latent inhibition and openness to experience in a high-achieving student population. *Personality and Individual Differences, 28,* 323–332.

Peterson, J. B., Smith, K. W., & Carson, S. (2002). Openness and extraversion are associated with reduced latent inhibition: Replication and commentary. *Personality and Individual Differences, 33,* 1137–1147.

Pinker, S. (1999). *How the mind works.* New York, NY: Norton.

Pinker, S. (2003). *The blank slate: The modern denial of human nature.* New York, NY: Penguin.

Pinker, S. (2007). *The stuff of thought: Language as a window into human nature.* New York, NY: Viking.

Pinsky, S., & Young, S. M. (2009). *The mirror effect: How celebrity narcissism is seducing America.* New York, NY: Harper.

Pipitone, R. N. & Gallup, G. G., Jr. (2008). Women's voice attractiveness varies across the menstrual cycle. *Evolution and Human Behavior, 29,* 268–274.

Place, S. S., Todd, P. M., Penke, L., & Asendorpf, J. B. (2010). Humans show mate copying after observing real mate choices. *Evolution and Human Behavior, 31,* 320–325.

Place, S. S., Todd, P. M., Penke, L., & Asendorpf, J. B. (2009). The ability to judge the romantic interest of others. *Psychological Science, 20,* 22–26.

Platek, S. M., & Singh, D. (2010). Optimal waist-to-hip ratios in women activate neural reward centers in men. *PLoS ONE, 5,* e9042.

Ponitz, C. C., McClelland, M. M., Matthews, J. S., & Morrison, F. J. (2009). A structured observation of behavioral self-regulation and its contribution to kindergarten outcomes. *Developmental Psychology, 45,* 605–619.

Prokosch, M. D., Yeo, R. A., & Miller, G. F. (2005). Intelligence tests with higher g-loadings show higher correlations with body symmetry: Evidence for a general fitness factor mediated by developmental stability. *Intelligence, 33,* 203–213.

Promislow, D. E. L., & Harvey, P. H. (1990). Living fast and dying young. *Journal of Zoology, 220,* 417–437.

Pronk, T.M., Karremans, J.C., & Wigboldus, D.H.J. (2011). How can you resist? Executive control helps romantically involved individuals to stay faithful. *Journal of Personality and Social Psychology, 5,* 827–837.

Provine, R. R. (2000). *Laughter: A scientific investigation.* New York, NY: Viking.

Pruett-Jones, S. (1992) Independent versus non–independent mate choice: Do females copy each other? *American Naturalist, 140,* 1000–1009.

Przygodzki-Lionet, N., Olivier, J., & Desrumaux, P. (2010). The effects of facial attractiveness, sex, internality of applicants on hiring decisions for managerial and non-managerial jobs. *Studia Psychologica, 52,* 53–57.

Purnine, D. M., Carey, M. P., Jorgensen, R. S., & Randall, S. (1994). Gender differences regarding preferences for specific heterosexual practices. *Journal of Sex and Marital Therapy, 20,* 271–287.

Rammstedt, B., & Rammsayer, T. H. (2000). Sex differences in self-estimates of different aspects of intelligence. *Personality and Individual Differences, 29*, 869–880.

Raskin, R., & Novacek, J. (1989). An MMPI description of the narcissistic personality. *Journal of Personality Assessment, 53*, 66–80.

Raven, J., Raven, J. C., & Court, J. H. (2003). *Manual for Raven's progressive matrices and vocabulary scales. Section 1: General overview.* San Antonio, TX: Harcourt Assessment.

Rawlings, D., & Freeman, J. L. (1997). Measuring paranoia/suspiciousness. In G. Claridge (Ed.), *Schizotypy: Implications for illness and health* (pp. 38–60). Oxford, UK: Oxford University Press.

Regan, P. C. (1998a). Minimum mate selection standards as a function of perceived mate value, relationship context, and gender. *Journal of Psychology and Human Sexuality, 10*, 53–73.

Regan, P. C. (1998b). What if you can't get what you want? Willingness to compromise ideal mate selection standards as a function of sex, mate value, and relationship context. *Personality and Social Psychology Bulletin, 24*, 1294–1303.

Regan, P.C. (1998c). Willingness to compromise ideal mate selection standards as a function of sex, mate value, and relationship context. *Journal for Personality and Social Psychology, 24*, 1294–1303.

Regan, P. C., & Berscheid, E. (1997). Gender differences in characteristics desired in a potential sexual and marriage partner. *Journal of Psychology and Human Sexuality, 9*, 25–37.

Regan, P. C., Levin, L., Sprecher, S., Christopher, F. S., & Cate, R. (2000). Partner preferences: What characteristics do men and women desire in their short-term and long-term romantic partners? *Journal of Psychology and Human Sexuality, 12*, 1–21.

Reiber, C. (2010*). A new perspective on menopause: Female gamete competition.* Presentation given at the annual meeting of the NorthEastern Evolutionary Psychology Society (NEEPS), March. New Paltz, NY.

Reiber, C., & Garcia, J. R. (2010). Hooking up: Gender differences, evolution, and pluralistic ignorance. *Evolutionary Psychology, 8*, 390–404.

Reitman, J. (2006). Sex and scandal at Duke. *Rolling Stone, 1002*, 70–109.

Reyes-Garcia, V., Molina, J. L., Broesch, J., Calvet, L., Huanca, T., Saus, J., et al. (2008). Do the aged and knowledgeable men enjoy more prestige? A test of predictions from the prestige-bias model of cultural transmission. *Evolution and Human Behavior, 29*, 275–281.

Rhodes, G., & Simmons, L. W. (2007). Symmetry, attractiveness and sexual selection. In R. I. M. Dunbar & L. Barrett (Eds.), *The Oxford handbook of evolutionary psychology* (pp. 333–364). Oxford, UK: Oxford University Press.

Rhodewalt, F., & Morf, C. C. (1995). Self and interpersonal correlates of the Narcissistic Personality Inventory: A review and new findings. *Journal of Research in Personality, 29*, 1–23.

Richards, L., Rollerson, B., & Phillips, J. (1991). Perceptions of submissiveness: Implications for victimization. *Journal of Psychology, 125*, 407–411.

Ridley, M. (2003). *The red queen: Sex and the evolution of human nature.* New York, NY: Harper Perennial.

Riggio, H. R., & Riggio, R. E. (2002). Emotional expressiveness, extraversion, and neuroticism: A meta-analysis. *Journal of Nonverbal Behavior, 26*, 195–218.

Ritter, S. M., Karremans, J. C., & van Schie, H. T. (2010). The role of self-regulation in derogating attractive alternatives. *Journal of Experimental Social Psychology, 46*, 631–637.

Robins, R. W., & Beer, J. S. (2001). Positive illusions about the self: Short-term benefits and long-term costs. *Journal of Personality and Social Psychology, 80*, 340–352.

Robson, A. J., & Kaplan, H. S. (2003). The evolution of human life expectancy and intelligence in hunter-gatherer economies. *American Economic Review, 93*, 150–169.

Rokach, A. (1990). Content analysis of sexual fantasies of males and females. *Journal of Psychology: Interdisciplinary and Applied, 124*, 427–436.

Ronay, R., & von Hippel, W. (2010). The presence of an attractive woman elevates testosterone and physical risk taking in young men. *Social Psychological and Personality Science*, *1*, 57–64.

Roney, J. R., Mahler, S. V., & Maestripieri, D. (2003). Behavioral and hormonal responses of men to brief interactions with women. *Evolution and Human Behavior*, *24*, 365–375.

Roney, J. R., Simmons, Z. L., & Gray, P. B. (2011). Changes in estradiol predict within-women shifts in attraction to facial cues of men's testosterone. *Psychoneuroendocrinology*, *36*, 742–749.

Ross, L. (1977). The intuitive psychologist and his shortcomings: Distortions in the attribution process. In L. Berkowitz (Ed.), *Advances in experimental social psychology*. New York, NY: Academic Press.

Ross, L., & Nisbett, R. (1991). *The person and the situation*. New York, NY: McGraw-Hill.

Ross, S. R., Stewart, J., Mugge, M., & Fultz, B. (2001). The imposter phenomenon, achievement dispositions, and the five factor model. *Personality and Individual Differences*, *31*, 1347–1355.

Rowatt, W. C., DeLue, S., Strickhouser, L., & Gonzalez, T. (2001). The limited influence of self-monitoring on romantic partner preferences. *Personality and Individual Differences*, *31*, 943–954.

Rowatt, W., & Schmitt, D. P. (2003). Associations between religious orientation and varieties of sexual experience. *Journal for the Scientific Study of Religion*, *42*, 455–465.

Rueda, M. R., Posner, M. I., & Rothbart, M. K. (2005). The development of executive attention: Contributions to the emergence of self-regulation. *Developmental Neuropsychology*, *28*, 573–594.

Saad, G. (2011). *The consuming instinct: What juicy burgers, Ferraris, pornography, and gift giving reveal about human nature*. Amherst, NY: Prometheus Books.

Saad, G., & Vongas, J. (2008). The effect of conspicuous consumption on men's testosterone levels. *Organizational Behavior and Human Decision Processes*, *110*, 80–92.

Sadalla, E., Kenrick, D., & Vershure, B. (1987). Dominance and heterosexual attraction. *Journal of Personality and Social Psychology*, *52*, 730–738.

Sakaguchi, K., & Hasegawa, T. (2006). Person perception through gait information and target choice for sexual advances: Comparison of likely targets in experiments and real life. *Journal of Nonverbal Behavior*, *30*, 63–85.

Salmon, C., & Symons, D. (2001). *Warrior lovers: Erotic fiction, evolution, and female sexuality*. London: Weidenfeld & Nicolson.

Salovey, P., & Mayer, J. D. (1990). Emotional intelligence. *Imagination, Cognition, and Personality*, *9*, 185–211.

Samuels, J., Bienvenu, O. J., Cullen, B., Costa, P. T., Eaton, W. W., & Nestadt, G. (2004). Personality dimensions and criminal arrest. *Comprehensive Psychiatry*, *45*, 275–280.

Saucier, G. (1992). Openness versus intellect: Much ado about nothing? *European Journal of Personality*, *6*, 381–386.

Schaich Borg, J., Lieberman, D., & Kiehl, K. (2008). Infection, incest, and iniquity: Investigating the neural correlates of disgust and morality. *Journal of Cognitive Neuroscience*, *20*, 1529–1546.

Scheib, J. E. (1994). Sperm donor selection and the psychology of female mate choice. *Sociobiology*, *15*, 113–129.

Scherer, K. R. (1986). Vocal affect expression: A review and a model for future research. *Psychological Bulletin*, *99*, 143–165.

Schmeichel, B. J., Vohs, K. D., & Baumeister, R. F. (2003). Intellectual performance and ego depletion: Role of the self in logical reasoning and other information processing. *Journal of Personality and Social Psychology*, *85*, 33–46.

Schmitt, D. P. (2004). The Big Five related to risky sexual behavior across 10 world regions: Differential personality associations of sexual promiscuity and relationship infidelity. *European Journal of Personality*, *18*, 301–319.

Schmitt, D. P. (2005). Sociosexuality from Argentina to Zimbabwe: A 48-nation study of sex, culture, and strategies of human mating. *Behavioral and Brain Sciences*, *28*, 247–275.

Schmitt, D. P., Alcalay, L., Allik, J., Angleiter, A., Ault, L., Austers, I., et al. (2004). Patterns and universals of mate poaching across 53 nations: The effects of sex, culture, and personality on romantically attracting another person's partner. *Journal of Personality and Social Psychology, 86*, 560–584.

Schmitt, D. P., Alcalay, L., Allik, J., Ault, L., Austers, I., Bennett, K. L., et al. (2003). Universal sex differences in the desire for sexual variety: Tests from 52 nations, 6 continents, and 13 islands. *Journal of Personality and Social Psychology, 85*, 85–104.

Schmitt, D. P., & Buss, D. M. (1996). Strategic self-enhancement and competitor derogation: Sex and context effects on the perceived effectiveness of mate attraction tactics. *Journal of Personality and Social Psychology, 70*, 1185–1204.

Schmitt, D. P., & Buss, D. M. (2000). Sexual dimensions of person description: Beyond or subsumed by the big five. *Journal of Research in Personality, 34*, 141–177.

Schmitt, D. P., & Buss, D. M. (2001). Human mate poaching: Tactics and temptations for infiltrating existing mateships. *Journal of Personality and Social Psychology, 80*, 894–917.

Schmitt, D. P., Couden, A., & Baker, M. (2001). Sex, temporal context, and romantic desire: An experimental evaluation of Sexual Strategies Theory. *Personality and Social Psychology Bulletin, 27*, 833–847.

Schmitt, D. P., Shackelford, T. K., Duntley, J., Tooke, W., Buss, D. M., Fisher, M.L., et al. (2002). Is there an early-30s peak in female sexual desire? Cross-sectional evidence from the United States and Canada. *Canadian Journal of Human Sexuality, 11*, 1–18.

Schulte, M. J., Ree, M. J., & Carretta, T. R. (2004). Emotional intelligence: Not much more than g and personality. *Personality and Individual Differences, 37*, 1059–1068.

Schützwohl, A., Fuchs, A., McKibbin, W. F., & Shackelford, T. K. (2009). How willing are you to accept sexual requests from slightly unattractive to exceptionally attractive imagined requestors? *Human Nature, 20*, 282–293.

Sefcek, J. A., Brumbach, B. H., Vasquez, G., & Miller, G. F. (2006). The evolutionary psychology of human mate choice: How ecology, genes, fertility, and fashion influence mating behavior. In M. R. Kauth (Ed.), *On the evolution of sexual attraction* [Special Issue]. *Journal of Psychology & Human Sexuality, 18*, 125–182.

Seligman, M. E. P., & Maier, S. F. (1967). Failure to escape traumatic shock. *Journal of Experimental Psychology, 74*, 1–9.

Senko, C., & Fyffe, V. (2010). An evolutionary perspective on effective vs. ineffective pick-up lines. *The Journal of Social Psychology, 150*, 648–667.

Shamosh, N. A., & Gray, J. R. (2008). Delay discounting and intelligence: A meta-analysis. *Intelligence, 38*, 289–305.

Shamosh, N. A., DeYoung, C. D., Green, A. E., Reis, D. L., Conway, A. R. A., Engle, R. W., et al. (2008). Individual differences in delay discounting: Relation to intelligence, working memory, and frontopolar cortex. *Psychological Science, 19*, 904–911.

Shaner, A., Miller, G. F., & Mintz, J. (2004). Schizophrenia as one extreme of a sexually selected fitness indicator. *Schizophrenia Research, 70*, 101–109.

Shaner, A., Miller, G. F., & Mintz, J. (2008). Mental disorders as catastrophic failures of mating intelligence. In G. Geher & G. Miller (Eds.), *Mating intelligence: Sex, relationships, and the mind's reproductive system* (pp. 193–225). New York, NY: Lawrence Erlbaum.

Shaver, P., & Mikulincer, M. (2006). Attachment theory, individual psychodynamics, and relationship functioning. In A. Vangelisti & D. Perlman (Eds.), *The Cambridge handbook of personal relationships* (pp. 251–271). Cambridge, UK: Cambridge University Press.

Sheng, T., Gheytanchi, A., & Aziz-Zadeh, L. (2010). Default network deactivations are correlated with psychopathic personality traits. *PLOS One, 5*, e12611.

Shenk, D. (2010). *The genius in all of us.* New York, NY: Doubleday.

Shiota, M. N., Campos, B., Keltner, D., & Hertenstein, M. J. (2004). Positive emotion and the regulation of interpersonal relationships. In P. Philippot & R. S. Feldman (Eds.), *The regulation of emotion* (pp. 127–155). Mahwah, NJ: Lawrence Erlbaum.

Shoup, M. L. & Gallup, G. G., Jr. (2008). Men's faces convey information about their bodies and their behavior: What you see is what you get. *Evolutionary Psychology, 6*, 469–479.

Sigal, J., Gibbs, M. S., Adams, B., & Derfler, R. (1988). The effect of romantic and nonromantic films on perception of female friendly and seductive behavior. *Sex Roles, 19*, 545–554.

Silventoinen, K., Posthuma, D., van Beijsterveldt, T., Bartels, M., & Boomsma, D. I. (2006). Genetic contributions to the association between height and intelligence: evidence from Dutch twin data from childhood to middle age. *Genes, Brain and Behavior, 5*, 585–596.

Silvia, P. J., Nusbaum, E. C., Berg, C., Martin, C., & O'Connor, A. (2009). Openness to experience, plasticity, and creativity: Exploring lower-order, higher-order, and interactive effects. *Journal of Research in Personality, 43*, 1087–1090.

Simon, H. A. (1957) *Models of man*. New York, NY: John Wiley & Sons.

Simpson, J. A., & Gangestad, S. W. (1991). Individual differences in sociosexuality: Evidence for convergent and discriminant validity. *Journal of Personality and Social Psychology, 60*, 870–883.

Simpson, J. A., & Gangestad, S. W. (1992). Sociosexuality and romantic partner choice. *Journal of Personality, 60*, 31–51.

Singh, D., & Singh, D. (2011). Shape and significance of feminine beauty: An evolutionary perspective. *Sex Roles, 64*, 723–731.

Smith, C. (2002). *Nice guys finish last*. Retrieved November 7th, 2010 from http://www.askmen.com/dating/curtsmith/getiton15.html.

Smith, D. L. (2007). *The most dangerous animal*. New York, NY: St. Martin's Griffin.

Smith, M. J. (1998). *Evolutionary genetics*. Oxford, UK: Oxford University Press.

Snyder, J. K., Kirkpatrick, L. A., & Barrett, H. C. (2008). The dominance dilemma: Do women really prefer dominant mates? *Personal Relationships, 15*, 425–444.

Snyder, M., Tanke, E. D., & Berscheid, E. (1977). Social perception and interpersonal behavior: On the self-fulfilling nature of social stereotypes. *Journal of Personality and Social Psychology, 35*, 656–666.

Spanier, G. B., & Margolis, R. L. (1983). Marital separation and extramarital sexual behavior. *Journal of Sex Research, 19*, 23–48.

Spearman, C. (1904). "General intelligence," objectively determined and measured. *American Journal of Psychology, 15*, 201–293.

Spence, J. T., & Helmreich, R. L. (1972a). The Attitudes Toward Women Scale: An objective instrument to measure attitudes toward the rights and roles of women in contemporary society. *JSAS Catalog of Selected Documents in Psychology, 2*, 667–668.

Sroufe, L. A., Bennett, C., Englund, M., Urban, J., & Shulman, S. (1993). The significance of gender boundaries in preadolescence: contemporary correlates and antecedents of boundary violation and maintenance. *Child Development, 64*, 455–466.

Stanik, C., Kurzban, R., & Ellsworth, P. (2010). Rejection hurts: The effect of being dumped on subsequent mating efforts. *Evolutionary Psychology, 8*, 682–694.

Stanovich, K. E. (2005). *The robot's rebellion: Finding meaning in the age of Darwin*. Chicago, IL: University of Chicago Press.

Stanovich, K.E. (2009). Distinguishing the reflective, algorithmic, and autonomous minds: Is it time for a tri - process theory. In J. S. B. T. Evans & K. Frankish (Eds.), *In two minds: Dual-processses and beyond*. Oxford, UK: Oxford University Press.

Stanovich, K.E. (2011). *Rationality and the reflective mind*. New York, NY: Oxford University Press.

Stanovich, K. E., & West, R. F. (2000). Individual differences in reasoning: Implications for the rationality debate? *Behavioral and Brain Sciences, 23*, 645–726.

Stanovich, K.E., & Toplak, M.E. (2012). Defining features versus incidental correlates of Type 1 and Type 2 processing. *Mind and Society, 11*, 3–13.

Stephenson, K.R., Ahrold, T.K., & Meston, C.M. (2010). The association between sexual motives and sexual satisfaction: Gender differences and categorical comparisons. *Archives of Sexual Behavior, 40*, 607–618.

Sternberg, R. J. (1997). *Successful intelligence: How practical and creative Intelligence determine success in life*. New York, NY: Plume.

Sternberg, R. J. (1998). *Cupid's arrow: The course of love through time*. London, UK: Cambridge University Press.

Sternberg, R. J. (1999). *Love is a story: A new theory of relationships*. Oxford, UK: Oxford University Press.

Sternberg, R. J. (2011). The theory of successful intelligence. In Sternberg, R. J., & Kaufman, S. B. (Eds.), *The Cambridge handbook of intelligence*. New York, NY: Cambridge University Press.

Sternberg, R. J., & Kaufman, S. B. (Eds.) (2011). *The Cambridge handbook of intelligence*. New York, NY: Cambridge University Press.

Sternberg, R. J., & Weis, K. (2008). *The new psychology of love*. New Haven, CT: Yale University Press.

Stewart, S., Stinnett, H., & Rosenfeld, L. B. (2000). Sex differences in desired characteristics of short-term and long-term relationship partners. *Journal of Social and Personal Relationships, 17,* 843–853.

Stinson, F. S., Dawson, D. A., Goldstein, R. B., Chous, S. P., Huang, B., Smith, S. M., et al. (2008). Prevalence, disability, and comorbidity of DSM-IV Narcissistic Personality Disorder: Results from the Wave 2 National Epidemiologic Survey on Alchohol and Related Conditions. *Journal of Clinical Psychiatry, 69,* 1033–1045.

Strack, F., & Deutsch, R. (2004). Reflective and impulsive determinants of social behavior. *Personality and Social Psychology Review, 8,* 220–247.

Strauss, N. (2005). *The game: Penetrating the secret society of pickup artists*. New York, NY: Harper Collins.

Strauss, N. (2010). *The pickup artist: The new and improved art of seduction*. New York, NY: Villard.

Stone, E. A., Goetz, A. T., & Shackelford, T. K. (2005). Sex differences and similarities in preferred mating arrangements. *Sexualities, Evolution & Gender, 7,* 269–276.

Sugiyama, L. (2005). Physical attractiveness in adaptationist perspective. In D. M. Buss (Ed.), *The handbook of evolutionary psychology* (pp. 292–342). New York, NY: Wiley.

Suls, J., Martin, R., & David, J. P. (1998). Person–environment fit and its limits: Agreeableness, neuroticism, and emotional reactivity to interpersonal conflicts. *Personality and Social Psychology Bulletin, 24,* 88–98.

Sundet, J. M., Kristian, T., Harris, J. R., Magnus, J. R., Torjussen, P., & Tore, M. (2005). Resolving the genetic and environmental sources of the correlation between height and intelligence: A study of nearly 2600 Norwegian male twin pairs. *Twin Research and Human Genetics, 8,* 307–311.

Sunnafrank, M., & Ramirez, A. (2004). At first sight: persistent relational effects of get-acquainted conversations. *Journal of Social and Personal Relationships, 21,* 361–379.

Swami, V., & Furnham, A. (2007). *The psychology of physical attraction*. London, UK: Routledge.

Swami, V., Furnham, A., & Joshi, K. (2008). The influence of skin tone, hair length, and hair colour on ratings of women's physical attractiveness, health and fertility. *Scandinavian Journal of Psychology, 49,* 429–437.

Swami, V., & Tovee, M.J. (2012). The impact of psychological stress on men's judgements of female body size. *PLoS One, 8,* 1–5.

Symons, D. (1987). If we're all Darwinians, what's the fuss about? In C. Crawford, D. Krebs, & M. Smith (Eds.), *Sociobiology and psychology* (pp. 121–146). Hillsdale, NJ: Lawrence Erlbaum.

Taylor, S. E., & Brown, J. D. (1988). Illusion and well-being: A social psychological perspective on mental health. *Psychological Bulletin, 103,* 193–210.

Thompson, A. P. (1983). Extramarital sex: A review of the research literature. *Journal of Sex Research, 19,* 1–22.

Thompson-Schill, S. L., Ramscar, M., & Chrysikou, E. G. (2009). Cognition without control: When a little frontal lobe goes a long way. *Current Directions in Psychology Science, 18,* 259–263.

Thorn, C. (2011). *Confessions of a pickup-artist chaser: Long interviews with hideous men*. CreateSpace.com.

Thornhill, R. (1981). Panorpa (Mecoptera: anorpidae) scorpionflies: Systems for understanding resource-defense polygyny and alternative male reproductive efforts. *Annual Review of Ethology and Systematics, 12,* 355–386.

Thornhill, R., & Gangestad, S. W. (2008). *The evolutionary biology of human female sexuality*. New York, NY: Oxford University Press.

Thornhill, R., Gangestad, S. W., Miller, R., Scheyd, G., McCollough, J. K., & Franklin, M. (2003). Major histocompatibility complex genes, symmetry, and body scent attractiveness in men and women. *Behavioral Ecology*, *14*, 668–678.

Thornhill, R., & Palmer, C. (2001). *A natural history of rape: biological bases of sexual coercion.* Cambridge, MA: MIT Press.

Tiger, L. (1987). *Men in groups* (2nd ed.). New York, NY: Marion Boyars/Rizzoli.

Tither, J. M., & Ellis, B. J. (2008). Impact of fathers on daughters' age at menarche: A genetically- and environmentally-controlled sibling study. *Developmental Psychology*, *44*, 1409–1420.

Todd, P. M., & Miller, G. F. (1999). Heuristics for mate search. In G. Gigerenzer and P. M. Todd and the ABC Research Group (Eds.), *Simple heuristics that make us smart.* New York, NY: Oxford University Press.

Todd, P. M., Penke, L., Fasolo, B., & Lenton, A. P. (2007). Different cognitive processes underlie human mate choices and mate preferences. *Proceedings of the National Academy of Sciences USA*, *104*, 15011–15016.

Tomasello, M., Carpenter, M., Call, J., Behene, T., & Moll, H. (2005). Understanding and sharing intentions: The origins of cultural cognition. *Behavioral and Brain Sciences*, *28*, 675–735.

Townsend, J. M., Kline, J., & Wasserman, T. H. (1995). Low investment copulation: sex difference in motivations and emotional reactions. *Ethology and Sociobiology*, *16*, 25–51.

Townsend, J. M. (1998). *What women want—what men want: Why the sexes still see love and commitment so differently.* New York, NY: Oxford University Press.

Tracy, J. L., Cheng, J. T., Robins, R. W., & Trzesniewski, K. (2009). Authentic and hubristic pride: The affective core of self-esteem and narcissism. *Self and Identity*, *8*, 196–213.

Travaglia, L. K., Overall, N. C., & Sibley, C. G. (2009). Benevolent and hostile sexism and preferences for romantic partners. *Personality and Individual Differences*, *47*, 599–604.

Trivers, R. L. (1972). Parental investment and sexual selection. In B. Campbell (Ed.), *Sexual selection and the descent of man: 1871–1971* (pp. 136–179). Chicago, IL: Aldine.

Trivers, R. L. (1985) *Social evolution.* Menlo Park, CA: Benjamin/Cummings.

Twenge, J. (2007). *Generation me: Why today's young Americans are more confident, assertive, entitled-and more miserable than ever before.* New York, NY: Free Press.

Twenge, J. M., & Campbell, W. K. (2003). "Isn't it fun to get the respect that we're going to deserve?"—Narcissism, social rejection, and aggression. *Personality and Social Psychology Bulletin*, *29*(2), 261–272.

Twenge, J. M., & Campbell, W. K. (2009). *The narcissism epidemic: Living in the age of entitlement.* New York, NY: Free Press.

Twenge, J. M., Konrath, S., Foster, J. D., Campbell, W. K., & Bushman, B. J. (2008a). Egos inflating over time: A cross-temporal meta-analysis of the narcissistic personality inventory. *Journal of Personality*, *76*, 875–901.

Twenge, J. M., Konrath, S., Foster, J. D., Campbell, W. K., & Bushman, B. J. (2008b). Further evidence of an increase in narcissism among college students. *Journal of Personality*, *76*, 919–927.

Urbaniak, G. C., & Kilmann, P. R. (2003). Physical attractiveness and the "nice guy paradox": Do nice guys really finish last? *Sex Roles*, *49*, 413.

Urbaniak, G. C., & Kilmann, P. R. (2006). Niceness and dating success: A further test of the nice guy stereotype. *Sex Roles*, *55*, 209–224.

Van den Bergh, B., Dewitte, S., & Warlop, L. (2008). Bikinis instigate generalized impatience in intertemporal choice. *Journal of Consumer Research*, *35*, 85–97.

van der Maas, H. L. J., Dolan, C. V., Grasman, R. P., Wicherts, J. M., Huizenga, H. M., & Raijmakers, M. E. (2006). A dynamical model of general intelligence: The positive manifold of intelligence by mutualism. *Psychological Review*, *113*, 842–861.

Vandermassen, G. (2005). *Who's afraid of Charles Darwin? Debating feminism and evolutionary theory.* Lanham, MD: Rowman & Littlefield.

Vandermassen, G. (2010). Evolution and rape: A feminist Darwinian perspective. *Sex Roles*, *64*, 732–747.

Vangelisti, A. L. (1990). Conversational narcissism. *Communication Monographs*, *57*, 251–274.

Vazire, S., & Funder, D. C. (2006). Impulsivity and the self-defeating behavior of narcissists. *Personality and Social Psychology Review, 10,* 154–165.

Vazire, S., Naumann, L. P., Rentfrow, P. J., & Gosling, S. D. (2008). Portrait of a narcissist: Manifestations of narcissism in physical appearance. *Journal of Research in Personality, 42,* 1439–1447.

Vernon, P. A., Villani, V. C., Vickers, L. C., & Harris, J. A. (2008). A behavioral genetic investigation of the Dark Triad and the Big 5. *Personality and Individual Differences, 44,* 445–452.

Vohs, K.D., & Ciarocco, N. (2004). Interpersonal functioning requires self-regulation. In R. Baumeister & K. Vohs (Eds.), *Handbook of self-regulation: Research, theory, and applications* (pp. 392–407). New York, NY: Guilford Press.

Volk, T., & Atkinson, J. (2008). Is child death the crucible of evolution? Special Issue: Proceedings of the 2nd Annual Meeting of the NorthEastern Evolutionary Psychology Society. *Journal of Social, Evolutionary and Cultural Psychology, 2,* 247–260.

von Hippel, W., & Trivers, R. (2011). The evolution and psychology of self-deception. *Behavioral and Brain Sciences, 34,* 1–56.

von Rueden, C., Gurven, M., & Kaplan, H. (2008). Multiple dimensions of male social statuses in an Amazonian society. *Evolution and Human Behavior, 29,* 402–415.

Voracek, M., Hofhansl, A., & Fisher, M. (2005). Clark and Hatfield's evidence of women's low receptivity to male strangers' sexual offers revisited. *Psychological Reports, 97,* 11–20.

Voracek, M., Fisher, M. L., Hofhansl, A., Rekkas, P. V., & Ritthammer, N. (2006). "I find you to be very attractive..." Biases in compliance estimates to sexual offers. *Psicothema, 18,* 384–391.

Wade, T. J., Butrie, L. K., & Hoffman, K. M. (2009). Women's direct opening lines are perceived as most effective. *Personality and Individual Differences, 47,* 145–149.

Wai, M., & Tiliopoulos, N. (2012). The affective and cognitive empathic nature of the dark side of personality. *Personality and Individual Differences, 52,* 74–799.

Walker, R., Gurven, M., Hill, K., et al. (2006). Growth rates and life histories in twenty-two small-scale societies. *American Journal of Human Biology, 18,* 295–311.

Walle, A. (1976). Getting picked up without being put down: Jokes and the bar rush. *Journal of the Folklore Institute, 13,* 201–217.

Walster, E., Walster, G. W., & Bershcheid, E. (1978). *Equity: Theory and research.* Boston, MA: Allyn and Bacon.

Watson, D. (1989). Strangers' ratings of the five robust personality factors: Evidence of surprising convergence with self-report. *Journal of Personality and Social Psychology, 57,* 120–128.

Watson, D., Hubbard, B., & Wiese, D. (2000). General traits of personality and affectivity as predictors of satisfaction in intimate relationships: Evidence from self- and partner-ratings. *Journal of Personality, 68,* 413–449.

Watson, D., Klohnen, E. C., Casillas, A., Nus Simms, E., Haig, J., & Berry, D. S. (2004). Match makers and deal breakers: Analyses of assortative mating in newlywed couples. *Journal of Personality, 72,* 1029–1068.

Waynforth, D. (2007). Mate choice copying in humans. *Human Nature, 18,* 264–71.

Webster, G. D. (2007). Evolutionary theory in cognitive neuroscience: a 20-year quantitative review of publication trends. *Evolutionary Psychology, 5,* 520–530.

Wedekind, C, Escher, S., Van de Waal, M., & Frei, E. (2007). The major histocompatibility complex and perfumers' descriptions of human body odors. *Evolutionary Psychology, 5,* 330–343.

Wedekind, C., Seebeck, T., Bettens, F. & Paepke, A. J. (1995). MHC-dependent mate preferences in humans. *Proceedings of the Royal Society of London: Biological Sciences, 260,* 245–249.

Weekes-Shackelford, V.A., Easton, J.A., & Stone, E.A. (2008). How having children affects mating psychology. In G. Geher & G. Miller (Eds.), *Mating Intelligence: Sex, Relationships, and the Mind's Reproductive System.* Mahwah, NJ: Lawrence Erlbaum.

Weiss, M. J., & Harris, S. L. (2001). Teaching social skills to people with Autism. *Behavior Modification, 25,* 785–802.

West-Eberhard, M. J. (2003). *Developmental plasticity and evolution.* New York, NY: Oxford University Press.

Wheeler, S., Book, A., & Costello, K. (2009). Psychopathic traits and perceptions of victim vulnerability. *Criminal Justice and Behavior, 36*, 635–648.

Wiederman, M. W. (1997). Extramarital sex: Prevalence and correlates in a national survey. *Journal of Sex Research, 34*, 167–174.

Wiederman, M. W., & Dubois, S. L. (1998). Evolution and sex differences in preferences for short-term mates: Results from a policy capturing study. *Evolution and Human Behavior, 19*, 153–170.

Wilcox, R. R. (2003). *Applying contemporary statistical techniques.* San Diego: Academic.

Wilhelm, H., Gschwendner, T., Friese, Friese, M., Wiers, R.W., & Schmitt, M. (2008). Working memory capacity and self-regulatory behavior: Toward an individual differences perspective on behavior determination by automatic versus controlled processes. *Journal of Personality and Social Psychology, 95*, 962–977.

Williams, K. M., Cooper, B. S., Howell, T. M., Yuille, J. C., & Paulhus, D. L. (2009). Inferring sexually deviant behavior from corresponding fantasies: The role of personality and pornography use. *Criminal Justice and Behavior, 36*, 198–222.

Williams, K. M., Palhus, D. L., & Hare, R. D. (2007). Capturing the four-factor structure of psychopathy in college students via self-report. *Journal of Personality Assessment, 88*, 205–219.

Wilson, D. S. (2007). *Evolution for everyone: How Darwin's theory can change the way we think about our lives.* New York, NY: Delacorte Press.

Wilson, D. S., Geher, G., & Waldo, J. (2009). EvoS: Completing the evolutionary synthesis in higher education. *EvoS Journal: The Journal of the Evolutionary Studies Consortium, 1*, 3–10.

Wilson, D. S., Dietrich, E., & Clark, A. B. (2003). On the inappropriate use of the naturalistic fallacy in evolutionary psychology. *Biology and Philosophy, 18*, 669–682.

Wilson, M., & Daly, M. (1985) Competitiveness, risk-taking and violence: The young male syndrome. *Ethology and Sociobiology, 6*, 59–73.

Wilson, M., & Daly, M. (2004). Do pretty women inspire men to discount the future? *Biology Letters, 271*, 177–179.

Wilson, T. D. (2002). *Strangers to ourselves: Discovering the adaptive unconscious.* Cambridge, MA: Harvard University Press.

Wolf, M., van Doorn, G. S., & Weissing, F. J. (2008). Evolutionary emergence of responsive and unresponsive personalities. *Proceedings of the National Academy of Sciences of the United States of America, 105*, 15825–15830.

Wolf, N. (1991). *The beauty myth.* New York, NY: Anchor Books.

Woody, E., & Claridge, G. (1977). Psychoticism and thinking. *British Journal of Social and Clinical Psychology, 16*, 241–248.

Wrangham, R. (2009). *Catching fire: How cooking made us human.* New York, NY: Basic Books.

Yorzinski, J. L., & Platt, M. L. (2010) Same-sex gaze attraction influences mate-choice copying in humans. *PloS One, 5*, e9115.

Youn, G. (2006). Subjective sexual arousal in response to erotica: Effects of gender, guided fantasy, erotic stimulus, and duration of exposure. *Archives of Sexual Behavior, 35*, 87–97.

Young, S. M., & Pinsky, D. (2006). Narcissism and celebrity. *Journal of Research in Personality, 40*, 463–471.

Zahavi, A. (1977). The testing of a bond. *Animal Behaviour, 25*, 246–247.

Zebrowitz, L. A., & Rhodes, G. (2004). Sensitivity to "bad genes" and the anomalous face overgeneralization effect: Cue validity, cue utilization, and accuracy in judging intelligence and health. *Journal of Nonverbal Behavior, 28*, 167–185.

Zerjal, T., Xue, Y., Bertorelle, G., Wells, R. S., Bao, W., Zhu, S., et al. (2003). The genetic legacy of the Mongols. *American Journal of Human Genetics, 72*, 717–721.

Ziv, A. (1980). Humor and creativity. *Creative Child & Adult Quarterly, 5*, 159–170.

INDEX